CHRISTIAN THEOLOGY
An Eschatological Approach

Volume I

CHRISTIAN THEOLOGY

AN ESCHATOLOGICAL APPROACH

VOLUME I

Thomas N. Finger

Thomas Nelson Publishers
Nashville • Camden • New York

© 1985 by Thomas N. Finger.

All rights reserved. Written permission must be secured from the publisher to use or reproduce any part of this book, except for brief quotations in critical reviews or articles.

Published in Nashville, Tennessee, by Thomas Nelson, Inc., Publishers and distributed in Canada by Lawson Falle, Ltd., Cambridge, Ontario.

Printed in the United States of America.

Scripture quotations noted are from the author's translation or from the Revised Standard Version of the Bible, copyrighted 1946, 1952, © 1971, 1973.

Library of Congress Cataloging-in-Publication Data

Finger, Thomas N.
   Christian theology: An eschatological approach

   Bibliography: v. 1, t. p.
   Includes index.
   1. Theology, Doctrinal. 2. Eschatology. I. Title.
BT75.2.F55   1985   230   85-21646
ISBN 0-8407-7505-9 (v. 1)

Contents

Preface

The two volumes of my eschatological approach to theology are designed for two main purposes. First, to provide a clear, readable beginning text for seminary and college religion courses, for pastors, for Christian workers, and hopefully for all persons having a good knowledge of Scripture and a desire to think and learn. Second, to do systematic theology in a manner which has never before been attempted. At first glance, two such purposes may seem incompatible. The introductory material needed by beginning students may seem overly cumbersome in an effort which stretches towards new frontiers. Contrariwise, an attempt to articulate problems and solutions in novel fashion may seem beyond the grasp of beginners.

These two emphases, however, mutually support and enrich each other. On one hand, in seeking to do theology differently, I do not pursue novelty for novelty's sake. I seek to wrestle with the major issues handed down through theological tradition, and to develop positions profoundly refined through this dialogue and thoroughly grounded in Scripture. To write theology in this way, however, involves reexamining its fundamental themes, historical schools, and biblical foundations in a thorough, patient manner. Accordingly, Chapters 1, 4, 5, 14, and 17 of Volume I consist largely of such material. Knowledgeable readers may wish to skim or skip them. But they should be aware that the exposition and dialogue which begin there is integral to the overall enterprise.

On the other hand, the effort to do theology freshly and creatively should not be left to experts in the field. As I shall argue (especially in Chap. 2), theology is rightly the activity of the entire Church. All Christians should be deeply sensitive to the challenges of their particular time and place, and searching for fresh understandings of what God's Word says to them. Indeed, theology has recently lost much of its interest and influence because its traditional forms seldom speak to such issues. If beginners and the Church as a whole are to find theology meaningful, the challenge to do it creatively should be present from the start. Accordingly, I seek to pose questions and articulate answers in a fresh way, not to give beginners one more complicated system to memorize but to encourage them to think creatively for themselves.

For their help in the exciting but laborious task of doing theology in a new way, my greatest thanks goes to many students who have challenged, criticized, applauded, and endured me. Were I to begin listing them individually, I would not know where to stop. I hope that they know–through my challenging, criticizing, applauding and enduring them–who they are!

CHAPTER ONE

Systematic Theology:
An Historical Introduction

W e often hear that this is an "apocalyptic" era. Uncounted journalists, political analysts, artists, and others join in portraying a world hurtling towards possible total destruction. The social conflicts which divide us, the psychological dis-ease which frightens us, the military escalation which is supposed to protect us—all threaten to combine in annihilating the human race.

At the same time, recent biblical and theological studies have been deeply influenced by the "rediscovery of eschatology."[1] Virtually all scholars agree that early Christianity arose amid an atmosphere highly charged with the anticipation that the end of all things was at hand (1 Pet. 4:7). At the same time, however, early Christians were energized by the paradoxical conviction that the old age of death and destruction had, in the most important sense, already ended and that the new age had already dawned.

Since the beginning of this century, when the importance of eschatology was rediscovered,[2] biblical scholars have reappraised practically every scriptural

---

[1] In the Greek New Testament, the *eschaton* means the final or ultimate event(s) in history. "Eschatology," then, means the study of or teaching concerning these final events. In today's popular speech, "apocalyptic" means about the same thing. Later we will distinguish precisely between the two terms (pp. 99-100 below), though we use them synonomously here.

[2] Above all, by Johannes Weiss, *Jesus' Proclamation of the Kingdom* (Philadelphia: Fortress, 1968 [originally published in 1892]); and by Albert Schweitzer, *The Quest of the Historical Jesus* (New York: Macmillan, 1968 [originally published in 1906]).

word and theme under its light. Systematic theologians have also been influenced by eschatology in numerous and highly diverse ways. Suprisingly, however, no one has yet attempted to restructure systematic theology as a whole from an eschatological perspective. No one has yet considered the details of a theological "system" written from this perspective. This is partly due to the present status of the discipline.

"Systematic Theology" is a little-used and even less understood term today. The average person will seldom know what it means. To most church-goers it conveys something abstruse and archaic. Of course, students of religion are acquainted with the term. But whereas systematic theology formed the curricular backbone of most seminaries and religion departments until recent decades, today subjects which are apparently more relevant—counseling, social ethics, world religions, etc.—command far more attention.

Perhaps this trend is not entirely bad. Christianity, after all, is more a way of living than a way of thinking. And for centuries systematic theology, the "Queen of the Sciences," has been *the* most encyclopedic, intellectual activity of all. No other discipline has sought to deal with as many subjects and to discover the ultimate significance of them all. Few disciplines have raised problems as difficult for human thought (the Trinity, Predestination, etc.) and have claimed as often to have solved them. And all this has often been done in a highly technical terminology which has been unintelligible to the average believer.

Possibly the decline of systematic theology is directly related to the increasingly eschatological character of our age. Perhaps our crisis-torn world can no longer make use of such an elaborate, cumbersome edifice. Time is running out. Urgent needs cry out on every hand. The Church must be on the move. Perhaps it needs only a small, light satchel of beliefs, as it were—not an enormous trunk crammed with complex mechanisms. If systematic theology no longer facilitates Christian involvement in our world, should it be seriously revised or even scrapped?

Churches and seminaries might simply drop the subject altogether or begin constructing something entirely new in its place. Yet in so doing they might simply be succumbing to the desperate urgency of our era. In contrast, Christian activity in the present and Christian hope for the future are always rooted in the past. Our very reasons for acting and hoping at all are intrinsically connected to events that occurred in the first century. And in between there lies a rich history of acting, hoping, and thinking.

We cannot decide how or whether systematic theology might be done in today's eschatological context without reconsidering how it has been done in the past. So questionable has the usefulness of this kind of thinking become that we can discern what purposes it was originally intended to serve only by retracing its origin and development. Only through observing how it functioned in other historical contexts can we begin to appreciate its strengths and weaknesses, and to determine what benefits, if any, such a discipline might contribute to our own. Accordingly, we begin with an historical overview of our subject.

I. The Bible

It is often said that the Bible contains no systematic theology.[3] As the term is frequently understood, this is indeed true. However, unless the Scriptures contain forms of presentation, discussion, and argument which are compatible with more "systematic" elaboration, the enterprise is doomed for anyone who takes Scripture seriously.

Within the biblical writings one does actually observe occasional attempts to pull together those events and beliefs which were central for different communities in various times and places, and to set them down in brief, orderly fashion. In the Old Testament one finds various "recitals" of those acts by which God had delivered and remained faithful to his people.[4] Very brief recitals may be found in passages such as Deuteronomy 6:20–24 and 26:5–9. As Yahweh's history with Israel lengthens, expanded recitals incorporate the more recent events and treat the entire series from broader, more profound perspectives (e.g., Josh. 24:2–13; Psalms 74, 77; Neh. 9:6–37).

Later in Daniel and Zechariah, and in the "apocryphal" writings of intertestamental times, Israel's history is placed within the broader framework of the history of all peoples. All history is interpreted as tending towards a time when Yahweh will alter the face of heaven and earth and establish a kingdom encompassing all nations. Up to the time of Christ repeated attempts are made to understand those things central to Israelite faith within ever expanding historical and cosmic horizons.

In the New Testament one finds brief recitals of those events connected with Jesus at the heart of the earliest preaching (Acts 2:22–24, 3:12–14, 10:36–41). These events are understood as the fulfillment of what God began in Old Testament times (Acts 2:14–21, 25–36; 3:18–26; Rom. 1:3–4). Thereby they form the climax of an expanded recital of God's acts throughout history (esp. Acts 13:16–41).

Several years after Jesus' resurrection the gospel began to spread beyond the Jewish community. Old Testament history was then unfamiliar to the Greco-Roman world. Furthermore, the notion of a God who acted through a decisive series of historical events was strange, even incredible. Consequently in communicating their message to the pagan world, Christians sought for ways to connect it with the experience and outlook of their audiences. To respond meaningfully to the gospel and to live it out daily, it was essential that people should hear the gospel phrased in concepts which they could understand and apply. Sometimes the gospel was presented by referring to such general aware-

---

[3] See especially G. Ernest Wright's classic case for biblical theology as opposed to systematic theology, *God Who Acts* (London: SCM, 1952). Although we are indebted to Wright, we will choose to redefine "systematic" rather than oppose it so sharply to "biblical." For an overview of the biblical theology movement, see Brevard Childs, *Biblical Theology in Crisis* (Philadelphia: Westminster, 1970).

[4] Wright, pp. 33-58.

ness of God as might be found in observing the natural world (Acts 14:15-17) or in Greek philosophies and religions (Acts 17:18-31). However, even when such "points of contact" with pagan cultures were utilized, the differences between them and the gospel stood out more sharply than did the similarities.

As the gospel spread ever more widely throughout Greco-Roman culture, it became necessary to connect it more broadly with the intellectual, religious, and social characteristics of those cultures. Historical study shows how this process was carried out in various ways and with varying degrees of comprehensiveness in all New Testament writings. It was done most comprehensively in Paul's letter to the Church at Rome.

In Romans Paul first describes the general awareness of God's existence that is available to everyone through the physical universe (Rom. 1:19-20). His terminology recalls that of current Stoic philosophy. He then argues that all humanity has turned from God since the creation of the world and the beginning of history (1:21—3:20). Paul also reflects on God's judgment at the end of history and discusses whether pagans who have known God's demands through their conscience might be acquitted at this event (2:5-10, 14-16).

In chapter 4, Paul recounts Israel's history, beginning with Abraham. Chapters 9-11 explore at length the relationship between this history and God's dealings with other nations. Meanwhile, chapter 5 traces human sinfulness back to Adam, while chapter 8 draws things forward to the comsummation of all things. In between, chapters 6 and 7 wrestle with the conflict between sin and righteousness in the Christian life. Finally, the concluding chapters (12-16) treat practical living at length, including the Christian's relationship to the state (12:14—13:10).

Paul's Roman epistle is not pure "recital." It does not move directly from beginning to end through God's historical dealings with the cosmos. Paul arranges material to suit his particular purposes. Some issues he explores in fairly intricate detail. Nevertheless, the overall historical framework is never lost from view. Any particular passage can be placed within it.

II. The Patristic Period

As the Church continued to spread throughout the Greco-Roman world, new situations continually required new explanations and applications of the gospel. Some of the earliest writings of this period were epistles (by Ignatius, Clement of Rome, etc.) similar to those of the New Testament. But as attacks from opposing philosophies, religions, and governments became increasingly severe, the "Apology" developed. ("Apology," from the Greek *apologia*, simply means "defense.")

Due to the sophisticated character of their opponents, Christian apologists sought to use concepts and arguments acceptable to the best philosophical schools of ancient times. Moreover, they found that by merely rebutting various charges in disjointed fashion, they were far less effective than when they stated the Christian position in a well-organized fashion. Accordingly, as the apologists strove to express their faith in more articulate and comprehensive ways, they laid down the rudiments of an overall Christian worldview that was couched in language similar to that of Greek philosophy.

The greatest apologist, Justin Martyr (100?–164?), is best known for such an attempt. In John's gospel (1:1–14) Jesus Christ is called the "Word," or *logos* in Greek. Now ancient Stoic and Platonic philosophies also spoke of the *logos*. For them it was the ultimate principle of order and rationality in the universe. Justin argued that the preexistent Christ and this Greek philosophical principle were the same. Therefore the Greek philosophers also knew of Christ, although only partially, whereas Christians know him fully. In this way Justin built a bridge between Christian revelation and Greek learning that allowed much of Greek wisdom to be accepted and incorporated into Christian theology.[5]

A second thrust of Justin Martyr's work was political.[6] He insisted that Christians were not, as was commonly thought, immoral and rebellious people who threatened the state. Instead, Christians were the sort of citizens any civilization should want. To be sure, Justin was critical of the Roman state. He felt it was partially controlled by demonic powers. And as his name indicates, Rome executed him for his faith. Nevertheless, even as Justin had constructed a bridge between revelation and Greek wisdom, he also built one between Christian ethics and Roman civic behavior.

Third, Justin responded to Jewish criticisms that the New Testament was not the proper fulfillment of the Old. Going into great exegetical detail, he sought to illustrate the continuity and coherence of both Testaments.[7] In all these ways, Justin moved toward a comprehensive statement of the Christian faith and its relation to the intellectual, political, and religious challenges of his day. However, such discussion was far from over. As Christians became increasingly educated, dialogue intensified between the biblical perspectives and the Greco-Roman religion and philosophy.

In the Greek worldview, generally speaking, the divine realm was incompatible with the realm of matter. The ultimate divine Principle could never come into this world. Therefore, if one wished to become like God, one would seek to become uninvolved in and unaffected by the material universe. Most Greek religions and philosophies sought to turn attention away from one's bodily needs and from the social, political, and domestic affairs of daily life. They did this by emphasizing contemplation or ecstatic experiencing of purely immaterial, spiritual realities. These activities would prepare one for full encounter with the divine, which could happen only after death, when the soul was completely freed from the world of matter.

---

[5] See Justin's *First Apology*, Chaps. 21-23, 46; and *Dialogue with Trypho*; Chap. 128; in *The Ante-Nicene Fathers*, Vol. I (Grand Rapids: Eerdmans, 1979).

[6] This is the major theme of Justin's *First Apology*, Chaps. 1-30.

[7] *Dialogue with Trypho*; *First Apology*, Chaps. 31-53.

Biblical faith, however, spoke of God's own entrance into the material world and of his intense concern for it. Accordingly, anyone who sought to be like the Christian God would seek to mirror this involvement with material reality. The Old and New Testaments regarded the natural world as God's good creation, and the body and social life as essential to human nature. Therefore, although Christianity also believed in a life beyond the present, it sought to transform affairs in this world rather than to escape them.

Conflict between these two orientations became intense by the time of Irenaeus (135?-202?). His opponents, the Gnostics, argued that the true God could not have created the world of matter; neither could Jesus, who clearly existed within it, have been fully divine. They elaborated complex systems of purely spiritual realities in which the Old Testament God and Christ (whom they often distinguished from Jesus) were lesser beings. Yet despite the sophistication of these gnostic systems, Irenaeus declined to formulate an alternative philosophy of immaterial entities. Instead he insisted that the work of Father, Son, and Spirit, are so unified both in creation and throughout salvation history that all three agents must be God. Irenaeus said little about the conceptual problem of how three agents could yet be one. He simply followed the lead of Justin's response to Judaism: an emphasis on the continuity of God's historical activity. His theology was thus much less philosophical than most in the Patristic period.[8]

Other Fathers such as Clement of Alexandria (150?–219?) and Origen (186?–232?) sought to combat Greek thinking more in its own terms, by adopting many of its concepts and assumptions but by using them to articulate a worldview which, they felt, was quite different. Origen's On First Principles took another step toward being a systematic theology by minutely exploring many issues which emerged in attempts to bring philosophy and revelation together.

Nevertheless, Christian doctrine became more Greek and philosophical in the process. For example, the complete, bodily humanity of Jesus and of other humans became less important. Origen also delved into highly speculative matters concerning the beginning and the end of all things: the original fall of evil angels, the eternity of the created world, the eventual salvation of the Devil, and more. To some extent, biblical revelation does deal with the origin and end of things and with superhuman powers of evil. But when the human mind delves into these matters, it naturally raises many intriguing questions which the Bible does not try to answer. The mind seeks to organize knowledge on all subjects into increasingly more comprehensive systems. In Origen we glimpse this kind of philosophical systematizing becoming a part of Christian theology. It goes well beyond the sort of reflection which grows out of biblical recital.

Nevertheless, so long as Christians sought to express the gospel within ancient culture, certain fundamental issues would not go away. The question of God's relation to the material world became acute whenever one spoke or

---

[8] All of Irenaeus' themes are found in his major work, *Against Heresies*, pp. 315-567.

thought seriously about the focal point of Christian faith, Jesus Christ himself. How could one understand and explain that which seemed so incomprehensible to Greeks; that he was both fully divine and fully human?

In A.D. 325 the Council of Nicea sought to indicate Christ's deity by insisting that he was "of the same nature (*homoousion*) as the Father." Although most of the terminology in the Nicene Creed came from Scripture, the crucial term *homoousion* had a long history in philosophy and philosophically-influenced theology. Nicea, however, did little to clarify the character of Jesus' humanity. Some of the most ardent defenders of his humanity were not even clear as to whether he possessed a fully human mind and will. Consequently, much theological effort was expended in clarifying such matters until the definitive Chalcedonian Creed of A.D. 451.

If one traces the history of these creeds, one recognizes a core of saving events that brings to mind the biblical recitals. They constituted the major portion of the early Apostle's Creed. Jesus

> was born by the Holy Spirit from the Virgin Mary, crucified under Pontius Pilate and buried. He descended to hell. On the third day he rose again from the dead; he ascended into heaven, where he sits at the Father's right hand, and from whence he shall come to judge the living and the dead.

This list, however, was shortened in the Nicene Creed. In the Chalcedonian Creed it all but disappeared. At the same time, increasing space was devoted to complicated interrelations of Jesus' deity and his humanity.[9] In Greco-Roman culture, of course, extended discussion of the latter issue was necessary. But emphasis on such issues of particular relevance to Greek thought began to seriously obscure the older framework of recital, producing theological documents unlike Paul's Roman epistle, with its emphasis on recital.

As Rome and ancient civilization as a whole began to decline, the most comprehensive writer of the Patristic period appeared. Augustine (354–450) wrote voluminously on such complex topics as the Trinity. A Platonic strain was evident in much of his thought; however, his massive *City of God* tied the history of biblical revelation into the ongoing history of the church. In contro-

---

[9] Chalcedon says of Jesus' history only that "in these 'last days,' for us and on behalf of our salvation, this selfsame one was born of Mary the virgin." At the same time, of Jesus' humanity and deity it says (in part) that he is: "perfect both in deity and humanity; this selfsame one is also actually God and man, with a rational soul and a body. He is of the same reality (*homoousion*) as God as far as his deity is concerned, and of the same reality (*homoousion*) as we ourselves as far as his humanity is concerned; thus like us in all respects, sin only excepted." Christ also exists "in two natures (*phusesin*), without confusion (*asunkutos*), without change (*atreptos*), without division (*adiairetos*), without separation (*acoristos*). The distinctiveness of each nature is not nullified by the union. Instead, the properties (*idiotetos*) of each nature are conserved and both natures concur (*suntrechouses*) in one person (*prosopon*) and in one *hypostasis*. They are not divided or cut into two persons (*prosopa*)." The increase of highly specialized, extra-biblical terminology is obvious.

versy with the British monk Pelagius, Augustine insisted on the bondage of the human will apart from God's renewing grace.[10] His complex arguments had affinities with those of the Stoics and other philosophical schools. Augustine was more pessimistic about the capacities of fallen human nature than were most Patristic writers.

Augustine lived well past the time when the Emperor Constantine had transformed Christianity from a persecuted sect to the foremost religion of the realm. From 313 on, almost all church leaders had accepted the authority of Christian emperors in theological and ecclesiastical affairs. (Constantine even played a leading role in formulating the Nicene Creed.)

Also by Augustine's day, the Roman church had attained a primacy in church affairs in the West. Its authority, however, was resisted by a North African group known as the Donatists. They objected that Rome's leaders were installed merely through the ceremony of ordination, without regard to their moral and spiritual qualifications. The Donatists insisted that only those clearly manifesting Christian character should be entrusted with church leadership. For years Augustine argued the Roman viewpoint against the Donatists. At first he felt that persuasion was the only weapon to be used against their schismatic activities. Gradually, however, he became convinced that the state might use physical force to subdue them. Christianity, he argued, had changed greatly from the days of the apostles. Then it had been persecuted by the Empire. But now God had given the church Christian Emperors who could use persecution to further its interests.[11]

By Augustine's day, then, Christianity had won most people's allegiance (nominally, at least) from other religions. It had permeated the Roman social system and called its political leaders to her side. It had absorbed and then further transformed the great intellectual traditions of antiquity. All these changes are clearly evident in Augustine's voluminous writings. Nevertheless, a complete system of Christian theology, systematic theology in the specific sense, had not yet appeared.

III. Medieval Theology

Following the fall of the Roman Empire, Western civilization swiftly declined. Many works of the ancients and the Fathers were destroyed or forgotten. In the East, however, their intellectual and spiritual contributions were preserved and integrated into an ecclesiastical heritage stretching down to the present. Eastern Christianity, however, tended to be more mystical and sacra-

---

[10] For the sources, see *The Nicene and Post-Nicene Fathers* (Grand Rapids: Eerdmans, 1956), Vol. V. For an excellent discussion, see Pelikan, *The Emergence of the Catholic Tradition* (Chicago: University, 1971), pp. 292-318.

[11] See Geoffrey Grimshaw Willis, *Saint Augustine and the Donatist Controversy* (London: SPCK, 1950), esp. pp. 127-43. For the sources, see *The Nicene and Post-Nicene Fathers*, Vol. IV, pp. 369-675.

mental than that of the West. Consequently, while theologians in the East debated certain theological issues in a highly refined manner, the desire to develop a comprehensive theological system never really developed there. In comparison with what later emerged in the West, Orthodoxy's most comprehensive work, *The Orthodox Faith* by John of Damascus (650?–749?), is "only a short textbook, not a theological system."[12] Nonetheless, Orthodoxy's way of theologizing in the context of worship should not be overlooked as we seek to re-evaluate the function of theology in the present.

By the twelfth century significant economic, artistic, and intellectual developments were once again underway in the West. In the forefront of this renaissance was the rise of the medieval university. Here students and teachers banded together to explore systematically all that was known in law, medicine, and theology. Much of Aristotle's work was rediscovered. Its profundity and scope far surpassed anything European scholars had seen.

Along with the medieval university, systematic theology in the specific sense also arose. In earlier medieval times theological discussion often centered on questions which originated from the exegesis of biblical texts. Peter Lombard (1100-1160?) initiated the discipline of systematic theology when he sought to arrange these questions according a certain plan and order. Lombard sought, first, to be comprehensive. The *Sentences* are a compendium of all the major questions which scholars had ever asked. Lombard also included all the relevant discussions on each question from church tradition, especially from the Fathers. Second, Lombard sought to disengage these questions from their original biblical contexts (and thus from any framework of "recital") and to arrange them in a *consistent, coherent,* logical sequence of their own. Finally, wherever the opinions from tradition differed, Lombard sought to synthesize such discrepancies. The resulting *Sentences,* then, were designed to be a comprehensive, coherent, and synthetically consistent account of all the major issues of the Christian faith. They remained at the core of Western theological education up to and even beyond that which culminated medieval systematic theology: the *Summa Theologiae* of Thomas Aquinas.[13]

During the twelfth century western Europe gradually rediscovered the writings of Aristotle (384–322 B.C.), the most comprehensive of all ancient philoso-

---

[12] John Meyendorff, *Byzantine Theology* (New York: Fordham, 1974), p. 4. For the general tenor of Eastern Orthodox theology, see also Vladmir Lossky, *Orthodox Theology: An Introduction* (Crestwood, N.Y.: St. Vladimir's Seminary Press, 1978); Ernst Brenz, *The Eastern Orthodox Church* (Chicago: Aldine, 1963) pp. 40-64; and Jaroslav Pelikan, *The Spirit of Eastern Christendom* (Chicago: University, 1974), pp. 1-36.

[13] Thomas' first systematic work, the *Summa Contra Gentiles* (Garden City, N.Y.: Doubleday, 1955-57) devotes the first of its four books to God, the second to creation, and the third to providence. In his *Summa Theologiae* (London: Blackfriars, 1964 [60 vols.]), Part I, Questions 1-43 deal with God and creation, Questions 44-102 and 103-19 with providence.

phers. This discovery was much like the earlier challenge Platonism and Stoicism posed to the Fathers. The principles underlying Aristotle's voluminous work were grounded (as were those of all ancient philosophers and scientists) on human observation and reason alone. Should Christianity, which was based on divine revelation, seek to absorb and appropriate this knowledge? Or were the principles of faith and those of reason so different that they could not be reconciled? Would Christianity have to reject scientific and philosophical learning, or at least let them become purely "secular" pursuits, while Christian faith occupied a purely "religious" compartment of life? Theology has always had to deal with these questions.

Generally speaking, Aquinas and most other medieval theologians followed the path broken by Justin and Origen. They regarded Aristotle's definitions of certain basic notions—cause, effect, motion, matter, mind, etc.—as valid for thought in all disciplines. They further argued that reasoning which employed these basic notions could demonstrate the truth of certain Christian beliefs; that God exists, that God is not composed of matter, etc. (Judaism and Islam shared most of these beliefs. Still, medieval theologians argued at length that correct interpretation of Aristotle favored understanding them with a Christian slant!) For Aquinas, systematic theology consisted not only of these results of philosophical or "natural" theology. It also included certain "revealed" truths: the events of biblical history, the Trinity, etc. This view gave theology a certain unique content which reason could not discover. Nevertheless, in order to develop a coherent, consistent theological synthesis, Aquinas used Aristotelian categories of explanation even when handling "revealed" content.

The procedure which developed from Lombard to Aquinas shaped systematic theology for centuries. It is crucial to remember that it arose as part of the medieval university. Within the university there was great concern to demonstrate the rational credibility of Christian faith and to clarify its relations to other branches of knowledge. Consequently, the relationship between faith and reason was usually discussed at the beginning of new theological systems. Systematic theology next took up the existence and attributes of God, issues which philosophical or "natural" reason could also handle. From there it proceeded to "revealed" truths about God, such as the Trinity, and then to the Creation of the world and God's providential guidance of it.

The existence and attributes of God are extremely abstruse subjects for human thought. Moreover, discussions of Creation and Providence require a good grounding in philosophy and the sciences. Once again, as in Origen, theological attention tends to become preoccupied with issues intelligible only to those who were intellectually sophisticated. Issues much closer to the average Christian—the events of biblical history, the process of salvation, the nature of the Church—were covered much later in the system. And by that time, the way they were handled was heavily influenced by the complex concepts and conclusions that had been developed in earlier sections.

These characteristics of early systematic theology were significantly influenced by the social location of the new discipline. Systematic theology, arose as a branch of academic study pursued in universities and not primarily as a task of the church involved in the world at large.[14] Nevertheless, the effects of this new "Queen of the Sciences" spread far beyond the walls of academia. It gave leaders of the church and society a unified worldview. Systematic theology stood at the pinnacle of the late medieval attempt, following the fragmentation and frequently miserable conditions of preceding centuries, to unify the social, political, and cultural dimensions of existence in an orderly, coherent way.

As time passed, and as objections to the use of the pagan Aristotle subsided, systematic theology served an orthodoxy that sought to unify Church doctrine and eliminate heresy. Theology attempted to preserve Christian truth and to delineate its every contour with increasing precision. This attempt fit nicely with other attempts to preserve and ever more carefully control a traditional society. And because the state had been promoting and protecting the Church ever since Constantine and Augustine, systematic theology could also aid rulers seeking to suppress religious and social dissent.

There were innovative philosophical and theological movements in the fourteenth and fifteenth centuries and innovative social and economic developments as well. But amid the main currents of systematic theology, the spark behind the brilliant syntheses of Aquinas and others often faded into rather sterile discussions over minor points of a largely fixed tradition.

IV. The Reformation

Since the Middle Ages, intellectual and social revolutions have shaken Western society and the Church, and their repercussions have affected theology greatly. However, the formal structure of systematic theology has remained substantially the same. Systematic theologians have sought for comprehensive development of all major issues raised by Scripture, tradition, and contemporary learning. By developing a set of coherent, consistent concepts, they have attempted to organize synthetic accounts of all major features of Christian faith. Theology has usually been pursued in academic settings and been much concerned with the relationship of faith and reason. Doctrinal treatment has normally begun with God (including the Trinity) and then moved to Creation and Providence. The biblical history of salvation, culminating in Christ, has come after this. The Christian life, the Church, and eschatology have appeared towards the end.

[14] Aquinas, however, belonged to the Dominican order, which had begun as a preaching movement to combat heresies. Aquinas' work can be interpreted as an extension of the teaching which was essential to this task (as the work of Fransiscan theologians was an extension of the teaching of their order). Our point, however, is that the theology of Aquinas and others quickly became far more at home in the university and far more preoccupied with the issues raised there than with those relevant to a travelling preacher.

The Reformation unleashed many new currents in the Church and combined with numerous social, economic and cultural forces which were disintegrating the medieval world. In a movement with so many aspects, it is perhaps impossible to single out the essential feature. However, the Reformation emphasized the human, experiential side of Christian faith: the awareness of sin and the need for forgiveness, the joy and freedom of salvation through faith, the roles of law and grace in Christian living. The spirit of the Reformation was best expressed in sermons and in brief, polemical pamphlets by leaders like Martin Luther (1483–1546).

Luther's chief contribution was his agonizing awareness of the paradoxes of sin and grace, judgment and salvation, divine wrath and divine love. Luther produced no systematic theology. Yet by 1521 his disciple Philip Melanchthon (1497–1560) constructed an outline of the new teaching. At first it seemed that this work, the *Loci Communes*, might put systematic theology on a new foundation. Melanchthon attacked the usual medieval order of treatment:

> We do better to adore the mysteries of the Deity than to investigate them....The Lord God Almighty clothes his Son with flesh that he might draw us from contemplating his own majesty to a consideration of the flesh, and especially of our own weaknesses....Therefore, there is no reason why we should labor so much on those exalted topics such as 'God', 'the Unity and Trinity of God', 'The Mystery of Creation', and 'The Manner of the Incarnation'. What, I ask you, did the Scholastics accomplish during the many ages when they were examining only these points?
> ...But as for one who is ignorant of the other fundamentals, namely, 'The Power of Sin', 'The Law', and 'Grace', I do not see how I can call him a Christian. For from these things Christ is known, since to know Christ means to know his benefits, and not as *they* teach, to reflect upon his natures and the modes of his incarnation.[15]

Yet in the much expanded *Loci* of 1555, Melanchthon's first three topics were lengthy treatments of God, the Trinity, and Creation—the same topics he had rejected as starting points in 1521! Protestant theology was beginning to resemble, at least in form, medieval Catholic theology. Why?

The main reason was the need to consolidate the Reformation. Protestants were seeking to cut through the theological authority which tradition and "natural" reason had claimed and to acknowledge that of Scripture alone. But in so doing they were continually debating the highly sophisticated, systematized Roman Catholic theology. It thus became necessary to apply the new principle of biblical authority to those areas which Catholic theologians had discussed. Accordingly, even though Protestants sought a theology whose content differed from Catholic theology, the efforts of both groups corresponded, to a significant degree, in form.

These consolidating efforts also proceeded on a second front. As people began reforming their ideas in light of Scripture, the Bible began to be read in

---

[15] *Loci Communes* in Wilhelm Pauck, ed., *Melanchthon and Bucer* (Philadelphia: Westminster, 1969), pp. 21-22.

more than one way. Lutheran and Reformed groups, for example, retained the medieval notion of the promotion and protection of the church by the state; yet more radical groups, like the Anabaptists, insisted that this exceeded the state's proper role. To keep the Reformation from splintering into numerous sects, Lutheran and Reformed theologians—not wholly unlike their medieval predecessors—sought for doctrines which could exclude such variant biblical interpretations. (The more radical groups, largely due to persecution, produced almost no systematic theology).[16]

These ecclesiastical concerns had socio-political parallels. The new Protestant territories were islands amid seas of Catholic power. Should the Catholic areas (France, Spain, Austria, the Papal States) unite, Protestant areas would almost surely be conquered. This intensified the latter's need for internal religious unity. Since Constantine, religious unity had been regarded as essential to political unity, but such internal unity appeared to be sorely threatened by the smaller, more radical new groups. Thus the achievement of a Protestant systematic theology served to unify both the Protestant church and state, countering the Catholic threat from without, and the sectarian threat from within.

Reformed systematic theology originated with John Calvin (1509–1564), and the appearance in 1536 of his first *Institutes of the Christian Religion*. Its basic structure remained unchanged in later, expanded editions. Like other Reformers, Calvin sought to emphasize Scripture's authority over that of any philosophy, especially Aristotle's. To do so, he devoted Book I of the *Institutes* to "The Knowledge of God the Creator." While Calvin acknowledged that some minimal awareness of God is available through reason, he insisted that Scripture alone is the source of all saving knowledge. By downplaying philosophical speculation, Calvin devoted little space to the attributes of God (although he developed a healthy section on the Trinity). He then discussed Creation and Providence before moving to issues closer to the heart of the Reformation.

In Book II, Calvin (like Luther and Augustine) emphasized the seriousness of sin and the inability of persons to overcome it. He then developed a biblical theology of redemption under the categories of Law and Gospel (the Old and New Testament principles, for him). He explored the relationship between the Testaments at length. Calvin then took up the Person and Work of Christ. Book III dealt with the human response to Christ's saving work: faith, repentance, justification, and the Christian life. Following this, Calvin pondered the abstruse but, for him, important doctrine of predestination. Book IV dealt with the church. Here Calvin insisted on obedience of Christians to the state. Eschatology was hardly mentioned in the *Institutes*.

Because of John Calvin's new grasp of faith, the content of his *Institutes* differed markedly from that of most medieval systems. His insights also left im-

---

[16] For the insights which such groups might contribute to systematic theology, see Chapter 5.

prints on the structure of a systematic theology. Speculations about God's nature were briefer and much more modest. Treatments of biblical history and its interpretation (hermeneutic) were much more extensive and central. The complex theme of predestination was handled only after describing the Christian life in detail. Nevertheless, the *Institutes*, somewhat like later editions of Melanchthon's *Loci Communes*, bottled the new wine in only partially redesigned vessels.

V. Protestant Orthodoxy

Not wholly unlike fourteenth and fifteenth century Roman Catholic theology, Protestant theology from the late sixteenth through the eighteenth centuries passed through a period of refinement and consolidation. The new doctrines were defined more precisely, and the new systems organized more minutely. All this accompanied and helped promote the ecclesiastical organization of Lutheran, Reformed, and Anglican regions and the accompanying emergence of self-consciously Protestant societies and cultures. Yet orthodoxy was not solely motivated by ecclesiastical or social needs but also by that desire for deeper apprehension of the gospel which always characterizes theology.

In face of Catholicism's reliance on both Scripture and Tradition as sources of authority, orthodox theologians rightly felt the continuing need to define and defend the superior role of the former. In so doing, they laid increasing emphasis on the cognitive, propositional assertions which could be found in the Bible and less on Scripture's historical or devotional character. They carefully defined the Bible as free from error, including its minute details.[17] Discussions of biblical authority came near the beginning of orthodox theologies. They were often supplemented by, of all things, philosophical arguments concerning God's existence and nature, inspired by Aristotle. Then orthodoxy, like medieval theology, moved to the nature of God.

Unlike Calvin, Reformed Protestant orthodoxy often discussed predestination in this context. (In the *Institutes*, we remember, it had appeared as a reflection on biblical history and Christian experience). But now orthodoxy treated it as an attribute of God's knowledge, from which the whole of salvation history (theoretically, at least) could be derived. Debates ensued as to the logical order of the different "decrees" in God's predestinating will. Did God "first" decree to elect some and condemn others—and "then" decree the fall and

---

[17] See Heinrich Heppe, ed., *Reformed Dogmatics: Set Out and Illustrated from the Sources* (Grand Rapids: Baker, 1978), pp. 15-20; Heinrich Schmid, ed., *Doctrinal Theology of the Evangelical Lutheran Church* (Minneapolis: Augsburg, 1875), pp. 51-66; Robert Preus, *The Inspiration of Scripture* (Edinburgh: Oliver & Boyd, 1955), pp. 76-88.

then the work of salvation (Supralapsarianism)? Or was it the other way around (Infralapsarianism)?[18]

Discussions of sin and grace in human experience usually appeared after many pages on such topics. Especially in Reformed orthodoxy, theologians focused on the relationship between the human will and God's predestinating sovereignty. As in Augustine's theology, these debates took on extreme philosophical complexity, intelligible only to the most learned.

Orthodox Lutheran theologians majored in several different issues. There was the "ubiquity" of Christ's body: Was it everywhere at once? How was it present in the sacrament? There was also the "exchange of attributes" (*communicatio idiomatum*): Which of the divine attributes were communicated to the historical Jesus? Which were not? The abstruseness of both these issues is obvious. Though they had both arisen from Luther's views [19], extended scholarly debate on their subtleties moved orthodox theology farther from Christian experience and daily life.

While orthodoxy was often allied with Church bodies whose structures were becoming more rigid and whose spiritual life was becoming more arid, vital Protestant movements were springing up largely outside these confines. Towards the beginning of the seventeenth century, the Baptists, the Puritans and then the Quakers appeared, and towards the end of the century, the Pietist movement arose. Formally, Pietism remained largely within the orthodox realm, but it helped spawn groups which did not: the Moravians, the Methodists, and the Church of the Brethren. Throughout the eighteenth-century, evangelical revivals from Puritan and Methodist roots swept the English-speaking world. Generally speaking, these movements, like orthodoxy, affirmed the Reformation's basic teachings. But, with the exception of Puritanism, they did little systematic theology. They stressed evangelistic mission and daily discipleship instead. Nevertheless, any attempt to rethink the value of systematic theology for today must ask whether these "Believers' churches" might also have something to contribute (see Chapter 5).

This question is especially pertinent in view of the resurgence of "evangelical" Christianity today. Protestant orthodoxy remained a minority voice throughout the nineteenth and into the twentieth centuries, and when evan-

---

[18] Since all agreed that God dwells in eternity and thus thinks and knows everything at the same instant, there could be chronological order among the decrees. Nevertheless, the logical order or, as it were, relative importance among the decrees was still thought to be significant. (See Justo Gonzales, *A History of Christian Thought* (Nashville: Abingdon, 1975, Vol. III, pp. 242-72.) Heppe, pp. 133-49; Charles Hodge, *Systematic Theology*, Vol. II (London: James Clarke, 1960 [originally published in 1874]), pp. 316-21.

[19] See Gonzales, pp. 226-41 for an excellent discussion; also Schmid, pp. 321-337; Edmud Schlink, *Theology of the Lutheran Confessions* (Philadelphia: Muhlenberg, 1961), pp. 187-93.

gelicals have done systematic theology, it has often been of this variety.[20] Otherwise, however, groups sponsoring orthodox theology have done comparatively little evangelism, while groups doing evangelism have done comparatively little orthodox theology. What might this mean for an "evangelical" theology today?

VI. Liberal Theology

The next major theological revolution was also connected with sweeping social and cultural changes, beginning with the scientific revolution of the sixteenth and seventeenth centuries. Science learned so much about physical nature by means of observation and reason that many wondered whether human nature might also be best understood by the same means. The Enlightenment (eighteenth century) philosophers sought to promote the study and advancement of humanity by scientific means.

However, orthodox Christianity, both Protestant and Catholic, stood in the way. On one hand, it often supported the political authority of traditional, despotic states. On the other, its doctrine of fallen human nature (accentuated in Protestantism via Augustine, Luther, and Calvin) seemed to undercut the possibility of human progress. Consequently, the Enlightenment struggle against traditional social structures was usually also a struggle against religion. By means of the Enlightenment, the scientific revolution led to those political revolutions which began in America (1776) and France (1789) and which have spread through most of the world.[21]

The scientific revolution also spawned the Industrial Revolution of the eighteenth and nineteenth centuries. Through it humanity seemed capable of transforming not only its own social environment but its physical environment as well. Revolution in both environments was accompanied by swelling confidence in humanity's ability to remake the world, leading to the birth of faith in the inevitable technological, moral, and social progress of humanity.[22] In Chapter 4 we shall discuss several liberal theologians in detail. For now we merely note that liberal theologies, like all others, sought to articulate the gospel in light of the challenges and problems of their times (from about 1800–

[20] See Donald Dayton, *Discovering an Evangelical Heritage* (New York: Harper, 1976), pp. 128-133; Claude Welch, *Protestant Thought in the Nineteenth Century*, Vol. I (New Haven: Yale, 1972), p. 25.

[21] Generally speaking, Believers' church groups even opposed movements towards social reform less than did those connected with Protestant orthodoxy, and they supported some such movements. This difference was due, in part, to their lesser affinities with most contemporary socio-political establishments and to their somewhat greater emphasis on the freedom of the human will.

[22] See J. B. Bury, *The Idea of Progress: an Inquiry into its Origins and Growth* (New York: Dover, 1955). In its mature form, this idea is the notion that progress is inevitable: that it is decreed by laws as unbreakable as those in the natural sciences were thought to be.

1917). They delved into the sciences, the political theories, and the philosophies of their day. Yet unlike Protestant orthodoxy, which generally championed traditional formulations against modern trends, liberal theology followed the general lead of Origen and Aquinas by adopting assumptions and concepts accepted by intellectuals in its day.

Liberal theologians spoke less directly of God's nature, the Trinity, and God's attributes. They were more concerned with human religious experiences and moral aspirations. They stressed the potential goodness of human nature, and they were constantly researching and reinterpreting past history (biblical, ecclesiastical, and social) in light of the new understandings of progress. In the process, they regained an appreciation of the Bible's historical character. Liberal theologians urged Christians to support advanced technological and social movements. They were at least as aligned with political forces as was orthodoxy, albeit with "progressive" rather than conservative ones.

Nevertheless, the basic structure of systematic theology remained unaltered. Since educational advances were central to progress, liberal theology strove to become at least as comprehensive, coherent, and synthetic as its predecessors. In an age of science, extensive discussions of how God might be known still prefaced the theological system. In an epoch which applied evolutionary theory to both nature and society, Creation and Providence needed to be rethought continually. Consequently, although theological systems directly asserted much less about God and his attributes, the Doctrine of God, followed by Creation and Providence, still comprised the first few sections of most works.[23]

VII. Neo-orthodox Theology

The successor to liberal theology, neo-orthodoxy (to be examined more fully in Chap. 5) arose with yet another cultural revolution. After World War I, it seemed that technology had contributed less to humanity's advancement than to its destruction. Humanity's supposed moral and political progress had seemed powerless to prevent or ameliorate that devastating war. Industry and culture were in shambles. Never, it seemed, could they be rebuilt on the foundations of the Enlightenment and its optimism. Harking back to the Reformation, neo-orthodoxy again stressed human fallenness and the need for *grace*. It severely critiqued the notion that humans could know God through philosophy and science. It sometimes denied the very possibility of natural theology and sharply contrasted reason with revelation.

Indeed, true faith was depicted as so contrary to what humans normally ex-

[23] A major exception is the influential work of liberal theology, Volume III of Albrecht Ritschl's *Justification and Reconciliation* (Clifton, N.J.: Reference Book Publishers, 1966 [originally published in 1874]). Ritschl organizes much of the material of systematic theology around the concepts "Justification" and "the Kingdom of God." (See Chap. 4.)

perience or think, that any conceptual, systematic expression of faith some-times seemed impossible. Neo-orthodoxy's foremost spokesman, Karl Barth (1886–1968), eschewed the very term "systematic theology." He defined it as "an edifice of thought, constructed on certain fundamental conceptions which are selected in accordance with a certain philosophy." Barth insisted that the-ology had to look away from all such supposed general principles, and base it-self instead upon the unique "history of the communion of God with man and of man with God."[24] And this history was initiated and guided by God, not man. For Barth the object of theology could never be the results of philosophy, science, history, or sociology, but only its unique revelation. He sought to ex-press this object in distinctly biblical categories. In fact, notions like "recital," which the contemporary biblical theology movement had discovered, played a role in neo-orthodoxy. Moreover, in contrast to the history of systematic theol-ogy, Barth insisted that theology could be properly pursued only within the church.[25] For this study, he preferred the name "dogmatics."

The structure of neo-orthodox dogmatics, however, proved strikingly similar to those of previous systematic theologies. Its very critique of natural theology demanded that at least as much time be devoted to faith/reason issues. Its em-phasis on the divine initiative called for a lengthy section on God, in which God's attributes and trinitarian character again came to the fore.[26] Predestina-tion and its complex implications also merited lengthy reconsideration. And in reaction against the liberal emphasis on human experience, the subjective dimensions of salvation usually came much later.

The cultural shock of World War I was repeated in World War II, and neo-orthodoxy remained at the theological center until the late 1950s. Since then, as neo-orthodoxy has waned, systematic theology has also declined. To some, this decline seemed sudden and inexplicable. But neo-orthodoxy's success in calling many to a more traditional kind of faith obscured the fact that forces which seriously threatened systematic theology had been at work for several centuries.

The reader may have noticed that systematic theology has been an almost entirely western, middle or upper class, male discipline. It has seldom, if ever, been pursued in eastern Christendom or in "third world" countries. Tradition-

---

[24] *Dogmatics in Outline* (New York: Harper, 1959), p. 5.

[25] Ibid., pp. 9-14. However, Friedrich Schleiermacher (1768-1834), often called "the father of liberal theology," had made the same claim (*The Christian Faith* [New York: Harper, 1963; originally published in 1830], pp. 3-5).

[26] Karl Barth's *Church Dogmatics* (Edinburgh: T. & T. Clark, 1936-69), for instance, begin with two lengthy volumes on the Doctrine of God, each of which is subdi-vided into two parts, and which also deal with prolegomena. They total 2,898 pages. See also Emil Brunner, *The Christian Doctrine of God* (Philadelphia: Westmin-ster, 1950) and Otto Weber, *Foundations of Dogmatics*, Vol. I (Grand Rapids: Eerd-mans, 1951), pp. 3-460.

ally, it has been done neither by minorities within western society, nor by women. In our pluralistic age, where too many differences of perspective already divide people, would it be helpful to pursue a discipline that might speak in a language foreign to many?

What value, then, might such a discipline have for our present "apocalyptic" era? Should we pursue it in this traditional form? Or is this form so far removed from contemporary attitudes and needs that it might best be scrapped? Or, finally, might it be best to keep pursuing some of systematic theology's fundamental goals—but in other ways, in a different form? These questions will occupy our next two chapters.

Suggestions for Further Reading

A. Works on the History of Theology

Bromiley, Geoffrey W. *Historical Theology: An Introduction.* Grand Rapids: Eerdmans, 1977.

Chenu, Marie Dominique. *Nature, Man, and Society in the Twelfth Century.* (Especially Chapter 7.) Chicago: University Press, 1968.

Congar, Yves. *A History of Christian Theology.* Garden City, N.Y.: Doubleday, 1968.

Gonzales, Justo. *A History of Christ Thought,* 3 vols. Nashville, Abingdon, 1970-75.

Harnack, Adolph. *History of Dogma,* 7 vols. New York: Russell and Russell, 1958 (Originally published in German, 1885.)

———. *Outlines of History of Dogma.* Boston: Beacon Hill, 1957 (originally published in German, 1893.)

Pelikan, Jaroslavl. *The Christian Tradition: A History of the Development of Doctrine,* vols. 1-4. Chicago: University Press, 1971-1983.

Tillich, Paul. *A History of Christian Thought* (also titled: *A Complete History of Christian Thought.* New York: Harper, 1966.

B. Works in Systematic Theology (Twentieth Century)

Barth, Karl. *Church Dogmatics,* 13 vols. Edinburgh: T&T Clark, 1936-69.

Berkhof, Hendrikus. *Christian Faith.* Grand Rapids: Eerdmans, 1979.

Berkouwer, C.G. *Studies in Dogmatics,* 14 vols. Grand Rapids: Eerdmans, 1952-1975.

Bloesch, Donald. *Essentials of Evangelical Theology,* 2 Vols. New York: Harper and Row, 1978.

Brunner, Emil. *Dogmatics,* 3 vols. Philadelphia: Westminister, 1950-1978. Vol. 1, *The Christian Doctrine of God;* Vol. 2, *The Christian Doctrine of Creation and Redemption;* Vol. 3, *The Christian Doctrine of the Church, Faith and the Consummation.*

Caster, Charles, ed. *A Contemporary Wesleyan Theology*. Grand Rapids: Zon-
dervan, 1983.
Erickson, Millard, *Christian Theology*, 2 Vols. Grand Rapids: Baker, 1983.
Küng, Hans. *On Being a Christian*. Garden City, N.Y.: Doubleday, 1976.
MacQuarrie, John. *Principles of Christian Theology*. (2nd ed.) New York: Scrib-
ner's, 1977.
Rahner, Karl. *Foundations of Christian Faith*. New York: Seabury, 1978.
Strong, Augustus. *Systematic Theology*. Westwood, N.J.: Revell, 1907.
Theilicke, Helmut. *The Evangelical Faith*, 3 vols. Grand Rapids: Eerdmans,
1974, 1977, 1982.
Tillich, Paul. *Systematic Theology*, 3 vols. Chicago: University Press, 1951-
1963.
Weber, Otto. *Foundations of Dogmatics*, 2 vols. Grand Rapids: Eerdmans, 1981,
1983.

C. Works in Movements Advocating Revision
of Traditional Systematic Theology

1. Black Theologies

Cone, James. *A Black Theology of Liberation*. Philadelphia: Lippencott, 1970.
———.*God of the Oppressed*. New York: Seabury, 1975.
Roberts, J. Deotis. *Liberation and Reconciliation*. Philadelphia: Westminister,
1971.
West, Cornell. *Prophesy Deliverance!* Philadelphia: Westminster, 1983.

2. Feminist Theologies

Christ, Carol and Plaskow, Judith, eds. *Womanspirit Rising*. New York: Harper,
1979.
Collins, Sheila. *A Different Heaven and Earth*. Valley Forge, Pa.: Judson, 1974.
Reuther, Rosemary. *Sexism and God-Talk*. Boston: Beacon, 1983.
Russell, Letty. *Human Liberation in a Feminist Perspective*. Philadelphia: West-
minster, 1974.

3. Third World Theologies

Elwood, Douglas, ed. *Asian Christian Theology*. Philadelphia: Westminster,
1980.
Fabella, Virginia and Torres, Sergio. *Irruption of the Third World*. Maryknoll,
N.Y.: Orbis, 1983.
Gutierrez, Gustavo. *Theology of Liberation*. Maryknoll, N.Y.: Orbis, 1973.
Segundo, Juan. *A Theology for the Artisans of a New Humanity*. Maryknoll,
N.Y.: Orbis, 1974.

CHAPTER TWO

Why Systematic Theology?

The preceding historical approach has sketched the discipline of systematic theology from Peter Lombard's time to that of Karl Barth. We have seen that systematic theology attempted, first, to be *comprehensive*. Not only has it discussed in detail the major beliefs of the Christian faith, but from medieval times onward systematic theology has sought to interact with the latest developments in philosophy and the sciences. It has laid down guidelines for moral, social, and political life. And in doing all this, systematic theology has sought to incorporate the vast heritage of theological tradition.

Second, systematic theology has striven for *consistent, coherent* conceptual expression. It has not been content to let different expressions of faith simply lie side by side. Systematic theologians have taken conceptual systems (from Plato, Aristotle, modern evolution, etc.) and overarching themes (salvation history, biblical authority, etc.) and sought to interrelate all of its doctrines coherently by means of them. Systematic theology has almost always been pursued in academic settings, and its pursuit has required prodigious education and intelligence.

Third, systematic theology has aimed at *synthesis*. When different assertions seemed to clash, whether among biblical writings or voices from tradition, faith, or the sciences, theologians have striven to harmonize them. Systematic theology has continually sought to smooth out paradoxes and to refine its various assertions. Such refinement has often served to consolidate religious movements by giving them a definite, normative shape. Along with this, the tendency has sometimes arisen to identify the degree of one's Christian commitment with the precision of one's intellectual beliefs. Systematic theology

31

has sometimes buttressed rigidified ecclesiastical hierarchies and gone hand in hand with authoritarian social structures.

Can systematic theology be a meaningful, useful undertaking in our swiftly-paced "apocalyptic" era? The three features just mentioned have long given rise to objections against it. While these objections have often been expressed in sophisticated fashion, most of them have been sensed by ordinary Christians. We shall seek, first, to express them in a straightforward, common-sense way; next we shall observe how they have intensified in recent decades. Then we will turn to this chapter's main task: to see if we can find starting point for contemporary theological reflection consistent with what is valid in these objections.

I. Objections to Systematic Theology

First, is not the vast enterprise of comprehensiveness, the attempt to deal with all possible issues from all possible viewpoints, quite removed from the simple trust and daily walk of Christian faith? Of what value is a lengthy review of the Fathers, the Scholastics, the Reformers (not to mention philosophers and scientists) for everyday worship and service? Does not continual concern with the international and cosmic implications of things blind one to needs that lie nearby?

Second, does not the emphasis on conceptual coherence and consistency overemphasize the intellectual realm? Is not Christianity more a matter of the way we act and feel than of the way we think? How do lengthy definitions and discussions couched in academic jargon help one live rightly and serve others or come to grips with the sorrow of sin and the wonder of grace? Does not the learning and intellectual effort required by systematic theology remove us from the arena of daily existence rather than help us deal with it?

Finally, is not the precisely interlocking synthesis of a system quite different from the fluidity and paradox of actual experience? Life does not always fit into neatly defined compartments, and faith often involves trusting God in situations which one does not understand. Does not the desire to put everything together, to have an answer for every possible problem, run counter to the risk and uncertainty of faith?[1] And does not systematic thinking stifle innovative ideas and actions and reinforce traditional ways of thinking and behaving?

Probably such objections have always been sensed by many ordinary Christians. But they have become much more widespread in recent years. If we look more closely at what has been happening ever since the Enlightenment, we shall understand why. Chapter 1 remarked that the Enlightenment of the late seventeenth and eighteenth centuries was a reaction against tradition, against philosophical and scientific schools, against authoritarian government, against

[1] Such objections to philosophical and theological systems have perhaps never been stated more sharply and effectively than by Soren Kierkegaard (1813-1855). See especially his *Concluding Unscientific Postscript* (Princeton: University, 1941).

semi-feudal economies, and against state religions and orthodox theologies. Never before had experimentation, discovery, and change been more celebrated. Seldom had the established and the enduring been so scorned and freedom from them so highly desired.

But the new age of democratic and industrial revolutions brought a paradoxical surprise. Economic, social, and ecclesiastical restraints gave way; capitalism, democracy, and religious pluralism arose. But these revolutions went hand in hand with the reshaping of the world through science and technology. And as the nineteenth century flowed into the twentieth, large-scale industry and commerce increasingly influenced all spheres of life. Masses crowded into large cities, many to work in mammoth factories or for gigantic corporations. Not only did new products such as radios, automobiles, and airplanes profoundly alter individual lives, but along with the new urban centers of production came a whole new host of social and economic problems. The unforeseen productivity of these rising industries created new issues for government and transformed the shape of international relations, where the gap widened between wealthy industrialized nations and those of less developed regions.

To deal with this new situation, the scientific method, which had made the rise of industry possible, was applied increasingly to social issues and to government. Every area of life was increasingly organized, rationalized, and systematized. Many an individual, freed from the restraints and comforts of traditional social, economic, and religious life, now felt lost in a world which was swiftly becoming ever more dominated by systems, bureaucracies, and other forces that depersonalize people.

And so a paradox of modern Western existence: It began with the desire to be free from traditional restraints and to remake the world through human intelligence and effort; yet the more these goals have been attained, the more stifled many people feel. The sense of helplessness and bondage has been greatest after the colossal tragedies of World Wars I and II and in the face of massive international problems and the nuclear threat of today. The social and industrial system, which a liberated humanity has created, appears uncannily to exist independently, and to have turned around and enslaved us.

Against this contemporary backdrop we can better appreciate the recent decline in popularity of systematic theology. First, the comprehensiveness at which it aims seems virtually unattainable. The enormous knowledge explosion ignited by the Enlightenment has made acquaintance with even the major fields of learning an awesome task today. Further, increasing specialization and compartmentalization has affected all fields and subjects, including religious studies. A synthetic overview of them seems beyond reach.

Yet suppose someone could compose a comprehensive, modern theological system. How desirable would it be? Given the massive social and intellectual problems that face us, one might suppose that most people would be keenly interested in explanations of how things fit together. Yet when many people search for meaning in life, their direction is often the opposite. Feeling adrift in our highly organized, impersonal and threatening technological world, they are searching for something more personal, more intimate, and more individual. Since the world may not last long anyway, they want concrete solutions to particular practical problems. They want something that makes their fragmented, frightened personal existence significant right now, whether or not it has any relation to what science, sociology, or religious tradition may say about the world.

For this reason, systematic theology's efforts at conceptual coherence and consistency also can seem remote from life's real issues. Knowledge has become a tool for subjugating, organizing, and depersonalizing the world. Numerous years of schooling seem necessary for making a living and coping with things. Thus many who turn towards religion are seeking anything but more knowledge. Our religious nature cries out for something vivid and alive. People seek fulfillment in their emotional and volitional lives, which often are poorly developed. So long as one's experiences seem meaningful, many care little as to whether their beliefs about them are coherent and consistent.

Third, systematic theology's synthetic tendencies—smoothing over apparent contradictions, resolving all difficult questions of truth and justice—are distasteful to most moderns. Ever since the Enlightenment, life has been changing at an ever more rapid pace. As traditional beliefs and customs have eroded, new social arrangements and technologies have presented humanity with fresh challenges and with moral dilemmas never thought of before. No sooner has one situation apparently been mastered than new learning, new inventions, or changing social circumstances alter its complexion entirely. Of course some discrepancy has always existed between the clarity of a theological system and the ambiguity of the life of faith. Yet existence today seems far more fluid and fast-paced than ever before. Modern means of communication continually alert us to the enormous variety of belief systems and moral standards existing among humankind. And today's global problems of hunger, poverty, and war seem so complex that one despairs of finding solutions. Accordingly, theological edifices which apparently inscribe correct thought and action within narrow boundaries seem to have little relevance today. And many people are reluctant to join churches which demand adherence to specific beliefs and practices, and which support traditional social institutions and behavior.[2]

In the face of all these objections, is it perhaps best to encourage the further decline of systematic theology? In their more general form, such objections have always existed. Is our modern situation simply intensifying these, helping us see more acutely the fundamental incompatibility between systematic theology and the living essence of Christian faith? Chapter 1 showed that theology has always arisen to help Christians articulate and live out their faith amidst a

---

[2] To be sure, as the world apparently becomes more fragmented and as individuals feel more isolated, many long for an integrated and stable worldview. Still, this need is usually met by rather unthinking adherence to ready-made moral, political, or religious views. Few people who adopt traditional religions, moral or social views study them with care.

specific culture. Is contemporary culture telling us that systematic theology is no longer needed? One thing seems clear: If systematic theology or something like it is still relevant, we can no longer assume that this is so because it has always been so. If we are to undertake this enterprise at all, we shall have to ask afresh why we should do it and just how we should do it.

II. The Fundamental Task of Theology

If we cannot simply accept the validity of a certain systematic tradition (protestant orthodox, liberal, neo-orthodox, etc.) and then proceed to work from within it, where shall we begin? Let us think back to the origins of theological reflection, antedating the rise of systematic theology. We observed that biblical writers occasionally set down the main items of their community's faith in concise, orderly fashion. Usually this statement took the form of a recital of those key acts through which God had delivered and remained faithful to his people. As time passed, new events were added to this narrative, and its overall course was envisioned from different and broader perspectives. Such new articulation took place not only because new events had occurred, but also because the events had to be expressed amidst different historical and cultural contexts.

As we followed this process, we observed that these saving events climaxed in the life, death, and resurrection of Jesus. The activity of interpreting those events amid different contexts, however, has continued down to the present. In other words, theological reflection has always involved two elements: (1) a basic message, grounded in certain historical events and (2) the orderly communication of this message in different ways appropriate to various times and cultures.

In searching for a theological starting point which lies outside any systematic tradition, we have two basic choices. We may seek to begin again from the original message. Or we may start from Christian existence as it is apprehended in our present context.[3] Certain problems confront either approach. The original message has come down to us as shaped by a series of historical traditions; all attempts to understand it are influenced by contemporary experiences and assumptions. Can we really get "back to the Bible" today?

Yet the second approach raises even greater difficulties. For Christian existence in any era, including the present, refers to certain biblical events as its source and norm. In some fashion, Christians seek to evaluate their culture and experience in light of this norm. If theology were to begin with an analysis of contemporary Christian experience, it would have difficulty distinguishing

[3] A third possibility might be to begin from some point in Christian history which lies outside the systematic theological tradition. One might take the experience of a Believers' church or of several Believers' churches as the starting point for theology. But one would encounter the same difficulties which arise in following the second option. For historical Christian movements refer in some way to the biblical events as their source and norm.

what was merely contemporary from what was truly Christian. In our swiftly changing world, it might soon prove to have done little more than analyze the outlook of an era being replaced rapidly.

Given the normative status certain biblical events have always had for faith, we must seek to begin from the original message. In accordance with common theological usage, we may call that message the "kerygma." But let us not underestimate the difficulties involved in hearing it correctly today. And let us remember that theology is never the mere repetition of the kerygma but the expression of it in the language of what we may call the "apologetic context."

A. The Early Kerygma

"Kerygma" is the basic New Testament word for "proclamation" or "message." In Greek, a *kerux* is a messenger or herald who speaks loudly and draws public attention to some definite announcement. The verb *kerussein* means "to proclaim" or "to preach," often with the connotation that those events most basic to Christian faith are being recited. Accordingly, *kerygma* often refers to a summary of those events. Thus biblical scholars and theologians have often used the word "kerygma" to denote the essential core of Christian truth.

A widely accepted outline of this kerygma has been provided by C. H. Dodd. He argues that the earliest and most basic message of the Christian community can be culled from Paul's epistles and from the early preaching recorded in Acts.[4] The kerygma announces that certain events have occurred: Jesus' ministry, death, and resurrection (Acts 2:22–25, 5:30–31, 10:36–41, 13:23–31). On one hand, these events point backward. They fulfill God's ancient promises to Israel (Acts 3:22–26, 4:11, 13:32–37; Rom. 1:2–3; 1 Cor. 15:3–4). On the other hand, they point forwards. The kerygma anticipates that this same Jesus will shortly return to judge the living and the dead (Acts 3:20–21, 10:42; 1 Thess. 1:10; Rom. 2:16).

But while the consummation of all things is not quite here, the decisive boundary between the old age and the new age has been crossed. Jesus' death has delivered us out of the old age (Gal. 1:3–4). The new age has begun with Jesus' resurrection and ascension (Acts 2:36, 5:31; Rom. 1:4, 8:34). Jesus, who is now at God's right hand, is already Lord of the universe, although that Lord-

---

[4] *The Apostolic Preaching and Its Developments* (New York: Harper, 1964 [originally published in 1935]), esp. pp. 7-35. Dodd finds the kerygma in Acts 2:14-39, 3:23–26, 4:10–12, 5:30–32, 10:36–43 and 13:17–41. Its primitive character is established by the fact that it is also the message presupposed by Paul (Rom. 1:1-4, 2:16, 8:34, 10:8-9, 14:9; 1 Cor. 1:23, 2:2-5, 15:1-7; Gal. 1:3-4, 3:1, 4:6; and 1 Thess. 1:10).

ship will not be fully manifest until his return. [5] This resurrection, which was accomplished by the Spirit (Rom. 1:4), has resulted in the pouring out of that Spirit, who enables life to be lived on a new plane (Acts 2:33, 5:32; Gal. 4:6).[6]

Finally, the kerygma closes with a call to repentance and the assurance that those who repent will obtain forgiveness and salvation (Acts 2:38, 10:43; Rom. 10:8–9). Dodd notes in passing that the emphases of the kerygma correspond broadly to those of Jesus, as summarized in Mark 1:15. Jesus' announcement that "The time is fulfilled" points backwards towards God's promises. His declaration that "the kingdom of God is at hand" affirms that something decisively new is occurring. His admonition, "Repent and believe the gospel" parallels the kerygma's call to its hearers.

B. The Earliest Confessions

Study of the early confessions confirms the primitive character of the kerygma. Kerygmatic preaching was directed primarily to those outside the Christian community. Confessions were recited within it. Yet both stressed the lordship of Christ, attained as a result of his death and resurrection. For Oscar Cullmann, "Jesus Christ is Lord" was the heart of the earliest confessions of

[5] The Aramaic term "maranatha," which means "Our Lord, come!," indicates that Jesus was acclaimed as Lord by the earliest Church. The fact that this exclamation appears untranslated in Paul's correspondence to Corinth (1 Cor. 16:23; cf. Rev. 22:20, Didache 10:6), a community far removed from Palestine linguistically, geographically, and in basic outlook, shows that it was widely known and used from the earliest time. Some, however, argue this early designation did not identify Jesus as the one presently reigning over the cosmos but merely as the one who would soon return (e.g., Reginald Fuller, *Foundations of New Testament Christology* [New York: Scribner's, 1965], pp. 157-58). In other words, Jesus Lordship over the cosmos was not part of the early kerygma; this meaning of his lordship arose only later, as the gospel spread among Greek-speaking Gentiles ("lord" was a common title for the gods of Greek religions; Fuller, pp. 184-86; see Wilhelm Bousset *Kyrios Christos* [Nashville: Abingdon, 1970; originally published in 1921]; and Rudolf Bultmann, *Theology of the New Testament*, Vol. I [New York: Scribner's, 1951, pp. 52-53, 121-28]).

However, had the earliest Christians merely been awaiting Jesus' return, they would never have gathered as a Church and invoked his presence in worship (see Oscar Cullmann, *Christology of the New Testament*, (Philadelphia: Westminster, 1959, pp. 207-22). At the root of their existence as a community was the conviction that God's kingdom had already broken into the present, and that Jesus, therefore, was already reigning. To be sure, it took time for all the implications of Jesus' reign to become clear; but the kerygma affirmed his reigning lordship from the beginning (see also Dodd, pp. 14-15; cf. Chap. 7, Sections I and II below).

[6] According to Dodd, while this element is prominent in the Acts speeches, it is not in the kerygma of Paul. It is, however, crucial to Paul's overall message (pp. 22-23, 26).

faith.[7] "Christ," of course, meant "Messiah," and identified Jesus as the fulfillment of Old Testament hopes. But beyond this:

> It is, then, the *present* Lordship of Christ, inaugurated by His resurrection and ex-
> altation to the right hand of God, that is the center of the faith of primitive Chris-
> tianity. The affirmation of the present reign of Christ, and of the power in heaven
> and earth conferred upon Him, is the historical and dogmatic core of the Christian
> confession.

Although Christ's return was not always explicitly mentioned in such confessions, it was nevertheless "*included* in the certainty of His resurrection and ele-
vation to the right hand of God already accomplished."[8]

These early confessions were not merely religious in character. Jesus' resurrection, exaltation, and present lordship were inseparable from the subjection
of the "Powers":

> Most of the developed confessions of early times are not content to say that
> Christ sits at the right hand of God; they emphasize with characteristic regularity
> the subjection of the invisible powers under Him. Here again we have to refer to the
> confession of Philippians 2:6ff., which reaches its climax in the formula *Kurios
> Christos* [Christ is Lord]. To make it clear that the formula has in view the complete
> sovereignty of Christ over all earthly *kurioi* [lords] and the invisible powers which
> stand behind them, it is pronounced in Philippians 2:11 by precisely these powers
> themselves, whose "every knee should bow", by every tongue of things in heaven,
> and on earth, and under the earth. The confession of 1 Peter 3:22 says: "who is
> gone into heaven, and is on the right hand of God; *angels and authorities and powers
> being made subject unto him.*"[9]

But what did these confessions mean by "the Powers"? This concept is difficult for modern people to grasp. Briefly, the New Testament understood that
invisible, spiritual forces lay behind most religious and political institutions of
the day. This especially included the Roman Empire, of which Caesar was the
"Lord." Confessing "Jesus Christ is Lord," then, meant that Caesar was not
Lord. This fact is primarily why such confessions brought frequent persecutions
upon the early Christians.[10]

[7] Rom. 10:9; 1 Cor. 8:6, 12:3; Phil. 2:9-11; 1 John 2:22. Cullmann finds the confession that Jesus is "the Son of God" (Acts 8:37, Heb. 4:14 1 John 4:15) substantially
similar to "Jesus Christ is Lord." For the former was originally understood in the
sense expressed by the early kerygma: Jesus was "declared to be the Son of God with
power, according to the Spirit of holiness, by the resurrection from the dead." (Rom.
1:4) (*The Earliest Christian Confessions* [London: Lutterworth, 1949], pp. 41, 55.)

[8] *The Earliest Christian Confessions*, pp. 57-58.

[9] Ibid., pp. 59-60.

[10] Ibid., pp. 25-30. We will explain the powers much more fully in Chaps. 15-17 and
in Volume II, Chap. 6. For a brief discussion, see Hendrikus Berkhof, *Christ and the
Powers* (Scottdale, Pa.: Herald, 1977).

C. Dimensions of the Kerygma

Careful analysis of the kerygma should reveal certain characteristics of the faith which theology seeks to explicate. First, the kerygma is grounded in events which lie within human history. Some of these also occurred in space just as do other human events. Such events include most of the ocurrences connected with Jesus' life and death, as well as most of those in Israel's history. Other events, however, while they occurred at a specific time, were not related to space in the usual way. These include Jesus' resurrection, his exaltation to lordship and, though the kerygma does not specifically mention them, the "miraculous" features of his ministry and of Israel's previous history. Finally, it is not entirely clear how the still future events, Christ's return and the final judgment, are related to either space or time. Scholars have differed widely over the nature of the last two groups of events. C. H. Dodd himself has largely denied their spatio-temporal character.[11] For now we merely note that even despite this, the historical character of most of the kerygmatic events is indisputable.

Second, the kerygma does not merely report historical events, if "historical event" means an occurrence fully describable in empirical terms. The fact that a Jewish carpenter died outside Jerusalem is not by itself kerygmatic. Provisionally, we may say that the kerygma involves both *historical facts* and *interpretations* of those facts. The life, death, resurrection, and exaltation of Jesus mean that the old age is past and the new age is here. This is their significance. The events recorded in Scripture are hardly ever bare, isolated, merely empirical occurrences. In their deepest nature they mean something. On the other hand, the Bible's spiritual message hardly ever involves free-floating truisms, intelligible apart from history. It consists instead of interpretations rooted in spatio-temporal happenings. (In fact, as we shall see, the fact/interpretation distinction cannot adequately express the deep intertwining between these two dimensions of biblical revelation [Chap. 12].)

Third, the kerygma points its hearers toward the future. The Spirit of the new age is already present. He draws one forward with heightened expectation towards the climax of the kerygmatic series: the return of Jesus the Lord. As Acts' early chapters and Paul's letters make especially plain, life is no longer to be guided by the standards of the old age. All actions strain towards the new reality which is already present and becoming more and more fully present. These actions include proclaiming the kerygma to everyone.

Fourth, the kerygma, while grounded in particular historical events, carries universal claims. Jesus is already Lord over the entire cosmos, over all dimensions of created existence. This rule will become manifest when he returns to judge everyone. Then God's purposes for all creation will be consummated.

Fifth, the kerygma is not only an announcement of events and their mean-

---

[11] Dodd, pp. 36-96. In coming chapters (7-9 and 18) we will explore their spatio-temporal character in detail.

ing, however earth-shaking and universal. It is also a living word. Even as it is proclaimed, it is already transforming lives and transforming reality. The power of the new age is present in the act of *kerussein* itself.[12]

III. The Value of Systematic Theology

To this point we have been exploring the kerygma in order to better apprehend the source and norm of Christian faith. We have left open the question of whether or how the kerygma might be expressed legitimately in a theological manner. However, when we ponder the above five dimensions, it becomes evident that the kerygma cannot remain isolated from theological reflection. By its nature the kerygma presses towards articulation in a variety of "apologetic contexts."

Since the kerygma proclaims God's purposes for all human history, it must be preached to all nations. Since it proclaims the lordship of Christ over all dimensions of creation, no aspect of life, whether physical, social, psychological, or political, can remain untouched by its implications. Since the kerygma draws us towards the future, calling us to view all things in light of Jesus' return, those who live by it will be transforming individual and collective ways of life into new ones. All of this proclamation, application, and transformation, however, will require some thought. It will not always be immediately evident what the kerygma, formulated in a first-century Jewish environment, might mean amid different cultural circumstances. And such translation will require some careful theological thinking, if not a mature systematic theology.

The intrinsic connection between kerygma and apologetic context, then, lies at the foundation of Christian theology and indeed of Christian existence in general. Wherever one encounters a group which is Christian in more than name, two things will be true of it. First, its members will already have understood and responded to the kerygma, at least to some degree. What God already has done, is doing, and will do in Jesus Christ will be the foundation of their new life. Second, they will already be seeking to more fully understand and live out this kerygma amid their contemporary cultural situation.

To be sure, some groups may place more emphasis on the kerygma. They may stress and seek to prove that what they believe is biblical, although they may relate somewhat poorly to their culture. Other groups may emphasize being relevant to their culture, although they neglect or even pervert certain aspects of the kerygma. Even though different groups may swing towards either the kerygmatic or contextual poles of Christian existence, these two elements and the

---

[12] A similar dynamic quality also characterizes the New Testament "gospel" (*evaggelion*) and the "word" (*logos*). On the former see this author's "Evangelical Theology: Where Do We Begin?" *TSF Bulletin* 8/2 (1984), pp. 10-14.

dynamic relation between them will mark Christian life wherever it is found.[13]

What specific implications does all this have for the practice of theology? In particular, might the interrelation of kerygma and context warrant reflection that could be called systematic? To find out, let us review the earlier objections to systematic theology in light of what just discussed.

A. Conceptual Coherence and Consistency

The second group of objections to systematic theology had to do with its highly logical, intellectual character. When one seeks to solve numerous complex issues in a conceptual manner, does not one overemphasize the intellect to the neglect of the emotions and will? Are not conceptual systems mere dry skeletons, dim and deceptive resemblances of the the living, organic reality that people crave and need?

Recall the kerygma. It is grounded in events. These are regarded as the fulfillment of other events and as the anticipation of still others. Many of these events happened at specific times and in specific places. They had certain definite features. Now when we respond to these events, they surely affect our wills and emotions. Yet we cannot respond to them in the first place unless we know something about them. And we cannot know about their specific, definite features unless we use our minds.

We have also seen that the kerygma is not mere information about bare, isolated occurrences. The events which it proclaims have profound meanings, or interpretations. To be sure, New Testament studies show that different writers could interpret the kerygmatic events in different ways. Their rich, overflowing significance could not be contained within a single formulation. Nevertheless, the diversity among New Testament writings is always diversity within a certain *range*. Passages referring back to the original gospel often contain strong warnings against erroneous interpretations (1 Cor. 15:1-7, 12-19; Gal. 1:6-9, etc.). Although the Bible contains and even celebrates diversity, it also draws broad but sharp distinctions between true and false. Response to the kerygma, then, involves grasping its interpretive dimension correctly. It involves distinguishing accurate interpretations from erroneous ones. But we cannot do this unless we use our minds.

In the apologetic context the kerygma must be proclaimed and understood in vastly differing settings. What if a given culture has no single concept of God (cf. Acts 13:15-17, 17:18-31)? What if its gods are crude or bloodthirsty? How does one proclaim the God of the kerygma to such people? Obviously,

---

[13] The distinction between these two poles in theology was developed by Paul Tillich (*Systematic Theology*, Vol. I [Chicago: University, 1951], pp. 3-27). Gordon Kaufman has spoken similarly of "historical" and "experiential" norms (*Systematic Theology: an Historicist Perspective* [New York: Scribners', 1968], pp. 75-80). The notion of "contextualization" is a key one in contemporary missiology (e.g., Gerald Anderson and Thomas Stransky, *Mission Trends No. 3* [New York: Paulist, 1976], pp. 1-61).

learning and dialogue about the relevant god-concepts must take place. And these activities will be, in large part, intellectual tasks. The need for such thinking is hardly restricted to pagan contexts. There the contrasts between kerygma and culture are often obvious. In Christian settings they are far more subtle. We have seen how those early Christians influenced by Greek philosophy had to wrestle with the Greek concept of God. Whenever this concept prevailed, those Christians tended to underemphasize or deny the historicity of the kerygmatic events.

The process of dialogue between kerygma and context, however, often becomes complex. Consider our own era. Many key kerygmatic terms such as resurrection, repentance, and salvation are little used and understood. To communicate, one must either use them and define their meanings carefully or find new, roughly equivalent terms. One does not need to pursue this process for long before one understands why theological reflection must sometimes employ unusual, complex, abstract concepts.[14]

The above considerations do not yet justify the discipline of systematic theology, and certainly not all the ways it has been practiced. But they do show that the intellect exercises an indispensable function in responding to the kerygma and in relating it to apologetic contexts. Some understanding of the kerygma, some understanding of the context(s), and some thinking about their relationships are necessary.

However, nothing yet suggests that such understanding and thinking are best acquired and pursued in a university. These intellectual tasks are those of Christians seeking to understand and communicate their faith to cultures which (along with their universities) might well be opposed to it. The church's primary intellectual task is not to articulate its faith in academically respectable terms nor to relate it to current scholarly trends. Of course the university is one context to which the kerygma is to be proclaimed and one in which many Christians live. The church may well profit from and enter into dialogue with much that is done in the academe. But its primary responsibility will be

---

[14] For instance, "alienation" can help convey some aspects of the notion of "sin" to today's culture. In our massive technological culture people frequently feel alienated from each other. Different groups, races, or classes are often alienated. People often feel alienated from any sense of meaning or purpose. A Christian might propose that the deepest root of all this is alienation from God. Still, alienation itself is a rather uncommon and sophisticated word. It has a significant background in Hegelian and Marxist philosophy. If "alienation" is to be used effectively, it is best to understand this background and to link this concept carefully to the Hebrew and Greek terms used for "sin."

to speak in a way and with a terminology that aids Christians in their concrete tasks.[15]

B. Comprehensiveness

Next, what about systematic theology's efforts to speak on a limitless range of issues, taking into account the major traditional and current theories in regard to each? Especially in a complex world like today's, does not such an enterprise go far beyond what is needed for the daily life of faith and service? Might it not divert one from facing the urgent needs all around us, plunging one instead into the endless process of "ever learning, and never [being] able to come to the knowledge of the truth" (2 Tim. 3:7)?

Let us recall the kerygma. Its claims are universal. Christ is already reigning over every dimension of the cosmos. Soon he will return to judge all humanity and to consummate God's purposes for history. The breadth and urgency of this message command its proclamation in every context. Since Christ is Lord of all, no aspect of any culture (or even of nature) is to remain untouched by the new age.

In other words, although authentic Christian faith is always lived out by individuals and groups in specific settings, and although these must always focus on concrete tasks and issues, all this takes place, as it were, against a universal horizon. The kerygma is not simply a message about how individuals may find meaning, although it surely offers them meaning. It does not merely inspire individuals and groups to tackle concrete problems, although it surely does this too. But it offers meaning to particular persons and tasks *because* God has not abandoned the world to evil and futility but has guided, is guiding, and will guide it towards fulfillment in Christ. The kind of meaning the kerygma offers is inseparable from this cosmic hope.

The importance of a comprehensive perspective is also clear in view of the current apologetic context. Upon close examination, the issues which individuals and groups experience prove to be interrelated. Personal loneliness and meaninglessness are but the reverse side of the industrial and social massification. Problems of health, education, and poverty all have economic dimensions. Social issues are also moral ones. And in today's global village the cultural and political issues facing any one country are interconnected with those of others.

To effectively proclaim and apply the kerygma, then, the Church must keep its cosmic dimensions in view. No intellectual, personal, or social issue is be-

---

[15] Perhaps any such carefully chosen terminology will appear to be "abstract." But such terminology should still be close enough to the experience and tasks of ordinary Christians that it can be clarified by referring to them. We agree with those philosophers of religion who have insisted that if religious language is to be meaningful, it must have "empirical anchorage," or reference to concrete situations (see Ian Ramsey, *Religion Language* [New York: MacMillan, 1957]).

yond its range. Accordingly no limits may be set to the issues on which the Church might have to speak and act. And often this speaking and acting will require much comprehensive thought.

However, the comprehensiveness for which the Church must strive need not be determined by academic notions of completeness or system. The Church often faces urgent situations with limited resources. It may need to think deeply now in one area, now in another, without being able to pull together all of the issues involved. What knowledge it does acquire should be ready for use, not deposited in storehouses so complex that it is difficult to find.

Nevertheless, there is no inherent virtue in acquiring knowledge in a haphazard and piecemeal fashion. The problems which faced churches of the past are often similar to those facing us today. Issues confronting churches in different geographical locations are often interrelated. So long as completeness and minute organization do not become ends in themselves, there is great value in assembling the knowledge available in some coherent, interrelated way.

However, when Christian groups organize their wisdom to best fit the needs of various situations, it need not conform to any one arrangement. In particular, if freed from academic environments, comprehensive theological thinking would not need to begin with the general issue of how God can be known. God and Creation, probably the most abstruse intellectual issues of all, would not need to be taken up immediately. Issues closer to Christian existence might be handled much sooner.

C. Synthetic Structure

But what about systematic theology's tendency to be tightly structured, even rigid and dogmatic? Are not the attempts to define articles of faith precisely, and the desire to require assent to these articles, opposed to the fluidity and constant growth of actual Christian experience? Does not systematic theology encourage and buttress rigid behavior, both ecclesiastical and social? How appropriate, then, can it be for our extremely fluid and swiftly changing era?

Let us again hear the kerygma. It announces the fulfillment and consummation of God's cosmic and historic activity. It announces that there always has been, is, and will be coherence and continuity in God's works. An early confession acknowledges "one God, the Father, from whom are all things...and one Lord, Jesus Christ, through whom are all things..." (1 Cor. 8:5-6). Even though humans cannot grasp it all, and although things do not always hang together as we might expect, coherence exists among the creations and the works of God. Every aspect of Christian faith is interrelated with every other.

When relating the kerygma to the apologetic context, there are dangers in isolating specific aspects from the whole. For instance, Christians may invest great energy in ameliorating social and economic situations but little of lasting value will be achieved if personal and religious dimensions are not touched. And the reverse is also true. In an age which is already deeply fragmented, if the church cannot grasp and articulate the connections among things, it is in danger of becoming a small sect concentrating narrowly on a few issues.

However, though all truth be related, humans cannot grasp all its connections. Even in the scientific realm there is much which will never be known. The Bible may tell us all we need to know. But it certainly does not tell us all we might like to know. At least since Origen, theologians have often tried to fill the gaps with speculation which went well beyond all biblical data. But the more that theological reflection denies the uncertainty and paradox which really do exist, the less suited it becomes to guide the life of faith, especially in an era so fragmented as ours.

Yet theological reflection might still be faithful to the kerygma (and thus synthetic) by seeking to explore and articulate relationships among those things which *can* be known. Such a theology would seek to acknowledge mystery where it truly exists. It would not deny unclarity and paradox in Christian faith. Rather, it would seek to discover more exactly just where these things lay. Part of its wisdom would consist in discovering the limits of its wisdom.

But what about systematic theology's attempts to define correct doctrines and to reject false ones? Does not this unduly cramp and restrict faith? Two things can be said in response. First, since the kerygma involves specific events, and since these can be truly expressed only by interpretations within a certain range, theological reflection will decide, at some point, that some interpretations are true and others false. Although kerygmatic truth is universal in its consequences, it is grounded in particulars. Yet far from being irrelevant in our modern era, such a stable and foundational reference point is what many people want and need.

Second, even though theological reflection can articulate what is true and false, it need not do so by constructing highly interconnected, narrowly defined dogmas which every true Christian must believe. Remember the kerygma. It encounters and demands the openness of the whole person to what God has done and will do. It claims one's will and emotion at least as much as one's mind. Consequently, response to the kerygma can never be equated with response to a doctrine. Properly understood, theological formulations are not direct objects of faith (see Vol. II, Chap. 8). Instead, theological reflection arises *after* the kerygma has been proclaimed and believed. It seeks to articulate more clearly that which has already occurred. If people strongly disagree with an adequate, understandable theological statement, their problem is not one of failure to assent to a doctrine. Rather, it probably indicates that they have never really responded to the kerygma. The problem lies in the original hearing and/or response. Thus it cannot be wholly solved on a theological level. Theological discussion can only seek to point people towards the kerygma, but it can never determine whether they will truly hear and respond.

Let us also remember that different but compatible formulations of the kerygma are found in Scripture. Similarly, theological truth can be expressed in various valid ways. Someone who disagrees with one formulation might assent to the same truth when presented in a different manner. Nevertheless, much as adequate biblical expressions fall within a certain range, so there are limits on what is theologically true. Neither theological affirmations, however, nor responses to them determine whether or not a person truly believes. Theological statements are conceptual descriptions of a reality which is far more than conceptual. They may help illuminate what occurs when a person believes or disbelieves. But faith and disbelief themselves rest upon other grounds.

Finally, what about systematic theology's tendency to support a given moral, social, or political system? Theologies of the past have certainly done so. Here again, two responses are appropriate. First, since the kerygma calls one to the life of the new age, certain actions are appropriate to it while others are not. Since the kerygma calls one to transform this life while hoping for Christ's return, it cannot be divorced from ethics, and it carries social implications.[16] Second, the kerygma announces Christ's lordship over the "powers"—all ideological, social, and political lords. At times features of certain social or political systems may be roughly in line with Christ's Lordship. Yet the kerygma is above every society and judges it critically; by it Christ will return to judge all nations. Theology which articulates the kerygma can never wholly endorse any social state or movement, whether conservative or liberal.

D. Summary

We have raised so many doubts about the traditional practice of systematic theology that we cannot simply locate ourselves in one of its streams (orthodox, liberal, neo-orthodox, etc.) and seek to carry it further. Instead, we have proposed a new basis for theological reflection: the original Christian kerygma, which inherently strives towards articulation in all possible apologetic contexts. We have shown that the kerygma legitimates, even demands, some degree of theological articulation.

We have indicated some ways in which such reflection might be practiced differently from, and thus overcome the objections to, traditional systematic theology. However, we have not yet shown whether something that still might be called systematic could be derived from it. And we have not yet said much about what such a system might be like. Might such a systematic theology be possible?

---

[16] We are disagreeing with the distinction between kerygma and teaching (*didache*) popularized by Dodd himself. See his *Law and Gospel* (New York: Columbia, 1951).

CHAPTER THREE

What Is Systematic Theology?

B y having learned how systematic theology has been done in the past and having pondered the character of our modern age, we discovered some good reasons against pursuing systematic theology in its traditional form today. Still we found that theological reflection of some sort always plays a part in Christian faith. In this chapter we must determine whether some forms of that reflection might compose a distinct discipline and whether it might be called systematic. To do so, let us examine more closely what we have already said about theological reflection. Theology arises in the midst of Christian living. Before anyone begins to theologize, the kerygma has already been heard and believed, and the life of its adherents has already been shaped by their apologetic context. Theology arises as an attempt to get clearer bearings on what is already believed and what is already happening.

Theology thus bears a two-way relationship to its apologetic context. On one hand it is undertaken within that context and aims to further shape that context. On the other hand theology seeks to evaluate that context and the life of the Church within it by something outside it: the kerygma. The activity of theology, then, cannot be separated from its context. However, the standard of theology, the kerygma, can. Generally speaking, theological reflection is the effort to guide the Church's activity and understanding within a given context by evaluating them against the foundation and norm of the kerygma.

Notice that we have not yet described theology as a discipline, but as an activity in which Christians engage. Christians pray and worship. They sing, preach, and witness. Christians share life with each other and minister to human needs. Now when such activities are accompanied by fairly serious and comprehensive thought about the kerygma and how it might best be understood and applied in their current situation, that thinking is theology.

Chapters 1 and 2 criticized various forms of systematic theology for not beginning sufficiently from within what we regard as theology's primary datum: the kerygma as it encounters and transforms various apologetic contexts. Had these theologies begun more properly, they would have given greater attention to Christian faith as a lived reality, to sin and salvation, to issues of ethics and mission, to worship and fellowship, and to the divine acitivity which grounds and guides them all. Instead we found that many systems began well outside the situation in which theology arises. Highly influenced by the academic world, such systems first discussed in detail the relationship of faith and reason (or of Creation, Providence, and science) before turning to those issues more at the heart of lived Christianity. We critiqued traditional theologies for presupposing the validity of sophisticated conceptual schemes (Platonic, Aristotelian, evolutionary, etc.) before reflecting on the acts of God and of humankind in history and in daily experience.

Theology, one might say, should adopt a somewhat more empirical approach. The lived realities of Christian faith should be investigated as they actually occur both in Scripture and in the church. The general concepts and methods which theology employs should be suited to the concrete, specific character of these realities. Concepts and methods derived from a science or philosophy should never be imposed upon such data from without, no matter how adequate they might be in other respects. In short, theological concepts and methods should not be fashioned before the main subject matter of theology has been investigated.

However, this approach is easier to insist on than to carry out. For it is impossible to explore any field without using concepts and a method of some sort, even if only in a provisional way. This is a major reason why most theologians, past and present, have asserted that beginning more directly with concrete data is not really possible. Since we must employ concepts and methods from the start, they argue, we might as well do this clearly by beginning our systems with discussions of faith and reason. Cautious as we are about beginning our own theologizing with a discussion of such issues, this objection deserves attention. For unless we can give at least a general response, we cannot perform this chapter's main tasks: to decide what kind of theology (if any) we might undertake and to show what it would be like.

I. Theological Reasoning

By its very nature the above question cannot be fully answered before we begin investigating theology's subject matter. For if it could, we would be trying to show how one can think from within by doing so from without.

Nevertheless, we can indicate the general kind of reasoning that we will seek to follow in coming chapters and its relationship to other kinds of reasoning common in theology. The ultimate validity of this approach cannot, of course, be determined in advance, but only by the success or failure of our actual procedure and its results.

A. Kinds of Reasoning

In order to reason clearly about things, most careful thinkers have sought first to base their thought on facts or truths which existed independently of their own particular perceptions or prejudices. Then they have attempted to move from such starting points to conclusions by methods of reasoning which have their own strict rules of validity, and are thus uninfluenced by their own wishes or shortsightedness. The most common kinds of reasoning in theology have been called deductive and inductive.

1. *Deduction* was especially prominent in the medieval theology shaped by Aristotle and in Protestant orthodoxy. Deductive reasoning begins from certain general assertions, or premises, which it regards as absolutely true. It then seeks, by means of correct reasoning, to derive, or unpack, other truths which are already implied, or entailed, by these premises.

To illustrate, popular forms of Protestant orthodoxy argued that because God is true, the Bible could contain no errors. The premise here is "God is true." This logically implies, one might argue, that "God always speaks the truth." Further one could define the words of the Bible as words that God spoke. One would then conclude that these words had to be true. For now, let us disregard the validity of this specific argument and the truth of its conclusion. We only wish to illustrate that its conclusion, like that of any deductive argument, must be true if: (1) its premise (s) is (are) true, and (2) the reasoning leading to its conclusion is correct. A deductive argument can be false only if one of these does not hold.

2. *Induction.* Beginning especially with the scientific revolution, deductive reasoning fell under suspicion. The problem was that its premises could not be checked. One simply had to accept their truth, because they seemed to be taught by reason, by Scripture, or by church authorities. But as scientists began examining nature by means of their senses, they discovered that many things which Aristotle had assumed to be true on the basis of reason alone simply were not. Suspicion spread to church authority and eventually to Scripture. No longer was their truth simply accepted. Inductive means of confirming or disconfirming them were sought.

Inductive reasoning begins from particular truths or facts. (Historical research, for instance, is inductive.) Induction then seeks, moving in the reverse direction from deduction, to establish general truths. Induction, strictly speaking, cannot establish absolutely true conclusions. For instance, archaeology might demonstrate ten instances in which the Bible has correctly reported historical fact. Yet one cannot conclude from this that the Bible always does so.

One can only assign a greater or lesser degree of probability to such a conclusion. But even though induction cannot attain absolutely certain conclusions, it can always point out the links between particular facts or statements and the conclusions that it does reach. It can give anchorage to general statements; it can show to what situations they refer. Thus many prefer it to deduction, which has no means of checking its assertions against the empirical, historical world.

Reformation theologians began to think inductively when they ceased using traditional dogmas and interpretations of biblical texts as premises for theology. Instead they used what historical tools they had to investigate the original contexts of these dogmas and texts. On the basis of what they could establish inductively, they rejected many of the dogmas and revised their understanding of other dogmas and of scriptural texts. The Reformers and their orthodox successors usually utilized these recovered meanings in the medieval way, as authoritative premises for deduction. But under liberal theology the meanings of biblical texts were far more radically revised and the authority of some rejected, on the basis of historical inquiry. In this way inductive reasoning of a scientific sort became the final criterion for some theologies. During the twentieth century various empirical theologies sought to revise and reinterpret traditional Christian beliefs by means of a highly refined concept of empiricism derived from discussion with philosophy and modern science.[1]

3. *Adduction.* Recent studies of many kinds have indicated that actual thinking often does not move in linear fashion either from particulars to generalities, or vice-versa. Both deduction and induction attempt to get outside our usual thinking situation where facts and interpretations, premises and conclusions are very mixed. They attempt to base reasoning on indubitable premises or on uninterpreted facts which lie outside it.

Often, however, thinking proceeds more from inside the shifting stream of facts, theories, hypotheses, and assertions which compose it. Frequently, thinking selects certain of these as "models" by means of which to explain larger ranges of data. Since these models are "brought to" the data which one wishes to explain, this method of reasoning may be called "adduction" (from the Latin *duco*, "to bring," and *ad*, meaning "to").[2]

---

[1] E.g., D. C. Macintosh, *Theology as an Empirical Science* (New York: Macmillan, 1919); Henry Wieman, *Religious Experience and Scientific Method* (New York: Macmillan, 1926), and *The Source of Human Good* (Chicago: University, 1946). For an excellent discussion of the contemporary relevance of this movement, see Bernard Meland, ed., *The Future of Empirical Theology* (Chicago: University, 1969).

[2] This term is suggested by Arthur Holmes, "Ordinary Language and Theological Method" in Ronald Youngblood, ed., *Evangelicals and Inerrancy* (Nashville: Nelson, 1984), pp. 129-36. For a critique, see Norman Geisler, Ibid., pp. 137-44. For a similar use of adduction (although he prefers to call it "abduction" or "retroduction"), see Paul Feinberg, "The Meaning of Inerrancy" in Norman Geisler, ed., *Inerrancy*, [Grand Rapids: Zondervan, 1980] pp. 272-76.

A model is a well-known object, image, or process which appears to have certain points of similarity with something much less known. Scientists, for example, have found that the well-known behavior of waves in water has certain similarities with the less known behavior of radiation and light. By assuming, as an hypothesis, that light behaves much as waves do, scientists have been able to set up experiments that have revealed much about the nature of light. These experiments, however, have also shown that light behaves differently from waves in certain ways. To explain some of these differences, scientists have hypothesized that these other activities might have much in common with another, quite different model: that of particles bouncing off things much as do billiard balls. This model has also helped explain certain characteristics of light. However, neither model has proved sufficient to explain all of light's activities. For over sixty years, scientists have employed both models in complementary ways.[3]

Thinking by means of models usually involves employing several at once, qualifying and balancing them against each other until those which have little explanatory range are eliminated, those of broadest range become central, and those of intermediate value occupy subordinate positions.[4] For example, in seeking to understand Scripture's authority, the notion of "the Law" might provide a model by which to conceptualize its character as something firm and fixed (cf. Psalm 119). Other images, however, might help one conceive of Scripture's more dynamic dimensions: the "hammer which breaks the rock in pieces" (Jer. 23:29) or the "two-edged sword" (Heb. 4:12). Through searching out and interrelating the implications of these images, theology might develop something like a "living letter" model (2 Cor. 3:2–3) to help express the stable and dynamic features of Scriptural authority.

A model, then, is not an exact replica or diagram of the lesser-known reality it helps explain. The fulness of that reality remains a mystery which no one model can fully describe. On the other hand, an object, image, or process attains the status of a model only when it corresponds quite precisely to certain

---

[3] For an excellent brief explanation, see Ian Barbour, *Myths, Models and Paradigms* (New York: Harper, 1974), pp. 29-91. See also Frederick Ferre, "Mapping the Logic of Models in Science and Theology," *The Christian Scholar* (Spring, 1963), pp. 9-39; Ian Ramsey, *Models and Mystery* (Oxford: University, 1964); Mary Hesse, *Models and Analogies in Science* (New York: Sheed & Ward, 1963); Max Black, *Models and Metaphors* (Ithaca, N.Y.: Cornell, 1962). For further discussion of science and theology, see Chapter 7.

[4] For the application of models to theological issues see, e.g., Avery Dulles, *Models of the Church* (Garden City, N.Y.: Doubleday, 1974), pp. 19-37, and *Models of Revelation* (Garden City, N.Y.: Doubleday, 1983), pp. 30-35. Paul Minear means much the same thing by "images" (*Images of the Church in the New Testament* [Philadelphia: Westminster, 1960], esp. pp. 11-27, 221-49). We will use the term "model" only for those "images" (and objects, processes, etc.) that prove to have a broad explanatory range.

features of that reality, and when it helps investigators discover new things about it. A model, then, yields authentic, even if limited, knowledge of its object.[5]

B. Reasoning and Theology

No systematic theology has restricted itself to just one kind of reasoning. Medieval attempts at strict deduction and modern strivings for rigorous empiricism have always been influenced by the powerful images, or models, found in Scripture. And different models cannot be interrelated without using deduction and induction. Still, a dominant use of deduction or induction is characteristic of theologies which seek to ground themselves outside the active reality of the kerygma amidst a cultural context.

1. *Deduction* seeks to ground theology in clear and certain propositions (e.g., "God is true"). Insofar as these come from Scripture, they may well express the kerygma accurately. But while biblical propositions can provide accurate foundations for theology, they are not entirely adequate. For Scripture speaks of God's truth in many other ways; for example, as an object of worship and praise, and above all as something whose many facets are revealed through God's various historical activities (see Chap. 12). To deal with any subject adequately, theology must consult not only clear propositions but the wide range of material in which it is expressed indirectly but no less effectively.[6] Theology's history, moreover, shows that deductive theologies almost always employ other propositions, derived from reason, as premises. By such means highly sophisticated philosophies also provide starting points and foundational concepts for theology. (We will examine two such systems in Chap. 5.) In this way, deductive theology can move away not only from the concrete richness of its subject matter but also from its truth.

2. *Induction*, as we have seen, sometimes seeks to ground theological truth by means of historical or scientific criteria. These may critique the kerygma itself. Here again, theology is being grounded in something which may conflict with the kerygma before its claims have been adequately heard.

Inductive methodology, however, can be applied from within the context of Scripture. Rather than beginning from clear scriptural propositions, one can consult a wide range of texts on any given theme. One can seek to construct doctrinal assertions carefully from the diverse data which these texts provide.

Insofar as it seeks to take full account of particular assertions, events, and ex-

---

[5] Our general position on the relationship between models and reality may be called "critical realism" (Barbour, pp. 37-42, 67-70).

[6] "If deduction were the logic of theology....(2) we would have to ignore the historical narrative except for narrative purposes and work only with logically universal propositions, (3) we would have to reduce all Biblical analogy and metaphor and symbol and poetry and connotation to logically univocal as well as universal form, (4) we would have to regard all events in redemptive history...as logically necessary rather than contingent on the will of God" (Holmes, p. 131).

periences before beginning theological construction, an inductive orientation is really beginning from within theology's subject matter. One need not pursue this method very far, however, before various models begin to play a large role. The biblical texts themselves often speak by means of powerful images (God as king, shepherd, father, etc.). As biblical scholars seek to organize the metaphors provided by various passages, it often seems to constellate naturally around such images. Moreover, images (the cross, the good Samaritan, etc.) often lie at the heart of Christian experience and activity. In other words, in inductive approaches to the particulars with which one begins usually do not lead in linear fashion to generalities but cluster about various images and models.

3. *Adduction*, then, provides focal points of intermediate range by which theological reflection can move back and forth between particularities and general propositions. Models (God as Shepherd, the Bible as Law) are not particular facts or assertions, but complex realities having various dimensions. They help organize thinking by providing reference points, around which particular texts and experiences might be clustered. But models also are not general propositions. Instead, they pull together enough data of various sorts to allow theology to grasp and further articulate the relationships which exist among them.

Models also help explain how thinking can begin from within a reality that is already partially experienced and known. As the Church responds to the kerygma and interacts with its context, many images or models are already present in its experience. But in the course of its activities, new or apparently contradictory facts and assertions enter the stream of this experience. (A church, for example, may encounter suffering which seems to contradict its image of God as Shepherd.) Models do not suggest ways of understanding such things by going outside the interaction of kerygma and context and by rethinking the whole issue from its foundations. Instead they suggest ways of relating them with things known and experienced within this stream. (For example, suffering and God's care come together in the Shepherd who dies for the sheep; John 10:1–18.)

In summary, is it really possible to think about theology's subject matter from within, to apprehend it in its own terms and not to impose alien concepts upon it? Yes so long as this subject matter is rich with models, some of which are partially understood already. Then what is unknown or apparently discordant within this field can be illuminated by reference to its more clearly understood features. And, as we shall see, this rich proliferation of models can suggest numerous ways for responding to claims from other fields such as modern science that apparently lie outside theology.

II. The Norm and Criteria of Theology

Theological reflection consists in relating particular texts, events, and experiences to broader models. It then assesses the implications and the range of different models, compares them with each other, and decides which models or combinations of models express the kerygma most adequately in particular contexts. But whereas models are often presented more or less intuitively in Scripture and Christian experience, theology seeks to clarify their significance in conceptual language. In so doing, it formulates many propositions about which it reasons in deductive and inductive fashion. But how does theology decide which models and propositions are most adequate? The fact that it makes such decisions shows that all theological reflection is guided, at least implicitly, by certain norms and criteria. These have been emerging gradually throughout our study. We now state them explicitly.

A. The Norm of Theology

We have called the kerygma the norm of theology. On one hand we have seen that the kerygma is a living gospel or word. Reality is transformed as the gospel is sounded and appropriated. It is not simply a report of events, not simply a list of propositions. On the other hand the kerygma is not merely an unformulated sense of God's presence or power. It is not some general inspiration or truth with numerous parallels in other religions and philosophies. The kerygma's dynamism is rooted in specific events, resulting in the cosmic rule of a specific Lord. These events are unique, unrepeatable acts of God. They come to us from beyond ourselves, and demand that we conform our lives to them.

The significance of these events is connected with past ones which they fulfill and future ones to which they point. These events and their range of valid interpretations come to us from Scripture. Consequently, Scripture is the norm of theology.

Scripture, like the kerygma, is a dynamic reality. It is not merely a group of statements; nevertheless, its dynamism flows from the specific histories which it narrates, the particular images which it forms, the specific propositions which it asserts. Theological reflection must be grounded in and be evaluated by fidelity to the distinctive way in which the biblical writers speak.

At the same time, since the kerygma in Scripture is continually entering and transforming new contexts, it must be translated into new words and actions. Consequently, in order to say the same thing as Scripture does, theology finds that it must express it differently. In order for the kerygma's *substance* to be faithfully expressed, the *form* in which this occurs must differ. If the form does not differ, if Scripture or some past theological formulation is simply quoted, the kerygma will often sound archaic and irrelevant, unlike the living dynamism that it really is.

Accordingly one could speak not only of theology's kerygmatic norm but also of its contextual norm. The extent to which theology is intelligible within the experience and thought-world of its context is also a standard by which its adequacy may be measured. Yet this does not mean that its truth is to be judged by the norms of any context. At some points theology's intelligibility will consist precisely in articulating the conflict between the kerygma and any such standards. Thus the kerygma expressed in Scripture is the sole norm of the truth of theological statements. The experience and thought-world of various contexts serve as norms of their intelligibility.

B. The Criteria of Theology

Theological reflection is synthetic. It seeks to correlate different models and propositions with each other. In addition to theology's norms, do other criteria exist for deciding how well or poorly this is done? Such criteria began emerging as we started to delineate theological reflection's basic features (comprehensiveness, conceptual ordering, and synthesis). To state them more formally, we may usefully employ terminology developed by the philosopher Alfred North Whitehead. In so doing, we are not contradicting our resistance to basing theology on philosophy. We have regarded dialogue between theology and philosophy (and other areas of learning and experience) as not only inevitable but also as profitable. In its interaction with various contexts theology can often appropriate work done in other fields, so long as it does so consistently with its own norm. Accordingly, although the terminology for these criteria comes from a philosopher, we shall ground our reasons for using it and the specific way we use it on the kerygma.

Two important criteria are coherence and logical consistency. Coherence means that connections among the basic concepts which one uses should be clear. It should not be difficult to tell how (or whether) one notion is related to others.[7] (For instance, if theology employs diverse models such as the Law and a sword to help explain Scripture's authority, it must also explain how these two are related, hopefully by means of overarching models or concepts.)

Whitehead's second criterion, consistency, means that good thinking is logical in "its ordinary meaning, including 'logical' consistency, or lack of contradiction, the definition of constructs in logical terms, the exemplification of general logical notions in specific instances, and the principles of inference." Like coherence, consistency does not demand that a specific philosophical vocabulary be used or that one's material be arranged in a certain order. Many "language games" can be coherent and consistent. Topics can be ordered in various harmonious arrangements. Both coherence and consistency function less as specific standards to which thinking must conform than as indications of what it must avoid. From our perspective, good theology should be characterized by these features because the kerygma must be appropriated by the mind and articulated in different thought-worlds (Chap. 2). These activities require coherent, consistent thinking.

---

[7] More precisely, "Coherence... means that the fundamental ideas, in terms of which the scheme is developed, presuppose each other so that in isolation they are meaningless." This does not mean, however, "that they are definable in terms of each other." It merely means that they will not be "capable of abstraction from each other." (*Process and Reality* [New York: Macmillan, 1929], pp. 5-6. All the material taken from Whitehead is from these pages).

Whitehead also says that good thinking must be applicable. Its concepts and models must apply to certain ranges of experience in a direct and illuminating way. It must also be adequate. No area of experience can be unrelated or in contradiction to them.

Adequacy measures the *comprehensiveness* of theological reflection. Theology is comprehensive because the kerygma announces the universal reign of Christ and the consummation of all things in him. No aspect of reality may be excluded in principle from theology's range. However, Whitehead recognizes that any conceptual scheme will illuminate some aspects of reality better than others. Adequacy, accordingly, does not demand that all phenomena be conceptualized with equal precision, but only that no phenomenon be completely outside or in opposition to one's conceptual apparatus. Applicability also acknowledges differences in the precision with which any set of concepts can articulate different dimensions of reality. It indicates Whitehead's clear recognition that comprehensive thinking often employs models derived from one range of experience which it then seeks to apply to others. Clearly, such a model will be more applicable to the area from which it was first taken than to other quite different areas.

The distinction between adequacy and applicability helps express the tension between the universality of theology's claims and the particularity of its contexts. Theology arises to help clarify certain areas of faith and life with which Christians in a given culture are grappling. Good theology, then, must be applicable to this situation. Otherwise it would poorly fulfill its purpose. But theology should not focus on these issues so one-sidedly that it forgets the kerygma's universal dimensions. Then it would cease to be adequate.

None of these four criteria is equivalent to the theological activity of *synthesis*; however, thinking in accord with all of them would clearly result in a synthetic picture of things. Whitehead's aim, in fact, is "to frame a coherent, logical, necessary system of general ideas in terms of which....everything of which we are conscious, as enjoyed, perceived, willed, or thought, shall have the character of a particular instance of the general scheme." In light of what we have said about incompleteness, mystery, and paradox in theological knowledge, we cannot aim to construct so synthetic a system as Whitehead's.

While we can ground all four criteria on our understanding of kerygma and context, dialogue with this philosopher has helped us articulate them precisely. But having advocated a certain kind of theological reflection at length, and having outlined its starting point, its methods of reasonng, its norm and its criteria, we have still not decided: shall we call it *systematic*? Reasons for doing so arise from the need to differentiate between different branches, or divisions, of theology.

III. The Divisions of Theology

Although all theological reflection moves between kerygmatic and contextual poles, and strives towards comprehensiveness, conceptual ordering, and synthesis, it can focus more on one pole or tendency than on others. When different emphases predominate, it is helpful to speak of different divisions of theological reflection, even though distinctions among them are those of degree and cannot be made exact.

A. Biblical Theology

Since the kerygma expressed through Scripture is theology's norm, biblical theology has often been called the fountainhead of all other forms. Exegesis of particular passages probably should not yet be called theology. Here one seeks to follow as closely as possible the text's original form. But when general readers, preachers, or scholars begin to ask what basic themes are involved in various texts and begin to articulate them in a different form and order, theology has begun. The more widely this spreads, say, from a theology of Galatians to one of Paul to one of the New Testament, the greater will be the task of arranging diverse materials in a coherent, consistent *form* which differs from the original texts yet says the same thing in *substance*.

Recent biblical theology has increasingly stressed the diversity among biblical writings and declined to present its results in forms derived from systematic theology. For example, rather than focusing on overall teachings on God, Christ, etc., many recent New Testament theologies are subdivided into the theologies of the Synoptics, John, and Paul. These subsections are often organized differently, according to the themes and emphases of the different literatures.

Some will argue that biblical theology is merely descriptive, that it merely articulates the kerygmatic pole and does not enter into theology's contextual task; however, the thoughts of distant eras can hardly be communicated without a perceptive understanding and a skillful use of modern concepts. All attempts to get at the Bible's social-historical contexts utilize modern methods of research. These highly elaborate methods can yield rich insights into the contexts from which the various biblical writings come, and thus into the meaning of many of their words and basic themes. The development of these historical-critical tools, however, was intertwined with the Enlightenment, and modern assumptions quite different from those of the biblical writers sometimes underlie their use. If biblical theologians are not critically aware of such differences, they may find themselves reinterpreting the Bible by means of modern criteria rather than penetrating back to its original meaning. In any case, although biblical theology stays as close to the kerygmatic pole as possible, the other features of theological reflection are essential to it.

B. Historical Theology

The increasing plurality of forms, in which the kerygmatic substance has been expressed from Patristic times, is reviewed by historical theologians. Like biblical theology, it mainly seeks to describe what past thinkers have said. However, the more forms it examines, and the greater the diversity of contexts in which they appear, the greater is the theological creativity required. This creativity involves selecting which doctrines and which relations among them are most worthy of attention. But such estimates are influenced by theological judgments about one's own age and what it most needs to reconsider. Consequently, historical theology also involves selecting and rephrasing kerygmatic material in a coherent, consistent fashion comprehensible to one's context.

The angle through which any contemporary theological reflection approaches the kerygma is always refracted through the lenses of historical theology. The way in which one hears Scripture is always shaped by at least one tradition. Such refraction can be distorting; it can restrict attention to certain kerygmatic elements while blotting out others. However, since no one can initially hear all the kerygmatic elements in appropriate balance at once, such lenses are not only necessary but can also be helpful. In the various traditions different combinations of themes, images, or models have been selected from the kerygma, and the whole has been read in light of them. Many such angles of vision have arisen when specific cultural situations have forced Christians to wrestle anew with the kerygma and to discover new dimensions within it. Coming to Scripture through one tradition, then, can provide initial models for organizing its many dimensions and for deep insight into certain aspects of its truth. Theological reflection can then move towards comprehensiveness and synthesis by utilizing other models provided by historical theology. Through the interplay of various such angles of vision, one will gradually be freed from the restrictions of any one lens and be better enabled to hear the kerygma itself.

C. Practical Theology

This discipline is concerned primarily with theology's contextual pole. It seeks to establish principles to guide church worship, preaching, teaching, counseling, administration, evangelism, and social involvement. (Practical theology, of course, is not identical with these activities. It is their intellectual dimension.)

Practical theology is guided by the same kerygmatic norm as all theology, a norm from whence it derives its fundamental principles. However, it pays more explicit attention than other branches of theology to the contextual norms which determine whether its principles are meaningfully expressed and thus able to meaningfully guide church activity. Consequently, practical theologians can be heavily involved in contemporary activities and disciplines such as education, counseling, and sociology. However, insofar as they are theologians, they approach these areas on the basis of the kerygma and are concerned with the principles underlying them, not with their concrete implementation.

1. *Apologetics* is not listed often under practical theology. However, it first arose as a Church activity and not merely as a branch of study (Chap. 1). It rightly belongs with other tasks of mission and ministry. We learned that apologetics is usually more effective the less it rebuts objections disjointedly and the more it responds from a coherent, comprehensive world view. Consequently, apologetics formed one root of systematic theology. However, although apologetics takes its guiding principles from the kerygma, its particular concern is with contemporary intellectual viewpoints which pose challenges to faith. Since this concern, far more than any other, shapes its specific form in any context, apologetics belongs under practical theology.

2. *Christian Ethics* belongs here too. Although its guiding principles come from the kerygma, it is chiefly concerned with how these are to be embodied in light of the complex moral issues and challenges of a particular context. Sometimes ethics is treated as a separate discipline. This treatment may reflect an unstated assumption that worship and preaching are more essential to the church than is actual behavior amidst one's context. But if the kerygma calls one to transforming activity in this life in light of the coming consummation, ethics must be at the heart of practical theology.

D. Systematic Theology

Let us visualize the first two divisions of theology (biblical and historical) placed on one side of a large river. Let us imagine practical theology on the other. These disciplines often tend to be separated. The first two can plunge into masses of minutiae and say little to the present context. The last can be so absorbed by its context that it hardly says anything Christian to the present. Is there any way to bridge the river between them? In our rapidly changing modern world, the biblical past seems exceedingly remote. Even recent centuries of church history seem foreign. Especially in view of the modern knowledge explosion, relating all these generations to the present appears an extremely formidable undertaking. Yet if this cannot be done, neither the three divisions of theology nor the Church can rightly perform their tasks.

Some Christians will become absorbed in reading their Bibles, or in preserving their particular church traditions, but they will not know how to relate to the present. Others will plunge into contemporary concerns but will be swept away due to their lack of moorings in the Scripture. The bridging of this stream in its intellectual dimension is the specific function of what we can call systematic theology. As such it directly focuses on those activities which are essential to theology's other branches but the specific concern of none: the interrelation of kerygma and context and the movements towards comprehensiveness, conceptual ordering, and synthesis.

In Chapter 1 we distinguished systematic theology in the precise sense from these general reflective activities. The canons of comprehensiveness, ordering, and synthesis employed by the former were largely taken from reigning philoso-phies and sciences and pursued primarily within the university. We have de-clined to pursue "systematic" theology in this sense. Nevertheless there probably is no better adjective for the necessary branch of theology that we have just described. In the following chapters, we will often encounter tradi-tional terms whose meanings have become obscured or freighted with undesir-able connotations. We will frequently have to decide, Is a better term available? Or can the older one be made serviceable with some explanation?

We face the same choice with systematic theology. What other terms might be available? Neo-orthodoxy preferred "Dogmatics." Yet this is just as foreign to modern people and connotes just as much rigidity. "Christian theology" or "theology" are too vague to denote the specific role of our discipline. Until a better term is found, it is probably best to keep the old one and to work hard at redefining it. In a crisis-torn age which has largely lost hope for any ultimate, integrative meaning in the cosmos and yet which deeply longs for it, perhaps the old word is a way—imperfect though it is—of affirming that such a hope ex-ists.

CHAPTER FOUR

Contextual Theologies

M uch of the preceding material might better be called historical rather than systematic theology. By beginning another chapter that promises to delve yet again into history, perhaps the reader may wonder if we advocate theological reflection that arises out of the present life and tasks of Christian communities? Why these frequent backward glances? Is this theology, like many that are here criticized, becoming cluttered with academic details and missing the heartthrob of Christian worship, fellowship, and mission?

Like most issues of method, our approach can be ultimately vindicated or critiqued only in light of its results: namely to the degree that our present procedure eventually aids the Church's intellectual and practical tasks. For now, let us recall what Chapter 3 said about tradition: Theological reflection cannot really begin exclusively and directly either from Scripture or from present experience. For whether we are aware of it or not, our present understanding of Scripture and of Christianity's nature and task is already shaped by the way in which previous generations have understood them. To be sure, systematic theology seeks to press beyond the distortions of any historical tradition to the kerygma itself. However, we shall never get there unless we are aware from the beginning of the role played by traditions. The less aware we are, the more likely we are to mistake tradition for the kerygma.

Beyond this, historical perspectives open up depths of meaning in the kerygma that one might not otherwise find. For over nineteen centuries the Church has sought to articulate the kerygma in numerous ways in numerous contexts. It has often succeeded and often failed. The more we appreciate and wrestle with this past, the better insight we will gain into the concrete opportunities and dangers of attempting to articulate the gospel anew today. Nevertheless, the profusion of issues and viewpoints cascading upon us from the past is overwhelming. Can we find any way of channeling this flood of ideas so that it does not sweep us away?

In Chapter 3, we observed that some systematic theologies emphasize theology's kerygmatic pole, while others stress its contextual pole. Since by definition all theology involves both, we must not overdraw this distinction. Yet the recognition that some theologies are generally kerygmatic and others contextual can help us discern overall patterns among past theologies. And the better we understand why and how certain ones have moved in one direction or the other, the more prepared we will be to reflect on the interaction of these two poles today. The present chapter will examine a few representative theologies which are best classified as contextual. Several kerygmatic approaches will occupy the next.

Contextual theologies endeavor above all to speak in relevant, meaningful terms to their own times. Points of contact between the kerygma and one's culture are stressed. But ways in which the kerygma differs from and critiques one's culture can be forgotten.

I. Traditional Catholicism

We have seen how systematic theology in the precise sense began with Peter Lombard (1100–1160?) and reached a classical expression with Thomas Aquinas (1225–1274). For centuries Thomas' system provided the backbone of most Roman Catholic philosophy and theology. By today most Catholic theologians have diverged from Aquinas at various points; nevertheless, Thomism's broad outlines are usually visible in their writings.[1] The contextual orientation of Aquinas' theology, then, has long shaped Christendom's largest body.

Thomists might reject our classifying their approach as contextual. They might insist that Thomism's major strength lies in its precise balancing of kerygmatic and contextual elements. These two elements can be visualized as constituting two closely related levels of theological knowledge. On the lower level (as we mentioned in Chap. 1) lies natural knowledge; that which is available to everyone, regardless of religious orientation, who uses the senses and reason correctly. At the start of his first synthetic work, the *Summa Contra Gentiles*, Thomas argued at length, following Aristotle, that God's existence could be proved. Aquinas began from various empirical starting points such as the observable fact that things change. He then analyzed these phenomena carefully, arguing that they could not be what they were unless a changeless

---

[1] "Thomism" is the name for the philosophical and theological system developed by Thomas Aquinas. In Volume II, which discusses Anthropolgy and Ecclesiology, we will distinguish traditional from contemporary Catholicism in detail.

Source, which all people call God, existed.[2] Aquinas then discussed those attributes of God which also could be known through natural theology. Here his reasoning was largely deductive. For example he had already argued that change could not exist unless there existed a Source which did not change. In the course of this argument Thomas had also said that only material things change. Now he could deduce that God was immaterial.[3]

Only after exhaustive discussion of what could be known about God through natural theology did Aquinas pass on to the second level of revealed theology. The truths discussed here, such as the Trinity, were above the scope of human reason. They were known only through revelation. And revelation could only be known through faith. The content of this second (kerygmatic) level, however, was discussed in the sophisticated conceptuality developed for the first. Faith, for instance, was described in much the same terms as natural knowledge. Those volitional, emotional, and personal elements which often characterize faith in Scripture were minimized. Faith became, by and large, cognitive belief in facts and propositions. Similarily, revelation, which is the object of faith, came to be understood largely as a collection of propositions.[4]

For Aquinas, then, knowledge came to be the highest attainment of the religious life; although at its upper reaches knowledge merged into mystical contemplation. In this way, Thomas shared the general Greek orientation we outlined in Chapter 1: Religion was mainly an affair of the mind and spirit; it consisted primarily in attuning them to the spiritual realm, which could be fully enjoyed only after death. In numerous other ways, however, Aquinas was more "this-worldly" than most of the Fathers. We have seen how his natural theology began with empirical sense-experience. Here he was following the lead of Aristotle, who had been a biologist. (In contrast, most early Fathers followed Plato, who had far less respect for physical science.) Aquinas always emphasized the essential role of the body in human existence, even in the after life.

The more earthly, ethical side of Aquinas emerges when he looks at human life from the standpoint not of knowledge but of morality, not of intellect but of will.[5] Here "the Good" is the highest goal towards which humans strive. For Aquinas this process occurs on two levels. On the natural level, human nature is perfected as all people, regardless of religious orientation, strive to develop four virtues: wisdom, courage, temperance, and justice. These were the "cardinal virtues" common in Greek philosophy. On this level, one can define "the

---

[2] *Summa Contra Gentiles*, Book I, Chaps. 10-13; *Summa Theologiae*, Part I, section 1, Question 2.

[3] Thomas' general discussion of God's attributes is found in *Summa Contra Gentiles*, Book I, Chaps. 13-102; in *Summa Theologiae*, I, 1, QQ. 3-26. His deduction of the immateriality of God is found in *SCG*, I, 17; and in *ST*, I, 1, Q. 3, article 2.

[4] *ST*, I, 2, QQ. 1-7.

[5] *ST*, I, 2, QQ. 1-67.

Good," following Aristotle, as "happiness." Happiness involves physical well-being and participation in a just and orderly society. These allow one to engage in artistic and intellectual pursuits. The highest of these, in good Greek fashion, is contemplation. Nevertheless, the moral life engages one in many spheres of concrete existence.

Considered from the level of revealed theology, however, "the Good" turns out to be the Christian God. From this plane one can see that all of human life is really a search for God, although most people perceive it dimly or not at all. Hence all strivings for wisdom, courage, temperance, and justice participate in this movement towards God. Yet people will not enjoy true divine fellowship unless these four cardinal virtues are elevated into three "theological virtues": faith, hope, and love. The search for wisdom, for example, can only be elevated into true faith by the action of divine grace. Consequently, although the orientation of all humans towards God is grounded in their "nature," this quest can be consummated only by God's free bestowal of "grace."

The more one ponders Thomas' intricate system, the more one is impressed by the manner in which reason and faith, cardinal and theological virtues, nature and grace, are continually distinguished, yet continually intertwined. Thomas establishes continuity between the kerygma and every cultural context by regarding all human activities as imperfect, often badly aimed, but nevertheless real movements towards God. He seeks to assert their discontinuity by making completion of those journeys wholly dependent on God. Yet he again affirms their continuity by insisting that the grace bestowed by God's acts "does not destroy, but perfects nature."[6]

However much we admire Thomas' effort, we must ask to what extent his system is based on the kerygma. To what extent does the kerygma provide the standpoint from which Aristotle's philosophy is critiqued and illuminated? Or to what extent does Aristotle provide a basis for altering and correcting the kerygma?

We have called Aquinas' theology contextual because the conceptuality he develops to describe nature molds his articulation of the realm of grace. The reader, of course, is free to disagree with our classification. For the very complexity of Thomas' effort demonstrates that whole systems can be classified as kerygmatic and contextual only in a very general way and that some might well be classified as neither.

II. Liberal Theology

Regardless of how the reader may judge, the Protestant Reformers criticized Aquinas for overemphasizing the contextual pole at the expense of the kerygma. They sought to eliminate natural foundations for theology and to base the entire enterprise on the revealed and revealing Word of God. As we saw in Chapter 1 (and will detail in Chap. 5), Reformation theology sought to achieve

---

[6] *ST*, I, 1, Q. 1, a. 8.

this by articulating detailed doctrines of divine sovereignty, of biblical authority, and of human inability to know and serve God. The latter, of course,
clashed with Aquinas' notion that the mind and will naturally incline towards
God.

But as this emphasis on the divine side of things hardened into ever more
highly elaborated doctrines and church structures, the experiential side of
Protestantism became impoverished. In response the Pietist movement arose.[7]
Pietists meditated on their personal struggles with sin and grace. They met in
small fellowship groups to share their experiences, to study Scripture, and to
pray. They initiated a number of charitable activities. Pietists stressed experiences more than doctrines, activity more than theologizing, feelings more than
thoughts. In this broad sense, the Pietist emphasis was contextual.

By the late eighteenth century many sectors of Western culture were also
stressing feelings more than thoughts. The Enlightenment's application of reason and science to all of life seemed to be going too far. The Industrial revolution was reorganizing economic and social life around its machines and around
the dismal factories and cities that had sprouted to house them. Enlightenment philosophy had raised grave doubts about traditional relegous doctrines,
and now it was reducing human beings themselves to machines. The late
eighteenth century, in fact, was an era like our own. Amid the depersonalization spawned by machines, amid the uncertainty spawned by continual advances in knowledge, the time was ripe for someone to proclaim that religion
was, after all, a matter of feeling. And the time was ripe for someone to rethink
theology as a whole on that basis.

A. Friedrich Schleiermacher (1768–1834)

Though the experiential emphasis of Schleiermacher's first pietist teachers
was attractive, their accompanying orthodox theology did not survive in his
thought. Advancing to the University, Schleiermacher became involved with
the growing Romanticist movement. Assemblages of intellectuals, artists, and
poets were searching for some dimension of life which could neither be controlled by machines nor analyzed and dissected by reason. They turned to the
wild, untamed worlds of the emotional life and of nature. Here one could find
meaning in soaring inspirations (and agonizing depressions) which seemed to
defy scientific analysis.

In their search for meaning, however, many Romanticists had accepted the
Enlightenment critique of Christianity. Schleiermacher undertook the apologetic task of persuading them that Christian faith, when correctly understood,
was directly relevant to their searchings and their aspirations. In his first major
work, On Religion: Speeches to its Cultured Despisers (1799), Schleiermacher

---

[7] The best-known leaders of early Pietism were Philipp Spener (1635–1705) and
August Francke (1663–1727). For an overview of the movement's theology, see Dale
Brown, Understanding Pietism (Grand Rapids: Eerdmans, 1977).

claimed that what Romanticists experience in their most intense moments of feeling is what religion calls God. Schleiermacher did not argue philosophically or doctrinally. He pointed his hearers to what they already felt:

> We shall endeavor to descend into the inmost sanctuary of life. There, perhaps, we may find ourselves agreed....I must direct you to your own selves. You must apprehend a living moment. You must know how to listen to yourselves before your own consciousness.[8]

In our normal experience we make distinctions between ourselves and the world around us and among different things in the world. But, says Schleiermacher, there are moments which lie below the threshhold of daily awareness. Here we do not feel separate from other things but at one with the entire universe. Described in terms which appeal to his Romanticist audience, such a moment

> is the first contact of the universal life with an individual. It fills no time and fashions nothing palpable. It is the holy wedlock of the Universe with the incarnated reason for a creative, productive embrace. It is immediate, raised above all error and misunderstanding. You lie directly on the bosom of the infinite world. In that moment, you are its soul. Through one part of your nature you feel, as your own, all its powers and its endless life. In that moment it is your body. You pervade, as your own, its muscles and members and your thinking and forecasting set its inmost nerves in motion. In this way every living, original moment in your life is first received. Among the rest, it is the source of every religious emotion.[9]

Religion, then, is

> to take up into our lives and to submit to be swayed by them, each of these influences and their consequent emotions, not by themselves but as a part of the whole, not as limited and in opposition to other things, but as an exhibition of the Infinite in our life....The sum total of religion is to feel that, in its highest unity, all that moves us in feeling is one...to feel, that is to say, that our being and living is a being and living in and through God.[10]

When we apprehend things through feeling, all things flow together. But when we apprehend things through reason, we must break them up, analyze them, dissect them. Theological doctrines were, for Schleiermacher, just such dissections of living religious experience. One could come to faith through theological study alone no more than one could produce a living body from the dissected remains of a corpse. Accordingly, Schleiermacher proposed that the content and function of theological statements be understood in a strikingly new way:

[8] *On Religion: Speeches to its Cultured Despisers* (New York: Harper, 1958), p. 41.

[9] Ibid., pp. 43-44.

[10] Ibid., pp. 48-50. Schleiermacher used "feeling" not to speak of just any emotion, but for that special sense of the Infinite experienced through the finite which he describes here.

Whence do those dogmas and doctrines come that many consider the essence of religion? Where do they properly belong?...They are all the result of that contemplation of feeling, of that reflection and comparison, of which we have already spoken. The conceptions that underlie these propositions are...nothing but general expressions for definite feelings.[11]

Some people criticized Schleiermacher's *Speeches* for taking the apologetic task too far, for speaking in Romantic terms so often that nothing distinctively Christian was left. Later in life, he endeavored to articulate his faith by means of a systematic theology more consistent with Christian tradition. Here Schleiermacher spoke less of religion in general. He sought to focus on the uniqueness of Christ. "Christianity", he wrote, "is essentially distinguished from other such faiths by the fact that in it everything is related to the redemption accomplished by Jesus of Nazareth."[12]

However, the heart of faith is still found in feeling, more specifically in "the feeling of absolute dependence." This is "a consciousness...that the whole of our spontaneous activity comes from a source outside of us" (p. 16). Schleiermacher sought to make the concept "God" meaningful for sceptical modern people by insisting that it need not refer (as it did for Aquinas) to a particular being characterized by definite attributes. Instead God simply denotes the mysterious source of religious feeling: "the term God...is nothing more than the expression of the feeling of absolute dependence..." (p. 17).

Much as in the *Speeches*, "Christian doctrines are accounts of the Christian religious affections set forth in speech" (p. 76). Theology is useful only as it helps express and convey those feelings at the core of religious life. Indeed the whole of theology consists in articulating those feelings involved, first, in the sense of sin; second, in the awareness of grace. Schleiermacher defines sin as that which hinders the development of God-consciousness; it is "a kind of imprisonment or constraint of the feeling of absolute dependence" (p. 55). Grace, on the other hand, increases God-consciousness. The more one's God-consciousness is developed, the more integrated and the better related to other persons one will be (pp. 18-29). For a generation intently seeking personal meaning in life, Schleiermacher tied these fundamental theological notions directly to what we today would call self-realization.

The significance of Jesus Christ was also understood in relation to this process. Jesus is significant because he can increase one's God-consciousness. This occurs when his own God-consciousness, which was unhindered and complete, comes to us through "the picture of Christ" which conveys "the impression of the sinless perfection of Jesus..." (p. 364). By its contrast with our lack of God-consciousness, this impression convicts us of our sin. Yet by communicating sufficient God- consciousness to overcome sin, it begins to remove sin at the same time. This picture, of course, comes to us primarily from Scripture. In

[11] Ibid., p. 87.

[12] *The Christian Faith* (New York: Harper, 1963), p. 52. This first appeared in 1821-22, and was revised in 1830. (The following page references in our text are to this work).

Schleiermacher's day, historical criticism was beginning to cast doubt on some of Scripture's features. But for him the efficacy of this portrait was untouched by such research. There are no rational or historical proofs for faith's reality; faith is "a certainty of a fact which is entirely inward" (p. 68).

Faith, however, is not a purely private, individualistic affair. Schleiermacher emphasized that the impression of Christ reaches and sustains one only through the Church. The Church, moreover, as the community of those whose God-consciousness is most vitally renewed, is also the company of those striving towards psychological and moral maturity. It therefore has the social task of "forming all things into an organ of the divine Spirit...thus bringing all into unity with the system of redemption" (pp. 736-737). In this way, Schleiermacher integrated the theological notion of redemption with those movements which the optimistic nineteenth-century thought were promoting moral and social betterment.

Like Thomas Aquinas, Schleiermacher displayed great ingenuity in seeking to express Christianity's fundamental beliefs in the terminology of his time. In one major respect, however, he differed greatly. Thomas' theological concepts were very similar to the ones then used in science and ethics. In the Thomistic worldview, significant continuity existed among all spheres of existence and all fields of knowledge. But by Schleiermacher's day scientific investigations of nature and history were challenging some traditional doctrines of faith. Schleiermacher sought to solve these modern conflicts by assigning theology and science their own separate, autonomous spheres. When he insisted that theology had only to do with feelings, Schleiermacher was denying that scientific theories about nature and history affected its content at all.

Schleiermacher assigned ethics to a third autonomous sphere. He affirmed that Christians would be moral; only so could they form the vanguard of worldwide moral and social progress. However, the principles of morality could be determined by practical reason alone. Christianity contributed no distinct contents or judgments to ethics.[13] In brief, Schleiermacher found a great deal of continuity among scientific, moral, and religious *activities*. In concrete reality according to his nineteenth-century vision, they were all working together to produce a better world. But the *principles* according to which each activity operated were distinct and autonomous.

Today we can sympathize with Schleiermacher's contextual approach. We are engulfed in an even more complex, impersonal industrial world. Traditional religious doctrines make even less sense to many people today. Unless theology can help show how such beliefs might affect people at an intense, personal level, Christian faith will have little appeal and effect. But we must also ask

---

[13] *On Religion*, pp. 35-40. Schleiermacher accepted the basic analysis of scientific reasoning developed in Immanuel Kant's *Critique of Pure Reason* (1781), and that of moral reasoning developed in his *Critique of Practical Reason* (1788). For a brief overview of Kant's impact on liberal theology, see Thomas Finger, *Dialectical Theology's View of Reason* (Ph.D. Dissertation: Claremont, Ca, 1974), pp. 13-34.

Schleiermacher some questions. Can Jesus' significance be based on, or reduced to, his effect on one's consciousness of sin and grace? Do the historical
assertions of Scripture really have very little to do with faith? Does theology
(and thereby the Church) have nothing specific to contribute to science or ethics?

In general we are asking to what extent Schleiermacher's theology is based
on the kerygma. To what extent does the kerygma provide the standpoint
which illuminates and perhaps critiques the life of feeling as most people experience it? On the other hand, to what extent does a Romanticist view of feeling provide a basis for altering and correcting the kerygma? To what extent
does Schleiermacher surrender the informative and critical Word which the
kerygma utters on science and society?

These questions probably have no simple answers. One might answer differently for different aspects of Schleiermacher's work. Nevertheless, these questions must be asked of all theologies, and especially of contextual theologies.

B. Albrecht Ritschl (1822–1889)

By the time the three volumes of Ritschl's monumental *Justification and Reconciliation* had appeared (1870–1874), the Romantic protest had subsided. Optimism about technology's potential to better human life was bubbling over.
Social and political structures were being dramatically altered. Yet religious
certainties continued to be shaken by scientific theories and historical criticism. The time was ripe for a theology which could envision science, change
and progress in a positive, enthusiastic light.

Ritschl could not separate science, ethics, and theology as had Schleiermacher. In an era which praised science, he strove to make theology a thoroughly
scientific discipline. Ritschlian theology met the challenges of biblical criticism on its own ground and defended the basic historicity of the gospels. For
Ritschl ethics was also a strict science. Its concepts of value were as objective
as the concepts of physical science (although the two, of course, were quite different in character). Making theology scientific, then, meant expressing it
largely in ethical conceptuality.

Ritschl regarded the whole of history as a struggle between the Spirit[14] and
the world of nature. The Spirit struggles to subdue nature so that it serves human needs rather than opposing them. The Spirit also struggles to form civilizations and cultures which express human creative potential. And, guided by
moral values, the Spirit struggles to produce societies and a world order of
equality and justice. To an age pursuing these tasks with special enthusiasm,
Ritschl explained that the meaning of religion could be found in the midst of
them:

[14] The German word for spirit, *Geist*, can mean either the collective human spirit or
the divine spirit. In Ritschl, and in of much liberal theology, the two meanings
often intermingle.

In every religion what is sought, with the help of superhuman spiritual power reverenced by man, is a solution of the contradiction in which man finds himself, as both a part of the world of nature and a Spiritual personality claiming to dominate nature. For in the former role he is a part of nature, dependent upon her, subject to and confined by other things; but as Spirit he is moved by the impulse to maintain his independence against them. In this juncture, religion springs up as faith in superhuman spiritual powers, by whose help the power which man possesses of himself is in some way supplemented and is elevated into a unity of its own kind which is a match for the pressure of the natural world.[15]

Ritschl felt that a society free from physical want and enjoying the benefits of justice and culture was what Scripture meant by "the Kingdom of God." And "the Kingdom of God," according to the synoptic Gospels, was the main theme of Jesus' ministry.

Schleiermacher had sought to explain the significance of Jesus in terms of his impact on human God-consciousness. Ritschl set out to conceptualize it in terms of Jesus' kingdom-bringing activity.[16] For Ritschl this could only be done by means of ethical, and hence scientific, concepts. The chief one was that of fidelity to one's vocation. Ritschl rejected older, more supernatural categories as means of explaining Jesus' deity. He argued instead that Jesus' vocation was that of bringing God's kingdom and that in identifying himself so fully and faithfully with God's ultimate purpose, Jesus was in fact God.[17]

Like Schleiermacher, Ritschl argued that Christ's saving work reaches one by means of the Church and brings one into its fellowship. A chief aim of Jesus' ministry was to found such a society of those who have made God's kingdom their ultimate goal. Only so could the kingdom which he initiated expand and transform the whole world. Whereas Schleiermacher had separated the realm of religion (which is the realm of feeling) from the realms of science and ethics, Ritschl articulated much of theology's subject matter by means of ethical con-

---

[15] *The Christian Doctrine of Justification and Reconciliation*, Vol. III (Clifton, N.J.: Reference Book Publishers, 1966), p. 199.

[16] Schleiermacher also recognized the centrality of God's kingdom in Christianity (*The Christian Faith*, p. 43). He defined Christianity as a "teleological" religion, meaning that it always involves moral striving towards the future (p. 52). Ritschl, however, argued that these themes were too marginal in Schleiermacher and then proceeded to make them central in his own theology (*The Christian Doctrine of Justification and Reconciliation*, pp. 8-10). Ritschl thought that Jesus communicated redemption to individuals in much the way that Schleiermacher said (pp. 387, 562-63, 607). But quite unlike his predecessor, Ritschl spent little time describing this.

[17] Ibid., pp. 450-51.

cepts.[18] Nevertheless, Ritschl, like his predecessor, felt that Christian faith did not contribute distinct principles or content to ethics. The concepts which ethical science had developed were entirely adequate for expressing theology's subject matter. (Later critics would claim, however, that his central notion of the kingdom was very different from the one found in the Gospels.) Also like Schleiermacher, Ritschl felt that the principles and methods of the physical sciences were autonomous. Christianity made no claims which disputed their results, just as none that they made could affect faith.

The liberal theology inspired by Albrecht Ritschl sought to articulate the social concerns of Jesus and the prophets in a nineteenth-century context. Liberal theology said much in criticism of the evils of the day: urban poverty, alcoholism, the lot of workers, lack of quality education, conditions in hospitals and mental institutions, and so forth. Yet the same criticisms were voiced by the most enlightened and progressive elements in late nineteenth-century Western society.

Living in a world hurled forward by even more rapid technological transformation than Ritschl's generation knew, and confronted by staggering global issues of social and economic justice, we can appreciate his attempt to articulate Christianity's essentials in a manner relevant to such situations. Nevertheless, we must ask Ritschl, much as we asked Schleiermacher, to what extent the kerygma provides the standpoint from which he reflects on the technological and moral state of society. To what extent does the kerygma illuminate and perhaps critique the notions of morality current in his generation? To what extent does a socio-ethical theory and proceed to provide the basis for altering and correcting the kerygma? To what extent does Ritschl surrender the informative and critical Word which the kerygma utters on science and society? As with Schleiermacher, evaluating Ritschl on such points is no simple task.

III. Existential Theology

Rudolf Bultmann (1884–1976) did not write during a period of cultural synthesis like that of Thomas Aquinas, where every sphere of life and every branch of study was neatly distinguished from yet closely interrelated with every other. Neither was his time like that of Schleiermacher and Ritschl, where science, ethics, and religion seemed to be cooperating in building a better human future, even though these fields were defined as autonomous from each other. Rudolf Bultmann's early writings appeared, in fact, during and after the Great War which plunged the latter era and its dreams of harmony into chaos. From

---

[18] Ritschl insisted, however, that people are brought into the church only by means of "Justification," and that this is a distinctly religious notion. Only insofar as they have been justified can they direct their lives towards the Kingdom of God (Ibid., p. 13). Ritschl felt that this emphasis on the priority of God's saving activity followed the Reformation and contrasted sharply with Catholicism, whose basic principles were not religious but moral.

the 1920s through the 50s, Bultmann addressed a society that was shattered, its hopes for human perfectibility dashed, its optimism about technology transformed into fear of its destructive power. In such a time, God seems to be absent. Where might God be found? Certainly not as an element in a general religious consciousness; not as the general force of Spirit which overcomes and transforms nature. But perhaps if one listened closely enough, God might still be uttering a silent word of hope somewhere in the inner recesses of the isolated individual.

Surprisingly, however, Bultmann's overall conceptuality diverged little from the nineteenth century's. He adopted much of it but radicalized it.[19] For Bultmann, as for Scheiermacher and Ritschl, the methods of physical science were wholly adequate for explaining the natural world. This meant that the modern person could never accept what the Bible said about

> the intervention of supernatural powers in the course of events; and the conception of miracles, especially the conception of the intervention of supernatural powers in the inner life of the soul....This conception of the world we call mythological because it is different from the conception of the world which has been formed by science...and which has been accepted by all modern men. In this modern conception of the world the cause-and-effect nexus is fundamental.[20]

In addition Bultmann regarded modern methods of historical science as wholly adequate for investigating biblical history. He himself took their sceptical tendencies to extremes. The gospels, in his view, contained almost no reliable information about Jesus of Nazareth. Finally, not only was science (including historical science) autonomous and independent from religion, but so was ethics. For Bultmann the Bible was not really a source for moral guidelines.

The significant but modest boundary line by which much liberal theology marked off religion from ethics and science became a broad, gaping ditch for Bultmann. The autonomy of historical science now meant that religion has nothing to do with relationships among historical events. The autonomy of ethics means that moral teachings have nothing to do with the kerygma. The whole godless modern world is evolving along its destructive course according to autonomous historical and social laws. Is there any way that modern humanity can again hear the kerygma?

When he delved deeply enough beneath the historical events and the ethical teachings found in Scripture, Bultmann found an essential kerygma that said, You have been forgiven! Open yourself to God's grace! Live freely and openly towards the unknown future, trusting in God to be with you! No matter how different modern times may be from ancient ones, no matter how many

[19] See "Religion and Culture" in James Robinson, ed., *The Beginnings of Dialectic Theology* (Richmond: Knox, 1968), pp. 205-22.

[20] *Jesus Christ and Mythology* (New York: Scribner's, 1958), p. 15.

traditional Christian beliefs one may need to abandon today, this proclamation and this challenge are still addressed to contemporary people.

But can theology find a conceptual system for better understanding and communicating this message? Bultmann finds one in what he calls "existentialism." According to it, every person

> has his own history. Always his present comes out of his past and leads into his future. He realizes his existence if he is aware that each "now" is the moment of free decision: What element in his past is to retain value? What is his responsibility toward his future, since no one can take the place of another?...Existentialist philosophy shows human existence to be true only in the act of existing. ...Self-understanding of my very personal existence can only be realized in the concrete moments of my "here" and "now."[21]

More generally speaking Bultmann has adopted a conceptual system which distinguishes sharply between the visible, public world grasped through the senses and known by reason and the private, invisible world of personal decision. It is this outer world which may be described by scientific and ethical laws. (We might call it the world of things.) But for Bultmann God "is beyond the world and beyond scientific thinking. At the same time...the self of man, his inner life, his personal existence is also beyond the visible world and beyond rational thinking."[22] Consequently this inner world can be conceptualized in existential terms alone. (We might call it the world of persons.)

For modern people, then, the kerygma is a call to cease placing one's ultimate trust in the things one can observe and control: technology, social and political movements, ethical codes. In contrast, true faith

> is the abandonment of man's own security and the readiness to find security only in the unseen beyond, in God....This faith can become real only in its "nevertheless" against the world. For in the world nothing of God and of his action is visible or can be visible.[23]

Rudolf Bultmann sought to make the gospel intelligible in a time when God seemed to have vanished. Few people expected to find evidence of God in the broad processes of nature, history, and culture. And modern forms of thought, when followed strictly, seemed to eliminate God's direct activity from these realms in any case. Somewhat like Schleiermacher, Bultmann searched for a sphere of existence untouched by reason and technology. He found this in the inner sphere where individuals decide, at the most fundamental level, how they shall understand themselves, their destiny, and their world. Here the kerygma's call to repentance and promise of forgiveness could still be heard.

Today we are not far removed from Bultmann's time. The rubble of two world wars may not surround us, but the threat of a final, apocalyptic war continually

---

[21] Ibid., p. 56.

[22] Ibid., pp. 40-41.

[23] Ibid.

hangs over us. And the rubble of numerous regional wars frequently appears on our television screens. Poverty and starvation have taken on mammoth proportions. And all the while the world-process seems to be hurried on by massive technological and social forces over which humanity's better impulses seem to have little control. We can empathize with the cry: Has God vanished? We can appreciate Bultmann's efforts to identify and describe a sphere where God may be found.

Nevertheless we must ask of Bultmann, To what extent does the kerygma provide the standoint from which he reflects on this state of affairs and on the existential life of individuals? To what extent does the kerygma illuminate and perhaps critique contemporary views on these matters? Or to what extent do Bultmann's theories of science, ethics, and existentiality provide a basis for altering and correcting the kerygma? To what extent does he surrender the informative and critical Word which the kerygma utters concerning reason and existence? As with Schleiermacher and Ritschl, interacting with Bultmann on these issues will require much thought.

IV. Liberation Theologies

So far in these first four chapters systematic theology seems to be a wholly Western phenomenon. Is this discipline incompatible with the way in which Christianity is lived and understood in other cultures? Is it immune to contributions from minorities within our own? If so, in view of Christianity's global character and the cross-cultural nature of its task, this discipline should at least drop the adjective *systematic*. More likely, the entire task should be abandoned.

However, we have been seeking a style of systematic reflection less rooted in academia and closer to Christianity as experienced and lived out. In this task the voices of those who have historically expressed their faith in less elaborate conceptual fashion are especially important. Significantly, however, just at the point when traditional systematic theology is apparently declining, many nonwestern and minority groups have begun expressing their faith in non-traditional, yet generally systematic fashion. We can most usefully consult those expressions which have been called "theologies of liberation." Most of these come from three main groups: Latin Americans, blacks, and women.

Liberation theologies are written from the standpoint of groups who feel themselves to be oppressed. Their proponents insist that the social location of the theologian is important. The academic environment is not, as has often been supposed, truly objective. We have seen that academic theologians can become absorbed in sophisticated philosophical and scientific issues. But they have often neglected issues of race, sex, and class.

This, according to liberation theologians, has hardly been accidental. Academic theologians seldom dealt with the latter because they and their audiences almost always were white, male, and at least middle-class. The problems of being black, female, or poor did not touch them. And the sophisticated problems which did could only arise amid a broader class which was well educated, socially powerful, and wealthy. In this way academic theology was a product of a social establishment; theology served to perpetuate interests and concerns of the establishment while neglecting those of the oppressed.

But when one looks at Scripture from other angles, issues of discrimination, oppression, and poverty appear at its heart. Biblical literature, generally speaking, comes from a nation and from groups who were often on the "underside" of history. They frequently experienced political and social oppression. They faced economic hardship and social ostracism. Consequently the perspectives of oppressed groups today are (to use our own language) traditions providing angles of vision by which certain dimensions of the kerygma can be discovered. Unless theology can bring these perspectives to light, it can hardly be objective.

But how does one reflect on things from the underside? In seeking to do so, liberation theologies are developing a new methodology. In a general sense it might be called inductive. It

> is *experimental in nature*. It is a process of seeking out the right questions to ask and trying out different hypotheses that arise. It becomes a theology of constantly revised questions and tentative observations about a changing world, rather than the type of theology described by Thomas Aquinas as a science of conclusions.[24]

More precisely liberation methodology is not just a way of thinking but an intertwining of action and reflection known as *praxis*. This is opposed to the notion that truth can be discerned and articulated on one level, an intellectual level removed from practical concerns, and only later applied to specific situations. Instead *praxis* originates as involvement in some concrete situation which people are trying to change. Thought arises as one element of these efforts towards change. It analyzes and criticizes these actions and that situation. Yet such thinking is always employed to further that process of change.

For most the notion of praxis implies "that there is no truth outside or beyond the concrete historical events in which men are involved as agents. There is, therefore, no knowledge except in action itself, in the process of transforming the world through participation in history." Or, even more pointedly, "action is itself the truth. Truth is at the level of history, not in the realm of ideas. Reflection on praxis, on human significant action, can only be authentic when it is done from within, in the vicinity of the strategic and tactical plane of human action."[25] To be sure, it is problematic to say that action is itself truth. In order for truth to critique and guide action, truth, it seems, would need to be distinguishable from action. Yet liberation theologies provide intriguing suggestions as to how thinking might be a dimension of the Church's

[24] Letty Russell, *Human Liberation in a Feminist Perspective: A Theology* (Philadelphia: Westminster, 1974), p. 54.

[25] Jose Miguez Bonino, *Doing Theology in a Revolutionary Situation* (Philadelphia: Fortress, 1975), pp. 88, 72.

overall life, and how it might be done from within the encounter of kerygma and context.

Another common theme in liberation theologies is "humanization."[26] Chronic unemployment, poor education, poverty, and discrimination stifle many North American blacks. And many women all over the world have been barred from developing and expressing their human potential. In Latin America the very means of subsistence are denied to many. Aspirations for better living conditions, for self-expression, and for political freedom are often met with brutal repressions. It is hardly surprising that Latin American theology, which is largely Catholic, has emphasized Aquinas' notion that the Good towards which all human actions are directed is God. By means of this conceptuality it has urged, more strongly than Catholic tradition usually has, that the development of the potential of all people, regardless of their religious orientation, is the concern of the Church.[27]

The first step towards humanization is often called "conscientization," or consciousness-raising.[28] The self-awareness of oppressed peoples tends to be defined by the dominant clases and the overall social structures in which they find themselves. They are conditioned to think of themselves as "things" which fit only into those subordinate roles which the larger society ascribes to them. Conscientization involves becoming aware of the extent to which this conditioning has shaped one's own self-image. This growing self-awareness is but the reverse side of becoming conscious of and beginning to exercise one's unique human potential. This conscientization usually involves great struggle against one's ingrained habits and society's expectations.

Many liberation theologies also contain an equivalent of Thomas' natural theology. It is not philsophical but sociological. Latin American theologians in particular often claim that the social and economic forces in any society can be described by analytical tools available to everyone, regardless of their faith. These outline the situation within which the specifically revealed dimensions of Christian faith are to attain realization by means of *praxis*.[29] Liberation theology's emphasis on humanization and its realization in social situations has affinities with Ritschl's concern for the moral development of individuals and society and his consequent articulation of much theology in ethical concepts.

[26] Russell, pp. 62-65; Juan Segundo, *Grace and the Human Condition* (Maryknoll, N.Y.: Orbis, 1973); James Cone, A *Black Theology of Liberation* (Philadelphia: Lippincott, 1970), pp. 152-96.

[27] Gustavo Gutierrez, A *Theology of Liberation* (Maryknoll, N.Y.: Orbis, 1973), pp. 43-78; Segundo, *The Community Called the Church* (Maryknoll, N.Y.: Orbis, 1973).

[28] The seminal work on this theme is Paulo Freiere, *Pedagogy of the Oppressed* (New York: Herder & Herder, 1970).

[29] For thoughtful discussions of this issue, see Jose Miguez Bonino, *Doing Theology in a Revolutionary Situation*, pp. 21-37, 106-53; *Christians and Marxists* (Grand Rapids: Eerdmans, 1976); James Cone, *God of the Oppressed* (New York: Seabury, 1975), esp. pp. 39-61.

For Schleiermacher also, increases in God-consciousness brought about advances in human self-realization. From a broad historical perspective the aspirations underlying liberation theologies can appear as expansions of those impulses towards personal and social freedom flowing from the Enlightenment. But when these impulses reach contexts of oppression, they seldom find expression in the optimistic, progressive manner of the nineteenth century. And when they are felt to correspond with the gospel, the gospel attains conceptualization as a message with revolutionary social implications.[30]

Given this emphasis on radical historical change, it is not surprising that liberation theologies stress the historical dimensions of the kerygma. They emphasize the biblical narratives of God's deliverance of the oppressed.[31] They see all things as directed towards God's eschatological renovation and liberation of the cosmos.[32] Since the oppressive situations from which liberation theologies are written are all around us today, we can admire their efforts to articulate the kerygma in ways which can help heal things. But we must also ask liberation theologians, To what extent does the kerygma provide the standpoint from which they reflect on these social realities? To what extent does the kerygma illuminate perhaps critique these situations and contemporary theories? Or to what extent do they seek to alter and correct the kerygma? Current social theories and situations provide a basis for liberation theologians. To what extent do they surrender the informative and critical Word which the kerygma utters concerning the present? Answering such questions in regard to liberation theology will be no easier than doing so for any other theology discussed in this chapter.

Suggestions for Further Reading

Bultmann, Rudolf. *Kerygma and Myth.* New York: Harper, 1961.

———.*Theology of the New Testament,* 2 vols. New York: Scribner's, 1951.

Kirk, J. Andrew. *Liberation Theology: An Evangelical View from the Third World.* Atlanta: Knox, 1979.

Livingston, James. *Modern Christian Thought.* New York: Macmillan, 1971.

MacQuarrie, John. *An Existentialist Theology: A Comparison of Heidegger and Bultmann.* New York: Macmillan, 1955.

---

[30] In the popular mind, liberation theology is often associated with revolution. Given its broad sociological understanding of the structures of oppression, this movement can hardly conceive of liberation without significant social change. It can hardly locate the kerygma in the individual sphere, as did Bultmann. Nevertheless, liberation theologians seldom make explicit appeals for violent revolution. Critics who quickly assume that they really mean to might remember that words like revolution have many meanings, and that it is not the business of theology, as theology, to give specific advice for particular situations.

[31] See Cone, *God of the Oppressed*, pp. 62-83.

[32] Russell, pp. 41-49, 56-62; Gutierrez, pp. 213-50.

Mahan, Brian and Richesin, L. Dale. *The Challenge of Liberation Theology: A First World Response*. Maryknoll, NY: Orbis, 1981. Philadelphia: Fortress, 1975.

Miranda, Jose. *Marx and the Bible: A Critique of the Philosophy of Oppression*. Maryknoll, NY: Orbis, 1974.

Mollenkott, Virginia. *Women, Men, and the Bible*. Nashville: Abingdon, 1977.

Mueller, David. *An Introduction to the Theology of Albrecht Ritschl*. Philadelphia: Westminster, 1969.

Niebuhr, Richard R. *Schleiermacher on Christ and Religion*. New York: Scribner's, 1964.

Rauschenbusch, Walter. *Christianity and the Social Crisis*. New York: Harper, 1964. (Originally published in 1907).

———.*A Theology for the Social Gospel*. New York: Abingdon, 1917.

Redeker, Martin. *Schleiermacher: Life and Thought*. Philadelphia: Fortress, 1973.

Roberts, Robert. *Rudolf Bultmann's Theology: A Critical Interpretation*. Grand Rapids: Eerdmans, 1976.

Welch, Claude. *Protestant Thought in the Nineteenth Century*, Vol. 1, 1799-1870. New Haven: Yale, 1972.

CHAPTER FIVE

Kerygmatic Theologies

C hristian faith, many would claim, is unique among the religions and phi-losophies of the world. Through it alone can we truly learn how the tran-scendent God views us and our world. (And we hear that our world is in a miserable state and under judgment). Through Christian faith alone can we be rescued from the evil of our ways and be reconciled to this God. But (such peo-ple would continue) human nature always tends to resist this God, to tone down the divine judgment on sin, to vainly imagine that things are better than they are. People want to live according to their own philosophies and values, to reduce the transcendent, sharply challenging gospel to something with which they feel comfortable. Now, according to this perspective, contextual theolog-ies do just this. Some human philosophy or socio-political perspective becomes the dominant criterion by which the kerygma is diluted and reshaped to suit the fancies of one's own age. But, such persons protest, theology's main task cannot be to make the gospel relevant. Theology's chief task must be to allow the transcendent Word of God to be heard in its radical otherness.

This chapter will explore four theologies that attempt this. Of course since all theological reflection involves contextual elements, none of them can be purely kerygmatic. Perhaps the reader may feel that an approach covered here belongs in the preceding chapter. However, our placing of several theologies in these two groups is intended as no hard and fast classification. It is merely a provisional means of alerting us to the elements involved in all theologizing and of beginning to wrestle with what it might mean to interrelate them in our own reflections. As much as contextual theologies risk distorting the kerygma in order to speak to their situations, kerygmatic theologies risk isolating it from their situations. In seeking to recover what is unique and distinct in the gospel, they may express it in ways which are virtually unintelligible. Insofar as this occurs, such theologies cease performing their central task: to enable the kerygma to be heard afresh.

I. Early Reformed Theology

According to John Calvin (1509–1564), medieval theology had greatly exaggerated the human capacity to know God (through natural theology) and to do God's will (through pursuit of the Good). By this means Catholicism had sought to shield itself from acknowledging humanity's deep ignorance of God and the depravity of our wills. This had enabled it to develop a theology of salvation through works. To counter this, Calvin developed his own theological system: the *Institutes of the Christian Religion* (first published in 1536 and revised up through 1559). It generally followed the traditional systematic order, beginning with the question of how God is known.

But when one looks more closely, Calvin's system reveals several significant differences from the usual medieval *Summa*. In speaking of knowledge of God, for instance, Calvin does not begin outside the concrete knowing situation— neither with the facts and arguments of natural theology nor with biblical passages. Instead, he begins within, by perceiving that knowledge of God and of oneself are deeply intertwined.[1] Very often, Calvin formulates and expresses doctrines in pastoral ways that rebuke, challenge, and comfort his readers. His theological formulations are designed to guide the lives of individuals and of the Church. Yet this hardly means that Calvin is concerned only with what is practical. He is certain that he is dealing with absolute truth. And although personal and ecclesiastical experience deeply color the way he says things, he seeks to ground his words in a norm transcending all experience.

Calvin acknowledges a certain natural awareness of God. In every person an intuitive "seed of religion" exists (pp. 43–47). Moreover the natural world's structure gives abundant evidence of its Creator (pp. 51–63). By knowledge of God, however, Calvin means neither mere information nor mere intellectual conviction. To know God is also to love God—it is a positive relationship.[2] It involves the heart as well as the mind. Therefore if the human heart cannot truly love God, humans cannot know God. Calvin is convinced that this is Scripture's emphasis. Consequently true knowledge of God can begin only as we become aware of our true relationship with God. And this involves seeing ourselves as we truly are in God's sight:

---

[1] *Institutes of the Christian Religion* (Philadelphia: Westminster, 1960), pp. 35-39. (The following page references in our text are to this work.)

[2] One can "not say that, properly speaking, God is known where there is no religion or piety" (Ibid., p. 39). Now piety is "that reverence joined with love of God which the knowledge of his benefits induces" (p. 41).

man never achieves a clear knowledge of himself unless he has first looked upon God's face, and then descends from contemplating him to scrutinize himself. For we always seem to ourselves righteous and upright and wise and holy—this pride is innate in all of us—unless by clear proofs we stand convicted of our own unrighteousness, foulness, folly and impurity....And because nothing appears within or around us that has not been contaminated by great immorality, what is a little less vile pleases us as a thing most pure—so long as we confine our minds within the limits of human corruption....

Suppose we but once begin to raise our thoughts to God, and to ponder his nature, and how completely perfect are his righteousness, wisdom and power—the straight edge to which we must be shaped. Then, what masquerading earlier as righteousness was pleasing in us will soon grow filthy in its consummate wickedness (pp. 37–38).

Human beings will never begin to know God unless they become aware of their sinfulness. And whatever natural awareness of God is available, it cannot bring us fully to this point (p. 68). This is because an authentic relationship with God can be initiated only when God reveals himself more directly to us. And according to Calvin, "God bestows the actual knowledge of himself upon us only in the Scriptures" (p. 69).

Calvin does argue that the Bible's credibility can be established by reason (pp. 81–92). But just as God is not really known through general religious awareness or through nature, so God is not known through a merely intellectual grasp of biblical concepts:

The highest proof of Scripture derives in general from the fact that God in person speaks in it....We ought to seek our conviction in a higher place than human reasons, judgments or conjectures, that is, in the secret testimony of the Spirit....For as God alone is a fit witness of himself in his Word, so also the Word will not find acceptance in men's hearts before it is sealed by the inward testimony of the Spirit. (pp. 78–79).

Calvin, in short, is thinking through the subject matter and method of theology in a new way. Theology can no longer be grounded by rational proofs concerning God and Scripture. This is not because such proofs are wholly invalid. It is because they have little, if anything, to do with theology's proper subject matter. This subject matter centers around God's living encounter with human beings. This is the only means by which humans can become truly aware of their own sin, of God's character, and of the new life which God offers. Therefore theology can properly be done only from within this encounter, from within a circle of faith. This prescription does not mean that theology is primarily reflection on Christian experience, as Schleiermacher would say. Calvin is convinced that genuine Christian experience occurs only as humans are confronted by God's Word and conformed to God's will. And this Word and will come to us only as mediated through Scripture.

From the Knowledge of God, Calvin follows the traditional systematic order on to the Nature of God, to Creation, and then to human nature. He is not primarily concerned to describe some human faculty (will, feeling, etc.) or striving (for self-realization, social liberation, etc.) and then show how the gospel fulfills it. Rather, Calvin emphasizes that Original Sin has rendered humankind miserably corrupt and spiritually helpless. Consequently, "Man has now been deprived of freedom of choice and bound over to miserable servitude" (p. 255). As a result, "only damnable things come forth from man's corrupt nature."[3] This pessimistic anthropology, however, is not intended to leave readers in despair but to emphasize the necessity of seeking redemption through Christ.

Calvin does not value Jesus primarily for his human qualities, for his profound "God-consciousness" or his vocational devotion to the kingdom. Christ's chief significance is that he alone could bridge the gaping gulf between God and humanity. To do this, he had to be both divine and human (pp. 465–67). Calvin focuses chiefly on the former. Calvin subdivides the Work of Christ into three functions: those of Prophet, Priest, and King. As Prophet, Jesus came to reveal God's will. As King, he now reigns over the universe and over the spiritual lives of believers. But Christ's chief work was that of priest: to atone for the sin which separates humanity from God:

> God's righteous curse bars our access to him and God in his capacity as judge is angry toward us. Hence, an expiation must intervene in order that Christ as priest may obtain God's favor for us and appease his wrath. The Christ to perform this office had to come forward with a sacrifice ....By the sacrifice of his death he blotted out our guilt and made satisfaction for our sins (pp. 501–02).

Having described this mediating work of Christ, Calvin shows how it has meaning for us: "As long as Christ remains outside of us...all that he has suffered and done...remains useless..." (p. 537). Much as in Calvin's view of Scripture, only God the Holy Spirit can make this saving work come alive for anyone. This happens chiefly through faith. Faith is not primarily feeling (as for Schleiermacher) or decision (as for Bultmann). Faith has a definite object in Jesus Christ. "Faith rests upon knowledge, not upon pious ignorance" (p. 544). Yet faith is also deeply personal. It cannot be a mere acknowledgement of God's existence, or of God's love in general, or even that God loves me. One must be assured of God's love on a deeper level.

> Believers know themselves to be God's children....The knowledge of faith consists in assurance rather than in comprehension....Here, indeed, is the chief hinge on which faith turns: that we do not regard the promises of mercy that God offers as true only outside ourselves...rather that we make them ours by inwardly embracing them (p. 561).

Calvin then moves on to the Christian life, to Repentance, Justification,

---

[3] Ibid., p. 289. Calvin also wrestles with the fact that even pagans possess certain admirable capacities and virtues (pp. 270-77, 292-94, etc.). For this dimension of Calvinism, see Vol. II, Chaps. 2 and 11.

and Sanctification. Only after this does he turn to "Eternal Election, by which God has predestined some to salvation, others to destruction" (p. 920). Calvin defends this doctrine strenuously. Clearly, he regards it as objectively true. But it is noteworthy that Calvin did not introduce Predestination at the beginning of the *Institutes*, as a premise from which other truths could be deduced. Instead he arrives at it by pondering from within the deepest mysteries of God's saving work. He discusses it not to solve all the interesting issues which human reason can raise. Rather, Calvin thinks that belief in this doctrine helps assure readers of their salvation.[4]

Finally, Calvin turns to the Church. For Schleiermacher and Ritschl, incorporation in the Church was essential for participation in Christ's saving work. But Calvin regards the Church (along with civil government) as "external means or aids by which God invites us into the society of Christ and holds us therein....Since...in our ignorance and sloth (to which I add fickleness of disposition) we need outward help to beget and increase faith within us...God has also added these aids that he may provide for our weaknesses" (p. 1011).

Given Calvin's kerygmatic perspective, which differentiates sharply between divine righteousness and human sin, one might suppose that the Church differs markedly from the world around it. But as the previous quotation intimates, Calvin regards sin as so pervasive even among Christians that they must submit to the discipline not only of the Church but also of the state. For Calvin, God's kingdom is primarily spiritual in nature. Believers dwell there in an inward way. But it is not a force which drastically alters the behavior of Christians or, as liberal and liberation theologians would urge, that of society.[5] Accordingly, God has established civil government to restrain sin and keep order. And because the sin in the world also threatens the Church, government's "appointed end" is also "to cherish and protect the outward worship of God, to defend sound doctrine of piety, and the position of the church" (p. 1487). Consequently civil magistrates have a divinely appointed function: "The magistrate cannot be resisted without God being resisted at the same time" (p. 1511). No matter how corrupt a ruler may be, this still holds:

[4] "We shall never be clearly persuaded, as we ought to be, that our salvation flows from the wellspring of God's free mercy until we come to know his eternal election, which illumines God's grace by contrast: that he does not indiscriminately adopt all into the hope of salvation but gives to some what he denies to others" (Ibid., p. 929).

[5] Despite his general insistence "that Christ's spiritual Kingdom and the civil jurisdiction are things completely distinct" (Ibid., p. 1486; cf. pp. 496-501 on Christ's kingly office), Calvin acknowledges in a few places that the church "is already initiating in us upon earth certain beginnings of the Heavenly Kingdom" (p. 1487). Although such themes appear fairly seldom in Calvin, he himself sponsored many social reforms in the Geneva of his day. Later Reformed movements elaborated on such themes and championed many impulses towards social justice (see Vol. II, Chap. 1).

If we are cruelly tormented by a savage prince, if we are greedily despoiled by one who is avaricious or wanton, if we are neglected by a slothful one, if we finally are vexed for piety's sake by one who is impious and sacrilegious, let us first be mindful of our own misdeeds, which without doubt are chastised by such whips of the Lord (Cf. Dan 9:7)....Let us then also call this thought to mind, that it is not for us to remedy such evils; that only this remains, to implore the Lord's help, in whose hand are the hearts of kings, and the changing of kingdoms (Prov. 21:1).[6]

Although Calvin's teachings may sound quite traditional today, we can appreciate his effort to reconceptualize the whole sweep of Christian doctrine in his own time. We can appreciate his effort to ground the whole of Christian life in God's initiating grace and to appraise all spheres of life afresh from this vantage point. Yet just as we put critical questions to our contextual theologians, we must put several to Calvin. In his efforts to stress the divine initiative, how accurately has he portrayed the human response? Has he underplayed the role of freedom? Has he underplayed or overplayed religious experience? How effectively does his theology address his apologetic context? Does it make contact with issues which are really alive there, or does it speak in a foreign language? Finally, despite Calvin's attempt to illumine and critique his theological and social context on the basis of the kerygma, to what extent might his own theological and social assumptions really be altering and critiquing the kerygma?

II. Believers' Church Theologies

During the Reformation both the Lutheran tradition (through Melanchthon's *Loci Communes*) and the Reformed tradition (through Calvin's *Institutes*) attained systematic theological expression. Each classical work initiated a Protestant orthodox tradition which has persisted until today. Their growth was intertwined with the consolidation of Lutheran and Reformed Protestantism as the two dominant branches of Christianity's new expression. The Reformation, however, had coincided with and contributed to numerous social, economic, and religious changes which were sweeping Europe. With established traditions breaking down, a wide variety of religious expressions emerged at that time and over the next few centuries. Some of these earnestly sought to be kerygmatic: to reject religious teachings and practices founded on human tradition and philosophies and to reshape Christian existence from the resources of Word and Spirit alone.

We have already briefly mentioned some such groups (pp. 12-13 above): Anabaptists, Baptists, Quakers, Pietists, Church of the Brethren, Moravians, Methodists. For the most part they can be classified as "Believers' churches":

---

[6] Ibid., pp. 1516-17. Theoretically, however, Calvin favored not monarchy, but aristocracy, or some mixture of aristocracy and democracy (p. 1493). And where present political structures already included "magistrates of the people, appointed to restrain the willfulness of kings..." (p. 1519), he encouraged them to raise their voices. Later Reformed movements often followed these inclinatons.

They restricted membership to those who clearly confessed their faith and their intention to act in a Christlike manner.[7] This restriction excluded young children and also many adults who had been baptized and thereby were members of Lutheran, Reformed, Anglican, and Roman Catholic churches.

Attempts to outline the theology(-ies) of Believers' churches soon encounter some features which also characterize liberation theologies. Both movements are primarily concerned with matters of action. Theological reflection is undertaken in order to guide action and is often evaluated by how well it does so. These theologies are also concerned primarily with matters relevant to practice. Yet Believers' churches have traditionally done less theology than one finds among contemporary liberation movements, partially because many became targets of persecution and access to education and freedom to publish were severely curtailed. Moreover, the highly refined theologizing of their day emanated from ecclesiastical institutions which opposed them; its results were often used to convict them of error. Add to this the tendency of systematic thought to remove one from concrete living. Believers' church adherents could easily regard theology as something abstract and inherently opposed to the breaking forth of the Spirit to energize new kinds of worship and behavior.

But although they seldom expressed themselves by means of elaborately formulated, explicit theology, Believers' churches have surely been guided by an implicit theology: a set of firm convictions for which they risked, and sometimes paid, their lives. Current attempts to do systematic theology in a manner more responsive to the church's tasks may not need to start from scratch. Some of this may already have been done, although in an implicit fashion that needs to be recovered and reconceptualized today.

What, for Believers' churches, functions as the source(s) and norm(s) of religious authority? Like Calvin, they tend to reject natural theology. As Calvin said, only God's Word, which often breaks radically into our sin-darkened lives, can grant us the true perspective on God and ourselves. Despite their relative lack of education, Believers' church adherents have often displayed a prodigious knowledge of Scripture, acquired through frequent preaching, study, and meditation. And they insist that God's Word cannot be understood and obeyed apart from God's Spirit. Yet while tending to agree with Calvin on the general correlation of Word and Spirit, they sometimes differ on the relation between the written Word and experiences of the Spirit.

In stressing that only the Spirit can make the Word alive, some contrast the "inner word" with the "outer" or the "living" word with the "written," in such

---

[7] Except for the majority of Pietists and some Moravians, all the above group become distinct denominations of this sort.

a way that the latter, by itself, becomes a mere dead letter.[8] Quakers can argue that although the "inward revelations" at the basis of their faith "neither do nor can ever contradict the outward testimony of the scriptures," they nevertheless are not "to be subjected to the examination...of the outward testimony of the scriptures...as to a more noble or certain rule or touchstone."[9]

To be sure, most Believers' churches give greater priority to the written Word than this.[10] But at one extreme the written Word merely illuminates, makes concrete, and witnesses to what the Spirit has already said. Since the Spirit may have spoken with great clarity, the biblical witness can become unimportant. The Bible is to be explained, and perhaps critiqued, by these experiences. For Calvin, however, experiences illuminate, make concrete, and witness to what the written Word already says. In theology experiences are to be explained and critiqued according to the biblical standard.

In any case Believers' churches have historically kept the interplay between Word and Spirit alive in a way (as we shall shortly see) that Protestant orthodoxy generally has not. They raise the question as to which is truly more kerygmatic, which more adequately grounds theology and life on the unique activity of God: an emphasis on what is written about God? or an emphasis on God as experienced?

Believers' churches have generally disagreed with Calvin on human freedom. Much of their concern is very practical. For if people are wholly "deprived of freedom of choice," why be concerned about evangelism? Why strive towards sanctification? The Anabaptists complained that Luther and Calvin's emphasis on Predestination, Original Sin, and the Bondage of the Will gave better excuses for sinful behavior than the Pope had ever invented. Calvin stressed these things, in part, because he felt that if he did not, people would not take sin seriously. Believers' churches, however, have often pronounced harsher judgments on sin than even Calvin. They have often raised behavioral expectations higher than he did. Is it because they hold an unrealistically optimistic view of human good? Or is the basis for this hope more kerygmatic? Might they expect more from the Spirit's renewing work?

In fact many Believers' churches have viewed "the natural man" much as

[8] See esp. selections 7.1, 7.2, and 7.13 in Walter Klassen, ed., *Anabaptism in Outline* (Scottdale, Pa: Herald, 1981), pp. 140-61. The conclusion was occasionally drawn that "a person, who has been chosen by God, may be saved without preaching and Scriptures" (p. 142). See also Dale Brown, *Understanding Pietism*, pp. 64-82.

[9] Robert Barclay, *Apology* (Philadelphia: Friends' Book Store, 1908 [originally published in 1675]), pp. 13-14; this is because "this divine revelation and inward illumination, is that which is evident and clear of itself, forcing, by its own evidence and clearness, the well-disposed understanding to assent, irresistibly moving the same thereunto."

[10] See Donald Durnbaugh, *The Believers' Church* (New York: Macmillan, 1968), pp. 30-33; James Garett, ed. The Concept of the Believers' Church (Scottdale, Pa.: Herald, 1969), pp. 201, 319.

Calvin did. Baptist theological anthropology has often been heavily Reformed.[11] John Wesley emphasized total depravity and original sin. Quakers can go even further than Calvin. All humankind is

> degenerated, and dead, deprived of the sensation or feeling of this inward testimony or seed of God, and is subject unto the power, nature and seed of the serpent...from whence it comes, that not their words and deeds only, but all their imaginations are evil perpetually in the sight of God.[12]

But given such a view of natural humanity, how can freedom come into the picture? The general answer: when freedom itself is conceived as a gift of grace. John Wesley, for example, spoke of prevenient grace by which a person's ability to choose for or against salvation through Christ is restored. This grace, however, was made available only through Christ's work. Thus even one's faith in Christ is not a human work, but made possible by God alone.[13] Furthermore this grace is normally regarded as universal. Consequently everyone has a chance at salvation. According to Wesley, no one is predestined to condemnation.

It is possible, of course, that despite these teachings many Believers' churches really do disagree with Calvin about human freedom. These brief references, however, do show that the issues are not simple and that theology may learn much through a fresh appraisal of Believers' church positions.

Because of their emphasis on sanctification, many Believers' churches have related Jesus' teaching and example more directly to daily living than did Calvin. Calvin spoke of Christ as Prophet and King. But this prophetic role did not include his attitude towards evil and injustice. And Christ's kingship, for Calvin, had little to do with the coming of his kingdom on earth. The Anabaptists, however, understood God's eschatological kingdom to be already existing among the hostile kingdoms of this world.[14] Those called to it were to literally follow Jesus' commands, including those forbidding self-defense and swearing of oaths. Christ was known by believers primarily as they suffered

---

[11] See William Lumpkin, ed., Baptist Confessions of Faith (Philadelphia: Judson, 1959), pp. 83, 103-04, 157-58, 162-63.

[12] Barclay, p. 15; for the Anabaptist view see Alvin Beachy, The Concept of Grace in the Radical Reformation (Nieuwkoop, the Netherlands: B. De Graff, 1977), pp. 6-79.

[13] For Wesley's views on prevenient grace, see "Working out our Salvation" in The Works of John Wesley (London: Wesleyan Methodist Book Room), Vol. VI, pp. 512; and "On Predestination Calmly Considered" (Vol. X, pp. 229-30); cf. Brown, pp. 87-101.

[14] Robert Friedmann regards the opposition between these kingdoms as the heart of Anabaptism's "implicit theology." (Theology of Anabaptism [Scottdale, Pa: Herald, 1973], pp. 36-46. Most historians, however, would agree that his phrase "uncompromising ontological dualism" (p. 38) expresses this opposition incorrectly. Cf. Lumpkin, pp. 164-65.

amidst an hostile world much as he did.[15] Later the Quakers interpreted Jesus' example and teachings and experienced him amidst suffering, in much the same way. The Pietists also focused on the concrete sufferings of Christ, although they understood these in a largely spiritual sense and experienced them more in worship and prayer than in the social arena.

Believers' churches were far less in tune with the societies and governments of their day than were Lutheran, Reformed, Anglican, and Catholic churches. Indeed until the present century, the existence of more than one church body in any political territory was considered a threat to social order in most of Europe. Believers' churches were often illegal. They were often persecuted by governments—sometimes openly and savagely, sometimes covertly and indirectly. Consequently, Believers' churches seldom held, as did Calvin, that it was the state's duty "to cherish and protect the outward worship of God, to defend sound doctrine of piety, and the position of the church." Instead, they usually insisted that government had no right to promote one religion and discourage others, for religious conviction is a matter of conscience. Consequently civil magistrates lost much of their honor as God's special servants.

Their emphasis on sanctification and their sense of conflict with the world drew believers into close fellowship groups living by standards quite different from those around them, believing that Christian discipleship could not be practiced alone. For them the Church was no external aid, as for Calvin; it was the essential context for the practice and transmission of Christianity, as for Schleiermacher and Ritschl.

Believers' groups sometimes became virtually isolated from their apologetic contexts. Their relative lack of education and of direct participation in social affairs crippled their ability to speak meaningfully to their day. Even today some such groups have perversely regarded their isolation as a mark of superiority or as an excuse for avoiding the challenge of mission. But even though they have seldom articulated it with theological precision, Believers' churches have kept alive the distinctions between Christian living and ordinary social behavior and between the kingdom of God and the kingdoms of this world.

Finally we may put to Believers' churches some of the questions we put to John Calvin. They too have sought to emphasize the divine initiative. But how accurately have they portrayed the human response? Have they overplayed or underplayed the roles of freedom or religious experience? Do they make contact with issues which are really alive in their apologetic context, or do they speak in foreign languages? Finally, despite attempts to illumine and critique the churches and societies of their day on the basis of the kerygma, to what extent do emphases from their experience or their context really critique and reinterpret the kerygma?

III. Protestant Orthodoxy

Following the original efforts of Melanchthon and Calvin, Lutheran and Reformed theologies passed into periods of increasing systematic refinement and

[15] See esp. Klassen, ed., pp. 85-100; cf. Lumpkin, pp. 111-12, 170; Brown, pp. 120-36.

organization. Concepts were defined and subdivided with ever greater precision. Reasoning fell into ever more lucid deductive patterns. Aristotle's influence revived, and varying amounts of natural theology were incorporated into dogmatics. And as the Enlightenment mounted its attack, Protestant orthodoxy took special pains to be scientific.

According to most histories, orthodoxy was gradually extinguished by liberalism during the nineteenth century. In that era, however, orthodoxy still represented the faith of most Protestants. During the twentieth century, orthodoxy has provided intellectual articulation for much of American evangelicalism. Because of this influence we may most profitably examine the orthodox theologian whose impact is probably greatest on the present: Charles Hodge (1797–1878) of Princeton.

Hodge's monumental *Systematic Theology* appeared in 1874. So did Volume III of Ritschl's *Justification and Reconciliation*. Both were seeking to articulate the faith amidst a highly scientific era. Hodge, however, resisted reinterpreting it as extensively in moral categories. He wanted to retain traditional affirmations about the being of God, especially over against what he regarded as the excessive subjectivism of Schleiermacher.

Many of Calvin's themes reappear in Hodge but are presented in a different form. Hodge does not begin with the interrelation of knowledge of God and knowledge of self. He begins by explaining how theology is a science. Science, for Hodge, consists of two elements: (1) facts and (2) laws which describe relationships among facts.[16] The scientific approach is inductive. The scientist observes a great many facts; eventually the laws which connect them emerge (Vol. I, pp. 9–10). According to Hodge, "The theologian is to be guided by the same rules as the man of science" (p. 11).

Hodge does not think of scientific laws as hypotheses or models which best explain certain data and which may be modified when new data and/or a better way of describing them is found. He does not spell out different criteria (such as consistency, coherence, applicability, adequacy) which different theories may satisfy in varying degrees. Theories (Hodge prefers "laws") seem to be either true or false. False theories arise when one misunderstands the facts, when one does not consider enough of them (when induction is incomplete), or when one disregards some facts due to prior commitment to a theory (pp. 10–15). For Hodge, "The Scripture contains all the facts of theology" (p. 15). In other words if the theologian examines all the biblical data objectively, the underlying connections among them will emerge and will enable one to state them as doctrines. This inductive method, Hodge insists, is the way to avoid interpreting biblical data in light of non-biblical concepts and assumptions.

Hodge acknowledges of course, that theologians, like all scientists, are

---

[16] *Systematic Theology* (London: Clark, 1960), Vol. I, pp. 3-4. (The following page references in our text are to this work.) Among more recent influential orthodox works are Augustus Strong, *Systematic Theology* (Westwood, N.J.: Revell, 1907); and Louis Berkhof, *Systematic Theology* (Grand Rapids: Eerdmans, 1939).

guided by certain assumptions. Some concern the physical universe: e.g., "That there are laws of nature (forces) which are the proximate causes of natural phenomena. Secondarily, that those laws are uniform; so that we are certain that the same causes, under the same circumstances, will produce the same effects" (p. 4). In addition there are many "first truths, which God has implanted in the constitution of all moral beings, and which no revelation can possibly contradict." Two of these are the following: "the essential distinction between right and wrong," and "that sin deserves punishment" (p. 10).

Comparing Hodge's opening pages with those of Calvin's *Institutes*, one is struck by the contrast between the former's insistence that theology is scientific; and the latter's that true knowledge of God involves a love of God which can be engendered only by the Spirit. Yet Calvin had affirmed that reason yields some knowledge of God; for him also, reason and faith did not conflict. Hodge acknowledges a favorite emphasis of Calvin's: "the inward teaching of the Spirit." He affirms that "the facts of religious experience should be accepted as facts, and when duly authenticated by Scripture, be allowed to interpret the doctrinal statements of the Word of God" (p. 16). Nevertheless Hodge seldom stresses this because he opposes Schleiermacher's "subjectivism."

What, then, functions for Hodge as the source(s) and norm(s) of religious authority? We have seen that "The Scriptures contain all the Facts of Theology." Yet the principles of physical and moral science inscribed in our nature and also religious experience can teach theological truths. What is the relationship among these sources? Hodge phrases it thus:

> All the truths taught by the constitution of our nature or by religious experience, are recognized and authenticated in Scripture. This is a safeguard and a limit. We cannot assume this or that principle to be intuitively true, or that conclusion to be demonstrably certain, and make them a standard to which the Bible must conform (p. 15).

Hodge, that is, acknowledges several *sources* of theology. But the Bible is its only *norm*.

As Hodge moves through specific doctrines, however, those truths "taught by the constitution of our nature" often play a large role. To catch the flavor of his methodology, ponder this fairly elaborate argument for God's existence deduced, or unfolded, from moral awareness:

1. We have, by the consitution of our nature, a sense of right and wrong; we perceive or judge some things to be right, and others to be wrong. This perception is immediate. As the reason perceives some things to be true, and others false; and as the senses take immediate knowledge of their appropriate objects, so the soul takes immediate cognizance of the moral character of feelings and acts....

3. No man can will to...think that black is white, or white black....In like manner, no man can will to believe that to be right which his conscience tells him to be wrong; nor can he argue himself into the conviction that he

has done right, when his conscience tells him he has done wrong.

4. Conscience has an authority from which we cannot emancipate ourselves....It commands, and it forbids. And we are bound to obey. It has power also to enforce its decisions. It can reward and punish.

5. Our moral judgments involve the idea of a law, *i.e.*, of a rule or standard to which we are bound to be conformed....

6. This law has an authority which it does not derive from us....It is something imposed upon us.

7. Our moral nature involves, therefore, a sense of responsibility... not to ourselves, not to society, nor to being in general. It must be to a person...a Being who knows what we are, what we do, and we ought to be and do...and who has power and purpose to reward and punish us according to our character and conduct...It is plain that we are under necessity of assuming the existence of an extramundane, personal God, on whom we are dependent, and to whom we are responsible (pp. 237–238).

As Hodge moves from the question of how God can be known to specific attributes of God, it becomes clear that many were already implied in that basic awareness just described. In reading Hodge one often wonders, To what extent are his doctrines derived inductively from biblical passages, as he says they usually should be? To what extent are they derived deductively from intuitive, rational first truths?

But whatever Hodge's methodology, he intends to describe God as Calvin did. God is supremely exalted and holy, separated from humanity by the vast chasm of sin. However, in common with most Protestant orthodoxy, Hodge handles predestination under the doctrine of God. The decrees through which God governs the cosmos can be deduced from God's other attributes. They are, for example, eternal and immutable, because this

necessarily follows from the perfection of the divine Being. He cannot be supposed to have at one time plans or purposes which He had not at another. He sees the end from the beginning; the distinctions of time have no reference to him who inhabits eternity (p. 538).

Consequently the predestination of some to salvation and others to damnation was irrevocably decided before history began.

Hodge's anthropology, like Calvin's, primarily emphasizes humanity's fallenness. Hodge defines sin as "transgression of the Law" (cf. 1 John 3:4). Even apart from Christ or Scripture, our moral sensitivity grasps its consequences:

Law, as it reveals itself in conscience, implies a lawgiver, a being of whose will it is the expression, and who has the power and the purpose to enforce all its demands. And not only this, but one who, from the very perfection of his nature, must enforce them. He can no more pass by transgression than he can love evil (Vol. II, p. 184; cf. p. 478).

And so the fundamental issue of Hodge's theology is stated. God, whose holiness is mirrored in moral law, must condemn those who fall short of it, that is, everyone. The chasm between God and humanity seems unbridgeable. Hence,

Jesus Christ functions chiefly, as in Calvin, to bridge that chasm. Like Calvin, Hodge discusses Christ's work under the titles of Prophet, Priest, and King. But the space allotted to each gives some idea of his emphasis: Two pages are devoted to Christ as Prophet, 14 to Christ as King, and 131 to Christ as Priest. Christ's priestly work means primarily his suffering and death. Whereas all humanity had broken God's Law and justly deserved punishment, the sinless and divine Christ took that punishment in our place.

Like Calvin, Hodge deals with the Christian life (with "experience") after the work of Christ. Hodge insists more strongly than Calvin (and in opposition to Schleiermacher) that faith is not mere feeling. It involves knowledge.[17] Nevertheless, through the Spirit's work, "every true Christian, passes from a state of unbelief to one of saving faith, not by any process of research or argument, but of inward experience" (Vol. III, p. 70).

Along with Protestant orthodoxy in general, Hodge speaks of the whole Bible as the object of faith: "All Christians are bound to believe...everything taught in the Word of God....The object of faith is the whole revelation of God as contained in his Word." More precisely, however, "the special object of faith...is Christ, and the promise of salvation through Him" (Vol. III, pp. 94, 95).

Again like Calvin, Hodge does not discuss the church until the Christian life has been covered. Unlike Believers' churches, he makes little reference to the church as a living, witnessing fellowship. Prior to the Church, Hodge discusses "the Law." Here an additional significance of his "first truths" comes to light. He finds such truths at the basis of the Ten Commandments. They ground a social conservatism typical of Protestant orthodoxy. In the fifth commandment ("Honor your father and mother"), for instance, Hodge finds that

> The general principle of duty enjoined...is that we should feel and act in a becoming manner towards our superiors....There are certain feelings, and a certain line of conduct due to those who are over us....To superiors are due...reverence, obedience and gratitude. The ground of this obligation is to be found....In the nature of the relation itself. Superiority supposes...on the part of the inferior, dependence and indebtedness (Vol. III, p. 348).

Here Hodge joins Calvin, who had also grounded Christian ethical behavior on general principles which he felt lay behind the Ten commandments.[18] (Both differ from Believers' churches which generally fund their ethical norms in

---

[17] Faith "includes the conviction of the truth of its object. It is an affirmation of the mind that a thing is true or trustworthy." Further, "knowledge being essential to faith, it must be the measure of it. What lies beyond the sphere of knowledge, lies beyond the sphere of faith" (Hodge, Vol. III, p. 85). This does not mean, however, that one comes to faith through reasoning.

[18] *Institutes*, pp. 367-423. Unlike Calvin, however, Hodge does prescribe limits outside of which "a magistrate ceases to be a magistrate," and where disobedience and even revolution become permissible (Hodge, Vol III, pp. 359-60).

Christ's teaching and example.) Hodge, however, occasionally took this kind of argument much further than Calvin, such as when (in his exposition of the eighth commandment) he sought to establish the right to private property. Humanity, he argued, is placed on earth

> as its lord and owner. The things of the outer world are given to him for the satisfaction of his physical wants, and of his spiritual necessities. He, therefore, has power and right over things external, and they must be permanently and securely under his control....Property is the means for the development of the individuality of man. The manner in which it is acquired and used, reveals what the man is; his food, clothing and habitation; his expenditures for sensual enjoyment, for objects of taste, of art, and of science; and for hospitality, benevolence, and the good of society...these in their totality as they rest on the right of private property make out a man's portrait. Property, however, is specially designed to enable a man to discharge his moral duties....Therefore, he must have what is exclusively his own (Vol. III, pp. 425–26).

Needless to say, Hodge would be uneasy with those liberation theologians for whom the Marxist critique of private property forms part of theology's "scientific" basis!

By being aware of the highly scientific character of Hodge's era, we can appreciate his efforts. Like Ritschl, he sought to articulate many theological themes in moral terms. Hodge also sought to resist many of the trends of the day, including Schleiermacher's subjectivism, and to defend the kerygmatic themes of Scripture and the Reformation. But the large role played by intuitive "first truths" in Hodge's theology moves one to ask whether, despite his intention, such concepts might really critique and reinterpret the kerygma. Would Hodge be better classed as a contextual theologian? On the other hand, one must ask Hodge whether he really did make contact with his context, or was he speaking in a foreign language? Hodge again he shows that the line between kerygmatic and contextual can hardly be made absolute.

One further issue will occasionally emerge as we proceed. Although Protestant orthodoxy has often provided theological articulation for evangelicalism, how adequately can it do so? Historically evangelicals have stressed things like radical conversion, thoroughgoing sanctification, and formation of committed fellowship groups. Where they have been socially active, they have usually opposed the status quo. In other words evangelical movements have often been, and often overlapped with, Believers' church movements. Protestant orthodoxy, however, has generally emerged from more established structures. If theology properly arises within the life of a church and in order to help guide that life, to what extent ought today's evangelicals rethink their theological foundations?

IV. Neo-orthodoxy

Attempts to do kerygmatic theology—to begin thinking, insofar as possible, from the divine perspective—will be more radical the more its proponents feel that their church and culture are thinking and acting from a purely human perspective. This was certainly true of early neo-orthodoxy. Most pioneers of the movement had originally held liberal views. In their early years, they had all but identified God with the development of nineteenth-century Western civilization. But when those technological and social forces exploded into the barbarity of World War I, it became shockingly clear that God—if God existed at all—had to be somewhere else. But where? Friedrich Gogarten vividly depicted the agony of his contemporaries:

> It is the destiny of our generation to stand between the times. We never belonged to the period presently coming to an end; it is doubtful whether we shall ever belong to the period which is to come....So we stand in the middle—in an empty space. We belong neither to the one nor to the other. Not to the one which precedes us, which would like to make us its disciples and the heirs of its thoughts and convictions. We cannot follow them. We never could.

He aimed his sharp critique of liberal theology at his former professors:

> Did you not teach us to see the work of man in each and every thing? Was it not you who sharpened our sight for the human element by subjecting everything to history and development?...We are so deeply immersed in humanity that we have lost God. Yes, really lost him; there is no longer any thought of ours which reaches him. None of our thoughts reach beyond the human sphere. Not a single one.[19]

In other words once one begins, like Schleiermacher, to regard theological doctrines as mere "accounts of the Christian religious affections," soon one has nothing left but those feelings. Once one begins, like Ritschl, to conceptualize theology in ethical terms, one soon has nothing left but human moral aspirations. God, the original source, object and criterion of those feelings and aspirations, disappears.

Neo-orthodoxy, then, arose as a radical effort to cease grounding theology on descriptions of the anthropological side of the divine-human encounter. Neo-orthodoxy sought for ways to allow God's unique, inbreaking Word to be heard in its sovereign, initiatory power. As Karl Barth (1886–1968) expressed it:

> The gospel is not a religious message to inform mankind of their divinity or to tell them how they may become divine. The gospel proclaims a God utterly distinct from men. Salvation comes to them from Him, because they are, as men, incapable of knowing Him, and because they have no right to claim anything from Him. ...The Gospel is the Word of the Primal Origin of all things, the Word which, since it is ever new, must ever be received with renewed fear and trembling....It is the clear objective perception of what the eye hath not seen nor the ear heard.[20]

But by the 1920s, almost every corner of existence had been subjected to the

---

[19] "Between the Times" in *The Beginning of Dialectic Theology*, pp. 277, 279.

[20] *The Epistle to the Romans* (New York: Oxford, 1968 [originally published in 1922]), p. 28.

explanatory efforts of some science. Even feeling, which Schleiermacher had isolated from the scientific sphere, might perhaps be explained by psychology. Neo-orthodoxy struggled to find a conceptuality for articulating the uniqueness of God.[21]

Karl Barth resisted expressing the kerygma in concepts from any other discipline, including natural theology. He regarded this attempt to move from general philosophical notions to Christianity's unique God as a way of reducing God to the measure of ordinary thought and experience and of silencing divine judgment on them. Barth insisted that

> God is not to be regarded as a continuation and enrichment of the concepts and ideas which usually constitute religious thought in general....It is not that there is in humanity something like a universal natural disposition, a general concept of the divine, which at some particular point involves the thing which we Christians call God...."God"...signifies a priori the fundamentally Other, the fundamental deliverance from the whole world of man's seeking, conjecturing, illusion, imagining and speculating....What is involved is man's meeting with the reality which he has never of himself sought out or first of all discovered.[22]

Throughout thousands of pages Barth sought to express the specificity of kerygmatic reality in language which can neither be reduced to nor critiqued by languages of other disciplines. Such efforts make Barth's writing voluminous, sometimes torturous, and often profound. Barth does not mean, however, that kerygmatic reality occurs in some spooky, invisible realm. The gospel, he insists, concerns the ordinary world where we live. Barth affirms the historicity both of Jesus' resurrection and of the Virgin Birth.[23]

Yet Barth refuses to express his theology in concepts which can be translated into or precisely compared with those of other disciplines. Thus it is difficult to tell what Barth's assertions *mean*: to determine their concrete, empirical reference points. And so contextual theologians have charged, Barth fails to speak to his situation. The uniqueness of Barth's theological expressions, however, is consistent with his claim that theology (he prefers "Dogmatics") can rightly be done only within the church. Schleiermacher and Ritschl, with their emphasis on Christianity's corporate dimension, had also said this. Yet the theologies still relied heavily on concepts derived from secular disciplines. Barth extended this claim to theology's concepts and methodology themselves.

[21] Rudolf Bultmann made one attempt (Chap. 4). Not unlike Schleiermacher, he sharply separated all science and ethics from the realm of revelation. Yet he found the categories of existentialism adequate for articulating the latter. Because he fully adopted common scientific, ethical, and existential concepts, we classified Bultmann as a contextual theologian. Yet during the 1920s, at least, his aims were similar to Barth's. He is often called "neo-orthodox." (Again, the provisional character of the kerygmatic/contextual classification is apparent.)

[22] *Dogmatics in Outline* (New York: Harper, 1959), pp. 35-36.

[23] *Dogmatics in Outline*, pp. 25, 98-99, 123.

For Barth, theology's only subject matter is God's Word. This Word is already present, heard, and at least partially known in the Church. Theology does not seek to establish how this is possible from outside; for example, by psychological analyses of how it arouses God-consciousness and whether this process is valid. Theology begins from within; it seeks to measure what is said and done by the standard of the Word itself. The Word is present in the Church in a three-fold form. It reaches Christians through hearing (through preaching) and writing (through Scripture). Yet both of these flow from and point to the Word Himself: Jesus Christ. Christ, Barth insists, is the source of the other two. Yet we know him as he reaches us through these forms. By equating the Word with more than Scripture, Barth seeks to speak of God's revealing activity as personal and dynamic, somewhat as did Calvin and the Believers' churches. Yet God's Word does not break forth in any way which is not dependent on the Bible. Although attempts to interpret his statements about biblical authority have engendered endless controversy, in his actual theologizing Barth turns repeatedly to Scripture as his primary source and norm.

To be sure, theological language rooted largely in Scripture and preaching will be very "churchly." It may not communicate to the world at large. Still, as Barth's theology developed, he did find a way of relating God's otherness and uniqueness to the human situation. He did this not by borrowing from ethics or existentialism. He focused increasingly on the One who was at the same time God and human. We can know what human nature ought to be, Barth insisted, only in light of Him who alone was "truly and fully human."[24] And we can become aware of how far we fall short (we can truly understand sin) only by comparison with the same Source. For Barth, then, Jesus' priestly role does not overshadow all others, as it does for Calvin and Hodge. Jesus as the norm for human existence and conduct—a favorite theme of most Believers' churches— looms large in Barth. Barth derives most of his ethics from Christ.

Yet, like Calvin and Hodge, Barth also emphasizes Christ's substitutionary suffering. For Barth, as for his Reformed predecessors, humans are deeply depraved, wholly unable to turn their wills towards God, and deserving of the penalty of God's wrath. Christ bore this wrath in our place. Barth, however, draws conclusions which depart from most Reformed tradition. Since Christ was condemned in place of everyone else, no one else (in all probability, at least [25]) will be condemned. Barth, that is, seems to hold a universalist view of salvation. Barth's treatment of predestination is similarly colored. He refuses to treat it as a decree which can be known and discussed apart from redemption through Christ. But in light of this universal goal, it appears that only Christ (in his substitutionary suffering) was actually predestined to condemnation. The rest of the human race, then, is predestined to salvation.

Finally, the implications of Barth's theologizing for social issues are debated.

---

[24] The Humanity of God (Richmond: Knox, 1960), pp. 37-65.

[25] Dogmatics in Outline, pp. 134-36.

In the 1930s his sharp refusal to identify God's work with any socio-political movement and his insistence that only Christ is Lord of the Church helped many resist the claims of another potential lord: Hitler. Barth became a leader in the "Confessing Church" which resisted the rise of national socialism. He helped author the 1936 Barmen Declaration. But despite this, and despite Barth's later efforts to develop a detailed social ethic grounded in Christ, many have argued that his refusal to relate theologizing directly to politics helped isolate the Church from social affairs. More broadly some say that neo-orthodoxy, by insisting that God breaks into human affairs unpredictably and vertically, left society and culture devoid of the divine from World War I on and intensified the atheism and despair of western civilization.

Karl Barth, like kerygmatic theologians in general, sought to articulate the gospel within a context which, he was convinced, had lost its sense of God's transcendent reality. Yet his primary strategy, like the others we have studied, was not to rephrase the kerygma in more familiar terms. It was to reassert with special energy the transcendence which had become dim and contemporary humanity's dire need of it. We can appreciate Barth's courage, even though we must ask him some questions. As we proceed we shall have opportunity to ask how well his grounding of anthropology in Christ enables him to grasp the human side of things; the roles of freedom, of religious experience, etc. For now, our chief question is whether the way in which Barth understood the uniqueness of theology really helped him make contact with his apologetic context. Or was he speaking a language foreign to his audience? To what extent did efforts to think continually from God's unique perspective enable theology to understand and address situations in strikingly illuminating ways? And to what extent do they distance theology from what is really going on? Finally, despite his efforts to illumine and critique his theological and social context on the basis of the kerygma, to what extent might his own theological and social assumptions really be altering the kerygma?

Suggestions for Further Reading

Balthasar, Hans Urs von. *The Theology of Karl Barth*. New York: Holt, Reinhart, and Winston, 1971.

Barth, Karl. *Evangelical Theology: An Introduction*. New York: Holt, Reinhart, and Winston, 1963.

———.*The Word of God and the Word of Man*. New York: Harper, 1928.

Beachy, Alvin. *The Concept of Grace in the Radical Reformation*. Niewkoop: B. DeGraf, 1977.

Bender, Harold. *The Anabaptist Vision*. Scottdale, Pa.: Herald, 1944.

Berkhof, Louis. *Systematic Theology*. Grand Rapids: Eerdmans, 1939.

Brown, Dale *Understanding Pietism*. (Grand Rapids: Eerdmans, 1978).

Dowey, Edward. *The Knowledge of God in Calvin's Theology*. New York: Columbia, 1952.

Durnbaugh, Donald. *The Believers' Church: The History and Character of Radical*

Protestantism, New York: MacMillan, 1968.

Friedmann, Robert. *Theology of Anabaptism*. Scottdale, Pa.: Herald, 1973.

Klassen, Walter. *Anabaptism in Outline: Selected Primary Sources*. Scottdale, Pa.: Herald, 1981.

Langford, Thomas. *Practical Divinity: Theology in the Wesleyan Tradition*. Nashville: Abingdon, 1983.

Littell, Franklin. *The Origins of Sectarian Protestantism: A Study of the Anabaptist View of the Church*. New York: Macmillan, 1974.

Lumpkin, William, ed. *Baptist Confessions of Faith*. Philadelphia: Judson, 1959.

Noll, Mark, ed. *The Princeton Theology, 1812-1921*. Grand Rapids: Baker, 1983.

Rideman, Peter. *Account of our Religion, Doctrine and Faith*. Rifton, New York: Plough, 1950, 1970 (originally published 1540-41).

Smart, James. *The Divided Mind of Contemporary Theology: Karl Barth and Rudolph Bultmann, 1908-1933*. Philadelphia: Westminster, 1967.

Wenger, J.C. *The Doctrines of the Mennonites*. Scottdale, Pa.: Mennonite Publishing House, 1950.

———.*Introduction to Theology*. Scottdale, Pa.: Herald, 1954.

Williams, George. *The Radical Reformation*. Philadelphia, Westminster, 1962.

Van Til, Cornelius. *Christianity and Barthianism*. Philadephia: Presbyterian & Reformed, 1962.

Williams, Colin. *John Wesley's Theology Today*. Nashville: Abingdon, 1960.

CHAPTER SIX

An Eschatological Approach to Theology

Chapters 1 and 2 raised serious objections to the discipline of systematic theology, as it has usually been pursued. But we also argued, beginning from the biblical kerygma itself, that the kerygma's proclamation and application are best facilitated by some kind of comprehensive, coherent, synthetic theological reflection. We began to outline a new way of doing this in Chapter 3. Now Chapters 4 and 5 have sensitized us in concrete ways to the manner in which movement between the kerygmatic and contextual poles lies at the heart of theology. We have seen why and how theological reflection must involve both. And we have observed some concrete strengths and weaknesses that arise from stressing either one.

Kerygmatic theologies emphasize that Christian revelation and existence have their origins in the Divine, which is uniquely "other" than any dimension of created existence. Revelation is not simply an interpretation of the world, no matter how profound. It is fundamentally a message from beyond the human situation and stands over against it. Revelation contains and implies norms which judge every dimension of creation. God's transcendent reality stimulates radical change and growth in all who open themselves to it. But if kerygmatic theologies point to the utterly transcendent Source of Christian existence, they sometimes fail to show concretely how that Source is related to life in a given context. They can emphasize a spiritual or ecclesiastical existence whose connections to other dimensions of reality are hazy. At other times their reverence for transcendent authority merges into deference to traditional social and political authorities. While castigating evil on a personal level, they can condone it on a social one. Life on earth may be not revitalized but routinized.

Contextual theologies, on the other hand, usually analyze contemporary life with insightful clarity. Aware of current trends, they often respond to change; they keep the Christian message alive and relevant. Frequently their followers are active in contemporary affairs. However, by adapting so well to what is current, contextual theologies risk losing their transcendent Source and norm. Deeply concerned with present trends, they may merely offer a religious version of a contemporary philosophy or social movement. Though contextual theologies may join forces with laudable causes, they may lose a perspective from which to evaluate them and collapse when they go out of vogue.

Is there any way of articulating the Christian faith which can both emphasize its transcendent Source and illuminate concrete existence? Can theology elaborate norms which are firm yet applicable and adaptable? As we search for an appropriate way of doing systematic theology today, let us search for an orientation and a method which can do both.

An adequate contemporary system must balance two other emphases. We have seen (in Chap. 2) that many modern people hunger for meaning on a personal, experiential level. If theology is to apply to their daily lives, it must be phrased to touch these existential longings. These longings, however, are hardly unrelated to broader social issues which face us all. Often, the individual's search becomes intense precisely because the economic and political forces which shape our lives seem so massive and impersonal, so threatening and yet so insoluble. Nonetheless Christ is Lord not just over individuals but also over the cosmos. An adequate contemporary theology, then, must speak to both the individual and the cosmic poles of existence. Can we find a balanced way of emphasizing not only both these poles but also the kerygmatic and contextual poles of theology?

I. The Eschatological Perspective

We remember that the biblical kerygma was intensely existential and broadly cosmic at the same time. Christ's life, death, resurrection, and ascension had inaugurated a new age. The ascended Christ was Lord of the universe. From on high he sent the Holy Spirit, who restored and energized life at the deepest levels.

This outlook and this experience were eschatological. The earliest proclamation of the resurrection and the new lifestyle that went with it were rooted in the joyous conviction that the final age of history had arrived. This final age, however, was present in a somewhat paradoxical manner. On one hand, the earliest Christians were convinced that it was "already" present. On the other, since Christ was still to return, it was "not yet" fully consummated. To be sure, early Christian communities were so filled by the Spirit and with the expectation of Jesus' coming that their thoughts and actions were little influenced by the "not yet." Since the new age was already so real, it must have seemed that all things would shortly be consummated. As time passed, however, the interval of the "not yet" became more real.[1]

In this sense the outlook and lifestyle of the earliest Christians were saturated by eschatology. Traditionally eschatology has also been a section of systematic theology. In the themes discussed under this heading, however, the vivid interplay of the "already/not yet" has usually disappeared. In systematic theologies, eschatology has included only those events which have not yet occurred: Christ's return, the final resurrection, the last judgment, heaven, hell, the millennium. Because the eager expectation of these events has usually faded among systematic theologians and the groups they represent, such events have seldom been near the center of concern. Eschatology normally came at the end of the system. By then, many theologians, exhausted (or dead) from hundreds or thousands of pages of writing, had little or nothing fresh to say. Often

> these teachings about the end led a particularly barren existence at the end of Christian dogmatics. They were like a loosely attached appendix that wandered off into obscure irrelevancies. They bore no relation to the doctrines of the cross and resurrection, the exaltation and sovereignty of Christ.[2]

In general, eschatology has suffered from two attitudes in the Church: neglect and overemphasis. In established, stable churches and theological systems, formal belief in end-time events has usually been retained. But they have often been removed to the heavenly stratosphere or the distant future. They have lost any direct influence on conduct and thought. However, smaller groups outside the mainstream, especially in unstable times, have stressed little but eschatology. Concern over the exact details amd timing of coming events has often been all consuming. Yet here also such concerns have had little influence on other areas of life and doctrine. Since both approaches have separated eschatology from the core of church life and teaching, its hopes have often been taken over by other groups in secularized form. The intense biblical desire for a final age of universal justice, fellowship, and peace has become an impor-

---

[1] The eschatological character of the early kerygma and the "already/not yet" character of the *eschaton* have been commonly acknowledged by biblical scholars in recent decades. A classic expression of these themes is Oscar Cullmann's *Christ and Time* (Philadelphia: Westminster, 1964).

[2] Jürgen Moltmann, *Theology of Hope* (New York: Harper, 1967), p. 15.

tant root of many humanistic, socialistic, and communistic movements.[3]

In the Bible, however, eschatology is not merely a set of beliefs which may be pushed aside when certain events are delayed or which push aside everything else when they are thought to be near. Although the kerygma does not specify exactly when the consummating events will occur, it insists that the last times are already here. The eschatological atmosphere of the "already/not yet" pervades every action and thought. Ultimately it does not matter whether the consummation is near or far off. In either case hope of Christ's return puts all things in a new perspective. If Jesus has already conquered the powers of evil and if he will surely return to consummate all of God's plans, then no situation of evil, tragedy, or despair can be as threatening as it looks. It must pass away. If the final evil, death, has already been conquered and if the power of the resurrection now lives within us (cf. Eph. 1:19-21), then nothing, not even death, can defeat the life and love which now flow through us. Energized by this hope and this experience of new life, Christians cannot put up with the sufferings and death of the old age which persist. The person

> who thus hopes will never be able to reconcile himself with the laws and constraints of this earth, neither with the inevitability of death nor with the evil that constantly bears further evil. The raising of Christ is not merely a consolation to him in a life that is full of distress and doomed to die, but it is also God's contradiction of suffering and death, of humiliation and offence, and of the wickedness of evil. Hope finds in Christ not only a consolation *in* suffering, but also the protest of the divine promise *against* suffering.... That is why faith, whenever it develops into hope, causes not rest but unrest, not patience but impatience.... Those who hope in Christ can no longer put up with reality as it is, but begin to suffer under it, to contradict it. Peace with God means conflict with the world, for the goad of the promised future stabs inexorably into the flesh of every unfulfilled present.[4]

In short the eschatological expectation of the first Christians bestowed a unique vantage point from which to view every dimension of reality and a unique impulsion to act in light of this hope. Their eschatology was not merely a set of beliefs concerning future events but also the attitude or atmosphere aroused by these events. Consequently,

> eschatology means the doctrine of Christian hope, which embraces both the object hoped for and the hope inspired by it. From first to last, and not merely in epilogue, Christianity is eschatology, is hope, forward looking and forward moving, and also revolutionizing and transforming the present. The eschatological is not one element *of* Christianity, but it is the medium of Christian faith as such, the key in which everything is set, the glow that suffuses everything here in the dawn of an

---

[3] Liberation theologians sometimes argue that this is why Marxist and Christian movements can be involved in many of the same causes: both go back to some common roots. For a thoughtful advocacy of some degree of Christian-Marxist cooperation, see Jose Miguez Bonino, *Christians and Marxists* (Grand Rapids: Eerdmans, 1976).

[4] Moltmann, p. 21.

expected new day....Hence eschatology cannot really be only a part of Christian doctrine. Rather, the eschatological outlook is characteristic of all Christian proclamation, of every Christian existence, and of the whole Church.[5]

As we ponder how to begin theologizing in a way which is both biblically faithful and also meaningful to modern people, two aspects of the eschatological outlook, so central to the Bible, strike us. First, the personal and the cosmic are inseparably intertwined. Precisely because Christ's triumph is universal, the individual is filled with intense hope. Because individuals are so moved, they begin to act differently in every area of life. By this means Christ's triumph continues to be actualized in a universal way.

Second, the Divine initiative and the human response are intertwined. It is because of God's unique acts—the living, dying, rising, ascending and expected return of Christ; and the outpouring of the Spirit—that human existence is so transformed. The kerygmatic Source of such experience is clear. It is not merely a deeper or more intense form of human experience in general. At the same time, this experience leads Christians into specific activities in our concrete world. Christians initiate acts of courage, hope, and love. They are not passive. And their experience is not enclosed in an inner or religious sphere.

Because the eschatological perspective was the one within which the kerygma was proclaimed, received, and lived out; because it unites the personal and cosmic dimensions of reality; and because the kerygmatic source and the contextual response of faith are inseparably intertwined within it, we propose it as a starting point for theological reflection in the late twentieth century.

II. The Order of Systematic Theology

Since all of God's acts are interrelated and since theology seeks to correlate them, to some degree, in *synthetic* fashion, all of its doctrines are also interconnected. This fact means that systematic reflection, in principle, may begin with any doctrine. Consequently when we propose an eschatological starting point, we are merely arguing that it is especially apt for our times, not that it is the only valid one. But if we actually propose to begin a system with eschatology, we will be starting at the reverse end of the traditional order. To clarify and justify such an unusual procedure, we had better take account of the arguments offered for beginning in the usual way, with God.

A. The Beginning and the End Points

It is often said that because God is the Origin and Source of all things, theology's structure should mirror this. This was especially emphasized by neo-orthodoxy. If theology begins from man, it was argued, one will never reach the ultimate, transcendent Source of all. Theology, to be true to its subject matter, should mirror in its structure the procession of reality from Source to result, or from Cause to effect. (Sometimes this order is called the "logical" one.) It is

[5] Ibid., p. 16.

also frequently argued that since systematic theology seeks to be comprehensive, it should seek to view reality from the standpoint of God, from whom and unto whom are all things. Any other starting point might well yield a fragmented, one-sided perspective. To sustain this standpoint throughout, the entire systematic corpus has sometimes been subdivided under the headings Father, Son, and Spirit.

We thoroughly agree that God is the Source and Origin of all. We agree that beginning with anthropology, in the sense of making human experiences or philosophies the basis of theology, must be rejected. We also agree that comprehensiveness of some sort is an aim of theology. However, theology's task is not to produce an exact transcript of reality. Theology is not primarily a branch of academic science. Rather, its task is to help facilitate church worship, fellowship, and mission. Therefore the question concerning systematic form should not be, Which structure most closely mirrors reality? but, Which structure best helps Christians in a given culture understand and apply their faith?

For both the Church and individuals, knowledge of God does not begin with a detailed understanding of the divine fulness, which is subsequently (deductively) applied to concrete tasks and events. Usually God is first apprehended in a particular aspect of life in a very limited way. As individuals and groups grow in faith, they apprehend God in more and more situations and in increasingly deeper ways. Detailed knowledge of God is mediated through and built up out of many such experiences. Moreover, God is perhaps the most complex and difficult concept of all for human thought. Without some fairly sophisticated conceptual tools and without some fairly well-developed notion of its content, one cannot begin theological discussion of the doctrine of God. From whence, then, might these concepts and this content come? For most systematic theologies, it has come from highly developed philosophies. And we have rejected this procedure because it tends to obscure and misrepresents what is distinctive about the biblical God.[6]

Scripture itself, however, suggests a way of acquiring knowledge of God. The

---

[6] Gordon Kaufmann insists, somewhat as we do, that theology cannot begin its reflections directly from lofty and concepts such as God, assuming that their meaning is "self-evident and clear and already given." (An Essay on Theological Method [Chico, Ca.: Scholar's, 1975], p. 2.) Kaufman also argues, again much as we do, that the concept God is meaningless unless theology can indicate how it is related to the world in which we live (p. 54). As a remedy, however, he proposes that theology begin by constructing a concept of the world through general philosophical procedures. In the final stage of Kaumann's enterprise, his God-concept will critique, or "relativize," this world-concept. For Kaufmann, however, the concept God is a product of general cultural processes; it has "been created in the efforts of men and women to comprehend and grasp their developing experience" (p. 8). Kaufmann, then, while looking to developing historical awareness of God as a source for theology, depends on philosophical and cultural concepts of God and the world far more than we do. For a critique of Kaufmann (and also of the approach of David Tracy), see this author's "Is Systematic Theology Possible from a Mennonite Perspective?" in Occasional Papers No. 7 (Elkhart, In.: Institute of Mennonite Studies, 1983).

Bible does not, generally speaking, move from cause to effect, from God's nature to the world and God's acts within the world. Rather God is usually known through his specific historical acts. As biblical history proceeds, and as God encounters humankind in different situations, knowledge of God deepens. It is often summarized by means of recitals. The Bible's most detailed statements about God's nature (which are not terribly detailed and of which there are few) appear in some of its latest writings (e.g., John 1:1-14, Col. 1:15-20, Hebrews 1). In other words, while God is undoubtedly the Cause of biblical history, biblical revelation generally does not move from cause to effect, but (largely by means of narrative) from effect to cause. Throughout the Bible the true God is contending with false gods who claim to control nature and history and with false human conceptions of God. Only as God, through his revealing and saving acts, overcomes these false gods and these false concepts does his distinct identity become known.

Consequently while God is indeed first in the "order of being," detailed apprehension of God often comes last in the "order of knowing." Accordingly we shall endeavor to speak of God "in himself" only when we have attained the fullest possible knowledge of God's acts—at the end of our theological system. We do this not to diminish the priority of God but to give that subject the richest and most profound articulation possible.

In general, we are seeking to begin at neither pole of theological reflection; neither kerygmatically, from God (and then moving deductively) nor contextually, from humanity (and then moving inductively). In beginning with eschatology we have chosen a point from within, where kerygmatic initiative and contextual response are deeply intertwined (and from which we will move adductively—Chap. 3). As we turn to biblical narrative for material on various doctrines, we will be reflecting on a history that is neither simply human nor simply divine but a unique history of God with humanity and humanity with God. Yet it is a history initiated by God's acts. Accordingly when we reflect on human experience, it will be experience as uniquely encountering the divine. We shall not seek to articulate it entirely in concepts which can be quite well understood apart from this encounter (e.g., Schleiermacher's feeling, Ritschl's ethics, Bultmann's existentialism, liberation theology's humanization).

Finally even though our reflections will make use of biblical narrative, our system will not simply follow the course of that narrative. In beginning with eschatology, we begin with that narrative's goal. We begin with the culmination of all of God's acts. We will then seek to understand all dimensions of God's work in light of that goal. We will work, generally speaking, from the end back towards the beginning. This method also contrasts with that of traditional systematics, which has generally moved from the beginning (God, Creation, Fall) towards the end. But despite our reversal of systematic theology's customary beginning and end points, we will make no strained attempt to reverse everything that comes in between. We have no desire to be novel simply for novelty's sake. In what follows we will briefly outline our proposed order. We do not assume that it is the only good one.

B. Relationships Among Specific Doctrines

Eschatology deals not only with the things hoped for but also with the hope that they arouse. Chapter 7 will explore the relationship of these objective and subjective dimensions. Chapters 8–9 will discuss the objects—the coming events—which arouse eschatological hope.[7] From consideration of what will happen in the future, we will turn to the question of how God is known in the present, to the question of "revelation." We will explore three dimensions of revelation: personal, historical, and propositional (Chaps. 10, 11, and 12). Then while discussing General Revelation (Chap. 13) we shall draw some tentative conclusions about the topic with which most systems begin: how God is known (often covered in a section called Prolegomena).

The three dimensions of revelation each point towards a Revealer, Jesus Christ. Traditional systems have discussed his Person (his divine and human natures, etc.) before his Work (his life and death). We shall attempt, however, to follow the course of biblical revelation, which generally moves in reverse order. Following an overview of general Christological perspectives (Chap. 14), we will discuss Jesus' life (Chap. 15) and death (Chaps. 16–17). We will conclude Volume I with Jesus' triumphant resurrection (Chap. 18). Jesus will function for us not only as the revelation of God but also as the revelation of what humans ought to be. Discussion of his Work, then, will provide the foundation for theological anthropology. We will outline traditional and contemporary anthropologies (Volume II, Chaps. 1–2), our own Christological approach (Chaps. 3–4), and the time-honored issues of body-soul-spirit and freedom of the will (Chap. 5).

Only in light of what human nature ought to be can we truly understand the nature of sin (Chap. 6) and move on to a precise understanding of salvation or soteriology. Chapters 7 and 8 will cover justification and sanctification. We will be unable, however, to regard sanctification as an individual affair. Since it involves relationships with others, sanctification flows directly into ecclesiology, or the doctrine of the Church (which we will discuss in general in Chap. 9). While many systems speak first of the Church's structure and then discuss (sometimes briefly) its activities, we will argue that the New Testament speaks primarily of church activities and only secondarily of its structure. Accordingly we will first discuss the Church as a community of fellowship (Chap. 10); its mission amidst society and to non-Christians (Chaps. 11–12); and its worship, including the sacraments (Chap. 13). Chapter 14 will then cover the structure of the Church.

Finally having learned as much as we can about the works of God, we will be ready for the most difficult and exalted topic of all: God's very being. Chapter 15 will discuss the "Persons" of the Spirit and the Son. Chapter 16 will consider the Trinity's historical work, including creation. This will prepare us for a discussion of the Trinity's eternal character and the deity and humanity of the

---

[7] For our definition of object and objective see Chap. 7.

Son (Chap. 17); and, finally, of the nature and attributes of God (Chap. 18). To clarify our overall procedure and its differences from the traditional order, we sketch their relationships as follows:

Traditional Order	Our Order
Prolegomena	Eschatology
Revelation	Revelation
God	(Prolegomena)
Person of Christ	Work of Christ
Creation	Anthropology
Anthropology	Soteriology
Soteriology	Ecclesiology
Work of Christ	God
Ecclesiology	Creation
Eschatology	Person of Christ

III. Approaches to Eschatology

Eschatology is full of strange images: bodies rising from graves and sailing on clouds; angels flying about with trumpets; fantastic beasts, scrolls, and bowls. Because it is straining towards things which have never occurred, hope must reshape and apply language in unusual ways. But how shall theology interpret such extraordinary speech? We begin by noticing that eschatological language is marked by three pairs of contrasting features.

First, as we have said, eschatological statements are expressions of hope. Most eschatological passages in Scripture are not straightforward, didactic descriptions of the end time. Instead they appear amid expressions of longing, dread, joy, exhortation, warning, comfort (1 Cor. 15:12-19, 51-58; 1 Thess. 4:13, 18—5:11, etc.). At the same time, these (subjective) expressions of hope are aroused by the (objective) things hoped for. The basis and object of hope are things which God has done, is doing, and will do.

Second, the *eschata* sometimes seem to stand in continuity with the present and past—and at others to be radically discontinuous with them. Paul, for instance, speaks of all creation groaning in anticipation of the final revelation of "the glorious liberty of the children of God" (Rom. 8:18-23). Here the *eschaton* seems to be the culmination of a process already in motion. Peter, however, declares that "the Day of the Lord will come like a thief, and then the heavens will pass away with a loud noise, and the elements will be dissolved with fire, and the earth and the works that are upon it will be burned up" (2 Pet. 3:10).

Third, eschatological language can be literal or figurative. Many Old Testament passages about a coming era of peace and prosperity seem to be literal. Yet no our would interpret Revelation's cacophany of angels, beasts, thrones, and trumpets in an entirely literal way.

Beginning our reflections with eschatology, then, immediately plunges us into issues of how biblical language is to be interpreted, of how different biblical emphases relate to one another, and of how all of this can be expressed in language intelligible for today. We are beginning "from within," and our reasoning must be largely adductive. We can sharpen our sensitivity to all these issues by briefly examining three widely contrasting intepretative schemes.

A. Dispensationalism

To interpret eschatological language literally. is to expect God's climactic reign to occur on earth. In other ways, however, Dispensationalism anticipates a good measure of discontinuity between the end and the present order of things. It is a form of "Premillennialism." During the second and third centuries most Christians were premillennial. That is, they expected the persecution of the Church to intensify and affairs in general to get worse. They expected that Christ would then suddenly return to defeat his enemies and establish the thousand-year reign (the millennium) prophesied in Revelation 20. Because it hopes for Christ's return before ("pre-") this "millennium," this view is called "Premillennialism." (Not all premillennialists, however, expect this period to last a literal thousand years).

After Constantine made Christianity the favored religion of the Empire, the popularity of this eschatology, which saw Christ in direct conflict with Rome, rapidly declined. Until the nineteenth-century the premillennial vision seldom flashed brightly except among fanatical sects and Believers' churches. It was revived in systematic and specifically dispensational fashion by John Nelson Darby (1800–1882). Darby sensed a distressing contrast between the New Testament Church, which was spiritually united with the heavenly Christ, and the worldly state church, Anglicanism of his own day. Ecclesiastically this led Darby to become a leader in a new Believers' church, the Plymouth Brethren. Theologically he began to feel that the contrast between the true Church and the state church in his time was similar to the one between the New Testament Church and Old Testament Israel.

Dispensationalism can be described as an interpretation of history and eschatology which makes important distinctions between God's way of working in at least two "dispensations": those of Israel and the Church.[8] Systematically, however, this distinction seems to be based on the hermeneutical principle of literal interpretation.[9] Many Old Testament prophecies predict the return of Israel to Palestine, the rebuilding of the Jerusalem temple, and the literal reign of a Davidic king over an era of universal justice, prosperity, and peace. Not all of

[8] Robert Saucy, "Contemporary Dispensational Thought," TSF Bulletin 7/4 (March-April, 1984), pp. 10-11.

[9] Earl Radmacher, "The Current Status of Dispensationalism and its Eschatology" in Kenneth Kantzer and Stanley Gundry, eds. Perspectives on Evangelical Theology (Grand Rapids: Baker, 1979), pp. 163-76. For a good description and defense of this principle, see Charles Ryrie, Dispensationalism Today (Chicago: Moody, 1965), pp. 86-109.

these were fulfilled before Jesus came. Most theologians have thought that they applied from that time on in a more general and spiritual way to the Church. But for dispensationalists this cannot be the basic meaning of these prophecies. If they say that Israel will flourish in Jerusalem, this can mean only that this particular biological people will enjoy material prosperity in that geographical center. If this fulfillment has not yet occurred, then it will surely occur in the future.

As this principle of literal interpretation is applied very broadly, it gives rise to, or at least seems to be consistent with, numerous differentiations between God's work with Israel (his kingdom work) and God's work with the Church.[10] Israel lived according to the Law; the Church lives according to grace. Israel was a distinct nation; the Church includes people from all nations. Israelite life was concerned with the earthly, the physical, and the social; the Church is concerned with the heavenly, the spiritual, and the individual. The principle of literal interpretation also leads to a significant discontinuity in God's historical activities. According to dispensationalism Jesus first offered himself to Israel as its earthly king. Had Israel accepted him, an Israelo-centric kingdom (which could have subdued the Romans by force) would have been established. When Israel rejected Jesus, however, the "Church age" came into being. God's particular dealings with the nation Israel have been put on hold ever since. (Individual Jews, however, have and can become part of the Church.)

According to most dispensationalists, the Church age will end when Christ returns secretly to "rapture" the Church out of the world. God will then reactivate his Israelite, or kingdom, program. During a few intense, trouble-torn years of "Great Tribulation" many Jews will be converted. Then Christ will return visibly to defeat Antichrist and set up his earthly, millennial, Israelo-centric kingdom. The Jerusalem temple will be rebuilt. Many Old Testament sacrifices will be revived.[11]

Dispensationalists have usually drawn a thick line between God's kingdom program and God's program for the church.[12] Recently, however, some have spoken of some degree of overlap. Some are now emphasizing that God's kingdom, though it will be established primarily through Israel, is the final goal of

[10] See Ryrie, pp. 132-48; also Herman Hoyt, "Dispensational Premillennialism" in Robert Clouse, ed., *The Meaning of the Millennium* (Downers Grove, Il.: InterVarsity, 1977), pp. 63-92.

[11] J. Dwight Pentecost, *Things to Come* (Findlay, Oh.: Dunham, n.d.), pp. 512-31; John Walvoord, *The Millennial Kingdom* (Findlay, Oh.: Dunham, 1959), pp. 309-15; Clarence Bass, *Backgrounds to Dispensationalism* (Grand Rapids: Eerdmans, 1960), pp. 38-45.

[12] Ryrie, pp. 132-55. But Alva McClain, *The Greatness of the Kingdom* (Grand Rapids: Zondervan, 1959), a classic attempt to outline relationships between these two programs, finds it hard to pinpoint exactly when Israel refused her king (cf. pp. 313-19 with 344 and 353). McClain also speaks of a brief revival of God's kingdom plan, or elements of it, in Acts (pp. 403-13).

God's work. Thus some prefer to speak of the present (church) age "as the first phase of the fulfillment of the one promised Messianic kingdom." This phase, however, involves only "the spiritual aspects of that Messianic kingdom...(i.e., regeneration, the indwelling spirit, etc.)." Its physical and social dimensions "will find their fulfillment following the second advent."[13]

We will examine dispensationalism's view of the millennium in Chapter 9 and its hermeneutic in Chapter 11. For now we observe that this interpretive system has strongly emphasized the literal dimension of eschatological language. When the Bible stresses discontinuity between the future and the present course of things, dispensationalists do not reinterpret how this is said. Millions of Christians suddenly disappearing from earth, Jesus landing on Mount Olivet—dispensationalists insist that this is exactly what will happen. But dispensationalism also interprets the continuity between present and future in a literal way. Peace and justice will someday reign on this planet among peoples organized in socio-political ways. In fact, dispensationalists often criticize more figurative interpretations for minimizing the earthly and social dimensions of God's kingdom work.[14]

B. Existentialism

While dispensationalism interprets eschatological language literally, modern existential intepretation construes it figuratively. While dispensationalists seek to discern the sequence of the (objective) things hoped for, existentialists focus almost entirely on (subjective) hope. So diverse are these two schemes that one may wonder how they can refer to the same Bible.

As represented by Rudolf Bultmann, existential interpretation regards the New Testament's eschatological worldview as mythological. Angels, demons, supernatural events shattering cause-effect sequences—all these contradict the modern scientific conception of the universe. Since Bultmann unquestioningly accepts this modern worldview, he insists that biblical mythology must be reinterpreted if eschatololgy is to have any meaning for the present. He calls his scheme of reinterpretation "demythologization." Demythologizing does not seek to simply eliminate the "mythical" elements in Scripture. For Bultmann myth is a crude, pictorial way in which ancient people sought to express deeper, existential truths. Accordingly, demythologizing's "aim is not to elimi-

[13] Saucy, p. 11. Robert Gundry also argues for more overlap between dispensations in *The Church and the Tribulation* (Grand Rapids: Zondervan, 1973), pp. 12-28. For a critique of Gundry from a more traditional dispensationalist perspective, see John Walvoord, *The Blessed Hope and the Tribulation* (Grand Rapids: Zondervan, 1976), esp. pp. 66-68.

[14] Radmacher, pp. 171-76; Ryrie, pp. 168-75.

nate the mythological statements but to interpret them."[15]

More precisely, Bultmann argues that when ancient people were moved by deep inner realities, they tended to picture them as events taking place in space and time.[16] For instance, a culture might apprehend the importance of doing good and avoiding evil; people would express the significance of this insight by elaborating vivid stories about a Last Judgment when the good would be rewarded and the evil punished. All of this happened, of course, in an unconscious manner. Those who invented and heard these stories really believed that such a judgment would occur at some future date. But modern knowledge, Bultmann insists, has shown that we cannot take such things literally. Thus theology's task, when confronted with the Bible's eschatological passages, is to disregard whatever is said about future events and specific places, and to search for their deeper existential message.

Existential eschatology, then, need not minutely exegete numerous recondite, highly symbolic texts, nor need it decipher a precise chronology of coming events. Existentialism can reduce the welter of eschatological predictions, images, and occurrences to a few simple, personally relevant truths. Assertions about a coming judgment or hell can be interpreted as vivid ways of expressing the dire consequences of going against God's will. The millennium and heaven become picturesque means of describing the joys of obeying God. The Great Tribulation and other end-time woes become imaginative pictures of the difficulties by which a Christian's obedience is tested. But no one need suppose that such events will really happen.

Perhaps it sounds as if existential interpretation, by making contact with the contemporary context in this way, emphasizes the continuity between the present course of things and that which eschatological language conveys. Bultmann argues, however, that the eschatological message is radically discontinuous with any present context. To understand this we must briefly examine how he interprets different kinds of eschatological language in the Bible.

In recent decades, scholars have argued much over the distinction between the "prophetic" and "apocalyptic" perspectives. The former is prevalent in the Old Testament. The latter was widespread in the intertestamental period. Prophecy tends, first of all, to be directed at specific historical situations. Apocalyptic is more concerned with the final, cataclysmic events to occur at the end of present history. Second, prophecy anticipates God's imminent action within the earthly order. Apocalyptic, however, often regards the present as devoid of God's presence and frowns pessimistically on the degenerating course of things. Third, prophecy calls for obedience and involve-

---

[15] *Jesus Christ and Mythology*, p. 18; for a further explanation of demythologizing and some critical responses, see Hans Werner Bartsch, ed., *Kerygma and Myth* (New York: Harper, 1953); and John Macquarrie, *The Scope of Demythologizing* (New York: Harper, 1960).

[16] Ibid., pp. 11-34.

ment in current social and religious affairs. But apocalyptic tends to withdraw from society and to wait for God's final intervention. Finally, while prophecy envisions a better future, it paints it in relatively sober, this-worldly colors. Apocalyptic, however, is often embellished with images of fantastic cosmic conflagration and renovation.

To be sure, precise lines between prophecy and apocalyptic cannot be drawn. Many scholars regard the latter as a gradual outgrowth of the former.[17] Bultmann, however, distinguishes them sharply. He argues that the prophets spoke of literal, identifiable, earthly events and hopes.[18] Apocalyptic, however, was wholly dualistic. For it the end of history

> no longer belongs to history as such. Therefore it cannot be the goal of history towards which the the course of history moves by steps. The end is not the completion of history but its breaking-off....The old world will be replaced by a new creation, and there is no continuity between the two Aeons....In the new Aeon...times and years will be annihilated, and months and days and hours will be no more.[19]

Most significantly Bultmann regards Jesus' perspective as thoroughly apocalyptic.[20] When Jesus proclaimed that "the Kingdom of God is at hand!" (Mark 1:15), he did not mean that a religious and social order of existence, the fulfillment of the earthly kingdom promised to Israel, was being established. Instead his teachings, healings, and exorcisms portended the end of the present spatiotemporal order and the inbreaking of a wholly different reality. The same sort of apocalyptic expectation, moreover, was held by the earliest Church and was expressed in its kerygma.

Bultmann acknowledges that the earliest communities (and perhaps Jesus himself) understood the coming of judgment and of the kingdom somewhat mythologically. They really expected that the new age, despite its radical otherness, would also have spatio-temporal features of some kind. Bultman argues that demythologization can show us the real significance of this imagery. It means that not a social order but God's forgiving grace is now present as an absolute gift. This grace is thoroughly discontinuous with anything else we may have experienced, no matter what our apologetic context. It means that we

---

[17] George Ladd, *The Presence of the Future* (Grand Rapids: Eerdmans, 1974) outlines the differences between prophecy and apocalyptic and argues that the latter grew out of the former (pp. 45-101); H. H. Rowley, *The Relevance of Apocalyptic* (New York: Association, 1964), pp. 13-53; R. H. Charles, "Apocalyptic Literature" in James Hastings, ed., *A Dictionary of the Bible*, Vol. I (New York: Scribner, 1903), pp. 109-10.

[18] *History and Eschatology* (New York: Harper, 1957), pp. 18-22, 27-28.

[19] Ibid., p. 30.

[20] Ibid., pp. 31-33; *Jesus and the Word* (New York: Scribner's, 1934, 1958), pp. 27-56.

must choose absolutely and radically for God's way, uninfluenced by the ethical standards of our culture.[21]

Because eschatological language, when interpreted literally, may sound incredible to modern people, Bultmann has sought for a figurative meaning which might still be significant today. Yet he has sought to preserve the sharp biblical discontinuity between the present and the ultimate order of things. Under the influence of science and technology, contemporary people tend to feel that all things, including themselves, are mere products of mechanistic, deterministic forces. But the eschatological kerygma announces that, however things may appear, we are not really machines meshed with the faceless mechanism of nature. By addressing us as deciding individuals, this new reality, this Word of forgiveness and freedom, actually brings the old age of determinism, sin, and despair to an end. Therefore this Word of grace *is* the new age, it is the *eschaton*, the utterly transcendent divine order which brings the old order to an end.[22]

C. Postmillennialism

The vivid, diverse, and largely unsystematized language of biblical eschatology can be interpreted according to a third distinctive scheme. This one emphasizes the literal intention of much eschatological language, especially its reference to the earthly, social realm. Unlike existentialism, it stresses continuity between current history and the end of things. Yet it does not press all the details as dispensationalism does. Postmillennialists understand the millennium to be some period of earthly history during which the gospel increasingly penetrates all culture. Christ's return is expected after ("post-") this millennium.

Augustine was the first to formulate a widely influential postmillennial teaching.[23] We have seen that Christians in the first three centuries were often persecuted by the state. They envisioned the millennium as a sharp contrast to their present situation. Christ would arrive before ("pre-") the millennium to defeat his enemies, including Rome. Augustine, however, noticed that without any such divine intervention the Church had ceased being persecuted and attained a position of supremacy under Constantine. By Augustine's day, the Church seemed to be on the verge of taking over the socio-political functions of its tottering former enemy, the Empire of Rome. Augustine concluded that the millennium had already arrived. The saints were already reigning with Christ. The Catholic church was now the kingdom of God.

Postmillennialism became the common position of the medieval Catholic church and also of the established Protestant denominations. It generally

---

[21] *Jesus and the Word*, pp. 27-56.

[22] *History and Eschatology*, pp. 149-55; *Jesus Christ and Mythology*, pp. 80-83.

[23] For a brief history, see Millard Erickson, *Contemporary Options in Eschatology* (Grand Rapids: Baker, 1977), pp. 58-62.

characterized Protestant orthodoxy, including that of Charles Hodge.[24] In the nineteenth century most liberals held similar views.[25] Perhaps postmillennialism comes naturally to churches which see themselves as allied with the positive forces in society and working along with them for the sake of God's kingdom.

Postmillennialism has not been expounded in as minute detail as has dispensationalism. Few have developed it into an interpretive system as precise as the one Bultmann has provided for existential eschatology. Until the late nineteenth century, postmillennialism was not even clearly differentiated from other approaches.[26] The name stands more for a general perspective than for one specific orientation. Consequently, it is best to describe it in general terms.

Like dispensationalists and unlike Bultmann, postmillennial interpretation regards the kingdom of God as a social, historical actualization of God's reign on earth. But postmillennialists reject dispensationalism's claim that God's kingdom program was put on hold, wholly or in part, when Israel rejected its Messiah. Instead, they insist, what Jesus proclaimed as beginning in his ministry came to pass. His resurrection confirmed him as the king reigning over God's kingdom.[27] Jesus also commanded the church to spread the gospel to all nations. "All authority in heaven and on earth" has been given to accomplish this task (Matt. 28:18–20). Therefore postmillennialists do not see how the church can ultimately fail in executing it. Some final, dramatic intervention of Jesus himself should not be necessary. For Christ has already endowed the Church "with all the gifts necessary for the proper discharge of this duty, and promised to send his Spirit to render their preaching effectual."[28]

Moreover, postmillennialists often argue that Jesus himself expected the kingdom to spread gradually. Of the seven kingdom parables in Matthew 13, for instance, four depict it in terms of organic growth. The difference between the "already" and the "not yet," one might say, will be bridged by a gradual

---

[24] *Systematic Theology*, Vol. III, esp. pp. 800-05.

[25] During most of the century, evangelicals were often in the forefront of numerous social causes. They tended to be postmillennial. Towards the end of the century, the revival of premillennialism, frequently in dispensational form, occasioned much conflict among evangelicals. Eventually, evangelicalism in general inclined towards the latter.

[26] Erickson, pp. 73, 76.

[27] For instance, Jesus quoted Psalm 110 to emphasize his Messianic identity (Mark 12:35-37 and par.), and the apostles quote it again to explain the significance of Pentecost (Acts 2:34-35). Throughout the New Testament this Psalm underlines Christ's present rule over the powers (1 Cor. 15:25; Eph. 1:20; Col. 3:1; Heb. 1:3, 1:13, 10:12-13, 12:2).

[28] Hodge, Vol. III, p. 801.

transition. And this calls the Church to hopeful action in the present. As a liberal "social gospel" theologian put it:

> the Kingdom of God is always both present and future....It is the energy of God realizing itself in human life....No theories about the future of the Kingdom of God are likely to be valuable or true which paralyze or postpone redemptive action on our part....It is for us to see the Kingdom of God as always coming, always pressing in on the present, always big with possibility, and always inviting immediate action.[29]

But even though the transition between "already" and "not yet" occurs largely by means of quantitative increments...(and not through a qualitative leap), conservative postmillennialists do anticipate dramatic occurrences at the very end. Many expect a large-scale conversion of Jews. They base this rather straightforwardly on texts which assert this kind of thing (Romans 11, etc.), not on dispensationalist reasoning. They also anticipate a brief flareing of apostasy under Antichrist (cf. Rev. 20:7–10), after which Jesus will personally return.[30]

Yet in emphasizing a progressive transformation of the world into the kingdom and in urging Christians towards this task, systems which call themselves postmillennial are akin to many activist theologies that fit under no precise eschatological label. Such a general orientation, for example, characterizes most liberation theologies. In this broad sense, then, Postmillennialism is an important contemporary option for interpreting the complex language of eschatology.

Suggestions for Further Reading

Bartsch, Hans Werner. *Kerygma and Myth*. New York: Harper, 1953.
Bass, Clarence. *Backgrounds to Dispensationalism*. Grand Rapids: Eerdmans, 1960.
Boettner, Loraine. *The Millennium*. Philadelphia: Presbyterian & Reformed, 1957.
Bultmann, Rudolph. *History and Eschatology: The Presence of Eternity*, New York: Harper, 1957.
———.*Jesus and the Word*. New York: Scribner's, 1934, 1958.
Clouse, Robert, ed. *The Meaning of the Millennium*. Downers Grove, Il.: Inter Varsity, 1977.
Erickson, Millard. *Contemporary Options in Eschatology*. Grand Rapids: Baker, 1977.

---

[29] Walter Rauschenbusch, *A Theology for the Social Gospel* (New York: Macmillan, 1917), p. 141.

[30] Loraine Boettner, *The Millennium* (Philadelphia: Presbyterian & Reformed, 1957), pp. 67-81.

Macquairrie, John. *The Scope of Demythologizing.* New York: Harper, 1960.
Marty, Martin and Peerman, Dean. *New Theology No. 5.* New York: Macmillan, 1968.
Moltmann, Jürgen. *Hope and Planning.* New York: Harper, 1968.
———.*Religion, Revelation and the Future.* New York: Scribner's, 1969.
Ruether, Rosemary, *The Radical Kingdom: The Western Experience of the Messianic Hope.* New York: Harper, 1970.
Ryrie, Charles. *Dispensationalism Today.* Chicago: Moody, 1965.
Schwarz, Hans. *On the Way to the Future: A Christian View of Eschatology in Light of Current Trends in Religion, Philosophy and Science,* rev. ed. Minneapolis: Augsburg, 1970.
Smith, Timothy. *Revivalism and Social Reform.* New York and Nashville: Abingdon, 1957.
Walvoord, John F. *Israel in Prophecy.* Grand Rapids: Zondervan, 1962.
———.*The Millennial Kingdom.* Findlay, Oh. Dunham, 1959.

CHAPTER SEVEN

Subjective and Objective Eschatology

B eginning theological reflection with eschatology immediately plunges one into a number of tasks. Eschatology is intertwined with numerous other issues: biblical interpretation, the kingdom of God, the relationship of Church and society, etc. Complex issues of religious language immediately arise: To what extent is it literal and/or figurative? To what extent are its referents subjective and/or objective? If systematic theology begins with eschatology, it does not start reflecting on such issues from outside, in an introductory Prolegomena but from inside, as it wrestles with issues which deeply concern our apocalyptic age.

We have begun with eschatology because here the personal and the cosmic, the contextual and the kerygmatic are intertwined. Eschatology engenders profound hope which transforms personal existence in any context; yet this hope is aroused by and directed toward God's kerygmatic, cosmic acts which transcend and transform all contexts. Now we must elaborate on this notion of eschatology in three ways.

First, in contemporary theology our starting point, the early kerygma, is understood and used in various ways. We will need to clarify how we understand it and how we are using it. Second, we will explore eschatology's personal or "subjective" side. How does eschatological hope affect people? How does it affect the way they understand themselves and lead their lives? Since people today hunger for meaningful experience, we will probably make better initial

117

contact with them by first discussing this subjective dimension.

Third, however, we will insist that eschatological hope is grounded in something "objective."[1] We will investigate the general character of things hoped for. Here serious problems will arise. For modern people (as Bultmann insists) are not supposed to believe that most eschatological events could occur in any literal fashion. How, then, are we to understand the implications of eschatology for nature, history, and society? We will need to explore such issues in depth.

I. The Theological Function of the Kerygma

Our efforts to reflect on the heart of Christian faith begin with the early kerygma. However, much of what the New Testament says on eschatology is not part of this primitive kerygma. The kerygma can be reconstructed largely from the early speeches in Acts and the letters of Paul (Chap 2.). But for the most part, the kerygma is not directly recited in the New Testament; one must delve into the documents we now have in order to discover it.

What relationship, then, exists between the kerygma and the Bible's more detailed eschatological teachings (as elaborated, say, in Mark 13, 1 Corinthians 15, or throughout Revelation)? For some, such as Rudolf Bultmann, the earliest kerygma (which he desribes differently than we do) operates as a criterion by which the validity of the other teachings may be judged. Bultmann, along with C. H. Dodd and others, bases his reasoning on the so-called Delay of the Parousia. (The Greek *parousia* can mean simply "arrival" or "coming"; but the English term refers to Jesus' second coming.) According to Bultmann the problem of New Testament eschatology

> grew out of the fact that the expected end of the world failed to arrive, that the "Son of Man" did not appear in the clouds of heaven, that history went on, and that the eschatological community could not fail to recognize that it had become a historical phenomenon and that the Christian faith had taken on the shape of a new religion.[2]

---

[1] "Objective" can have two meanings. In the most general sense, something is objective when it is different from, when it is other than, the subject (s) (the person [s]) who perceive or experience it. In a second sense, however, something can be considered objective insofar as it is constituted or constructed according to the categories of human perception and can be controlled or manipulated once the laws governing this construction are discovered. In modern philosophy and theology, "objective" is often used in the second way. When it is, theologians deny that God or eschatological events have an objective character—for if they did, humans could manipulate and control them. We, however, are using the word in the first sense. Consequently, if we insist that God or the *eschata* are objective, we mean that they cannot be controlled by humans, for their reality is distinct from ours.

[2] *History and Eschatology*, p. 38.

We remember how, in Bultmann's view, the apocalyptic perspective of Jesus and the early Church anticipated the end of the present earthly order and the imminent arrival of a completely different reality. But, says Bultmann, that end failed to occur. Consequently many New Testament passages on eschatology originally arose to give an explanation for this delay. (For example, 2 Thessalonians 2 exhorts its readers "not to be quickly shaken in mind or excited" about the coming of the parousia, for certain other events must first occur.) These explanations, according to Bultmann, were the genesis of those detailed eschatological schemes which dispensationalists still seek to decipher.

Many other features of our New Testament can be traced to the same roots. According to the Delay theory the earliest Christians were not concerned about ethics, for they did not expect to be living much longer in this world. Only when it became plain that they might be here for a while did they begin laying down rules for conduct. The origins of theological doctrines and ecclesiastical structures can be similarly explained. The early communities, ecstatically prompted by the Spirit, needed to define neither their faith nor their organizational structure. But as years lengthened, the communities experienced theological and sociological conflicts among themselves and also with the outside world. The New Testament's doctrinal teachings and its remarks on church order originated largely through this process.

For us this sort of reconstruction is significant because of the theological use that Bultmann and others make of it. They tend to set the original kerygma over against these later developments: The kerygma expresses the essential Christian message, but many more developed New Testament teachings are regarded as flawed human attempts to adjust it to a time-bound ancient culture.[3] (For Bultmann, of course, even the earliest expressions of the kerygma, involving as they do a bodily resurrection and conflict with demonic forces, were products of mythological thinking. Theology must probe even behind these to find a few fundamental, existential truths, which alone constitute the real Christian message.)

We have acknowledged the apparent apologetic advantages of such an approach. It allows modern people to disregard supposedly fantastic eschatological teachings and also many ethical, doctrinal, and ecclesiastical claims. They can be directly confronted with a message full of challenge and comfort for the distressed individual.

But we wonder if this approach does justice to the kerygma. We observed that at least several essential kerygmatic events (Jesus' ministry and death) are clearly historical. The kerygma fulfills the lengthy history recorded in the Old Testament. Can one really assume that the other events, Jesus' resurrection, ascension, and return, have no real relationship to the spatio-temporal order?

The Delay of the Parousia theory assumes that Jesus and the earliest Christians were rabid apocalpyticists. They expected the entire spatio-temporal uni-

---

[3] The classic attempt to reconstruct the early history of doctrine in this manner is Martin Werner's *The Formation of Christian Doctrine* (New York: Harper, 1957).

verse to pass away. That is why so many later New Testament expectations that the universe will continue cannot be valid expressions of the early kerygmatic perspective. But did Jesus and the earliest communities really envision such absolute discontinuity between the kerygma and reality as we know it? Postmillennialists, among others, certainly do not think so. Many people would argue that the kingdom which Jesus announced, and which the first believers entered, has continued to transform this world up to the present.

But if the early kerygma is compatible with and even anticipates some continuation of history, then further explanation of coming events by later writers is consistent with the kerygma. And if God intended the kerygma to create a group of people who would act and think within history, God might well use their experiences and writings to unfold the kerygma's ethical, doctrinal, and ecclesiastical implications.

At this point we can hardly solve all the questions raised by this fundamental issue. They will affect almost every doctrine we will consider. At present we can describe our theological use of the kerygma as follows: It will provide the fundamental vantage point from which to explore the development of Christian doctrine. It will be our primary clue to what is distinct about and essential to Christian faith. But unless other biblical assertions contradict the kerygma, we will regard them as valid explanations, elaborations, and applications of its meaning from different angles.

II. The Subjective Dimension of Eschatology

The kerygma announces certain events and their consequences. But as we have noted, it is no mere communication of information. The kerygma is also a dynamic reality, transforming those whom it touches. But how can we learn what this subjective dimension is like? It is accomplished by following roughly the same method that scholars have used in detecting the kerygma itself. Paul's epistles and the first chapters of Acts also contain glimpses into the early response to the kerygma. We have seen that the hope aroused by God's eschatological acts is marked by the interplay of the already and the not yet. We can best penetrate the nature of this hope by considering each pole in turn. As we proceed, it will become evident that they cannot be separated.

A. The "Already"

The earliest Christians experienced the already of the *eschaton* through worship. They met daily in the temple and in private homes, and "devoted themselves to the apostles' teaching and fellowship, and to the breaking of bread and prayers." (Acts 2:42; cf. 2:46–47, 5:42). The "breaking of bread" refers to worshipful commemoration of the disciples' last meal with Jesus.[4] While this

---

[4] Oscar Cullman feels that not only the "last supper" but also Jesus' post-resurrection meals with his disciples (Luke 24:30–31, John 21:12) were sources of these feasts (*Early Christian Worship* [London: SCM, 1953], pp. 14-20).

"love-feast" was the origin of the communion practiced in churches today, it focused more on Christ's resurrection and his joyous presence than on his death. It was part of an actual meal, not just a religious ceremony. In this worship, Jesus was personally experienced and addressed as "Lord."[5]

From the beginning, then, Jesus Christ was experienced and addressed personally in worship—an act appropriately offered to God alone. Moreover this title "Lord" indicates that his rule over the cosmos, including the powers, was essential to early awareness of Christ.[6] From the beginning, in other words, eschatology contained both intensely personal and broadly cosmic elements.

The "already" of the new age brought together those who responded not only for worship but also for fellowship. Not only did they meet and eat together frequently, but their sharing of new life involved sharing on an economic plane: "There was not a needy person among them, for as many as were possessors of lands or houses sold them...and distribution was made to each as any had need" (Acts 2:44–45; cf. 4:32–5:11). The reality of the New Age, when divisions among human groups should vanish and universal fellowship should reign, was so profound that the earliest Christians left their old socioeconomic positions. They joined communities where these distinctions were being reshaped and where Christian commitment extended to all areas of life.[7]

The deep commitment of early Christians to each other, however, did not isolate them from their context (as sometimes has happened with Believers' churches). On the contrary, the quality of their life together appealed very strongly to many around them (Acts 2:47). The earliest communities were constantly engaged in missionary outreach. Missionary preaching itself seems to have been done by their leaders. But their worship and fellowship not only undergirded missionary efforts; it was itself a visible actualization of their message: The new age is here!

The vitality of these subjective dimensions was rooted in the outpouring of the Holy Spirit.[8] The Spirit conveyed a vivid sense of God's power and motivated the works done by the apostles. These included healings and other works which affected the spatio-temporal dimensions of earthly existence. The gift of tongues made their preaching intelligible to those from all nations (Acts 2:5–11). Like early Christian experience of Christ, the experience and work of the

---

[5] Ibid., pp. 12-14. Some have argued that "the exalted Jesus was never a direct object of worship." (Fuller, *Foundations of New Testament Christology*, p. 158). Cullmann, however, points out that Paul sometimes prayed directly to the Lord Christ (2 Cor. 12:8, 1 Thess. 3:12, 2 Thess. 3:2–5) and argues that the early Christian exclamation "maranatha!" (1 Cor. 16:22) is best understood as a prayer (*Christology of the New Testament*, pp. 208-213).

[6] Ibid., pp. 203-22; see the argument on p. 39, note 7.

[7] Wayne A. Meeks, *The First Urban Christians: The Social World of Paul* (New Haven, CT: Yale Univ. Press, 1982).

[8] Acts 1:5, 8; 2:4, 17-18, 33, 38; 4:8, 25, 31; 5:3, 32, etc.

Spirit was not only intensely inward but had broad outward manifestations and implications as well.

The above characteristics of the "already" show that we must modify Bultmann's understanding of eschatology's subjective side. First, early Christian experience was not that of individuals making solitary decisions in face of the unknown future.[9] It was largely corporate. It involved not only personal encounter with Christ and the Spirit but also included joining and participating in closely-knit groups, sharing common experiences and devoted to common tasks.

Let us adopt a simple terminological distinction. Let us reserve the adjective "individual" for those experiences and decisions where people are acutely aware of their own uniqueness and solitariness. But let us use "personal" for profound and meaningful experiences which are shared. For existentialists, who are repulsed by the impersonality of modern mass society, authentic feeling and decision are often possible only in the isolated depths of the solitary soul. Subjectivity, however, need not be diluted but can be greatly enriched through experiences that are shared. And early Christian experience is far more "personal" than "individual."

Second, the personal character of subjective eschatological experience cannot be sharply separated from its objective side. Not only does what people consider to be true profoundly affect their experience and behavior, but that behavior itself begins to transform their objective situation. Worshiping the risen Lord, sharing experiences and goods, proclaiming the kerygma—all these profoundly subjective activities have objective manifestations as well.

B. The "Not Yet"

During their first few years, the atmosphere among the earliest communities was probably so highly-charged that the "not yet" aspects of the new age were little noticed. To be sure, Jesus was absent. Longing for his return (*maranatha!*) was intense. Yet his presence through the Spirit was so vivid, and his return was so certain, that the gap between the presence and the consummation of God's Kingdom seemed negligible. Eschatological experience, however, is not just absorption in undiluted bliss. It includes struggle and suffering. It is paradoxical existence in an Age when God's enemies have been decisively defeated, yet when they uncannily raise their forces for one final (and foredoomed) assault. It was not long before the harsh realization struck that the consummation was "not yet" here.

The early community soon learned that they were not as fully "of one heart and soul" as they had thought. Groups from differing social backgrounds complain about unequal distribution of common goods (Acts 6:1). The Church must still work at unity and love.

---

[9] "No one can take another's place, since every man must die his own death. In his loneliness every man realizes his existence" (*Jesus Christ and Mythology*, p. 56).

Soon after, persecution raises its head. The early Christians are scattered (Acts 8:1). Through this dispersion, the gospel spreads to Gentiles (Acts 10, 11:19-26). Yet persecution continues. It becomes painfully apparent that even in the New Age, "through many tribulations we must enter into the Kingdom of God" (Acts 14:22).

Paul's first letter to Corinth expresses this pointedly. Many Corinthians thought that they were, for all practical purposes, already reigning in glory (1 Cor. 1:5-7, 4:8). Paul reminds them that even in his initial visit, he pointed to the Christ who endured suffering and persecution (1 Cor. 1:23, 2:2-5; cf. Gal. 4:13-14). Paul himself, who follows in Jesus' footsteps, suffers similarly, and the Corinthians may expect to do likewise (1 Cor. 4:9-16). Joy at Jesus' resurrection must not obliterate the cross which preceded it. Paul relates this fact to the love feast. To be sure, it joyously anticipates Christ's return (1 Cor. 11:26). But many had turned this meal of rejoicing into one of carousing (11:20-22). Paul, accordingly, reminds them that the love feast is connected with Jesus' death. He emphasizes its seriousness (11:23-30).

The Corinthians' illusion that they were reigning in glory stemmed largely from their misinterpretation of the Spirit's work. Gifted with marvelous pneumatic powers, they felt that they had already reached perfection. In reality, however, this split them into factions, each claiming superiority over the others. Paul insists that the Spirit works most truly (yet often slowly) among those who are aware of their immaturity (1 Cor. 3:1-15). And the Spirit brings harmony among diverse persons and diverse gifts within the Church (12:4-13; 14). In later letters, Paul expresses this view by envisioning the Spirit as tending or struggling towards the future. The Spirit is the guarantee (better: "down-payment") of our final inheritance (2 Cor. 1:22, 5:5; Eph. 1:14). The Spirit is the first-fruit of God's final harvest (Rom. 8:23), just as Christ is the "first-fruit" of the final resurrection (1 Cor. 15:20, 23). The Spirit groans within Christians and throughout Creation as we all strive for liberation from bondage of every sort (Rom. 8:19-23).

From the vantage point of the "not yet," then, eschatological experience also proves not to be individualistic but corporate. Rightly apprehended, experience of the Spirit draws one towards harmonious relationships with others. Here also subjective and objective cannot be sharply separated. The suffering Church is enagaged in mission; her longings for consummation intertwine with those of all creation.

C. The "Already/Not Yet"

How does our subjective eschatology compare with the Delay of the Parousia theory? We cannot agree that experience of the new age, in its fundamental character, transports one from our spatio-temporal world into another realm. For the Spirit, who bestows the very life of the new age, inherently strives to shape this world towards a vision still future. We cannot regard the immaturities of Christians, their inward divisions, and their outward persecutions as un-

fortunate distractions from the eschaton's true meaning. They are vivid re-
minders that not all that God intends has yet been accomplished. Understood
not as interruptions of God's plan but as challenges, they keep pushing the
Church towards the universal goal of its mission and its members towards maturity. The Delay of the Parousia theory views eschatological experience too
much as an ecstatic Already! that delivers one from space and time.

This delay theory also wrongly understands the not yet. According to Bultmann and others, early Christian experience was so heavily based on Christ's
early return that when this failed to occur, it had to take on vastly different
ethical, doctrinal, and ecclesiastical form. It was adjusted, with varying degrees
of success, to a universe that unexpectedly kept on going. In our view, however,
early Christian experience was not so fully sustained by expectation of the
"not yet" that it had to be drastically revised when this failed to occur. Instead
subjective eschatology was grounded in the certainty of the already. Because
Christ's victory and lordship over Death and the powers were so definitive, because the Spirit was so decisively present, the new age was surely here! But if
this victory is certain, then it does not matter how much time elapses before it
is consummated. One's faith is based not on what has not yet happened but on
what has already occurred.[10]

Many early Christians probably did expect the parousia very soon. Its apparent delay must have caused significant psychological unrest. And many ethical, doctrinal, and ecclesiastical New Testament passages were written to help
come to grips with this. But there is a great difference between psychological
readjustment, when particular events do not occur as anticipated, and theological revision of one's entire view of reality. Early Christian experience was psy-
chologically readjusted. But the theological basis for the Church's continuing
historical struggles was already implicit in the kerygma. For the kerygma itself
was grounded in historical events, including the sufferings of the One at its
center.

What can all this sometimes technical discussion of subjective eschatology
say to our modern context, where so many long for meaningful personal experience? How can it help the Church articulate what the kerygma is all about? It
affirms, first, that kerygma offers a deep sense of the presence of Christ and the
Holy Spirit. In an age when God may seem to have vanished, God can be experienced at work within the individual. Yet the kerygma offers no lasting help
for those who seek refuge within their private selves, sheltered from the challenges of interpersonal relationships and social issues. For as we noticed in
Chapter 2, the modern desire for intensely personal meaning is often the reverse side of cosmic despair. And the kerygma strikes at the roots of this cosmic
despair. It can offer hope and meaning only because Christ has overcome its
deepest causes.

[10] Oscar Cullmann, *Christ and Time*, pp. 81-93, 139-43. We can substantiate our view
in detail only through a detailed exploration of Christ's work (chaps. 15-18). For
Bultmann's response to Cullmann, see "History of Salvation and History" in *Existence and Faith* (Cleveland: Meridian, 1960), pp. 226-40.

Consequently any real apprehension of this hope thrusts people into social and interpersonal challenges and into the tasks of personal growth. This hope, however, is not oriented so wholly towards the "not yet" that it conists primarily in desperate striving, all the while fearing that its goals may not be attained. It is rooted, rather, in what God has already done; because all forces opposing Christ's reign have already been conquered, one may confidently challenge their lingering though potent effects.

Christians have often understood the already or the finished character of Christ's work to encourage passivity. Because Christ has done it all, people may reason, things must be generally as God wants. Christians then lose their sensitivity to grief and injustice and begin to put up with things as they are. But properly apprehended, the presence of the Spirit and the joy of the resurrection make it impossible to put up with the pain and despair that afflict so much of humankind. Because Christians believe that a different kind of world is not only possible, but real

> hope causes not rest but unrest, not patience but impatience....Those who hope in Christ can no longer put up with reality as it is, but begin to suffer under it, to contradict it. Peace with God means conflict with the world.[11]

We have begun with eschatology's subjective side in hopes of making contact with our present context. People today long for personal meaning. Yet they often find eschatological language unintelligible and eschatological events incredible. As much as we disagree with Bultmann, we appreciate his search for such a "point of contact." Still we have repeatedly insisted that subjective eschatology is based on objective events, claims, and hopes. Unless we can clarify this basis our eschatology will sound unreal and incredible too.

III. The Objective Dimension of Eschatology

Our initial awareness of eschatology's subjective side has come from some passages in Paul and Acts. But in our modern age systematic theology cannot so easily draw objective eschatological data directly from Scripture. For unlike biblical theology, systematic theology seeks to expound the Scripture's meaning in terms intelligible to our context. But when most people read of Christ returning on the clouds, of the moon turning to blood, of stars falling from the sky, they immediately wonder what this language signifies? How literally must one take it? So even should systematic theology wish to interpret it literally, it must show why such a reading is appropriate and what it really means today. Today's questions about the objective reference of eschatological language arise largely from the influence of science. They are so complex that the general relationship between the two will fill the rest of this chapter. The more specific objective (as well as subjective) features of particular eschatological events will occupy Chapters 8 and 9.

Traditionally systematic theology has handled the relationship of science and religion under the heading of Creation. Here the relations among different

[11] Moltmann, p. 21.

realms of reality and among differing kinds of causality were solved in a general way before proceeding to the experiential and eschatological dimensions of faith. Initial questions about the courses of nature and history, however, fit better under eschatology. When most Christians raise them, they are not academic questions about science. They are questions of the form; for what may I hope? Is my character wholly determined by my genes and environment? or might I change myself and my circumstances? Will the nations follow a foredoomed path to mutual annihilation? Or can other factors modify this apparently relentless course?

Subjective questions about meaning and hope are deeply intertwined with objective ones about the openness or closedness of the future. If the future course of nature and history is entirely predetermined, the extent of my joy and the scope of my actions will probably be quite small.[12] Systematic theology, then, rightly raises issues of science and faith when it speaks about Eschatology. It can expand on these under such topics as General Revelation (Chap. 13) and Creation (Vol. II, Chap. 16).

A. The Development of Modern Science

The modern objection to many traditional eschatological beliefs has been succinctly stated by Rudolf Bultmann. This objection has been around for about 300 years:

> Modern man acknowledges as reality only such phenomena or events as are comprehensible within the framework of the rational order of the universe. He does not acknowledge miracles because they do not fit into this lawful order. When a strange or marvelous accident occurs, he does not rest until he has found a rational cause.[13]

Bultmann claims that "the cause-and-effect nexus is fundamental to this rational order." He insists that even though, in this century,

> modern physical theories take account of chance in the chain of cause and effect in subatomic phenomena, our daily living, purposes and actions are not affected. In any case, modern science does not believe that the course of nature can be interrupted or, so to speak, perforated, by supernatural powers.[14]

The widespread influence of the scientific perspective on modern life stems largely from the work of Isaac Newton (1642–1727). Newton supposed that all bodies were subdivided into tiny, invisible particles. All forces which combined or separated these particles could be determined by some variant of a single formula which Newton had first discovered to hold for gravitation:

[12] Moltmann, pp. 67-69, 92-94.

[13] Jesus Christ and Mythology, pp. 37-38.

[14] Ibid., p. 15.

$F = k \frac{m_1 \cdot m_2}{d_2}$, known as the Inverse Square Law.[15]

For most Newtonians (although not for Newton himself) the laws governing these particles were invariable. If one could calculate the position and momentum of all particles in the universe at a given instant, the entire past and future of the cosmos could be infallibly described. For these particles and their laws never changed over the course of time. During the eighteenth and nineteenth centuries laws of this kind were found to be operative in one field after another, until the ultimate validity and infinite extension of Newtonian explanation seemed assured.[16] This success formed a major strand in the optimistic outlook which stretched from the Enlightenment to nineteenth-century liberalism.

Note that the Newtonian explanation was reductionistic. That is, it assumed that no matter how complex a physical body or process, its behavior could be explained by breaking it down into smaller particles, and discovering what forces held among them. Complex phenomena were always built up from and reducible to simpler phenomena.

The Newtonian world picture, second, was isomorphic. That is, scientific theories were thought to provide exact descriptions of the way things were. Although no one can observe the smallest particles, it was often assumed that all things really were composed of them and that they moved on precisely the paths that scientific laws described. Finally Newtonianism was deterministic. All phenomena which could be observed through the senses had to obey such laws. And since the particles which constituted them never changed, their future behavior was entirely determined by what had occurred in the past.

In the early years of this century, however, physics was amazed to find that subatomic phenomena and light did not fit Newtonian models. For example some features of subatomic entities could be explained when it was assumed that they were behaving like particles (somewhat like Newton's tiniest bits of matter). Others, however, could be explained only when they were treated like waves (that is, more as forms of energy than as bits of matter).[17]

The truly surprising consequence of all this was that neither explanatory model, particle nor wave, could be reduced to or derived from the other. In some ways the particle and wave models were incompatible. Yet both were nec-

[15] The force (F) between any two bodies is the product of their masses (m_1 x m_2) divided by the square of the distance between them (d^2). See Cecil Schneer, *The Evolution of Physical Science* (New York: Grove, 1960), pp. 103-30; A. Rupert Hall and Marie Boas Hall, *A Brief History of Science* (New York: New American, 1964), pp. 154-69; and Stephen Toulmin and June Goodfield, *The Architecture of Matter* (New York: Harper, 1962), pp. 186-98; and *The Fabric of the Heavens* (New York: Harper, 1961), pp. 228-72.

[16] Schneer, pp. 131-232; Hall and Hall, pp. 170-97, 215-51; *The Architecture of Matter*, pp. 270-303.

[17] Schneer, pp. 266-378; Hall and Hall, pp. 252-327; *The Architecture of Matter*, pp. 270-303, cf. Chap. 3.

essary for adequate explanation.[18] In addition, it was soon discovered that whether one sought to treat such phenomena as waves or particles, their exact behavior could not be traced in Newtonian fashion. The more precisely one determined the position of such an entity, the less precisely could one calculate its momentum. And the more accurately one calculated its momentum, the less accurately could its position be determined.[19]

This discovery meant that scientific laws concerning the behavior of such entities could not be descriptive. One could never predict exactly how any single such phenomenon might act. It was still possible, however, to develop laws which were statistical. Given a very large number of them, one could accurately predict their collective effects. The mathematical laws which applied to such "quanta," however, were so complex that any connection between them and actual events which one could picture became extremely indirect.

B. The Implications of Modern Science

Newtonians had supposed that scientific formulations more or less mirror the data which they explain. But the above discoveries overturned this isomorphism. Although a subatomic entity behaves like a particle in some ways and like a wave in others, it does not behave entirely like either. People became less confident that science could directly and fully grasp "the way things really are." New emphasis was laid on the fact (which had always been partially recognized) that scientific explanation is abstractive. It is not concerned with the concrete features of particular objects. Instead it selects certain features which many objects have in common and formulates general rules about their interrelations. Science is little concerned with what is unique and specific.

More importantly it appeared that scientific explanation frequently employs models (cf. Chap. 3). The "wave," for instance, had been developed as a scientific concept to explain sound. Because of certain similarities between sound and light, modern physicists then used it to explain the latter also. It explains some characteristics of light very well. Others it does not. The same can be said for the "particle." The wave and the particle are both models. Light and subatomic entities have some features in common with waves and others in common with particles. But in themselves they are neither. Science approaches them now from one angle, now from another, using models originally derived from other fields to do so. Thereby science comes to understand many things about light and subatomic entities. But it does not isomorphically describe what these things are in themselves.

Recognition of the often indirect relationship between scientific concepts

[18] This is often called the "Principle of Complementarity," developed by Niels Bohr (Atomic Physics and Human Knowledge [New York: Wiley, 1958]).

[19] This is Heisenberg's "Uncertainty Principle." For a brief explanation, see Ian Barbour, Issues in Science and Religion (Englewood Cliffs, N.J.: Prentice-Hall, 1966), pp. 279-82; and Schneer, pp. 250-65.

and empirical data led to a revised understanding of the scientific enterprise itself. According to the classical inductive understanding of scientific method (recommended for theology by Charles Hodge), theories are built by simple enumeration and comparison of large collections of facts. The greater the number of facts supporting a theory, the higher its probability; the fewer that support it, the lower. According to this inductive approach, a theory could be disconfirmed by a single "crucial experiment." Recent research into the history of science, however, has suggested that overarching, widely accepted theories or paradigms, exert far more influence on scientific discovery than once was thought.[20] Paradigms (such as Newtonianism itself) contain not only the major concepts of a science but define its procedure as well. They determine what problems are seen as significant, what kind of evidence counts, and what sorts of explanations are to be sought.

Paradigms, many have claimed, cannot be confirmed or disconfirmed by simple "crucial experiments."[21] If observations seem to conflict with theories, scientists will usually try to account for them by making slight adjustments in the reigning paradigm. (Around the turn of the century, for example, many scientists sought to explain subatomic particles in Newtonian terms for as long as possible.) Only when repeated conflicting data has accumulated do significant changes in theories occur—and then by means of a creative leap called a "paradigm shift." A "paradigm shift" involves seeing all the relevant facts and theories from a brand new angle. They are usually envisioned by means of new models. For instance, modern physics has largely replaced the Newtonian model of "solid" particles attracting and repelling each other with more fluid notions of waves undulating through force-fields. Since this new paradigm involves new notions as to what sort of evidence and argument support a good scientific theory, its validity cannot be strictly evaluated by criteria appropriate to the former paradigm.

The formation of scientific theories, then, involves intuition and imagination, as do the arts and theology. Not only the contents of science but the very notion of what science is changes somewhat in the historical course of research. Since science today is seen more as a changing activity and less as a set of definite assumptions, methods, and laws, one cannot easily assume that some feature of the scientific world-picture is or is not in conflict with religion. All this does not mean, of course, that science is entirely subjective, or that most theories are as good as others. Criteria exist according to which not only particular hypotheses but even shifts among paradigms may be evaluated. These, however, are somewhat general. They are similar to those which White-

[20] The most influential reading of the history of science in this way is Thomas Kuhn's *The Structure of Scientific Revolutions* (Chicago: University, 1962). See also Barbour, *Myths, Models and Paradigms*, pp. 92-118.

[21] Irving Copi, "Crucial Experiments" in E. H. Madden, ed., *The Structure of Science* (Boston: Houghton Mifflin, 1960).

head, himself a scientist, developed for metaphysics and which have suggested ways for evaluating theological systems (Chap. 3).[22]

To recapitulate: Modern scientific theories seldom mirror reality in isomorphic fashion. The relation of scientific concepts to empirical data is much less direct than once was thought. Science increasingly appears to be one way of abstracting certain features from the concrete fulness of reality and of elucidating their relationships by means of various models. Scientific methods for doing all this, of course, are rigorous. Their results are subject to repeatable public validation. Nevertheless, today's science appears to be one among several valid ways of apprehending reality and not the normative approach by which the validity of the others must be tested.

Second, the obstacles to saying what the ultimate components of reality really are also raise grave objections to affirming that they are interrelated in deterministic fashion. The laws of subatomic particles, we have seen, are statistical. They can predict what large groups will do. But they cannot describe the behavior of a particular entity.

Third, the objections to the isomorphism of Newtonian science also apply to its reductionism. If everything could be explained by means of the same model (small particles attracted and repelled by uniform forces), then the most complex phenomena could be broken down successively into simpler and simpler levels of the same kind. Human intelligence and creativity, for instance, could be reduced to atoms moving at certain speeds. But if phenomena must be apprehended by diverse models which explain them in various ways and are not reducible to each other, no such reduction is possible. Different forms or levels of existence might well have their own distinctness. In quantum theory, for example, the behavior of the total atom cannot be derived from the laws governing the behavior of its individual electrons. When new electrons are added to an atom, the whole entity functions in a very different manner.[23]

Many scientists argue that biology differs from physics in much the same way.[24] The subatomic particles that make up living beings obey the laws of physics. But they act differently than they do on the merely physical level, because they are organized in different ways. This higher organization is not simply a more complex form of what is found on the lower level. The higher

[22] Scientific theories, for example, must (1) agree with empirical data which are reproducible by other scientists. (This is part of what Whitehead means by applicability.) Scientific concepts must also (2) be marked by coherence and logical consistency. Many theorists also stress simplicity: the fewer the assumptions and concepts needed, the better. Finally scientific theories should be (3) comprehensive. They should be able to show underlying unity among diverse phenomena. And they should be fruitful; they should enable one to predict future occurrences. (This is part of what Whitehead means by adequacy.) Barbour, *Issues in Science and Religion*, pp. 144-48.

[23] Ibid., pp. 295-98.

[24] Ibid., pp. 324-37.

organization is qualitatively different, a unique structure which first emerges on the higher level. It can neither be analyzed into nor derived from combinations of lower-level activity. As the familiar saying has it: "the whole is more than the sum of its parts." Many very similar organs, for instance, are found in animals of various species. But they are organized so differently in each species that the whole organisms behave quite diversely.[25]

Finally we remember that the ultimate particles of Newtonian physics were unaffected by time. As long as the cosmos existed, they would combine and separate according to the same laws, and in the same ways. But for modern science, the fundamental character of things changes over time. Even subatomic particles are characterized by change and temporal duration; to the extent that they must be conceptualized not merely as things but as forms of energy. Everyone knows how geology and biology have altered conceptions of the age of the earth and of the enormous changes have marked earth's history. In addition current cosmology pictures the whole universe as continually expanding from some distant temporal point of origination. At the same time the amount of energy available for work has been continually decreasing.[26]

C. Eschatology and Modern Science

The preceding discussion has shown that modern science is open to the future occurrence of events whose uniqueness may, to some degree, transcend anything that has yet occurred. Science, in principle, can neither trace the entire activity of every entity nor wholly predict its future course. Science shows that lower levels of activity need not always follow their characteristic behavior patterns. They can be differently organized by higher levels operating according to other principles. If what we think of as physical and social levels be open to the influence a higher one, it is at least possible that such a reality could alter some of the former's normal patterns. Finally, if the universe changes over the course of time, it might well operate differently in the future than it does now.

This scientific openness overturns Bultmann's contention that once one adopts a modern scientific perspective, one must immediately regard all spatio-temporal features of the *eschata* as mythological. Science exhibits enough tolerance to novel future events that the truly modern person must at least ask whether eschatology might have spatio-temporal dimensions. It becomes clear that Bultmann, who stressed speaking the language of modernity, was actually assuming the validity of Newtonian science. Had he been truly modern, Bultmann could never have distinguished as sharply as he did between faith and existence on one hand and history and science on the other.

However, modern science manifests only a very limited openness towards anything like the literal occurrence of eschatological events. The not com-

[25] Eric Rust, *Science and Faith* (New York: Oxford, 1967), pp. 57-71.

[26] Ibid., pp. 71-84.

pletely traceable behavior of subatomic phenomena is a far cry from a universal bodily resurrection. The openness of lower-level processes to higher ones is a long way from the openness of the stratosphere to Jesus' descent.

Theology cannot use science to conclusively prove or disprove religious claims. Science and theology function largely as different approaches to understanding different dimensions of reality. At the outset neither need exclude the claims of the other. At some points both will make assertions about the same thing. And then theology must decide how it will interpret the procedures of science.

Science studies behavior which recurs regularly, and is thus open to repeated experimental testing and verification. Although science cannot disprove the possible occurrence of unique future phenomena, it makes predictions only on the basis of what has regularily happened and can be assumed to happen again. If being "scientific" means that one can only look forward towards events which can be predicted on the basis of repeatable empirical observation, events which are scientifically *probable*, then anything like the literal occurrence of the *eschata* must be "scientifically" incredible. A theology which regards science in this sense as its epistemological norm can expect eschatology to affect the spatio-temporal structure of things only in very limited ways.

However, science can also be regarded as one among several ways of knowing, and one which therefore cannot make exhaustive claims about realities that it investigates. Although science can hardly regard wide-ranging future transformations of space and time as likely, it cannot dismiss them as impossible. If theology has other reasons for anticipating such events, then it cannot regard scientific *probability* as its ultimate epistemological norm. Theology must go well beyond what science can assert. Such theology, however, need not contradict science; it must continually compare and contrast its claims and methods with those of science. Otherwise it will fail in its contextual task of explaining what its assertions mean.

Suggestions for Further Reading

Barbour, Ian. *Issues in Science and Religion*. Englewood Cliffs, N.J.: Prentice-Hall, 1966.

———.*Myths, Models and Paradigms: A Comparative Study in Science and Religion*. New York: Harper, 1974.

Bultmann, Rudolf. "History of Salvation and History," in *Existence and Faith*. Cleveland and New York: Meridan, 1960, pp. 226-40.

Cullman, Oscar. *Early Christian Worship*. London: SCM, 1957.

———.*Christ and Time*. Philadelphia: Westminster, 1964.

Gerhart, Mary and Russell, Ahin, *Metaphoric Process: The Creation of Scientific and Religious Understanding*. College Station, TX: TCU Press, 1985.

Kuhn, Thomas. *The Structure of Scientific Revolutions*. Chicago: University, 1962.

Mascall, Eric. *Christian Theology and Natural Science*. London: Longmans, Green and Co., 1957.

Ramsey, Ian *Religion and Science.* London: SPCK, 1964.
Torrance, Thomas. *Divine and Contingent Order.* Oxford: University, 1981.
Toulmin, Stephen. *The Return to Cosmology: Postmodern Science and the Theology of Nature.* Berkeley: University, 1982.
Toulmin, Stephen and Goodfield, June. *The Architecture of Matter.* New York: Harper, 1962.
————.*The Fabric of the Heavens.* New York: Harper, 1961.
Werner, Martin. *The Formation of Christian Doctrine.* New York: Harper, 1957.
Whitehead, Alfred. *Science in the Modern World.* New York: Macmillan, 1925.

CHAPTER EIGHT

The Resurrection, the Last Judgment, and Universalism

A mid the swiftly changing, uncertain, and potentially self-destructive currents of late twentieth-century existence, we have sought a meaningful
starting point for theological reflection. We have rejected any merely academic
procedure. We have resisted adopting any starting point simply because it was
traditional, even if it be the venerable Doctrine of God. We have sought an
orientation which might illuminate and energize the life and mission of the
Church in these dangerous but exciting times. We have sought a starting point
from within the interweaving of the personal and the cosmic dimensions of
Christian faith and also within the interplay between God's (kerygmatic) initiatory acts and the human (contextual) response. We proposed eschatology for
such a task.

The language of eschatology is at first glance strange and confusing to modern people. But as we examined it more closely, we began appreciating its rich
levels of meaning. Eschatological language has literal and figurative dimensions. It affirms of both continuity and discontinuity between the present and
the things to come. It strains towards the things that are hoped for and gives
moving expression to the character of hope. For eschatological reality itself is
"already" present and "not yet" at its climax.

But now we must become more specific. Enough has been said about eschatology's general features. People in our turbulent times want to know more specifically, For what may we hope? The next two chapters will inquire into six
things for which Christian faith hopes, and into the hope which they arouse.

I. The Resurrection of the Dead

Although eschatological existence strains and strives towards the future, the
previous chapter showed that it is not focused wholly on the "not yet." One is
able to move forward through a world of uncertainty and pain because Christ
has "already" lived, died, and risen. And of these acts of God in Christ, the
resurrection was the most climactic and decisive. Jesus' resurrection has in
some way established the *eschaton*. By it he has become the first-fruit of the eschatological harvest which shall be concluded "at his coming" with "those
who belong to Christ" (1 Cor. 15:23). We may appropriately begin our exploration into the things hoped for with the resurrection.

A. The "Already"

The resurrection has already occurred, and not only in the sense that Jesus
has been raised. According to the early kerygma Jesus' resurrection and and the
eschatological outpouring of the Spirit were inseparably intertwined. Jesus was
raised by the Spirit (Rom. 1:4); since his ascension, he continues to pour out
the Spirit (Acts 2:33). There is an important sense, then, in which the resurrection life of the new age is already among us. Paul writes that "if the Spirit of
him who raised Jesus from the dead dwells in you, he who raised Christ Jesus
from the dead will give life to your mortal bodies also through his Spirit which
dwells in you" (Rom. 8:11). Paul goes on to portray the transforming work of
this same Spirit throughout all creation (Rom. 8:19–24). John also emphasizes
the presence of the resurrection, probably more than Paul. When Martha refers
to the resurrection "at the last day," Jesus apparently corrects her perspective
somewhat by saying, "I am the resurrection and the Life" (John 11:24-25).

Rudolf Bultmann has observed that as one moves from early Christian eschatology through Paul to John, many "not yet" events, including the resurrection, are increasingly spoken of as present. For Bultmann this shows that
demythologizing was already taking place. That is, the New Testament writers
themselves were increasingly shedding their futuristic, spatio-temporal imagery
and realizing that eschatological events were really present, existential occurrences.[1] But Bultmann has difficulty with the fact that Paul clearly looked forward to coming *eschata*: He devoted a detailed chapter to the future
resurrection (1 Cor. 15). And even though John's emphasis is on the present (or

---

[1] *Jesus Christ and Mythology*, pp. 32-34.

realized) dimension of eschatology, he also spoke of the coming resurrection (John 5:28–29; 6:40, 54).[2]

Bultmann argues that these are mere relics of a more primitive eschatology; they do not represent the writer's basic views. But Bultmann's approach is grounded on the assumption that religious expressions must either depict events in time and space in mythological fashion or denote present, inward experiences in existential fashion. Consequently when Paul and John emphasize the latter, Bultmann must regard their other references to real future events as not expressing their true intentions.

If valid religious expressions can refer both to time and space and to inner experience; if, in fact, meaningful inner experience usually is grounded on and looks forward to spatio-temporal events, then Paul and John could have really meant to speak of both. It is most natural to intepret their increasing stress on the "already" of the resurrection as a deeper unfolding of the meaning of that coming event and not as the replacement of an historically-oriented faith by an existential one because of the Delay of the Parousia.

B. *Immortality of the Soul*

Perhaps Bultmann is closer to the truth than we are acknowledging. Down through the centuries the ultimate hope of most Christians has probably been not the future resurrection of the dead but "the immortality of the soul." Most Christians have believed that immediately after death, their spiritual self or "soul" would pass directly into eternity. Christians have usually assumed that the soul was inherently immortal.[3] According to this popular view the ultimate Christian hope is not a physical, cosmic, and future resurrection. It is something spiritual, individual, and, for each soul, immediate. The former expectation began to fade in early Christian centuries, along with the decline of premillennialism. Perhaps Bultmann (although he rejects mythological talk of "going to heaven") is somewhat true to the common Christian hope.

Certain biblical passages appear to teach that the individual soul will enter heaven, or Christ's presence, immediately after death. Paul longed to depart this life to "be with Christ, for that is far better." (Phil. 1:23) Elsewhere, he wrote in more detail that

> if the earthly tent we live in is destroyed, we have a building from God, a house not made with hands, eternal in the heavens. Here indeed we groan, and long to put on our heavenly dwelling.... We know that while we are at home in the body

---

[2] For the view that a historical "not yet" was both important for both Paul and John, see George Ladd, *The Pattern of New Testament Truth* (Grand Rapids: Eerdmans, 1968), pp. 64-111.

[3] For the theological teachings involved, see Aquinas, SCG, Book I, Chaps. 79-81; ST I, Q. 75; Heppe, pp. 225-27, 695-96, 707-09; Schmid, pp. 629-32; Hodge, Vol. III, pp. 716-43.

we are away from the Lord...and we would rather be away from the body and at home with the Lord (2 Cor. 5:1-2, 6-8).

Also Jesus told his sorrowing disciples, "In my Fathers' house are many rooms....When I go and prepare a place for you, I will come again and will take you to myself, that where I am you may be also" (John 14:2-3).

Do such passages clearly teach the immortality of the soul? Before deciding, we should be aware of the influence which the standard Greek worldview has had on this issue. For this worldview, as we remember (pp. 15-16), the human person is composed of two very different elements: body and soul. The former is physical, temporal, and corruptible; the latter is spiritual, eternal, and incorruptible. The body, then, is simply a temporary shell, or prison, in which the soul is housed. With its weaknesses, diseases, and lusts, the body chains down the soul. Death, therefore, releases the soul from its prison and enables it to unite with the purely spiritual world. Consequently wise and moral persons do not really fear death. They welcome it.

To what extent has Christian belief in the soul's immortality been shaped by the Greek worldview? To what extent is it based on Scripture? In the Bible, neither death nor life refer primarily to biological phenomena. Life denotes the fulness of fellowship with God, which includes, of course, the vitality and health of the body. Death, on the other hand, means being out of fellowship with and being cut off from, God. Death is the result of God's curse upon sin (Gen. 3:3-4, 19).

In the Old Testament, in sharp contrast to the Greek perspective, life is most fully experienced on this earth, when one walks according to the covenant and attains health, prosperity, and a goodly number of offspring. To experience disease or poverty, to die young or without descendants; these are at best tragedies, at worst effects of Yahweh's judgment. The Old Testament occasionally pictures an afterlife. But it is a weak, shadowy existence, and hardly the fulfillment of human destiny.[4]

In the New Testament, Death is portrayed as a terrible power which separates humans from God.[5] Paul speaks of sin and death reigning over humankind since Adam (Rom. 5:12-21). Sin enslaves one in a "body of death" (Rom. 7:5-25). Death is the fearsome "last enemy" (1 Cor. 15:26, 54-56). For John, death is the way of existence in separation from the life of God (John 5:24; 1 John 3:14). Accordingly even Jesus did not face death with equanimity. For he came to do battle with death:

> since therefore the children share in flesh and blood, he himself partook of the same nature, that through death he might destroy him who has the power of death,

[4] E.g., 1 Sam. 28:8-15; Isa. 8:19, 14:9-16, 29:4; Ps. 88:3-13. See Walther Eichrodt, *Theology of the Old Testament*, Vol. II (Philadelphia: Westminster, 1967), pp. 210-16; cf. pp. 496-529.

[5] Oscar Cullmann, *Immortality or the Soul of Resurrection of the Dead* (London: Epworth, 1958), pp. 19-27.

that is, the Devil, and deliver all those who through fear of death were subject to lifelong bondage....In the days of his flesh, Jesus offered up prayers and supplications, with loud cries and tears, to him who was able to save him from death (Heb. 2:14–15, 5:7; cf. Mark 14:32–42 and par.).

Now if death apart from Christ's conquest has such a grip on all humanity, Christian theology cannot regard dying as a natural transition to something better. On the contrary, it must be a final, irreversible deliverance into the hands of that power.

Scripture gives little warrant for thinking of an immortal soul at all. For one thing, no biblical writer clearly teaches that the human person is constituted of a physical component called a "body" and a non-physical one called a "soul."[6] Moreover immortality was an essential property of the Greek soul; its very nature was such that it could not die. But in the Bible the words sometimes translated as "soul" can also be rendered "life."[7] And all life is given and can be taken away by God.

If dying finalizes one's separation from the source of life, it is most likely that deceased persons (apart from Christ) are simply and wholly dead; unconscious, decaying, gone. At most they might lead some weak, shade-like existence under the final dominion of an alien power. But in either case death is hardly the transition of some nobler component of human nature into a superior realm. If death is the awful "last enemy," opposed to and choking out the life of God, then meaningful existence beyond dying is impossible unless death is first conquered. This is how the kerygma understands Jesus' resurrection. He was "crucified and killed by the hands of lawless men. But God raised him up, having loosed the pangs of death, because it was not possible for him to be held by it" (Acts 2:24). Jesus' resurrection is a triumph. It is God's powerful, creative inbreaking into a world dominated by Death. Consequently if anyone lives after dying, it can hardly be a matter of course. It is cause for wonder and awe:

> Death is swallowed up in victory!
> O death, where is thy victory?
> O death, where is thy sting?"
> Thanks be to God, who gives us the victory through our
> Lord Jesus Christ (1 Cor. 15:54–57)!

Now if this last, terrible enemy has been overcome, no wonder the early Christians had confidence that all lesser powers must inevitably yield to

---

[6] See Volume II, Chapter 5. There we shall not deny, precisely speaking, that human nature is composed of "body" and "soul." We shall argue that since no biblical writer teaches this, an attempt to affirm or deny it goes beyond the range of what theology can assert. Even though Scripture stresses the unity of all human functions or activities, it is still possible that human nature is so constituted. But arguments for and against this belong in philosophy, not in theology.

[7] TDNT, Vol. IX, 617-31, 637-56.

Christ's incontestable lordship. The last battle had been fought. The consummation was certain, even if postponed.

Christian hope, then, does not rest on some intrinsic property of human nature. It trusts in God's creative power. Neither is it restriced to the inner self, or soul. In marked contrast to the Greek perspective, it includes the body. This fact is clear from the "already" of the resurrection. Even now it begins to vivify our mortal bodies and to renew all creation. The final resurrection must culminate this process on a more all-encompassing scale.[8]

C. An Intermediate State

If the reasoning above is correct, the hope of the deceased also still lies in the future. At death Christians do not immediately pass into the full presence of Christ. There must be an intermediate state. But can these general theological assertions be squared with those biblical passages we cited above? What about that eternal house awaiting us in the heavens, the "heavenly dwelling" which we long to put on, so that we might be "away from the body and at home with the Lord" (2 Cor. 5:1-9)? Does not all this mean that we go straight to heaven after death?

Clearly according to the early Christian perspective, Christ and the full reality to be actualized at the consummation are presently in heaven. The Christian's longing is directed upwards (Col. 3:1-3). But does that mean that one longs to actually go upwards? Or does one anticipate the day when the Person and the reality now temporarily in heaven will come downwards?

Second Corinthians 5 is compatible with the latter perspective. Paul sighs "not that we would be unclothed" (not, that is, that our separable souls would fly up to heaven) "but that we would be clothed upon (*ependusasthai*), so that what is mortal may be swallowed up by life" (5:4). This imagery fits with that eschatalogical pattern whereby the life of heaven descends upon and transforms what is earthly. "To be away from the body," then, is not to escape physical existence altogether. It is to experience the final transformation of our present frame, which, through persecution and suffering, is already "carrying...the death of Jesus, so that the life of Jesus may be manifested in our bodies" (2 Cor. 4:10). Similarly, to be "at home with the Lord" is not to go where he presently is but to experience his full presence in time to come.

John 14:2-3 fits the same pattern. To be sure, Jesus went from his disciples to his "Father's house." This will be their final destination also. But he "will come again and take you to myself." Jesus can be pictured as bringing his Father's mansion from heaven to earth when he returns.[9]

It is less clear how to interpret Paul's desire "to depart and be with Christ, for

[8] The physical dimension of the coming resurrection and even of the present working of resurrection power is grounded in the bodily character of Jesus' resurrection. We will discuss this in detail in Chapter 18.

[9] Ladd, pp. 68-73.

that is far better" (Phil. 1:23). By itself it could mean that one fully experiences Christ immediately after death. But a later passage in this epistle expresses its eschatological framework more clearly. Although our citizenship is presently "in heaven," it is "from" there that "we await a Savior...who will change our lowly body to be like his glorious body" (Phil. 3:20–21). Paul's earlier statement expresses his subjective desire. It need not refer to any time interval. And indeed if one does not enter fully into life until the final resurrection, any passage between one's own demise and this climactic event may well seem very short.

The New Testament's eschatological framework, with which apparently discordant passages are consistent, thus includes some kind of intermediate state. Human curiosity inevitably wants to know more about it. But if theology respects the limitations of its data, very little can be said. Scripture gives no real insight about those who die outside Christ. There is little warrant for regarding them as other than under death's dominion, unconscious and decaying (or at most, subsisting as shadows).

Dead Christians, however, are in some way "in Christ," under his care.[10] To view them as separated from Christ, as lying wholly under death's dominion, would contradict the "already" of Christ's victory, the assurance "that neither Death nor Life...nor anything in all creation will be able to separate us from the love of God in Christ Jesus our Lord" (Rom. 8:38-39). Those who die in Christ are said several times to be asleep (1 Thess. 4:15, Acts 7:60). Revelation 14:13 pictures the martyrs as resting from their labors. Revelation 6:10–11 depicts them both as resting and longing for the final Judgment.

From the general considerations and sketchy images above, we may conclude that the dead in Christ are in some passive state. Perhaps it is not wholly unconscious. It may well approximate pleasant dreaming. It is a "rest from their labors." Their sufferings are over. Nevertheless they still exist within the tension of the "already/not yet."[11] Until Christ's cosmic victory is consummated, they too will not experience the fulness of his presence and the fulfillment of their individual destinies.

D. The Subjective Dimension

Perhaps the strongest objections to all this will be raised by practical theology. In our modern context, and perhaps in all contexts whatsover, people turn to religion primarily to find consolation in face of death. But we seem to have painted the "not yet" in very dark colors, even while underlining that Christ has "already" conquered death. We cannot assure people that their departed Christian loved ones are in heaven, fully enjoying God's presence. What kind of consolation for the grief-stricken is that?

We reply that our culture's treatment of death involves much escapism. By numerous devices modern western society insulates itself against brokenness,

---

[10] Cullmann, pp. 48-58.

tragedy and pain. Many come face-to-face with this side of things only when confronted with the reality or the serious possibility of dying. But our treatment of death normally seeks to smooth over this shock. We go to great lengths to pretend that everything really is all right. Religionists are eagerly sought to assure people that the deceased instantaneously and automatically pass into a better, wholly blissful state.

In this way conventional views of immortality and "going to heaven" can function as a broad shield against reality's darker side. They can suppress or hinder the working through of one's particular grief. To fully adjust to losing a loved one, people need to come fully to grips with their sorrow, confusion, rage, and despair. But if my departed one is enjoying total, final bliss, how can I be so overwhelmed with grief? How can I be so selfish, so negative? I ought to think only about how wonderful things are for my beloved, not about how awful I feel!

Yet what if my loved one, like me, is not yet fully released from death's lingering effects? What if my beloved, like me, also awaits the consummation of all things? What if my loved one's joy, like my joy, will only be complete when Christ comes fully into his reign? Then I can be glad that my departed one has ceased to suffer and probably experiences some bliss. But instead of looking upward at a happiness I cannot touch, or downward at my own emptiness and pain, my loved one, myself, and my Lord will look forward to the joy of his coming reign.

And might not our approach touch other cords in today's apologetic context? For does not the intensity with which people seek to shield themselves from pain and tragedy indicate how deeply aware they are (even if subconsciously) of the widespread scope of these things? Even if they try to believe in immediate immortality, how many can fully suppress the fear that decay, death, and ultimate annihilation are the final word in the present course of affairs? Yet our theology says that apart from Christ's victory this is exactly how things are! Insofar as Christ is "not yet" reigning, all things are still permeated by Death, who hurries them on towards oblivion. The eschatological perspective, with its stark realism, can agree on much with the modern pessimist. Pastorally speaking it can allow pessimists to express and explore their doubts and dreads. It does not need to immediately contradict them.

Beyond this our theology offers an ultimate word of hope. Yet it is not an easy optimism that declares pain and death to be unreal. It is based on God's creative inbreaking into the tightening cycle of sin and death in the past. It lives in anticipation of such inbreakings yet to come. It indicates that Christian faith is not general confidence in the automatic emergence of life out of death. It is faith in the God who creates anew out of the depths of despair, defeat, and hell. Such a faith may be difficult to attain. Yet precisely because it faces all the powers of defeat squarely, it is difficult to shake.

E. The Significance of the Coming Resurrection

The resurrection is not a marginal issue. Not only has Jesus' resurrection, the "first-fruit" of the coming resurrection, decisively inaugurated the eschaton. But most people initially turn to Christianity (and to most other religions) out of concern over what happens at and after dying. Their understanding of this issue probably shapes their overall orientation to Christian faith more than any other. If they are significantly in error here, their entire approach to worship, fellowship, and mission will probably be askew.

Briefly, we have argued that the most commonly held view, the "immortality of the soul," can distort our hope in four ways. It can replace the physical, bodily resurrection with something purely spiritual. It can replace the cosmic breadth of Christ's reign with something individual. Hope no longer need stretch toward the historical future but is fulfilled when each person dies. Finally it can dissolve hope's single, all-encompassing goal into numerous individual goals. In short, when "the immortality of the soul" becomes eschatology's guiding model, the biblical framework can easily become unhinged, and its capacity for guiding life and theology can collapse.

II. The Last Judgment

A. The "Already"

Like the resurrection, the Last Judgment has already occurred in an important sense. Later on we shall see how it came to pass in Christ's death and resurrection (Chaps. 17 and 18). This is why these events can provide ultimate "Justification" (Vol. II, Chap. 7).

The kerygma announces that not only salvation but also final judgment is continuing to occur. It speaks of "Jesus, who is delivering us from the wrath that is now coming" (1 Thess. 1:10).[14] Paul declares not only that the righteousness of God is revealed (Rom. 1:17, 3:21) but also that "the wrath of God is revealed from heaven against all ungodliness and wickedness of humans" (Rom. 1:18). Both are functions of God's continuing judgment. For John, who emphasizes the present reality of the *eschata*, "this is the judgment, that the Light has come into the world, and people loved Darkness rather than Light, because their deeds were evil" (John 3:19). The challenge of the kerygma is serious, in part, because irreversible separations between life and death, good and evil, Christ and the powers are already being made.

B. The "Not Yet"

Nevertheless, the kerygma also speaks of Jesus as the future Judge (Acts 3:21, 10:42; 1 Thess. 1:10; Rom. 2:16). In other passages, his return means not only vindication for those who are his own, but condemnation for those who are

[14] See Anthony Hanson, *The Wrath of the Lamb* (London: SPCK, 1957), pp. 69-71.

not (1 Thess. 4:14–5:3, 2 Thess. 1:6–10, 1 Peter 4:17–18, Matthew 25). And even Christians are warned not to take it lightly:

> Take heed to yourselves lest your hearts be weighed down with dissipation and drunkenness and cares of this life, and that Day come upon you suddenly like a snare....But watch at all times, praying that you may have strength to escape all these things, and to stand before the Son of Man (Luke 21:34–36, cf. 12:35–40; 2 Cor. 5:10; Rom. 14:10–13; 1 Peter 4:4–7).

At least until the Enlightenment, the prospect of this judgment wielded untold influence on Western peoples' lives. Sometimes it overshadowed God's love, plunging many into anxiety, even terror. An emphasis on judgment was fairly common in authoritarian societies. We have seen how John Calvin insisted that the magistrates' authority reflected and was granted by God. The socio-political effect of this was to help keep people in line (Chap. 5). Since the eighteenth century, with the growth of democracy, the leveling of social and political hierarchies, and greater faith in humanity's goodness, emphasis on the Judgment has faded.[15] Daily life is no longer encompassed by a framework of laws and customs backed by divine authority. Any sort of divine reality seems vague, distant, and perhaps non-existent to many in modern society.

For these reasons, the very notion of a Last Judgment often arouses indignant objections. A distant God who has shown little interest in his creation suddenly inflicts horrifying penalties on many good people who happen not to be Christians and rewards many louts who happen to profess Christ; so the standard protest runs. Given the obvious sufferings of our times, it seems cruel for this absent God to inflict yet more distress on a bewildered humanity.

This objection protests the apparent discontinuity between the future envisioned in this Christian doctrine and the present as many experience it. Our discussion of the resurrection, however, argued that the entire eschatological framework has become disjointed in much traditional teaching. Might the modern objection have arisen, in part, because Christians themselves have failed to adequately conceptualize the continuity linking the Judgment with the other features of the *eschaton*? If so, there is need for systematic theology to conceptualize it in a coherent, consistent manner.

Let us again consider the presence of the new age and the core of the Church's message: the kerygma. It proclaims that Christ is Lord of all and that salvation is extended to all peoples. But when we survey our globe, what do we perceive? Even in "Christian" countries, those who take Jesus seriously seem to be few in number. Where, wonder many people (Christians included), is the evidence that the gospel is truly universal?

The kerygma proclaims that the new age of justice has dawned. Evil has

---

[15] James Martin, *The Last Judgment: in Protestant Theology from Orthodoxy to Ritschl* (Grand Rapids: Eerdmans, 1963).

been defeated. The God who has overcome it is loving and good. But when we survey our globe, what do we perceive? Despite great advances in technology, food production, and medicine, the percentage of those suffering from serious poverty, malnutrition, and disease is probably as great as ever. And the threats which military technology pose to humanity's very existence seem daily to increase. For every person who doubts God's existence for theoretical reasons today, at least ten probably doubt God's goodness for the reasons above. Where, wonder many (Christians included), is the evidence that God is just and good?

Understood in its proper context, the Last Judgment not only rewards and punishes individuals but also provides some answers to these questions. To grasp this, we must appreciate the notions of justice and judgment central in Scripture. In western society justice and judgment have consisted largely in the passing of a legal declaration. An accused party is declared guilty or innocent. A specific, appropriate punishment or reward is handed out. But biblical notions of justice and judgment are broader than this in two respects. First, biblical judgment cannot be limited to the mere passing of a sentence. The coming of God's justice, or righteousness, involves the overturning, the defeat, of what is evil. And it includes the establishing of those who are vindicated in just and peaceful circumstances.[16] Biblical trials, in other words, are not merely courtroom trials. They are historical struggles, historical conflicts between forces of good and evil. These forces, of course, might sometimes confront each other in court. But their conflict is not resolved with the mere declaration of a verdict. It is resolved only with the defeat of evil and the triumph of good.

Second, while biblical trials involve the accusation of some and the vindication of others, many have an additional, overarching purpose. They are also vindications of God and of God's righteousness (e.g., Psalms 97–99; Isa. 43:20–25; 62:1–4). Throughout biblical history the apparently righteous often suffer. The apparently wicked prosper. These conditions raise questions not only about human character (Who is really righteous?) but about God's character. Does God really care about those who suffer? Does Yahweh keep his promises to them? Does Yahweh have the ability to overturn the wicked and to establish the righteous in peace?

The similarity between these questions and those which people ask today is clear. Whereas many in ancient Israel doubted Yahweh's justice and his rule over all nations, so many today doubt the goodness of the Christian God and the universality of his reign. Yet if the kerygma's claims really are true, then there must come a Day when evil is finally abolished, when righteousness finally holds full sway, and when the reality of all this becomes unmistakeably plain.

Now this is the comprehensive, theological significance of the Last Judg-

[16] Gerhard von Rad, *Old Testament Theology*, Vol. I (Edinburgh: Oliver & Boyd, 1962), pp. 357-59, 370-83, Roland de Vaux, *Ancient Israel* (New York: McGraw-Hill, 1961), pp. 155-58; Johannes Pedersen, *Israel: Its Life and Culture* (London: Oxford, 1954), pp. 406-10; Markus Barth, *Justification* (Grand Rapids: Eerdmans, 1971), pp. 14-21. Barth)

ment. Viewed in the overall context of God's eschatological acts, from the joyous "already" of Jesus' resurrection through the struggles of God's people during centuries of the "not yet," it is no sudden, arbitrary imposition of rewards and punishments. It is the Day when the significance of all history will be made plain. It is the Day when "the Lord comes, who will bring to light the things now hidden in darkness and will disclose the purposes of the heart" (1 Cor. 4:5).

C. The Subjective Dimension

Even for early Christians, much was shrouded in darkness. Why, even in the new age, should God's people still struggle against disunity and struggle towards spiritual maturity? Why should they still be wrongly persecuted and their opponents still receive praise? Toward what purposes still future was God guiding the cosmos? Belief in the coming Judgment enables one to persist through this "not yet," knowing that things will not always be this way. It gives individuals confidence not only that they will be vindicated but also that all of God's activity towards righteousness and peace will find consummation. It bestows the courage to act according to God's will in the world at large, although one's efforts may seem miniscule, perhaps even futile.

For "nothing is hid that shall not be made manifest, nor anything secret that shall not be known and come to light" (Luke 8:17). On that Day no longer will evil acts appear as noble, nor their perpetrators as just. No longer will those who were persecuted for righteousness' sake be outcast or regarded as criminals. "All excuses will be scrutinized, all motives known. In this way the parousia will not be strange; life, as it actually happened in its hourly, daily and yearly sequence, will be fully known."[17] Consequently Christ's parousia can be anticipated in two ways and sometimes in both ways at once. Insofar as someone longs for hidden truths to come to light, for wrongs to be righted, one looks forward to it. But insofar as one desires that secret wrongs remain hidden, that evil and ignoble motives and deeds appear benevolent and noble, one fears the coming of the Day.

This explains how Christians can anticipate Christ's return for judgment not only with joy but also with some measure of dread. Paul explains the possible negative consequences in a somewhat obscure but important passage:

> For no other foundation can any one lay than that which is laid, which is Jesus Christ. Now if anyone builds on the foundation with gold, silver, precious stones, wood, hay, stubble—each one's work will become manifest; for the Day will disclose it, because it will be revealed with fire, and the fire will test what sort of work each one has done. If the work which anyone has built on the foundation survives, one will receive a reward. If anyone's work is burned up, one will suffer loss, though one will be saved, but only as through fire (1 Cor. 3:11–15).

This passage is offered as one of the few biblical supports for the medieval

---

[17] Berkouwer, p. 161; cf. Karl Barth, *Dogmatics in Outline*, pp. 133-36.

doctrine of Purgatory. It was elaborated, in part, to deal with an obvious fact. Many who seemed to be sincere Christians were far from perfect when they died. Yet God called everyone to maturity, and the hope of Christ's return was a strong incentive "to be found by him without spot or blemish, and at peace" (2 Peter 3:14; cf. 1 Cor. 1:8, 1 Thess. 5:23).

Consequently (some reasoned) if many were not pure at death, they must undergo a further process of purification or purgation between their death and the Lord's return. Subjectively, however, this doctrine was often taught in such a way that expectation shifted from the joyous return of Christ to increasingly lengthy and gruesome years in Purgatory. Purgation "as through fire" sounded more and more like Hell. Complex schemes of pilgrimages, penances, fastings, and indulgences were worked out whereby people could shorten their own stays in Purgatory, and those of their departed loved ones.[18]

Such theories are prompted by the understandable anxiety and curiosity of the human heart and mind. Clearly they far exceed any biblical foundation. Nevertheless they contain grains of truth. At the coming Judgment God's righteousness will be climactically manifest and actualized. All activities, thoughts, and beings opposed to it may well experience it as a blazing, painful fire. Christians who have long harbored evil attitudes and thoughts, or who have long practiced certain sins, may well encounter God's presence with some pain. Further since everything will be made public, they may well be deeply shamed as these things become known. Perhaps some brief time span will be required for these things to be purged away.

Above all, however, Christians must remember Paul's assurance that even if their works be "burned up," they will be saved, even if it be "as through fire." Our dominant attitude is surely to be one of joy and positive expectation. Theology must reject any period of purgation which significantly postpones the establishment of the righteous in peace or which greatly dims their positive expectation. Christians can be confident that they themselves will be saved. As to their specific works, they may perhaps harbor some doubt. Systematic theology can do no more than establish the general interrelationship of these two paradoxical elements.

The issue of negative judgment, however, brings us to perhaps the most pressing modern question on this whole subject. Almost everyone can welcome the prospect of evil being destroyed. But in a democratic and pluralistic age many find it hard to think of persons, even evil ones, being destroyed. Is this a firm Christian belief? Or might there be a biblical basis for universalism?

---

[18] For a brief overview of the history of the doctrine, see Karl Rahner, ed., *Sacramentum Mundi*, Vol. V (New York: Herder & Herder, 1970), pp. 166-68.

III. Universalism

A. The Issues

Let us notice, first, that many biblical passages can be enlisted for either side. In his resurrection chapter Paul declares: "For as in Adam all die, so in Christ shall all be made alive"(1 Cor. 15:22). He speaks of God's "purpose which he set forth in Christ...to unite all things in him, things in heaven and things on earth" (Eph. 1:10; cf. Col. 1:20). Jesus "is the expiation for our sins, and not for ours only, but also for the sins of the whole world" (1 John 2:2). The living God "is the savior of all people...." (1 Tim. 4:10). Other passages affirm God's desire that all might be saved (2 Peter 3:9, 1 Tim. 2:4). And Paul, while speaking of God's condemnation before Christ's coming, emphasizes that "much more will those who receive the abundance of grace and the free gift of righteousness reign in life." He goes on to assert that Christ's "act of righteousness leads to righteousness of life [dikaiosin zoes] for all" (Rom. 5:17–18).

On the other hand, the Old Testament abounds with decisive, annihilating divine judgments (Exod. 14:23–28, Numb. 16:28–35, Josh. 7:24–26, Jer. 51:39–40, etc). Jesus proclaims negative judgment in many parables (Matt. 13:40–42, 49–50; 25:30, 41–43, etc.) and in many other sayings (Matt. 5:29–30, 10:28, 11:23, 23:33, etc.). Paul often speaks of condemnation to come (Rom. 2:5, 8; 5:9; 1 Thess. 1:10; 2 Thess. 1:8–9, etc.). The later New Testament books mention it often (2 Peter 3:7; Judges 8, 23; Rev. 6:16–17, 11:18, 16:17–21, 19:2, etc.). How shall we approach this apparent discrepancy? Are we confronted by two very different models, each of which expresses certain realities but which theology (if it respects its limitations) should avoid seeking to reconcile into a single doctrine?

Some recent theologians think that this is the case. They note, as we have, that most statements about judgment appear in contexts of exhortation, warning, encouragement, etc. They conclude that such passages are designed not to speak (objectively) about the things hoped for but only (subjectively) to stimulate our hope. We should not expect information about the future from them. We should let them arouse, at one time, wonder and awe at the wideness of God's grace and, at others, fear and repentance over the seriousness of our sin.[19] Perhaps, should the data available really lack objective implications, we should adopt some such perspective. But it sounds very like the existentialist one which we have already rejected. It supposes that authentic inner transformation will be elicited by appeals that have no reference to events about to occur in time or space.

---

[19] E.g., Emil Brunner, *The Christian Doctrine of the Church, Faith and the Consummation* (Philadelphia: Westminster, 1962), pp. 415-24; Karl Rahner, *Foundations of Christian Faith* (New York: Seabury, 1978), pp. 431-44. For an overview, see Berkouwer, pp. 396-403.

But surely the authenticity of one's response to eschatological claims has much to do with whether or not one expects them to actually occur. One who believes that some will really be condemned will normally be more earnest about repenting and more concerned to warn others. One who truly believes that all will be saved may be joyous and hopeful about the good news—or perhaps lackadaisical, feeling that everything will turn out well no matter what one does. But in any case the stronger their convictions about what really will occur, the deeper and more sincere the responses of most people will be. Let us see, then, whether systematic theology can determine anything objective about universalism on the basis of the biblical data.

B. The Universality of the Gospel

First, one may hope that God's saving work will spread very widely. Throughout biblical history, while human perversity grows darker, God's mercy often glows marvelously more brightly. Through Hosea, having recounted Israel's sins and coming judgment with dismal severity, Yahweh suddenly cries:

> How can I give you up, O Ephraim! How can I hand you over, O Israel! My heart recoils within me, my compassion grows warm and tender. I will not execute my fierce anger, I will not come to destroy (Hos. 11:8–9).

Several centuries later, as Israel languishes in well-deserved Babylonian exile, the glad word comes: "I, I am he who blots out your transgressions for my own sake, and I will not remember your sins" (Isa. 43:25).

Jesus reissued this word of forgiveness. In so doing he reversed many current expectations. Most religious people expected the kingdom to come to the morally righteous. But Jesus proclaimed undeserved grace for sinners. This offer of free, undeserved grace to those who least expected it constitutes a very strong argument for universalism.[20] Paul summed up the flow of biblical history by declaring that "where sin increased, grace abounded all the more, so that, as sin reigned in Death, grace might also reign through righteousness to eternal Life through Jesus Christ our Lord" (Rom. 5:20–21).

Consequently as Christians confront the vast scope of evil and injustice in our world, and perhaps also observe it being overcome by goodness and justice, they can hope that God will spread salvation very widely (1 Tim. 2:4, 2 Peter 3:9). It is hard to set limits to the mercy of God which may be revealed either in this present world or at the Last Judgment. Many would argue for no limits whatever by appealing to those passages which apparently extend salvation to "all" people (1 Cor. 15:22, Rom. 5:18, 1 Tim. 4:10, etc.). These texts, however, are not as conclusive as they seem. Scripture sometimes uses "all" in a distributive sense. That is, "all" may often refer to individuals "from every tribe and tongue and people and nation" (Rev. 5:9) and not to all people from every such group. Similarly, reconciling "to himself all things, whether on earth or in heaven," (Col. 1:20) need not mean reconciling every single creature in heaven and earth but creatures from all realms of the cosmos.

---

[20] So argued by Moltmann, The Crucified God (New York: Harper, 1974), pp. 128-35.

Other apparently universalist passages express God's desire that everyone find salvation (1 Tim. 2:4, 2 Peter 3:9). Still others stress the universal sufficiency of Christ's saving work (for instance, that he "is the expiation...for the sins of the whole world" [1 John 2:2]). But none of these assert that everyone will actually experience salvation. All the above passages extol the broad scope of Christ's work (extensively), but they need not extend actual salvation to every single person (intensively). They are compatible with the negative judgment of some, if other grounds for affirming this can be found.

C. Limitations to Universalism

Negative judgment of some is compatible with the overall course of biblical history. Old Testament offers of grace come to peoples whom Yahweh has often previously judged. Although these nations as a whole may survive, the majority of individuals are condemned in a way that usually sounds final.

The fact that the same God both condemns and pardons (and does the former more often) does not limit the wonder of grace. It enhances it. For the wonder of grace does not consist primarily in "quantity," in the number of people pardoned, but in "quality," in that it overflows to the undeserving. Grace is marvelous when it does not come more or less as a matter of course, as a necessary outflowing of God's benevolence, but when it intervenes despite brutally real rebellion and brokenness. And Yahweh's negative judgments, which are praised as just and are often exercised against a people for whom God has shown great love and patience, reveal the extent of that rebellion and brokenness.

Of course, Christian theology cannot be derived straight from the Old Testament. The scope of salvation, we have learned, may be far broader in the New Age. Still, Jesus, Paul, and the later New Testament writings proclaim God's grace against the backdrop of a wrath surely to come. They magnify this grace by contrast with the condemnation that humans surely deserve. Salvation's widening stream still flows within these broader banks.

Turning to a more existential standpoint, the kerygma's call to decision in light of future judgment loses its decisiveness if no negative verdicts will be rendered. To be sure, this call is not based chiefly on what has "not yet" happened; its reference to future judgment is not primarily a threat. But it is an important component of the kerygma's claim as to how reality is constituted. That Christ is Lord means, partly, that those who refuse to acknowledge it collide, like an automobile that runs head-on into a bridge, with the very essence of the way things are. The coming consummation of his lordship means that nothing which opposes him can ultimately survive.

Objections are raised to the possible condemnation of some people because it seems to demean them. The dignity of humanity created in God's image seems incompatible with the thought of anyone being forever annihilated or punished in hell. But on the contrary, the possibility of negative judgment is a consequence of human dignity. It is the reverse side of our capacity to choose and live in deep, vital fellowship with God. For this very potentiality also enables us to ally ourselves with monstrous evil. Humans can do extremely severe damage to other people, to other creatures, and to themselves. Thus the dignity of humanity, rather than being incompatible with eventual condemnation, entails the possibility of negative choices and of fitting negative consequences for them.

The weightiest considerations against universalism are those general ones which support the coming of the Last Judgment: If God is good and just, as the kerygma announces, evil must finally be exposed, condemned, and eliminated. It may seem attractive to think simply of *evil* and not of evil individuals suffering this fate. After all in today's massive technological environment, we are increasingly aware of the "structural" character of much that is bad. Individuals are often swept along by negative forces over which they seemingly exercise little control. And we have also indicated that supra-individual powers are behind much that is evil. Yet if one carries these essentially sound considerations too far, humans become little more than puppets. They become incapable of willing any of the unfortunate consequences which unwittingly follow from their acts. But humans also become incapable of resistance to the networks in which they are trapped. In other words if humans are incapable of significant response to evil, they are also incapable of significant response to God.

Personal and social evil cannot exist without humans, to some degree, being responsible for it. Great personal and social evil cannot exist without some persons being greatly responsible for it. The human capacity to choose for or against God includes the possibility of aligning oneself increasingly with the forces of evil. And, as Thomas Aquinas noted, human inclinations are strengthened by repeated choices.[21] The more often one chooses, the more fixed one's allegiance becomes, and the harder it becomes to break. The human capacity for good and evil is great enough that one can can be aligned irreversibly with the evil which God must finally destroy.

These considerations help answer Karl Barth's apparent support for universalism. Barth, as we saw (Chap. 5), argues that human evil is serious. God must judge it severely. Yet Jesus took this punishment in our place. For Barth this means that "the Judge who puts some on the left and others on the right, is in fact He who has yielded himself to the judgment of God *for me* and has taken away all malediction from me."[22] Here Barth apparently argues that if Christ suffered for all the evil I could ever commit, how could he turn around and finally condemn me?

In an important sense, he will not. Nonetheless, I can choose (and choose again and again) to reject what Christ has done for me and to align myself with forces which oppose him. In other words, I can condemn myself. In this way God's negative final judgment will not be suddenly and arbitrarily imposed, in

[21] *ST*, II, 1, QQ. 52-55; Q. 63, a. 2.

[22] Barth, pp. 135-36.

a way wholly discontinuous with one's existence to that point. It will simply confirm the attitude that one has already taken, the orientation by which one has lived. It will be like the clearing away and destruction of plant growth which has come to serve no useful function (Matt. 13:30, Heb. 6:7-8).

Perhaps some are a bit dissatisfied with these arguments. They have involved a notion of human freedom which we have not fully developed (and cannot until Vol. II, Chap. 5). Moreover, our argument, strictly speaking, has only been this: God's goodness, Christ's lordship, and human freedom are such that negative final judgment must be possible. We have not proved that anyone actually will be condemned. In addition, we previously affirmed that salvation's range might become exceedingly broad. Might we then possibly hope that God's love could somehow convert all evil persons and even all evil Powers whatsoever, if not in this present existence, then beyond death?

A thorough response must await our discussions of hell and the millennium (Chap. 9) and of evil and sin (Vol II, Chap. 6). For now we can only observe that from an eschatological perspective the conflict between God and evil is so sharp that the ultimate conversion of all God's opponents is not a viable option. The powers of evil sought to annihilate Jesus. The early Church experienced persecution designed to obliterate its existence. Through the subsequent centuries Christians have suffered similarly strong opposition from time to time. And evil has raised its head in numberless brutal and shocking forms. To be sure, no one can determine exactly which individuals and which evil forces have set themselves irreversibly against God. But surely there have been some; probably very many.

D. The Subjective Dimension

When people face death, many turn to religion (some for the first time) for consolation. Many want religion to soften this harsh confrontation with reality's darker side. We have argued that the "immortality of the soul," insofar as it promises automatic and immediate conquest of dying, constitutes an escape from the reality of death. Similarly universalism can offer an escape from the reality of evil. We instinctively shield ourselves from the magnitude of real and possible tragedy and suffering in our world. We seldom want to consider what terrible consequences our acts and those of our loved ones might and sometimes do have. To the extent that universalism offers everyone the automatic attainment of a positive, eternal destiny, it allows us to evade these realities.

Believing that the coming judgment will be negative as well as positive, however, underlines the seriousness of our decisions. It awakens us to the magnitude of evil in our present world, and thereby can arouse our compassion and concern. It normally enhances our efforts to communicate the gospel with explicitness and care. Belief in the negative and future dimension of judgment is subjectively damaging only when divorced from positive and present aspects of judgment. The complete kerygmatic proclamation of judgment is this: God has already defeated evil and established righteousness! This victory will attain absolute sway! Those who open themselves to this reign of righteousness need not fear the final destruction of evil. The message of coming negative judgment is like italics which warn: *Nevertheless, evil is still real. Therefore, you must really turn against it!*

The proclamation of coming negative judgment, then, offers a word of great hope. All evil and injustice will surely be abolished! Yet it is not an easy optimism that declares these things to be unreal. It is based on God's inbreaking into the tightening cycle of evil and injustice in the past. It lives in anticipation of such inbreakings yet to come. It indicates that Christian faith is not general confidence in the emergence of good from evil. It is faith in the God who establishes justice out of the depths of evil. Such a faith may be difficult to attain. But because it squarely faces the horrors and sufferings caused by injustice, it is difficult to shake.

People grasped by this universal message of judgment may face concrete situations with almost unlimited optimism and almost unlimited pessimism: optimism because God's limitless and saving love may spread far beyond one's expectations; pessimism because of the stark reality of injustice and evil. Christians may face any situation with great hope yet need not despair when their efforts are partially unsuccessful, or even apparently crushed. In situations of apparent failure Christians can bear realistically with much evil but need not give up all courage and hope.

Finally, even though evil and some evil persons will ultimately be punished, we cannot know who or how much or in what way. If every evil act received its just desert, none of us would attain salvation. If we insist that punishment must always fit the crime, we deny the grace that we have been shown. And we cannot be certain that anyone, no matter how apparently evil, never has turned nor will turn towards God. In the first days of the Church, no one would have seemed more opposed to Christ than Paul. Yet he later testified:

> I received mercy for this reason, that in me, as the foremost, Jesus Christ might display his perfect patience for an example to those who were to believe in him for eternal Life (1 Tim. 1:16).

> Therefore do not pronounce judgment before the time, before the Lord comes, who will bring to light the things now hidden in darkness and will disclose the purposes of the heart (1 Cor. 4:5).

Suggestions for Further Reading

Berkouwer, C. G. *The Return of Christ.* Grand Rapids: Eerdmans, 1972.

Brunner, Emil. *Eternal Hope.* London: Lutterworth, 1954.

Cullman, Oscar. *Immortality of the Soul or Resurrection of the Dead.* London: Epworth, 1958.

Jüngel, Eberhard. *Death: The Riddle and the Mystery.* Philadelphia: Westminster, 1974.

Martin, James P. *The Last Judgement: In Protestant Theology From Orthodoxy to Ritschl*. Grand Rapids: Eerdmans, 1963.

Martin-Aschard, Robert. *From Death to Life: A Study of the Development of the Doctrine of the Resurrection in the Old Testament*. London: Oliver and Boyd, 1960.

Moody, Dale. *The Hope of Glory*. Grand Rapids: Eerdmans, 1964.

Pittinger, Norman. *"The Last Things" in a Process Perspective*. London: Epworth, 1970.

Schep, J.A. *The Nature of the Resurrection Body*. Grand Rapids: Eerdmans, 1964.

Schwarz, Hans. *Beyond the Gates of Death: A Biblical Examination of Evidence for Life After Death*. Minneapolis: Augsburg, 1981.

Stendahl, Krister, ed. *Immortality and Resurrection*. New York: Macmillan, 1965.

Summers, Ray. *The Life Beyond*. Nashville, Broadman, 1959.

Thielicke, Helmut. *Death and Life*. Philadelphia: Fortress, 1970.

CHAPTER NINE

Heaven and Hell, the Return of Christ, and the Millennium

A lthough the Resurrection and the Last Judgment have "already" occurred, we argued in Chapter 8 that they are also real future events. We
maintained that the resurrection, which will transform (and already transforms) our bodies, will affect the spatial dimensions of the cosmos. And
though we said nothing about the spatial characteristics of the coming Judgment, we insisted that it will affect the course of time.

But Christian hope has traditionally been directed towards an eternal and
apparently spaceless realm called "heaven." It has dreaded another apparently
spiritual realm called "hell." Chapter 8 said nothing about either, except to critique the notion of an inherently immortal soul automatically "going to
heaven" immediately after death. But is not hope concerned with heaven and
hell? Or only with what may happen to our spatio-temporal world? We will explore this issue first.

Next, the present chapter will turn to the focal point of early Christian
hope: the return of Jesus Christ. Is his coming to be spiritual, bodily, or just
what? And what of other events that have often been thought to precede or
follow it, such as the millennium? Our chapter will close by considering what
else theology might say, or not say, about history's final events.

All along we will be probing in specific detail the relationship between the
literal and figurative dimensions of eschatological language and the extent to
which the consummation will be continuous and/or discontinuous with the

155

present. We shall find ourselves occasionally speaking of features of the universe which science also explores.

I. Heaven and Hell

A. Heaven

The traditional Christian notion of heaven owes much to the Greek world view. Heavenly reality has often been conceived as the opposite of earthly existence. Since things in this world have bodies which exist in certain places through limited periods of time, heaven must be a spiritual, timeless, spaceless realm. But (as we saw in Chap. 8) the more that such a heaven becomes the ultimate goal of God's saving work, the less important are events such as a bodily resurrection or an earthly history likely to become.

Liberal theology virtually reversed this traditional view when it reduced the scope of theological doctrines. Theology could no longer refer directly to any realm which transcended religious experience (Schleiermacher) or moral action (Ritschl). According to Schleiermacher, "we can have no doctrine of the consummation of the Church, for our Christian consciousness has absolutely nothing to say regarding a condition so entirely outside our ken.[1] Consequently statements about eternal life, or heaven, can be "useful only as a pattern to which we have to approximate."[2] In other words they must refer, symbolically, to some fulness or perfection of human capacities or experiences.

Similarly, Albrecht Ritschl acknowledged that "The aim of the Christian is conceived as the attainment of eternal life."[3] But since theology cannot speak about any realm transcending the present spatio-temporal order of things, eternal life must be interpreted as an affirmation about the value of the human individual. For Ritschl, to say that humans are destined for eternal life is to affirm that each individual is of greater value than the whole natural realm and is destined to participate in conquering it.[4]

Traditional orthodox theologies, then, present us with a heaven far removed

---

[1] Schleiermacher, The Christian Faith, p. 697. That is, eschatological propositions "are not doctrines of faith, since their content (as transcending our faculties of apprehension) is not a description of our actual consciousness." Schleiermacher does not like the phrase, " 'the Last Things'...for the term 'things' threatens to carry us quite away from the domain of the inner life, with which alone we are concerned" (p. 703).

[2] Ibid., p. 696.

[3] Justification and Reconciliation, p. 387.

[4] "Eternal life" refers to the "realization of the personal self-end, of which it is the test that the whole world does not compare in worth with the personal life, and that by this the acquisition of spiritual lordship over the world, this, the true worth of life, is vindicated" (p. 387). Such a view could have disastrous ecological consequences.

from this earth. In liberal theologies, however, heaven becomes so earthly that it seems to disappear. Do the biblical writings on this subject support either of these views? Or is Scripture best interpreted in another way?

The biblical writings speak of heaven in two main ways. The first is literal. According to it, heaven is a created realm. Although the heavens are superior to the earth, they too will one day "wear out like a garment." (Ps. 102:26; cf. Mark 13:31, 2 Pet. 3:7-10, etc.). The heavens are the home of created beings, including evil powers who constitute some kind of barrier between earthly creatures and God (esp. Eph. 2:2, 3:10, 4:9-10). The heavens, like the earth, participate in salvation history (Eph. 1:10, Col 1:16, 20). Because God will one day alter the heavens, and because disharmony as well as harmony reign there, heaven, in the literal sense, cannot be a specific realm with precise boundaries which is the fixed object of eschatological hope.

Despite this, Scripture speaks of heaven in a second, figurative way as the "place" where God is fully obeyed (Ps. 103: 19-20, Matt. 6:10). In this sense, heaven is "the starting-point of the divine work of salvation."[5] When Jesus came proclaiming that "the kingdom of heaven is at hand" (Matt 4:17),[6] the powers of heavenly life, as manifested in his healings, teachings, and exorcisms, began invading the earth.[7] As exalted to God's right hand in heaven, he now is the origin of that divine activity which presently reshapes the universe. When Jesus returns with the clouds of heaven (Mark 14:62), the fulness of divine life will even more thoroughly transform the earth. In this figurative sense, heaven is more nearly a verb than a noun. Heaven is a way of speaking not of a territory over which God rules but of the dynamic, transforming power of God's reign. Insofar as God's life streams forth and is answered by obedience, service, and joy (wherever in the universe and however this might occur) "heaven" is active.

This dynamic, figurative understanding of heaven corresponds with what we said about the resurrection of the body (Chap. 8). The dwelling prepared for us in the heavens will come down upon us; we will be "clothed upon, so that what is mortal may be swallowed up by life" (2 Cor. 5:4). It also corresponds with early Christianity's understanding of Jesus' presence in heaven. While the kerygma affirms that "the heavens must receive" him, this will only last "until the time for establishing all that God spoke by the mouth of his holy prophets from of old" (Acts 3:21). While the early Christians focused their gaze

---

[5] TWNT V, p. 520.

[6] We regard the term "kingdom of heaven," which is used almost exclusively by Matthew, as equivalent to the "kingdom of God" used almost always by Mark and Luke (see George Ladd, *Crucial Questions About the Kingdom of God* [Grand Rapids: Eerdmans, 1952], pp. 121-32). Biblical scholars generally agree that both terms refer primarily to the active rule of God, and little (if at all) to any realm over which God may rule. (Ladd, *The Presence of the Future*, pp. 122-48.)

[7] Ladd, *The Pattern of New Testament Truth*, p. 57.

towards Jesus in heaven, it was in eager anticipation of his return to earth (1 Thess. 1:10; cf. Phil 3:20–21, 1 Cor. 16:22).

In light of this biblical understanding, we can evaluate the traditional and the liberal views of heaven as models which account partially for different features of it. Like the liberal model, the biblical perspective regards heaven as in some sense continuous with earth: it has to do with the perfecting of what exists here. But like the orthodox model, Scripture depicts heaven as discontinuous with our earthly state of affairs. The coming of heaven to earth means a radical transformation of all that exists here.

The ultimate eschatological hope, then, is not that individuals will go to heaven but that heaven will fully and finally pervade earth. It is that "the earth will be filled with the knowledge of the glory of Yahweh, as the waters cover the sea" (Hab. 2:14; cf. Isa. 11:9).

This means, then, that "heaven" is very like what the Bible means by "life," or "eternal life." Both signify dynamic realities. Chapter 8 showed that life is opposed to what Scripture calls death. Accordingly, death might give us some clues as to what is meant by hell.

B. Hell

Two main New Testament words are translated as "hell." *Gehenna* refers to a valley outside Jerusalem. Here sacrifices were once offered to Moloch (2 Kings 16:3, 21:6). In Jesus' time, fires of rubbish were perpetually smoldering there. This term, and similar references to "everlasting fire" (Matt. 13:42) and "the lake of fire" (Rev. 20:10, 14), vividly depict the agony of the lost. But there is no need to interpret them literally as references to a specific place. In popular literature, *hades* was pictured as a compartment under the earth; here the dead led a shadow-like existence. The New Testament once uses *hades* to depict a place of fiery torment (Luke 16:23). The other New Testament uses show that hell was usually conceived in a far more general way. It is closely intertwined with Death (Acts 2:27, 31; Rev. 1:18, 6:8, 20:13–14), the Last Judgment (Matt. 11:23–24; Luke 10:14- 15), and the forces opposing God (Matt. 16:18). In other words, much as heaven is more properly a verb than a noun, and signifies the source of divine life, so hell is not primarily a realm but a force or state of existence opposing the divine life. This places it among the eschatological realities we have discussed so far.

1. The Coming of Heaven. Let us recall what we said about the Last Judgment (Chap. 8). It will be God's final triumph over death and evil. God's reality and purposes will become unmistakably clear. Nothing will remain hidden. No longer will evil seem good, nor injustice pass for justice. Theology can express much the same reality from a different angle by employing the model of heaven. At some time, we can say the powers of heaven will invade the earth in an unhindered way. Not only will a judicial sentence be passed against death and evil; the reality of life and righteousness will overcome them.

Now the Judgment will divide creatures into two groups. Those whose deepest orientation has been inclined towards God's righteousness will rejoice (although perhaps amidst trembling and astonishment) at heaven's unhindered coming. But those whose deepest orientation has opposed God will meet it with resistance and fear. Although it will separate creatures in this way, the coming of heaven itself will be one undivided, overpowering, irresistable reality. It will test everyone's works as by fire. And if anyone experiences it as painful, the pain will be due to the character of one's own works. We have seen that some Christians will undergo a good measure of pain. Their works will be "burned up"; although they themselves will be saved, it will be "only as through fire" (2 Cor. 3:12–15).

This understanding provides a major clue as to the nature of hell. Those outside Christ will not be suddenly condemned by an alien, hitherto absent God, by unknown and unreasonable standards. Instead the true character of Reality will be lit up with unmistakable brightness. It will become unavoidably clear that Reality is of one character and that their own deepest wills and works are irreversibly opposed to it. There will be no need to convince anyone about how things really are or about the certainty of God's justice. Even within those who have never heard of Christ, their conscience will "bear witness and their conflicting thoughts accuse or perhaps excuse them on that Day when…God judges the secrets of humans by Christ Jesus" (Rom. 2:15–16). Hell, we can say, will be the reality aroused by negative response to the climactic coming of heaven. Finally, "God is all in all" (1 Cor. 15:28). There is no place to hide. There is no way to oppose the overpowering, irresistible joy of life. For those who irreversibly oppose such energy and brightness, existence will be painfully, hellishly "burning".

2. *Eternal Conscious Torment?* Negative judgment and hell have aroused objections not only because they seem to condemn people by alien, arbitrary standards. Christians (often because they have thought the soul to be inherently immortal) have usually believed that final punishment would be eternally experienced. Objectors, however, have loudly protested: Eternal torture outweighs even the very terrible crimes which humans can commit; any God who consigns people to it must be a fiend!

Upon what biblical basis might one argue that the experience of hell is not only very painful, but also eternal? One thinks of passages like Revelation 20:10:

> the Devil who had deceived them was thrown into the lake of fire and brimstone where the beast and the false prophet were, and they will be tormented day and night for ever and ever.

It seems very similar to Revelation 14:9–11:

> If any one worships the beast and its image…one shall be tormented with fire and brimstone in the presence of the holy angels and of the Lamb. And the smoke of their torment goes up for ever and ever; and they have no rest, day or night, these worshippers of the beast and its image.

Upon close inspection, however, the first of these apportions eternal torment only to the devil, the beast, and the false prophet. The second does include humans who worship the beast, but, strictly speaking, it is only the "smoke" (the smoke of the same "lake" where the first three are consigned) that is clearly eternal. This observation may seem like a hair-splitting reservation, but only until one realizes that no other passage comes as close to ascribing eternally experienced punishment to humans. Other texts mention the everlasting character of "fire" (Isa. 66:24; Mark 9:43, 48; Jude 7). We hear of eternal "punishment" (Matt. 25:46) and eternal "destruction" (2 Thess. 1:9). But in no case is it absolutely clear that the experience of condemned humans will be eternal. Indeed it is hard to combine the notion of destruction with the eternal survival of anything.[8] "Eternal" in such passages may well not refer to consciously experienced time, but to the finality of God's judgment, which will stand for ever and ever.

The relevant biblical texts, then, do not conclusively support or deny the possibility of eternal conscious torment. Are there then perhaps broader theological considerations which can help decide this issue? It has been argued that everlasting conscious punishment is fitting because of the majesty and holiness of the Being whom one has disobeyed. That is, while other human acts could only do a finite amount of damage, and thus could merit only a finite penalty, the infinity and the character of the One offended make this a special case. This argument is deductive. It assumes as a premise that divine punishment will fit the crime. It also argues deductively from God's infinity and holiness alone, leaving aside divine love and mercy. It therefore shows that eternal conscious punishment is consistent with certain other theological truths. However, like many deductive arguments, it does not consider the full range of factors that might also help determine whether or not the thing that it shows to be possible really will occur.

On the other side, it can be argued that if hell is the pain of those who have aligned themselves with death, and if the Last Judgment is the final triumph of life, it sounds strange to speak of the everlasting experience of death. To be sure, we have described death not simply as non-being; it is a power which strives mightily against God. Accordingly, even at the full revelation of life, death might not immediately collapse into nothingness.

Nevertheless death inherently tends towards disintegration and oblivion. And death can have no power which was not originally derived from the Creator. Thus if God is finally to be all in all (1 Cor. 15:28), how could any such opposed reality exist eternally alongside him? It seems more likely that, at the triumph of life, death (and those held irreversibly in its snare) would decline towards ultimate annihilation. This might be a relatively slow, painful process.

Of course this argument itself is also somewhat deductive. It attempts to deduce consequences from the natures of life and death. Thus it too cannot pre-

---

[8] For an opposing argument, see Anthony Hoekema, The Bible and the Future (Grand Rapids: Eerdmans, 1979), pp. 265-73, on both "eternal" and "destruction."

dict what absolutely must occur. Yet it may well correspond to the real meaning of Revelation 20. Death and hell themselves are thrown into the lake of fire (verse 14)! If one presses this symbolic chapter too literally, one has hell itself burning up in a lake that also seems to be hell. Might not this eternal burning, then, rather than being something which endures throughout period that persons may experience, itself symbolize the ultimate abolition of all such hellish burning?

What can we conclude from all this? As in the case of the coming judgment of Christians, or of the quantities of the saved and the lost, theology cannot be nearly as precise as human curiosity would like. We cannot rule out the possibility of eternal conscious torment. But since the coming triumph of heaven is to be complete, it seems less likely that hell will be an eternal, consciously experienced process existing alongside it. "Eternal" most likely refers not to the duration, but to the final character of God's negative judgment. Some sort of gradual, at least partially experienced annihilation seems the most likely fate of the condemned.[9]

If this conjecture softens the pains of hell a bit, it is not meant to do so by much. To stand before the brightness and glory of God, knowing that one has irreversibly set oneself against that irresistible Reality, will surely be a horrifying experience. To be convinced that one has failed to reach the destiny for which one was created; to pass into oblivion (or perhaps endless conscious suffering) while others go on to an eternity of joyous fulfillment—such will surely arouse "weeping and gnashing of teeth."

C. The "Already"

While we have focused on the future character of heaven and hell, we have conceived them as final actualizations of dynamic, presently existing realities. Indeed heaven, as the point from which the powers of life emanate and to which some creatures positively respond, has existed since Creation. The Old Testament speaks of a heavenly court, or council, of angelic beings who obey God. When Jesus came to bring the kingdom of heaven and when he poured out the Spirit from on high (Acts 2:33), heaven came more fully to earth. For us heaven is not simply a future lying beyond the skies. It is "already" among us.

If heaven is definitively present among us, so is hell (Matt. 16:18, Rev. 6:8;

---

[9] C. S. Lewis has conjectured that those in hell might gradually decline from a human state to an animal to a vegetable one, and so on down to non-existence. They would thus gradually lose their intelligence, and eventually consciousness. But to assert or deny such a supposition lies beyond the range of theology. Lewis' general views on heaven and hell have shaped the present author's thinking. For excellent overviews, see Clyde Kilby, *The Christian World of C. S. Lewis* (Grand Rapids: Eerdmans, 1964), pp. 37-64; and William White, *The Image of Man in C. S. Lewis* (Nashville: Abingdon, 1969), pp. 50-55, 198-207.

though Jesus has already overcome it; Acts 2:27, 31; Rev. 1:18) This seems to mean not only that death continues to do its work but that it presently binds some with hell's irreversible finality. Just as people can now decisively choose life, so can they choose to definitively reject it.

D. The Subjective Dimension

Like belief in judgment, belief in heaven and hell underlines the importance of one's present decisions and actions. It does so by placing them towards the beginning of an (at least potentially) eternal future. On one hand the attitudes and motives from which we act become extremely significant. For we are beginning to chart a course whose goal lies beyond what we can dream. On the other hand the particular results of our actions, our concrete successes and failures, become less important. For we are only beginning our journey. It is important to start in the right way. Our path is lit up by the promise of joys eventually to come.

II. The Return of Jesus Christ

A. The "Already"

In discussing judgment, heaven, and hell, we have stressed some measure of continuity between our present existence and the consummation. Objections to these teachings often arise because they are presented in a disjointed manner, disconnected from the cosmic and historical activity which they climax. We have sought to articulate their inherent meaning by indicating how they sum up and reveal all that has been happening until that time. They bring to full harvest what has "already" been occurring.

There is also a sense in which Jesus Christ "already" has returned and is now returning. Salvation is not just something which Jesus won for us long ago. It involves present participation with him. The earliest Christians sensed this. "Maranatha!" expressed the longing not only for his climactic return but for his presence amidst worship. Paul used the phrase "in Christ" to indicate many dimensions of salvation and Christian existence. John linked the coming of Jesus closely to the coming of the Spirit (John 14:16–28). Precisely speaking Christ is now present through the Spirit (Vol. II, Chaps. 15–16). Yet this presence, or return, is very real.

B. Discontinuity

If Christ has already returned in some sense, what does this mean for the future course of history? Can we suppose, as the postmillennial model does, that his presence will gradually permeate the cosmos, perhaps making any climactic future return unnecessary? Or, along with premillennialism (and some forms of amillennialism), can we expect the discontinuity between the present and the consummation to increase in certain important respects, so that Jesus' triumphant inbreaking will be necessary to set things right?

We have seen that Scripture sometimes emphasizes continuity between the present and the future (Rom. 8:18–25, etc.) Nevertheless, this theme is subordinate to the dominant model which pictures the end-times as a period of suffering and persecution for God's people. Oppression by enemies is expected to increase, and the world situation in general is certain to worsen before God's final breakthrough.

And this is certainly the perspective of inter-testamental apocalyptic, which was largely forged under such experiences. Many sayings in the Synoptic Gospels maintain it. Before the end, they foresee a time of "such tribulation as has not been from the beginning of the creation...until now, and never will be. And if the Lord had not shortened the days, no human being would be saved." (Mark 13:19–20 and par.). Peter, Jude, and Revelation clearly express this overall perspective.

For Paul, even in his later letters, struggle with opposing forces always characterizes the Church.[10] His first letter expects Jesus' sudden return (1 Thess. 4:14–17), which will bring travail and destruction (5:2–7). As he dealt with the parousia's delay, Paul gave more attention to what might occur before that time. The explanation he probably gave first was that evil must increase to a climactic point of opposition (2 Thess. 2:3–11). Even in Romans 8 the continuity envisioned between present and future is a continuity of "groaning" amidst struggle (Rom. 8:18–39; cf. 5:1–5). Paul's later writings deal little with the precise situation preceeding Christ's return. He is more concerned (as Bultmann rightly noticed) to spell out the significance of Christ's presence in the Church. Nonetheless, there is no reason to assume the Paul ever dropped his expectation of the increase of evil before the end. We also find little about the course of final events in John. Yet this apparent lack is due to his special emphasis, not to his abandonment of future eschatological expectations. John expects the Church to be in frequent conflict with the course of this world.[11] And, in any case, he does not replace the penultimate increase of evil with another framework.

We may conclude that the New Testament writers generally expect the Church to exist in conflict with evil throughout the "not yet." The intensity of opposition will increase before the very End. Though the final Judgment will be in continuity with what God has been doing all along, it will be in sharp discontinuity with the course of much else in the world and with the way that

---

[10] E.g., Rom. 5:1-6, 8:18, 31-39; Phil. 1:27-30; Eph. 6:10-20; 2 Tim. 3:1-13, 4:1-6. Even when the congregation addressed in a letter is not undergoing persecution at that moment, Paul, in carrying on the larger missionary work of the Church, always is.

[11] John 15:18-25, 17:14-16; 1 John 2:15-19, 3:13, 4:1-6, 5:19.

events seem to most people to be proceeding.

This corresponds with what we have frequently observed concerning our present world situation. For while the coming judgment will reveal all continuities among past, present, and future, most of them are now hidden to Christians and non-Christians alike. A world in which poverty and violence seem to be increasing is not obviously being brought under the reign of God's justice. In a world where starvation, loneliness, and despair hurry so many towards death, the life of God is not clearly triumphing. Waiting for the "not yet" is painful, not just because it is future but also because the things hoped for are so different from, so opposed to, the way things are now. The continuity proper to eschatology, then, cannot be such as Postmillennialism supposes. Christ's peace and righteousness are not exercising an increasingly broader historical sway which flows steadily towards his final enthronement. Even allowing for temporary reversals of such a process or for a final outbreak of evil before the end (as more conservative postmillennialists do),[12] no such evolution of true goodness and justice is discernible.

C. A Personal, Bodily Return

If God's goal for our spatio-temporal world is to be attained, the large measure of discontinuity between it and the present points towards some unusual future acts of God. For several reasons the personal, bodily return of Jesus Christ will be at the center of these. Above all, the kerygma is primarily a proclamation about a person. This person's acts are at its core. So far we have been speaking of eschatology in general terms. We have spoken of the "things" hoped for: life, heaven, etc. We have done so, in part, to counteract the individualism of much traditional eschatology. While the kerygma is not merely a message about individual existence, neither is it a general theory about universal history.

Of course the kerygma claims that existence and history have new meanings. But they have them only because of Jesus and what he has done, does, and will do. The one who brought, brings, and will bring meaning to these things cannot be abstracted from those claims. Since Jesus has "already" brought the new age through his personal, physical activity, it would be strange for its consummation to occur apart from similar activities. To be sure, the consummation may well transcend the limitations of the personal and the physical as we now understand them. But if we are open to its true significance and novelty, we must allow it to also transcend our era's present understanding of what the personal and the physical are like.

The personal character of Christ's coming is also evident from early Christian worship. The risen Christ was no vague symbol. The same Jesus whom some had known several years (or months?) earlier was addressed personally. The early community beseeched him to come soon: "Maranatha!" Later, Peter

---

[12] Loraine Boettner, The Millenium (Grand Rapids: Baker, 1958), pp. 67-71.

wrote to many who had never known Jesus. "Without having seen him you love him; though you do not now see him you believe in him and rejoice with unutterable and exalted joy!" (1 Pet. 1:8). Even later, while John acknowledged that the parousia will bring the unexpected ("it does not yet appear what we shall be"), his focus was on reunion with this person: "but we know that when he appears we shall be like him, for we shall see him as he is" (1 John 3:2).

The personal character of Christ's return becomes more evident when we recognize that the kerygmatic events came to be perceived as the supreme manifestation of God's love.[13] Love is deeply personal. It is the self-giving, the faithfulness, the tender compassion of a person.[14] One who loves desires to know, to experience, to perceive as fully as possible the beloved person. Love for God, then, is not general reverence for an impersonal Force. It too will not be satisfied, will not come to full fruition, without the fuller manifestation of the beloved Person.

The bodily character of Christ's coming is evident from the nature of the resurrection. The resurrection "already" vivifies our bodies. At the consummation it will transform them. But our resurrection is grounded in Christ's. What happens and will happen to us has first happened to him. Further, we have seen that the biblical notion of person includes that of the body.[15] In contrast to the Greek perspective, for which the real person was a "soul," the body is intrinsic to the individuality and the specific character of each person. If the same Jesus who was crucified (and not some phantom) arose, and if the same person (not some vague symbol) will return, then his return will be "bodily."

D. The Objective Dimension

Since Christ's return will be bodily, and since it will effect the transformation of our bodies, it will be a spatio-temporal event. Few contemporary theologians assert this clearly; some who do say little more about its specific character However, if such an event will actually happen, its occurrence has momentous implications for all of nature and history. If systematic theology is to elucidate such a claim in the modern context, it must sketch at least a few of its implications for the modern scientific understanding of things.

First, what is the relationship between such a claim and the claims of science? We have noted that modern science (unlike Newtonianism) does not insist that unbreakable natural laws render Christ's bodily return impossible (Chap. 7 above). Laws in general are understood not as direct descriptions of

[13] This recognition dawned somewhat gradually. It focused most of all on Jesus' death (esp. Gal. 2:20, Rom. 5:6-11, 1 John 4:9-11); cf. p. 317.

[14] Volume II, Chap. 3 will show that we are not forcing some presupposed notion of love onto our relationship with God. We are deriving our notion of love from that relationship.

[15] In our discussion of the final resurrection (Chap. 8); for a more thorough discussion see Chap. 18 and Volume II, Chap. 5.

how phenomena must behave, but as statistical generalizations as to how certain selected features of them are likely to act. At least on the level of "microphenomena," science acknowledges its inability to fully predict the behavior of every event. We have also seen that lower level activities are open to reorientation and reorganization by higher ones. Science can conceive of things behaving differently due to the directing presence of some higher reality.

This notion has similarities with the coming of heaven. When heaven comes to earth, it will take what is earthly up into itself and transform it. What is mortal will not be destroyed but be "clothed upon...[and] swallowed up by Life" (2 Cor. 5:4). We may expect the return of Jesus, whose earthly body has already been transformed by heavenly reality, to be at the center of such a transformation.

In its objective character, then, Christ's return is analogous to events which science also can anticipate. However, due to the discontinuity between the present and the consummation, such transformations will occur far more rapidly, and with far broader effects, than anything which science can predict. For science predicts the future only by extrapolating from what has regularily occurred in the past and can be subjected to empirical verification in the present.[16] If being "scientific" means that he only spatio-temporal phenomena one can hope for must be of this sort, then Jesus' bodily return must conflict with science. Our efforts to clarify its meaning in contemporary concepts will lead not to its acceptance but to its rejection. But if one's thinking about all things can begin from God's unique kerygmatic acts, and if one can hold open the possibility that similar acts might affect the future spatio-temporal world, then science can provide several models for conceiving how these acts might occur. The most helpful, of course, is the reorganization and redirection of lower levels by higher ones in which the lower entities are not destroyed, but reoriented so that they participate in a very different overall complex.

The complex topic of dimensionality suggests another model. Imagine creatures who lived entirely in a two-dimensional world. Then suppose that a third dimension were suddenly introduced. The third dimension would not destroy the other two. Length and width would be there, just as before. But with the dimension of depth, everything, including the creatures themselves, would radically change. Everything would look and feel entirely different. Many new activities would become possible. Yet numerous characteristics of this new world could still be described two-dimensionally. Something like this will happen when Jesus returns. Heaven will likely bring so many new dimensions to our experience that our present ways of reckoning temporal sequence will seem highly inadequate. Yet its final coming and continuance will at least be identi-

---

[16] The contrast with theology, however, is not complete. All sciences, especially the social and historical ones, are concerned with uniqueness to some degree. And theology must also deal with general, frequently recurring phenomena (see Barbour, pp. 175-206).

fiable on our present chronological scale. Perhaps length, width, and depth will seem artificial abstractions from the far more complex reality of things. Yet such spatial coordinates will not be entirely meaningless.

If such suppositions sound utterly fantastic, readers should consider what alternatives to our eschatology exist. If Christ will surely establish a universal kingdom of justice and peace, and if it cannot come in the way we have said, how else might it come? Alternatives seem to boil down to two. Either all such language must be interpreted figuratively, or existentially, in which case this kingdom will not actually come in social history; or else it will come literally and gradually, as postmillennialism maintains. But in view of the continuing conflicts among nations and the awesome build-up of destructive nuclear power, how likely is this? Scripture's primary eschatological model corresponds closely with what humankind is experiencing today. Not only do life and heaven come to a point of ripeness, of harvest, but death and hell do too. From the very beginning, humanity's rebellion against God has been expressed through peoples' estrangement from and war against each other (Gen. 4:8, 23–24; 11:1–9). War leads to the production of ever more powerful armaments. Whether they are produced for offensive or defensive purposes, the manufacture of weapons by one side eventually leads to the manufacture of more powerful weapons by the other. Throughout history this process has spiraled to the point where earthly life can be destroyed many times over. In our current nuclear situation, has the intrinsic dynamism of sin and death evolved to its ultimate, inevitable climax? Are we on the verge of its final act; humanity's total self-destruction? Are these the days in which, if God does not cut them short, no human being will survive (Mark 13:20)?

Theology cannot prove that this is the case. No one knows when the end will come. But given the current situation, how reasonable is it to hope that God's kingdom can overcome all evil through anything but an unprecedented divine intervention?

E. The Subjective Dimension

In Chapter 8, we presented the coming resurrection and judgment as objects of great hope. Yet, we cautioned, such hope differs greatly from an easy optimism that blinds itself to the reality of death and evil. True eschatological hope is based on the God who has broken, breaks, and will yet break into the appallingly real, ever-tightening cycle of death and hell. This discontinuity between our present world and the consummation will not gradually transform itself into continuity. It must be conquered by the radical inbreaking of God. Perhaps our treatment of Jesus' return has portrayed this discontinuity most graphically. To hope in his personal, bodily coming amidst evil's final intensification is to acknowledge that the universe knows no real hope apart from Christ. Left to themselves, death and hell ensnare everyone and surge relentlessly and inevitably towards climactic self-destruction. To hope thus for Christ's return is to give oneself over entirely into his hands.

Such a hope can endure the darkest of times. When evil seems to have over-whelmed one's situation, when there seems to be absolutely nothing that one can do, even then there is still room for hope. For hope does not rest on what we can do but on what Christ has already done. And he has already faced and overcome death and hell in their most powerful form. Yet hope for Jesus' com-ing is not essentially passive. For it knows that life and peace, not death and destruction, are the final word. It knows that whatever is done for the cause of peace now will surely live on, taken up into heaven's life. Thus it must always be on the side of goodness and peace. It can work with almost unlimited opti-mism. Even the arms race might be reversed! Yet it can also continue to work, even when it must acknowledge almost unlimited practical pessimism about immediate results.

Finally, in hope for Jesus' personal, bodily return the inward, experiential di-mension of eschatology comes to life. It anticipates not the return of a symbol but deeper communion with One whom one already loves. At Christ's return not only will the veil that hides history's significance be done away (Isa. 25:6–9) but also the veil that presently hides him. We shall see him and rejoice in his presence, face-to-face.

III. The Coming of the Millennium

Eschatology, we said earlier, has suffered from two extreme attitudes in church life and theology: overemphasis and neglect. Practitioners of the former have often keenly calculated the precise sequence of events surrounding Christ's return. It is easy to scorn their excesses; detailed charts, crass literal-ism, and the rest. Yet we have insisted that Jesus' coming will affect the spatio-temporal world. Thus we too must ask whether theology might say more about other, related events.

A. Major Millennial Views

Millennial perspectives have been commonly divided into three: post-, a-, and pre- millennialism (cf. Chap. 6). The latter two can each be subdivided into two important varieties. We have already rejected postmillennialism. It cannot take seriously enough the discontinuity between our present world and a coming one more directly under Christ's rule.

"Amillennialism," literally understood, denies the existence of any specific period called "the Millennium." Sometimes "amillennialism" is applied broadly to almost any view which regards all language about a renewed cosmos as figurative. Since we have rejected wholly existential and spiritual interpreta-tions of eschatology, we also reject this kind of amillennialism.

Today, however, most who call themselves amillennial insist that all the es-chata will affect our present world. There are five such eschata: Christ's return, resurrection, judgment, the defeat of evil, and the final renewal of the cosmos. Amillennialists argue that all five will occur together. No one of them will be separated from others by a period called the Millennium. In fact amillennialism and the two common forms of premillennialism (historic and dispensational) may be distinguished by the ways in which they group these occurrences. The amillennial scheme is by far the simplest. Before Christ's return it anticipates a greatly troubled time called the Tribulation; during it antichrist will rule. It also expects a large-scale conversion of Jews sometime before the parousia. Then, as we just said, the five major *eschata* will occur more or less together.

Historic premillennialism also expects Israel's conversion and the Tribulation to occur before Christ's return. However, it divides each of the other final events—resurrection, judgment, the defeat of evil, and the renewal of the cosmos—into two phases:

(1) At Jesus' return only "the just" shall rise; they will be judged and rewarded for their works; antichrist will be defeated and Satan bound (though evil will not be wholly destroyed); the millennial kingdom will be established (though heaven and earth will not be wholly transformed). (2) Then after the Millennium "the unjust" will rise; they will be judged for their evil works; Satan and all his cohorts will be cast into the lake of fire; and the new heavens and earth will descend.

Dispensational premillennialism makes further distinctions in this scheme. It divides Christ's return into two phases. The first will occur before the Tribulation and Israel's conversion. At this advent he will not descend all the way to earth but will "rapture" Christians to meet him in the air. This will mark the end of the Church Age. God will then reactivate the "kingdom program" for Israel, which had been been suspended since about A.D. 33. Then the Tribulation will break out, and many Jews (along with some from other groups) will be converted. Next, Christ will return for a second time to defeat antichrist, bind Satan, and establish an Judeo-centric millennial kingdom. From then on events will proceed much as they do for historic premillennialism. Notice, however, that the resurrection now has three phases: at the "rapture," all who had died in Christ to that time will be raised; at Christ's second return, all who had been martyred during the Tribulation will rise; and finally, after the millennium, the "unjust" will be resurrected.[17]

Does Scripture provide the kind of data which can enable us to make assertions about these events or to decide among the schemes into which they have been arranged? Let us look carefully at those events which have the greatest bearing on these questions.

---

[17] While the judgment, as in historic premillennialism, still has two phases, the character of each is somewhat different. For dispensationalism, "the just" are rewarded at the rapture, not at the resurrection following Christ's return to earth. The martyred saints who are raised at this second return, however, are not rewarded until the second judgment, after the millennium. But for historic premillennialism, the final judgment consists only in the condemnation of "the unjust."

B. The Eschatological Events

1. *The Great Tribulation.* In arguing that evil will intensify before the end, we have already found evidence for a final tribulation such "as has not been from the beginning of the creation...and never will be" (Mark 13:19). We have noticed that just as Christ's lordship surges towards a climactic manifestation, so does evil. The notion of antichrist expresses this graphically. Not only will antichrist bring blasphemy to its climax, taking "his seat in the temple of God, proclaiming himself to be God" (2 Thess. 2:4), but his activity will be a reverse mirror-image of Christ's: Both he and Jesus will have a "coming" (parousia; 2:8, 9); he will come working apparent miracles (2:9); he is a "son" (of perdition [2:3]); his coming is a "mystery" (2:7; cf. 1 Cor. 2:7, Rom. 16:25-26, Eph. 3:3-4, etc.); he will finally be "revealed" (2:3, 6, 8; cf. 2 Thess. 1:7, etc.).

With different imagery the Book of Revelation describes a final, all but irresistible political "Beast" (Rev. 13:1-10) whose power is consolidated by a religious Beast having horns like a lamb but speaking like a dragon (13:11-18). Such symbolism is clear. Evil is neither shapeless nor merely individual. It takes corporate form. It underlies the grasping of political states for total power over their subjects. At its most potent it is consolidated by religious organizations which align total loyalty to themselves with total loyalty to such states. For only through religion can political organizations take captive the deepest springs of human fear and hope. In the final stages of present history, then, the true Church may expect the emergence of such a totalitarian power, supported by a religious body somehow resembling the Church.

This conclusion underlines some possible perils of postmillennialism. In searching for historical manifestations of Christ's advancing reign, it is easy to form alliances with what seem to be the progressive trends of one's era—especially if they bear the name or imprint of Christianity. But eschatology warns us that evil can cloak itself, and will attain its most overwhelming dominion, under such a disguise.

2. *The Conversion of Israel.* While a large-scale conversion of Jews towards the end fits smoothly into a dispensational scheme, it can be affirmed apart from this system. Paul asserts it emphatically in Romans 11. Sometimes this chapter has been treated as a minor digression, but this judgment is far from true. Throughout his ministry Paul inquired passionately as to what had become of God's plan for Israel. If God had "rejected his people whom he foreknew" (Rom. 11:2), then Yahweh's promises and Yahweh's faithfulness, the very realities on which the gospel itself was based, were unreliable. Paul began Romans by wrestling with this question (esp. Rom. 3:1-4). Though he did not return to it until Chapters 9-11, this is no indication that he dropped it. Rather, Paul found that he could not answer it until he had sketched the historical and cosmic breadth of God's saving work (Rom. 3:5—8:39).

Israel's coming "ingrafting" is another indication that eschatology has to do not merely with a heavenly or an existential realm but also with concrete history. It helps indicate that the *eschaton* is not the replacement of one kind of reality by another but the final interweaving of God's acts in all dimensions. It also indicates that the present history of Jewish people is not at all outside God's main concern.

3. *The "Already."* We have discussed the Tribulation, with its antichrist, and Israel's conversion as future events. Yet like other eschatological realities, they are "already" present in some sense.

John reports that many antichrists are already active (1 John 2:18, 4:3; 2 John 7; cf. Mark 13:21–22 and par.). Ever since Jesus came, not only has the gospel been proclaimed and lived but evil has sought to extend its range by appearing in similar dress (cf. 2 Cor. 11:14–15). Similarly, while we can anticipate a "Great Tribulation" of unique intensity before the end, "tribulation *(thlipsis)*" is a common experience of Christians in all generations (Acts 14:22, Rom. 5:3, John 16:33, etc.).[18] In both phases tribulation arises not merely from accident or misfortune but from the opposition of the powers (cf. 12:7–17). Finally, from the very beginning the Church has been constituted not merely of Gentiles but of both Jews and Gentiles united in profound harmony (Eph. 3:3–6). This union is a sign of God's continued faithfulness to Israel and a promise of Israel's final ingathering.

So far, however, our discussion has not indicated whether one of the three above schemes (amillennialism, historic premillennialism, or dispensational premillennialism) is preferable. Can theology decide for one over the others? We can find out by examining two more possible events.

4. *A Secret Rapture?* As far as the order of the events is concerned, dispensationalism differs from historic premillennialism by distinguishing two phases in Christ's return and by placing the first, the secret rapture of the Church, before the Tribulation and Israel's conversion.[19] We can evaluate the comparative strengths of both chronologies by examining the evidence for such a rapture. If one sharply distinguishes God's programs for Israel and for the Church, this return seems appropriate; it removes the Church from earth and facilitates the resumption of the Israel program. But apart from such an assumption, what evidence is there?

First, many gospel passages warn that Christ will return suddenly, or "imminently":

---

[18] See Erickson, pp. 152-56.

[19] Robert Gundry has denied a pre-Tribulation rapture while seeking to retain a basically dispensational eschatology. He expects God to deal with Israel during the Tribulation much as dispensationalists normally anticipate; he expects the millennium to be largely Israelo-centric; etc. (*The Church and the Tribulation*, esp. pp. 9-28). Perhaps, then, certain features of dispensationalism might be retained even apart from the pre-Tribulation rapture position. Our present chapter, however, deals only with the order of events which dispensationalists normally anticipate. We will discuss dispensationalism's other features in Chap. 11.

But of that day or that hour no one knows, not even the angels in heaven, nor the Son, but only the Father....Watch therefore—for you do not know when the master of the house will come, in the evening, or at midday, or at cockcrow, or in the morning—lest he come suddenly and find you asleep! (Mark 13:32–36; cf. Matt. 25:1–13, Luke 12:35–40).

Similarly, the epistles often speak of Christians eagerly awaiting Christ's return (Rom. 8:19–25, Tit. 2:12–13, James 5:8–9). But, dispensationalists argue, Christ's coming cannot be imminent if various other events (e.g., Tribulation, Israel's conversion) must occur first. Eagerness and urgency cannot be maintained if we know that Jesus will not come until certain other things happen. Consequently those texts which picture him returning following other occurrences cannot refer to that coming for which we are always to watch. There must be an earlier return.

Second, dispensationalists argue that the Bible teaches the Church's absence during the Tribulation. The Tribulation will be a time of God's wrath, but many texts promise God's protection from this wrath (1 Thess. 1:10, 5:9; Rom. 5:9), and from severe trials (Luke 21:36, 2 Pet. 2:6–9, Rev. 3:10). Third, one text seems to clearly teach a rapture:

the Lord himself will descend from heaven with a cry of command, with the archangel's call, and with the sound of the trumpet of God. And the dead in Christ will rise first; then we who are alive, who are left, shall be caught up together with them in the clouds to meet the Lord in the air (I Thess. 4:16–17).

Taken together, these texts and arguments can be enlisted to support an earlier, secret return of Christ to rapture the Church, even apart from dispensationalist presuppositions.[20] However, they are less than conclusive.

First, warnings about Christ's imminent return need not mean that he might come at absolutely any moment. They may simply indicate that, while other events must first occur, their exact number, nature, and duration is unknown. Second, while the Church is indeed to be protected from God's direct wrath, this provision need not imply removal from all circumstances in which it is poured out on others. For we have seen that Christians, rather than being removed from tribulation, may normally expect to experience it. Finally, if 1 Thessalonians 4 is speaking of a secret return, it is strange that Jesus will come "with a cry of command, with the archangel's call, and with the sound of the trumpet of God." Moreover, this picture of the saints meeting Christ in the air need not mean that they will remain there for several years; they may well be joining his victorious descent to earth.

In sum, apart from dispensationalism's sharp distinction between Israel and the Church, the above texts offer little support for a pre-Tribulation rapture. On the other hand Scripture usually represents Jesus' return as a single event.

---

[20] See John Walvoord, *The Return of the Lord* (Findlay, Oh.: Dunham, 1955), and *The Rapture Question* (Findlay, Oh.: Dunham, 1957); Rene Pache, *The Return of Jesus Christ* (Chicago: Moody, 1955).

So far as the order of coming events is concerned, then, dispensational premil-lennialism is weaker than historic premillennialism or amillennialism.

5. *A Millennium.* So far we have spoken in a unified manner of the coming *eschata*—Christ's return, resurrection, judgment, the defeat of evil, the renewal of the cosmos. For these events are often misunderstood when the theological significance that unites them is forgotten. Moreover, even many premillennial-ists acknowledge that Scripture usually pictures them as occurring together.[21] Is there any reason, then, to make chronological distinctions among them? Pre-millennialism offers the only important possible reason: Because an historical millennium follows Christ's return, the other four events must be divided into two phases. However, only one biblical text seems to definitely teach a millen-nium: Revelation 20. A decision between amillennialism and premillennial-ism, therefore, requires that we must consult this passage.

Premillennialists interpret the scenes pictured between Revelation 19:11 and 22:6 as occurring in chronological order. Following a decisive defeat of God's enemies (19:11–21), Satan is bound for "one thousand years" (20:1–3; for many, the "Millennium" need not be exactly this long.). Then those who had been martyred for their faith come to life; they reign one thousand years with Christ, sharing in his judging activity; this is "the first resurrection" (20:4–6). Following the millennium, Satan is set free, gathers the nations for battle against God but is defeated and thrown into the lake of fire (20:7–9). Then the rest of humankind is raised, and some are also thrown into this lake (20:11–14). Finally, the new heavens and new earth are ushered in (21:1–22:6).

Amillennialists argue that this section of Revelation cannot be interpreted as a continuous chronological sequence. For most amillennialists, in fact, Rev-elation as a whole consists of parallel accounts of the entire period from Jesus' coming onward.[22] Accordingly, Revelation 20:4–6 does not describe an histori-cal period following 19:11—20:3. Instead it symbolizes the way in which saints reign with Christ throughout the Christian era. But then what can coming to life and reigning with Christ mean? For most amillennialists, such expressions symbolize the present existence of Christian "souls" (20:4) in heaven.[23]

These interpretations leave two alternatives. Either, following premillennial-

[21] E.g., George Ladd in Clouse, pp. 189-91.

[22] Nevertheless Revelation as a whole involves "a certain amount of eschatological progress" so that the parallelism among its sections is a "progressive parallelism." Thus, "Since Satan is the supreme opponent of Christ, it stands to reason that his doom should be narrated last." (Anthony Hoekema in Clouse, pp. 156-159.) For such an interpretation of Revelation, see William Hendrikson, *More than Conquerers* (Grand Rapids: Eerdmans, 1940); G. R. Beasley-Murray, *The Book of Revelation* (Lon-don: Marshall, Morgan and Scott, 1974); and Robert Mounce, *The Book of Revela-tion* (Grand Rapids: Eerdmans, 1977). (Mounce, however, is a premillennialist.)

[23] A few interpret it as a "spiritual" birth occurring in this life; but then martyrdom and resistance to the beast would also need to be interpreted spiritually. Given the very real martyrdom occurring as the book was written, this seems highly unlikely.

ism's more literal, historical reading we must speak of a coming chronological millennium followed by the new heavens and earth, or, following amillennialism's more figurative, spiritual reading we must speak of an "intermediate state" far more active and triumphant than we have acknowledged (Chap. 8). It is not self-evident which of these readings is appropriate for Revelation 20. Decisions of this sort depend partially on overall eschatological considerations. Consequently we must ask whether reasons of this kind can help us decide. If they cannot, we shall have to regard premillennialism and amillennialism as different models whose overall implications theology should refrain from synthesizing.

In several ways amillennialism emphasizes the "already" more than the eschatology we have so far developed. Its proponents often argue that it focuses hope synoptically towards the future consummation rather than splitting it up among various events. However, its assertions about "souls" of Christians "already" reigning and judging with Christ is at least as likely to focus attention "upwards" and away from Christ's future victory and reign.[24] Moreover, by regarding Satan's binding and Christ's millennial rule as already actualized [25], amillennialism, which has often been indistinguishable from postmillennialism[26], can dim our sense of evil's reality and of our conflict with it. The more that the actualization of Christ's reign is stressed, the easier it becomes to regard current governments as his direct representatives, and their standards of justice as his. One can assume that the Last Judgment will be executed according to these same standards, so that those who conform most fully to the current *status quo* will receive the greatest reward. Conversely, one can use the threat of final judgment, as authoritarian societies often have, to discourage behavior which challenges the present system. Finally, in all these ways and in expecting the consummation to arrive all at once, amillennialism can regard eschatological fulfillment as something which occurs too instantaneously and is received too passively rather than as something which arrives only after a time of struggle and which involves our participation.

Premillennialism, on the other hand, accentuates the "not yet" somewhat more. The fulfillment of Christ's destiny and ours need not be actualized so fully in a present, heavenly, "intermediate state." It is easier to think of Christ's current reign as co-existing with the fact that evil seems to be increasing as the

[24] Hoekema admirably attempts (but in our view fails) to combine the present reign of "souls" with a strong emphasis on the future resurrection of the body (*The Bible and the Future*, pp. 86-108).

[25] Some have preferred the term "actualized millennialism" for the standard "amillennial" view. Rather than implying that its adherents believe in no millennial reality of any sort, it indicates that the realities expressed in Revelation 20 are largely actualized already. (Jay Adams, *The Time is at Hand* [Philadelphia: Presbyterian and Reformed, 1970], pp. 7-11).

[26] Erickson, pp. 75-76.

consummation nears. One is more likely to feel that Christians must often come into conflict with the ethical and political practices of their societies. Premillennialists will more often suppose that those who oppose the current status quo, rather than those who enforce it, are likely to be vindicated at the coming judgment. Finally, by indicating that even the consummation will not come all at once, premillennialism prevents our ultimate hope from focusing on some thing that will arrive too instantaneously and without struggle on Christ's part and ours. Even after Christ returns, life will still be a relationship with him; we will have to participate actively in it and will not be entirely isolated from the threat of evil. Premillennialism can remind us that our ultimate hope must always be for Christ himself, that it must rest on what he "already" has done and is doing for and with us, that it will always, even beyond the millennium consist in a relationship that involves our activity.

6. *The Nature of the Millennium.* Can theology say anything more about what the millennium, or any era beyond it, will be like? Although we must distinguish between this period and the final coming of the new heavens and earth, each will involve transformations of our present world. Thus both will (1) be continuous with its basic spatio-temporal structure and (2) exhibit discontinuous features which we cannot now describe. We can expect the new heavens and earth to exhibit greater transformations than the millennium (though perhaps some may be gradually introduced during the earlier period?). Should any spaceless, timeless realm lie even beyond the final coming of Heaven to earth, we have no biblical evidence for it.

Since each person's individual traits are bound up with their physical constitution, the resurrection of our bodies in a world with some spatio-temporal features means that individuality will be preserved. Christian hope is not merely for the survival of our deeds or influence, nor for our merging into an impersonal Brahman. We will be recognizable to each other and will rejoice in each other as the individuals we were, even if greatly changed. Our bodies, however, not only distinguish us, but as we shall see (Vol. II, Chap. 5), they also unite us with others. The millennium and the new earth, accordingly, will be eras of social activity and harmony. They will fulfill human hopes for justice, righteousness, and peace.

Since evil will not be fully conquered even in the millennium, some struggle with it may occur throughout. Perhaps the evil works of Christians will be "burned up" during this time. Towards the end we may expect a final outbreak and conquest of evil. Following this the premillennial scheme rightly anticipates a resurrection and judgment of all those not raised and judged at Christ's return. Should the millennium then merge gradually into the new heavens and earth, a gradual annihilation of those condemned could could then occur.

C. The Subjective Dimension

True hope requires an object. Without it hope becomes vague, wishful, and often unrealistic. True hope for history's future requires concrete events and visions. If biblical revelation does not provide them, human philosophy and speculation will. The above overview of coming events has given hope something concrete enough to kindle its energy. Since we believe that certain things will surely occur, we can undertake those projects which lead in their direction with confidence and enthusiasm.

At the same time hope rigidifies if one attempts to spell out the future too exactly. Joyous (or fearful) anticipation turns into hard calculation. It turns from the One who is coming and will come to the things that he will bring. Since it knows exactly what will happen, it can cease its watchful dependence on God and seek to bring the kingdom by its own efforts. The above overview has sketched the character and timing of coming events only within very broad limits. As we move towards the future, we must be ready for many surprises. The king who is coming, not the details of his kingdom, must remain the ultimate focus of our hope.

CHAPTER TEN

Revelation as Personal

W e have sought to begin theologizing by outlining a vision of the ultimate goal of all Christian hoping and striving. The coming eschatological consummation will bring all God's purposes for humanity and the cosmos to fruition. It will be breathtakingly universal in scope. All dimensions of the universe will be touched by the transformations it will bring. Yet if systematic theology is to guide the Church's worship, fellowship, and mission, it cannot stop with portraying the future. Even if the Church be fairly clear about what God will ultimately do, it is often far from clear as to what God is doing now. Numerous ideologies, movements, and groups claim to be promoting human wholeness and peace. But which are really in accord with the peace which Christ will bring?

And how should the Church respond to them? Other ideologies and persons seem to be working against Christ; but are they really? What is the proper response to them?

In other words, as the Church seeks to understand today's varied and swiftly-changing context, it inevitably raises the question of revelation. Where is God acting? How is God acting? How can we be certain? When these questions are raised in the context of the Church's life and mission, the issue of revelation is not merely an academic one. It has to do with more than the relationship of scientific, philosophical, and religious ways of knowing. It is concerned with more than theoretical probability or certainty. It is above all an issue of mission and of action. How can we discern God's leading? How can we assure people including, at times, ourselves that God is really speaking and that God's words are true?

177

Some, however, would object to defining the theological topic of revelation so broadly. Revelation, they would argue, is objective. God has already been revealed in the histories of Israel, Jesus, and the early Church. This revelation is definitively recorded in sacred Scripture (and, Catholics would add, in Church tradition). If we broaden revelation to encompass all those ways in which God speaks in the present all those intuitions, experiences, and events through which people think that they hear God's voice we will have difficulty distinguishing between what comes from God and what comes from ourselves.

For this reason, some conservative theologies distinguish Revelation from illumination.[1] The former is the content of what God reveals. The latter is the insight and appropriation of human subjects, guided by the Holy Spirit. This approach enables theology to stress (kerygmatically) that human awareness of God is based on, and is a response to, God's prior initiative. However, when we begin theologizing from the point where kerygma encounters context, we find that divine initiative and human response are continually intertwined. Were we to describe revelation's content in a wholly objective manner, we would immediately abstract ourselves from this context, only to return to it (under the heading of illumination) much later. But then questions about how God calls, challenges, and motivates about all those things that really happen when God becomes known would become separated from the topic of revelation. Systematic theology could easily become absorbed as it often has in delineating the precise contours of revealed knowledge, all the while forgetting what God's revelation really means for the worshiping, fellowshipping, and witnessing community.

To avoid this we prefer to handle under the heading of Revelation the broad range of issues that arise when one asks: How God is known? From the beginning, then, we must ask how revelation's objective and subjective characteristics are intertwined. Yet in this process (as those who distinguish revelation from illumination remind us), we must also carefully establish how they are distinct.

More precisely stated, the question of revelation will prove to have at least four aspects. Our present and future hope are revealed decisively in the kerygma. Yet the kerygma, while it points the Church forward, also directs it towards the past. First, then, revelation is historical. At the same time, these events and their significance are known largely through the Bible, where they are conveyed largely through verbal propositions. (Moreover, church tradition, if it be considered revelatory, also contains many assertions.) Revelation, secondly, is also propositional.

Third, questions about revelation are not merely requests for information. They arise from quests for personal and social meaning. Moreover, the keryma indicates that what God reveals transforms lives and energizes action (Chap.

[1] See Millard Erickson, *Christian Theology*, Vol. I (Grand Rapids: Baker, 1983), pp. 251-58. For discussion of the issue, see Donald Bloesch, *Essentials of Evangelical Theology*, Vol. I (San Francisco: Harper, 1978), pp. 51-56.

2). Revelation, in other words, encounters us not only externally, through history and the written word, but also inwardly, through the Spirit. Revelation is also personal.

Finally, we notice that revelatory events and propositions are surprisingly particular: they concern mostly the history of Israel, Jesus, and the early Church. Personal encounters with God are also unique and particular. Yet revelation's ultimate scope and aim is universal. Our study of revelation's first three dimensions, then, will repeatedly raise a fourth question: to what extent is revelation "special" and/or "general"? That is, to what extent is revelation focused through the Bible and perhaps tradition (special)? To what extent is it available to everyone apart from these sources (general)?

Since all the above dimensions of revelation are interrelated, none can be discussed in isolation. Accordingly our perspective on them all will develop gradually as we proceed. Constructive conclusions about revelation as personal, the subject of this chapter, will begin emerging as we consider revelation as historical, the subject of Chapter 11. Our perspective on both will be further developed as we explore revelation as propositional, the subject of Chapter 12. Throughout these chapters the relationship of special and general revelation will keep recurring. We will develop a synthetic perspective on all these dimensions (including the role of tradition) in Chapter 13. We can best get our bearings by first considering how these dimensions were emphasized in some of the historical movements with which we are familiar.

I. Revelation: An Historical Overview

The issue of special and general revelation has been around since the dawnings of Christian theology. This is quite understandable. Since theology seeks to communicate the kerygma to its contemporary context, theologians have usually asked whether any true knowledge of God which could serve as a "point of contact" was available to everyone in their context.

Justin Martyr said "Yes." When he claimed that the Logos which became incarnate in Jesus was the same Logos operative in all human reason, he laid the foundation for considering certain philosophical, scientific, and moral insights as products of general revelation (Chap. 1 above). We have seen that thinkers like Origen continued this emphasis; others, like Irenaeus, grounded their theological assertions very largely on the history known through Scripture. The dispute over general and special revelation became acute when certain Medieval theologians made insights from Aristotle (a form of general revelation) foundational for their theology. However when Thomas Aquinas distinguished two levels of revelation (Chap. 4 above), he settled the issue with a precision that satisfied many for centuries to come.

For Aquinas, we remember, revelation on the lower, or natural, level was available to everyone who utilized their senses, reason, and conscience correctly. By means of it, people who had never heard the kerygma could know certain things about God (that God exists, that God is immutable, etc.) and about human destiny (that we ought to pursue the cardinal virtues, etc.). However, saving knowledge of God was available only through the higher revelation known through the Bible and the Church. Here alone can we learn, for example, about God becoming incarnate in Christ or about the theological virtues. But whether speaking of lower or higher levels of revelation, Aquinas made some important assumptions about the form which revelation takes. For Aristotle, truth, the object of science and philosophy, was expressed in propositions. A proposition is a statement which asserts or denies the connection of a predicate with a subject. Now since theology deals with truth, Aristotle's Medieval followers assumed its truth must also be expressed in propositions. Consequently, although the contents of both levels of revelation differed, the form in which they were expressed was the same. Revelation of both sorts, that is, was understood to be the communication of principles, doctrines, and other sorts of information. Belief or faith in what God revealed was understood to be intellectual assent to these propositions.[2]

During the Reformation the issue of revelation took on a new dimension. For John Calvin true knowledge of God consisted not only of propositional information but involved personal reverence and love. Accordingly natural (or general) revelation could be evaluated from two standpoints. First, Calvin acknowledged that even in our fallen condition, general revelation teaches everyone that God exists must be obeyed. Nevertheless it can never bestow the love and reverence which lead to true obedience. Therefore (and second), general revelation is sufficient only to show us our shortcomings, to render us "inexcusable," but never to bring salvation.[3] Saving (or special) revelation, then, must have a different content. It will tell of God's redeeming acts through Christ. These can be expressed by means of propositions. However, more than communication of information must take place. For salvation occurs only when one's heart is touched, when true reverence and love for God are kindled. And this happens only when God's Spirit convinces each person that Christ's work is effective "for me."[4] Consequently special revelation must be not only propositional but also personal.

Over the next few centuries Believers' churches stressed revelation's personal dimension. Without the Spirit, they emphasized, the written Word with its

---

[2] In fact, it has always remained quite central in Eastern Orthodxy (Lossky, *Orthodox Faith*, pp. 13-25). Nevertheless, the highly propositional notion that emerged in Western Christianity, and especially in Thomism, has had greater impact on subsequent discussion of this topic. Cf. John Baille, *The Idea of Revelation in Recent Thought* (New York: Columbia, 1956), pp. 3-5; Thomas Aquinas, *Summa Theologia*, II, ii, Q. 1, a 2. For a general discussion, see Etienne Gilson, *Reason and Revelation in the Middle Ages* (New York: Scribners, 1948). A complete history of this subject would show that the "personal" dimension of revelation was acknowledged in various ways in Patristic and Medieval theology.

[3] *Institutes*, pp. 68-69.

[4] Ibid, pp. 74-75, 78-81; cf. p. 561.

propositions can become a mere dead letter. Protestant orthodoxy, however, in seeking firm theological foundations for its struggle against Catholicism, increasingly emphasized revelation's propositional character. Such propositions, we have learned, often served as premises for orthodoxy's deductive method (Chap. 5). Nevertheless, while insisting that saving knowledge of God involved assent to revealed propositions, like Calvin orthodox theologians also underlined the personal dimensions of reverence and trust.[5]

For Protestants, the Reformation had eliminated many items which Catholics had regarded as objects of special revelation: purgatory, hierarchies of saints and angels, etc. Then as the Enlightenment's critical and scientific mentality won wider acceptance, the Bible itself was criticized. Many of Protestantism's specially revealed beliefs were placed in doubt. The scope of "special"' revelation shrank. Yet at the same time reason seemed increasingly capable of explaining all things. Accordingly, liberally-inclined theologians tended to minimize or abandon the notion of "revelation" itself.[6]

Yet even though they seldom used the term, the leading liberal theologians prepared the way for a new notion of revelation. With its propositional, or "objective" content rendered questionable, revelation's personal, or "subjective" side came to be stressed. For Friedrich Schleiermacher, we remember, propositions cannot be direct objects of faith. God is truly revealed in moments which lie beneath explicit conscious awareness (Chap. 4). And for Albrecht Ritschl all knowledge of God involved value judgments. God is truly known only when we apprehend the significance that God has for our moral lives. Accordingly, Ritschl insisted that

> we ought not to strive after a purely theoretical and disinterested knowledge of God as an indispensable preliminary to the knowledge of faith. To be sure, people say that we must first know the nature of God and Christ before we can ascertain their worth for us.... The truth rather is that we can know the nature of God and Christ only in their worth for us.[7]

Ritschl, of course, did not feel that the value which God has for us could be perceived apart from some knowledge of how God had acted in history. Liberal theology in general placed great emphasis on historical research. On one hand this emphasis was often very critical. It sought to eliminate those elements in

[5] For Protestant orthodxy, the essential elements of saving faith were: (1) *notitia*, intellectual apprehension of things necessary to faith; (2) *assensus*, assent to their truthfulness; and (3) *fiducia*, personal trust in and approporiation of their truth for the individual. While orthodoxy insisted that the first two must be present in any act of saying faith, they also stressed that the goal of faith is reached only with the third. (Heppe, pp. 530-34; Schmid, pp. 410-15; cf. the discussion in Hodge, Vol. III, pp. 41-93.)

[6] Baille, pp. 9-18.

[7] *The Christian Doctrine of Justification and Reconciliation*, p. 212.

Scripture and in historic Christian belief which seemed incompatible with the modern, scientific outlook. But even as much that seemed mythological or superstitious was being eliminated, it became clearer that the biblical God is revealed largely through historical acts which point forward toward a comprehensive climax. The "History of Religions School" constructed an overall theology of history. It located the special revelation of God recorded in Scripture within the generally knowable framework of Western culture's forward march.[8]

Because it intertwined biblical with Western history so closely, liberalism's emphasis on revelation's historical dimension was generally rejected by early neo-orthodoxy. Nevertheless, neo-orthodox theology tended to follow liberalism's emphasis on the personal dimension of revelation. Revelation (which once again became a common theological term) tended to mean some kind of specific encounter. For most neo-orthodox theologians, it could scarcely be general in character. Moreover revelation could not be directly expressed in propositions. Neo-orthodoxy also helped stimulate the biblical theology movement, which once again emphasized revelation's historical dimension. Yet while this movement generally distinguished biblical salvation history (*heilsgeschichte*) from history as a whole, many more recent movements (such as liberation theology) have argued that God's revealing activity can also be discerned in other spheres of historical and cultural activity.[9]

Our overview has shown that many who have emphasized one dimension of revelation have seen it as opposed to others. Since each dimension has often been most forcefully articulated by those who saw things in this way, we will explore revelation's personal, historical (Chap. 11), and propositional (Chap. 12) dimensions in their more extreme forms. But through dialogue with them we will begin constructing our own synthetic perspective.

II. Revelation As Personal

Although different historical movements have acknowledged revelation's personal dimension in various ways, neo-orthodoxy tended to stress it, in sharp contrast to other possible dimensions, as *the* characteristic of authentic revelation. This insistence was hardly unrelated to the apologetic context in which neo-orthodoxy arose. By the 1920s science could seemingly explain away almost any claim to revelation. But even more seriously, God no longer seemed to be speaking, to Western culture at least, at all. Could theology make credible the claim that God really revealed himself to humankind, even amidst an apparently godless and scientifically regulated world? The moment was particularly opportune for conceiving revelation in personal categories. Theology

[8] Especially influential were the writings of Ernst Troeltsch (1866-1923). See Benjamin Reist, *Toward a Theology of Involvement* (Nashville: Abingdon, 1965), esp. pp. 19-77.

[9] See Gutierrez, *Theology of Liberation*, pp. 27-37, 153-87.

could claim, on one hand, that all the major themes of Christian faith (God, revelation, salvation, faith, etc.) are personal and interpersonal realities. On the other hand certain features of deep personal experience seemed to elude the reductionist explanations of science.

We shall first describe the dominant neo-orthodox perspective. It regarded personal revelation as largely special, as uniquely connected with the Bible, preaching, and Christian tradition. We shall then turn to a view (advanced by Paul Tillich) which saw revelation occurring in more general ways among various religions and human experiences.

A. Revelation as Specific Personal Encounter

1. *Revelation as Divinely Initiated.* Neo-orthodoxy insisted, above all, that revelation is not a product of human experience but that it originates in God. Revelation occurs not because humans seek it; revelation occurs only when God, in sovereign freedom, decides to reveal himself. If God does not decide to reveal himself, we shall never know him. In seeking to express the uniqueness of revelation and its irreducibility to knowledge of other sorts, many neo-orthodox theologians made use of a sharp philosophical distinction between things and persons, between an "it" and a "thou."[10] The usual presentation divided all phenomena in the universe into these two classes. On one hand there are conscious, volitional, affective beings: human persons and God. Everything else—animal, vegetable, or mineral—is a "thing." Things, so the theory runs, do not change their nature. A thing's basic material structure is always the same; all alterations which they undergo happen according to scientific laws. In principle, science can fully describe the nature and behavior of any thing. Once we know these facts we can manipulate these objects as we please. Things do not initiate relationships with us. They do not present surprises which we are unable (in principle) to grasp through science. They simply wait for us to learn about them and do what we want with them.

But one cannot know persons simply by describing their given character; for persons are always in the process of change. This change does not follow rigid scientific laws. For what a person becomes depends on free decisions.[11] At the core, a person is a mysterious, elusive "I." This "I" can never be known by simply observing one's outward features and behavior. It can be known only when persons open up or disclose themselves and only by other persons who respond with similar openness. We cannot manipulate persons as we do things. We can know them only through yielding to and cooperating with them.

We remember that Bultmann held such a perspective (Chap. 4): The natural, historical, and social worlds obey invariable laws; but there is also an existential world of encounter and decision. Modern people know that God does

---

[10] Macquarrie, pp. 59-62. This distinction was widely popularized through Martin Buber's *I and Thou* (New York: Scribner's, 1958).

[11] Macquarrie, pp. 62-66.

not act directly in nature, history, or society.[12] Religion, therefore, can deal only with the realm of self-understanding. In this existentialist perspective the realm of thought was usually assigned to the side of things. Thought utilizes concepts. These are more useful when they are as precise, clear-cut, and invariable as possible. Thought seeks to link concepts into propositions, into assertions that subjects and predicates invariably go together. But, as Schleiermacher had also said, when we reduce religious awareness to propositions or doctrines, we are dealing with a dry, brittle skeleton, not with vibrant, living reality.[13] Consequently, rational thinking which is expressed in propositions cannot deal adequately with the personal realm.

In speaking of revelation, then, neo-orthodox theologians insisted that it is God's self-revelation. God in his sovereign freedom decides to open and reveal his inner self. These theologians frequently emphasized the sharp contrast between knowing about a person (knowledge consisting of information expressible in propositions) and directly knowing a person. Revelation was of the latter not the former sort.[14]

This sharp contrast between knowing about a person and directly knowing a person led most neo-orthodox theologians to disparage any sort of general revelation or natural theology. Natural theologies begin with facts and laws of nature or of moral experience and seek to reason from there to some transcendent Source or Cause. But, neo-orthodox theologians protested, such reasoning never gets beyond the impersonal chain of effects and causes. It can never lead to the truly personal God, who may disclose himself in a manner dramatically unlike anything we normally experience.[15] Yet only such a self-revealing God can truly be the sovereign Lord. For if I can know God through my own reflections on nature, culture or history, then such a god will be limited to the range of my experience and thought. I will not need to surrender to a God whose

---

[12] "Modern man always makes use of technical means which are the results of modern science. In the case of illness modern man has recourse to physicians, to medical science. In case of economic and political affairs, he makes use of the results of philosophical, sociological, economic and political sciences. Nobody reckons with direct intervention by transcendent powers." (*Jesus Christ and Mythology*, p. 36).

[13] *On Religion*, pp. 47-49. For the relationship between Schleiermacher's view of revelation and Bultmann's, see the latter's "Religion and Culture," in *The Beginnings of Dialectic Theology*, pp. 210-18.

[14] Emil Brunner, *Truth as Encounter* (Philadelphia: Westminster, 1973), pp. 31-40; William Hordern, *The Case for a New Reformation Theology* (Philadelphia: Westminster, 1959), pp. 61-65.

[15] Cf. p. 95 above on Karl Barth. This general line of argument can also be found in Schleiermacher (*On Religion*, pp. 35-36; *The Christian Faith*, pp. 133-37), and in Ritschl (*Justification and Reconciliation*, Vol. III, pp. 211-26). All such arguments are indebted to Immanuel Kant's *Critique of Pure Reason*.

thoughts and ways are infinitely higher than my own.[16]

Neo-orthodox theologians maintained that this perspective was the biblical one. They emphasized the Old Testament "theophanies," unexpected appearances of God at various times and places, such as Moses' encounter at the burning bush (Exodus 3) or Isaiah's vision in the temple (Isaiah 6). They noted that Yahweh often appeared in in his "glory," in an awesome, overwhelming form of the divine presence (Exod. 24:15-18, 40:34-38; Isaiah 6). They emphasized the way in which God spoke directly through the prophets: "Thus saith the Lord!" They noticed how often revelatory passages contain the phrase "I am Yahweh."[17] Above all, they stressed that God's ultimate revelation was his coming to humanity in Jesus Christ. When God revealed himself most fully, he revealed himself as a person.

In these important revelations it was clear that God took the initiative. God opened himself up in a way that the recipients could never predict nor control. Moreover, according to many neo-orthodox theologians, God remained sovereign even on the subjective side of such encounters. For they could be truly appropriated only through the work of the Holy Spirit.

2. *Revelation as Event.* As personal, revelation is also an event. When persons address us from the depths of their being, something happens. It is not merely that certain items of information become knowable. If this were all that occurred, we could ignore the information or simply make a mental note of it. But when we are thus addressed, we are met by a promise, a threat, an offer of love, a rebuke, etc. In such encounters we cannot remain neutral. We must respond in some personal manner, even if that be rejecting or fleeing the address. Such revelation is dynamic. It is God's own self-giving. It does not inform us about a situation. It creates a new situation. Revelation, so conceived, *is* interpersonal communion and communication. It is neither an object nor a proposition but an activity.

Of course, the biblical authors sought to convey the significance of revelatory events. They sought to give them some sort of interpretation. People today do the same. Interpretations are usually expressed by means of propositional statements. Nevertheless, neo-orthodoxy stressed that revelation occurs in the event—in God's dynamic, transforming activity—and is expressed only very indirectly in the interpretation.

3. *Revelation as Call to Decision.* Finally, as implied in this notion of activity,

---

[16] Brunner, *The Christian Doctrine of God* (Philadelphia: Westminster, 1950), pp. 121-23; *Revelation and Reason* (Philadelphia: Westminster, 1956), pp. 42-45. For the classic discussion on this theme by neo-orthodox theologians, see Barth and Brunner, *Natural Theology* (London: Centenary Press, 1946).

[17] For a discussion of such themes in relation to neo-orthodox theology, see John Cobb and James Robinson, eds., *Theology as History* (New York: Harper, 1967), pp. 42-62.

revelation makes a demand which calls us to decision.[18] Neo-orthodox theologians emphasized that one cannot really remain neutral where ultimate religious issues are concerned. Sophisticated modern people may feel that they can examine every issue from an uncommitted, objective vantage point and then decide at leisure how, or whether, to respond. Yet God always addresses us not with general announcements but with very specific claims: an offer of life, an urgent warning, a demand for action. Consequently, we can know God only when we respond to such claims. For knowledge of another person is attained only when we open ourselves in a way which corresponds to the other person's self-opening: by loving, heeding, obeying. In short, God as person is known only through decisions which co-respond to God's personal self-disclosures.

For many neo-orthodox theologians those actions to which God calls us might conflict sharply with conventional moral or political values. Neo-orthodoxy tended to view such standards as things, as invariable rules which shield one from the unsettling uniqueness of many decisional situations. Adherents of the personal view, then, could become nonconformists or radicals on social and political issues. On the other hand neo-orthodoxy could stress the uniqueness of each decision so strongly that one's responses to God might never fall into any clear pattern. Neo-orthodoxy could breed individualistic non-conformists having little involvement with broader movements and issues. Revelation, along with the rest of religious life, could be confined to each individual's world.[19]

4. *Summary.* In general, revelation "as specific personal encounter" emphasizes some features central to the kerygma. The kerygma certainly proclaims God's unexpected inbreaking into our world. The initiative lies with the divine. The kerygma, moreover, is not just a verbal message. It is itself an event. And its propositions refer to events. Finally, the kerygma calls one to decision. We can affirm neo-orthodoxy's effort to emphasize these features of revelation. This movement was seeking to rephrase, in our modern context, the Reformation's insistence that God is fully known only as he comes to us in Jesus Christ, and when this becomes subjectively alive for us by means of the Holy Spirit. Later on we will evaluate the conceptuality by means of which they sought to rephrase these things.

B. Revelation through "Ontological Shock"

When theologians like Karl Barth and Emil Brunner spoke of revelation, they freely applied personal terminology to God. They spoke as if God were a

---

[18] Esp. Rudolf Bultmann, "What Does it Mean to Speak of God?" (in *Faith and Understanding* [New York: Harper, 1969], pp. 51-65).

[19] For an account of Rudolf Bultmann's ethics, see Thomas Oden, *Radical Obedience* (Philadelphia: Westminster, 1964). Cf. Bultmann's view of Jesus' ethics (*Jesus and the Word* [New York: Scribners, 1924], pp. 65-110).

particular being with specific purposes, intentions, activities, and character.[20] Others like Rudolf Bultmann felt that one could never speak directly of God. For Bultmann, revelation communicated a self-understanding; an awareness of oneself as limited by death and freed by grace. God, of course, was the origin of such a self-understanding. Yet one could directly describe not what God does but only what happens to oneself.[21] In either case, however, revelation was regarded as special, as occurring only at God's specific initiative and as contrasting with and often shattering God-concepts and self-understandings prevalent in other religions and philosophies of life. In the twentieth century, however, personal categories have also been used to explain a more general kind of religious awareness. Some features of this approach can be found more than a century earlier.

Friedrich Schleiermacher argued that religion was not limited to specific, unique doctrines and experiences. Rather religious awareness is

> immediate consciousness of the universal existence of all finite things, in and through the Infinite, and of temporal things in and through the Eternal. Religion is to seek this and find it in all that lives and moves, in all growth and change, in all doing and suffering.[22]

Now if religious awareness involves all possible objects and experiences, then any one of them can be a medium for revelation. For the "Father" of liberal theology, "Every original and new communication of the Universe to man is a revelation....Every intuition and every original feeling proceeds from revelation."[23] Moreover, since these intuitions occur below our consciousness' threshhold, their authenticity cannot be objectively demonstrated. Their significance cannot be directly expressed through propositions.

At the height of World War I Rudolf Otto outlined an immediately influential description of such revelatory encounters. Otto insisted that they had to do primarily with "the Holy," a reality whose significance went beyond anything expressible in scientific or ethical categories. Otto described encounter with the Holy by means of the three Latin words *mysterium, tremendum, fascinans.*

By *mysterium,* Otto meant that the Holy is "Wholly Other" than anything

---

[20] For a defense of such "anthropomorphism," see Brunner, *The Christian Doctrine of God,* pp. 124-27.

[21] Bultmann initially proclaimed his allegiance to the arising "Dialectical Theology" (later, neo-orthodox) movement by asserting that "The subject of theology is God, and the chief charge to be brought against liberal theology is that it has not dealt with God but with man" ("Liberal Theology and the Latest Theological Movement," in *Faith and Understanding,* p. 29). However, since there is no direct way to speak of God, Bultmann concluded this article by explaining that "the subject of theology is God. Theology speaks of God *because* it speaks of *man* as he stands before God" (p. 52, italics ours). See also "What Does it Mean to Speak of God?"

[22] *On Religion,* p. 36.

[23] Ibid., p. 89.

else. By *tremendum*, he meant that when the Holy encounters us, it over-
whelms us; it strikes us with awe, even terror; it confronts us with a majesty, an
urgency, an energy before which humans are but "dust and ashes." At the same
time, however, such encounters are also *fascinans*. The Holy attracts us; it com-
municates mercy and love.[24] The Old Testament and Luther provided Otto
with dominant models of religious experience. Nevertheless he also spoke of
revelation occurring through a number of objects and experiences.

Influences from Schleiermacher and Otto were systematized in Paul Tillich's
account of revelation. According to Tillich every human is confronted by the
threat of "non-being." Although most people seldom face it consciously, at a
deep level everyone is anxious that their existence might disintegrate into
meaninglessness, absurdity, oblivion. Therefore revelation occurs in moments
of "ontological shock." These are moments when non-being threatens to
engulf everything. The individual, and perhaps the universe itself, seems to be
permeated with futility and purposelessness. Life seems about ready to collapse
into chaos. But precisely at such moments, when the threat of non-being is felt
most intensely, one can experience the power of being, of life and meaning
overcoming the threat. Just when one feels overwhelmed by nothingness, the
power of being reaches out and sustains, supports, and encourages one.[25]

Such experiences can occur, especially in the modern world, in a manner
which has no religious overtones. However, they have many features which
Christianity has associated with salvation. Being's acceptance and sustaining
of the distraught individual, for instance, seem to be what Christians call
"grace." For such individuals feel helpless, permeated to their core by non-being, and unworthy of deliverance. Moreover, being seems to take the initiative.
Being is experienced as coming from beyond one; reaching out, rescuing, and
drawing one into a pre-existing fullness of life and love.[26]

C. Comparisons and Contrasts

Revelation as "ontological shock" and as "specific personal encounter" are
most alike in their claim that revelation occurs in experiences which are
unique in kind and which therefore cannot be explained away or modified by
science or by criteria relevant for any other kind of truth. For both views, then,

---

[24] *The Idea of the Holy* (London: Oxford University, 1950), pp. 1-40; Otto felt that
Schleiermacher had understood revelation merely as an experience affecting one's
self-consciousness; one did not encounter God directly but could only infer, indirectly, that God must be its source. In contrast, Otto insisted that experience of the
Holy "indubitably has immediate and primary reference to an object outside the
self" (Ibid., p. 10). Consequently Otto's views greatly impacted the emerging neo-
orthodox movement, which often called God the "Wholly Other."

[25] *Systematic Theology*, Vol. I (Chicago: University, 1951), pp. 110-11, 113-14; cf. pp.
186-89.

[26] See also John Macquarrie, pp. 84-88.

revelation tends to be self-authenticating. When one is encountered by the self-revelation of another person, or by the Holy, or is by being, one tends to know it. It usually seems inappropriate to ask for evidence that this has really happened. Such experiences provide their own evidence.

To be sure, if one stresses that revelation occurs through Scripture or through preaching based on Scripture, one has some way of testing what has occurred. Alleged revelations must somehow be in accord with the Bible's basic themes. And even the validity of what occurs through "ontological shock" can be supported by certain rational arguments such as, for instance, that such experiences need not be illusory but may accord with accepted psychological data.[27] Nevertheless the more one emphasizes the distinctness of personal knowing from any other kind of knowing, the harder it is to determine how any other kind of experience, argument, or truth-claim could support or challenge its truth.

Revelation as "ontological shock" differs from revelation as "specific personal encounter" in its insistence that what is revealed is Being, not a particular being. Of course one can hardly avoid speaking of the initiative, deliverance, and grace which one experiences in personal terms. Tillich regards this as inevitable and even appropriate, so long as one realizes that personal language is symbolic. For revelation does not have a specific object. Instead the whole of reality is seen in a new way, from a new perspective, in a new depth. Revelation, one might say, is a manifestation and apprehension of the meaning of things. In such an encounter, then, "the person who receives the revelation sees and hears no more than any other person in the situation might see and hear."[28] Revelation does not interfere with the laws governing normal spatio-temporal processes. If it did, "the manifestation of the ground of being would destroy the structure of being."[29] Tillich emphatically calls such a supposition "demonic."

In other words, unique historical events or propositions about them cannot themselves be objects of revelation. In fact any sort of "Knowledge about nature and history, about individuals, their future and their past, about hidden things and happenings—all this is not a matter of revelation but of observations, intuitions and conclusions."[30] In this respect revelation as ontological shock is very similar to revelation as specfic personal encounter. For Bultmann unusual historical events cannot be objects of revelation:

> The thought of the action of God as an unworldly and transcendent action can be protected from misunderstanding only if it is not thought of as an action which happens between the worldly actions or events, but as happening within them. The

[27] See Macquarrie's discussion, pp. 90-103.

[28] Ibid., p. 89.

[29] Tillich, p. 116.

[30] Ibid., p. 110

close connection between natural and historical events remains intact as it presents itself to the observer. The action of God is hidden from every eye except the eye of faith. Only the so-called natural, secular (worldly) events are capable of proof. It is *within* them that God's hidden action is taking place.[31]

Bultmann, however, and more so Brunner and Barth speak more often of God, or of God's specific actions, being revealed. For the more common neo-orthodox view, revelation may not show us much about reality as a whole, but it does tell us something unique about God. For Brunner revelation is primarily God's manifestation of his own character, the announcement of his own "Name."[32] For Barth all revelation is of the Word who is Jesus Christ. In this sense, revelation has a distinct object, although this object is first and foremost the revealing Subject.

Finally, to this distinction between revelation as "ontological shock" and as "specific personal encounter" corresponds the fact that the former can occur in connection with a larger range of experiences and objects. Since "every person and every thing participates in being itself...(so says Tillich, reminding one of Schleiermacher) There is no reality, thing, or event which cannot become a bearer of the mystery of being and enter into a revelatory correlation."[33] Accordingly, Tillich can think of revelation as a process occurring places, in numerous cultures and religions. To be sure, being is most fully manifest in the revelation of the New Being in Jesus as the Christ.[34] Nevertheless for Tillich Jesus is more a symbol or a manifestation of a "general" revelatory process than he is the "special" agent and object of God's unique intrusion into this world. For Tillich God may be revealed most clearly in connection with the Christian tradition. But divine reality is being revealed far more universally: wherever individuals sense that the threat of non-being is overcome by a power beyond themselves.

D. A Critique

When systematic theology deals with the question of revelation, it seeks to answer the broad question of how God is known. In doing so, it cannot treat revelation simply as a body of information. Authentic questions about revelation, as Tillich rightly says, are questions of "ultimate concern." God's revelation(s) affect the whole person; our wills and feelings as well as our minds. They address and claim us at the core of our beings. The emphasis on revelation as personal has focused on this living context in which revelation occurs. It has helped theology broaden its traditional preoccupation with propositional content.

---

[31] *Jesus Christ and Mythology,* pp. 61-62.

[32] *The Christian Doctrine of God,* pp. 117-27.

[33] Tillich, p. 118.

[34] Ibid., pp. 135-37.

Nonetheless this modern view may have narrowed revelation in another way. For most of its proponents, revelation as personal encounter is opposed to revelation as propositional or revelation as historical event.[35] But in virtually identifying the sphere of revelation with the personal sphere, might they not have removed it from many other spheres of modern life? Might they have restricted God to a corner of contemporary existence, leaving social and economic forces to proceed unhindered along their frequently destructive paths? Let us reconsider the sharp distinction they make between persons and things or between knowing a person and knowing about a person. To be sure, this philosophic description says much that is true about persons. But on close examination, it proves to be overdone.

Even though opening oneself to another's mysterious, elusive "I" is at the core of personal relationships, those relationships involve more than this. They also involve accepting and relating to others in light of their specific physical, emotional, and cultural characteristics. This is especially true of Christian love, or *agape*. Agape as we shall see, is accepting others as they are and not as I might like them to be; love of others for their own sake, and not for what they can contribute to me (Vol. II, Chap. 3). In relating to others who remain distinct and different from myself, I need some awareness, for instance, of their emotional characteristics: Are they even-tempered or do they go "up and down?" I need to appreciate their physical and intellectual strengths and limitations. I need some grasp of how their upbringing and their culture have shaped them. And all of this information can be expressed in propositions. But if I have little awareness of such factors, I will be far more likely to relate to others as I wish they were, and not as they truly are. In short, true knowing of human "persons" involves knowing about and appreciating their thing-like characteristics.

What relevance might these general considerations have for questions as to how God is known? At first glance perhaps very little—for many of the thing-like characteristics just mentioned seem closely intertwinded with finitude. However, we remember that Jesus Christ, who shared our human finitude, is the supreme actualization of revelation as personal. Could this indicate that God's revelation, and perhaps even God himself, are also characterized in a fundamental way by features at least analogous to some of the thing-like phenomena we have discussed? In any case, the above considerations seriously challenge the dichotomy between persons and things so important for both theories. They raise questions as to whether one can truly encounter an Other without confronting a reality with specific, definite features. And they raise

---

[35] E.g., Hordern, p. 63: "what God reveals is not propositions and information—what God reveals is God.... When God's revelation comes to us, it does not come as propositions to subdue the mind; it comes as a challenge to the 'heart', it appeals to the whole man. The faith to which it calls us is not the submissive believing of propositions but the commitment of the self in trust to the God who is encountered."

the question whether this reality could be known unless these features were formulable in propositions. Said otherwise, a close look at human personal encounters leads us to ask whether the personal model of revelation can really articulate the kerygmatic concerns it desires to defend.

It desires, first, to stress the divine initiative. But if one cannot say what encounters one—if God's revelations have no formulable content—cannot one interpret them much as one wishes? How does one distinguish between what God is saying and one's own experiences? As conceived by the personal model, God may not appear as truly other and as challenging us decisively but as confusedly mixed with one's own moods and wishes.

The personal view desires, second, to assert the active, transforming character of revelation as event. But to do so it separates each event as personal experience from any interpretation formulated in propositions. Interpretations, however, by expressing the significance of events in general terms, link them together. They indicate patterns of significance and meaning.

But if revelation has to do only with events, and if interpretations are never part of revelation, what effect will these isolated occurrences really have? If revelatory events display no coherent patterns, if they do not point in certain directions, will they really transform their recipients' self-understanding and behavior? On the personal model, revelation may not bring real newness and change but may simply jolt one with unusual, unconnected experiences.

Finally, personal views set out to emphasize that revelation demands decision. Yet if the "Wholly Other" who encounters one is so little connected with historical events, or with social or ethical claims, or with anything at all that propositions can formulate, how can such encounters call one to meaningful decision in the rest of one's life? On the personal model God and any decisions to which we are called may simply be irrelevant to modern life.

All these questions recall our discussions of eschatology's subjective and objective sides. We insisted that eschatology must deal with the dynamics of hope (subjective), but that hope becomes empty and individualistic unless it is directed towards things that one can hope for (objective). In this chapter the personal view has helped us understand revelation's subjective dimension: When God becomes known, the persons involved will be transformed. Nevertheless we have suggested that revelatory experiences may become empty and individualistic unless they are initiated by and directed towards a definite Reality closely connected with particular events and situations.

But does revelation really have some such object(s)? So far we have only suggested, by analogy from our understanding of human interpersonal relations, that it perhaps might. But this suggested critique of the personal view cannot be substantiated, nor can an alternative understanding of revelation be articulated, until we carefully consider whether revelation might also have historical and propositional dimensions.

Suggestions For Further Reading

Baille, John. *The Idea of Revelation in Recent Thought.* New York: Columbia, 1956.

Barth, Karl. *Church Dogmatics.* Volume I, Pt. 1. New York: Scribner's, 1936 (esp. pp. 51-140).

Brunner, Emil. *Revelation and Reason.* Philadelphia: Westminster, 1943.

———. *Truth as Encounter.* Philadelphia: Westminster, 1943.

Bultmann, Rudolf. "The Concept of Revelation in the New Testament" in *Existence and Faith.* Cleveland: Meridian, 1960, pp. 58-91.

———. "What Does it Mean to Speak to God" in *Faith and Understanding.* New York: Harper, 1969, pp. 51-65.

Dulles, Avery. *Models of Revelation.* Garden City, New York: Herder & Herder, 1983.

Gilson, Etienne. *Reason and Revelation in the Middle Ages.* New York: Scribner's, 1948.

Hordern, William. *The Case for a New Reformation Theology.* Philadelphia: Westminster, 1959.

McDonald, H.D. *Ideas of Revelation: An Historical Study, A.D. 1700 to A.D. 1860.* London: Macmillan, 1959.

McDonald, H.D. *Theories of Revelation: An Historical Study, 1860-1960.* London: Alben and Union, 1963.

Neibuhr, H. Richard. *The Meaning of Revelation.* New York: Macmillan, 1941.

Oden, Thomas. *Radical Obedience: The Ethics of Rudolf Bultmann.* Philadelphia: Westminster, 1964.

Otto, Rudolf. *The Idea of the Holy.* London: Oxford, 1950.

Ramm, Bernard. *Special Revelation and the Word of God.* Grand Rapids: Eerdmans, 1961.

Schillebeeckx, Edward. *Revelation and Theology.* New York: Sheed and Ward, 1967.

Tillich, Paul. *Systematic Theology,* Vol. I. Chicago: University, 1951 (pp. 71-159).

Troeltsch, Ernst. *The Absoluteness of Christianity and the History of Religions.* Richmond: Knox, 1971 (first published in 1902).

CHAPTER ELEVEN

Revelation As Historical

S pecial revelation, as Chapter 10 demonstrated, must encounter and affect us personally. Yet most who emphasize this effect sharply distinguish the personal dimension from any sort of general revelation, and from revelation through propositions and historical events. While they intend to emphasize God's sovereignty and the dynamism of his revelatory will, we wondered if they might not really isolate God in a highly individualized corner of existence, leaving the modern forces of secularization, depersonalization, and cosmic destruction to go their way unhindered.

Is there a way to conceive revelation as occurring in more direct connection with the history in which we all participate? An initial clue can be found in the common New Testament word for revelation, *apokalupsis*. Literally this word means "removal of the veil." Apparently, then, revelation must be "the disclosure of what is veiled, the opening up of what is hidden."[1] A face behind a veil is fully and completely there. It is unknown only because something blocks our vision. Similarly it seems natural to assume that whatever knowledge or reality is to be revealed must be fully existent and complete. It must be unknown only insofar as human limitations or sins block access to it. Revelation through "ontological shock" fits this definition fairly well. Nothing new is revealed. The recipient perceives nothing that was not already there. But a "veil" is lifted from these things so that one now apprehends, in and through them, the conquest of non-being by being. Yet such an interpretation of *apokalupsis*, while apparently derived straightforwardly form the word's etymology, is

[1] Rudolf Bultmann, *Existence and Faith*, p. 59.

195

only partially correct. For while it adequately describes revelation as it occurred in many contemporary Greek religions, it pays insufficient attention to
the New Testament usage of this word. Frequently *apokalupsis* (and the verb
apokalupto) refer not to the unveiling of something already existing but to a future event. The return of Jesus is often called "the revelation of our Lord Jesus
Christ" (1 Cor. 1:7).[2]

Of course this coming revelation will involve unveilings. We have described
it as the Day when "the Lord comes, who will bring to light the things now
hidden in darkness and will disclose the purposes of the heart" (1 Cor. 4:5).
The deepest meaning of present and past reality, of "life, as it actually happened in its hourly, daily and yearly sequence" will become unmistakably
clear.[3] Nevertheless, Christ's coming revelation will be far more than an unveiling. As we have already shown, it will also be a judgment, a righting of
wrongs, a final conquest of enemies (Matt. 10:26; Luke 17:30; Rom. 2:5; 1 Cor.
3:13; 2 Thess. 1:7, 2:8). It will involve the resurrection of the body and a transformation of earthly reality whose character we can neither fully anticipate nor
predict (Rom. 8:18-19; 1 Peter 1:5-13, 4:13, 5:1). In short, this final revelation
will also be a new event—not merely the disclosure of something which already
exists. And as we have argued, this new event will affect the "objective" course
of history and the shape of the cosmos.

Of course, we are not insisting that the theological theme "revelation" coin-
cide exactly with the definition of *apokalupsis*. As we have just said, the former,
in our usage, covers all issues relating to the broad question of how God is
known. Still, the dominant usage of a central biblical term cannot help but
provide a clue for our kind of theology. If *apokalupsis* refers to a new, climactic
historical event having cosmic dimensions, what of other occurrences that
might be called revelation? Might some of them be connected with a stream
which flows in this direction? In other words, might revelation be not only personal but also historical?

In this chapter, we will first examine the "special" revelatory history found in
Scripture. Then, in Section II, we will ask what bearing this history might
have on that critique of revelation as personal with which we closed Chapter
10. This discussion, however, will not solve all questions as to how "special"
revelatory history might be connected with God's more "general" historical
work. So we will close this chapter by examining some important proposals as
to how biblical history might be connected with God's revealing activity today.

I. "Special" Revelation Through History

Neo-orthodoxy, as we know, generally sought to assert the uniqueness of biblical revelation. In so doing it tended to critique the earlier liberal notion of
revelation as historical. For liberalism, as neo-orthodoxy saw it, had subordi-

[2] Moltmann, *Theology of Hope*, pp. 44-45.

[3] Berkouwer, quoted on p. 146 above.

nated whatever historical themes it found in Scripture to its general theory of Western progress and superiority. Neo-orthodoxy, however, stimulated the rise of the biblical theology movement, which carried the search for the distinctive biblical mentality further. As it proceeded, biblical notions on almost every subject seemed deeply permeated by the theme of God's revelation through history.[4] Eventually a theme which had been rediscovered due to neo-orthodoxy's emphasis on biblical authority began to turn against its original parent.

Moving even beyond biblical theology, a newer "revelation as history" emphasis attacked neo-orthodoxy's personal view of revelation where it was most vulnerable: by examining those Scripture passages where God's revelation seemed most clearly personal.[5] Let us consider the classic instance of Moses at the burning bush. This encounter is indeed overwhelming (a *mysterium tremendum et fascinans*). Moses must approach with humility and awe (Exod. 3:5). Things are disclosed which he could not otherwise have known. Moses must make a difficult, decisive response to God's address (Exod. 3:11–12; 4:1,10).

But what is the substance of this revelation? It is not merely awareness of God's personal presence and the need to obey. God begins by identifying himself with Israel's past history (3:6). Then God unfolds a plan to deliver Israel from Egypt in the future (3:9–10). Even the subsequent announcement of God's name ("I am who I am," or "I will be what I will be") is not only a "dust and ashes" experience. It is given to aid Moses in explaining the historic task to which God is calling Israel (3:13–17).

Most dramatic personal appearances of God in Scripture occur in the context of calls to similar historical tasks whose particular features and far-reaching significance are also announced. Biblical theophanies interpret and describe history and employ propositions in doing so. This is obviously the case with Abram (Gen. 15, etc.), Jacob (Gen. 28:12–16), Samson's parents (Judges 13), Isaiah (chap. 6), Jeremiah (chap. 1), Ezekiel (chap. 1), Mary (Luke 1:26-38), Jesus (Matt. 3:13-17), Paul (Acts 26:12-18) and many others.

Clearly, then, the significance of these revelations cannot be limited to a personal kind of knowledge, understood as quite different from historical or propositional knowledge. But what positive understanding of revelation can closer examination of them give us? Notice first that many such encounters contain promises. God does not merely describe the present or predict the future in detached fashion but gives words of hope, challenge, comfort, and encouragement. Later on in biblical history, these promises are fulfilled. Nevertheless they often are not fulfilled in just the way that their addressees

---

[4] Childs, *Biblical Theology in Crisis*, pp. 39-47.

[5] See esp. Wolfhart Pannenberg, *et. al.*, *Revelation as History* (Philadelphia: Westminster, 1968). Our remarks below follow the general approach taken especially in Rolf Rentdorff's article "The Concept of Revelation in Ancient Israel." Pannenberg's own position, however, moves beyond these findings from biblical (special) revelation into a more general theory which we will examine in Sections III and IV.

anticipate. How, for instance, would Abram and Sarai have understood the following promise?

> I will make of you a great nation, and I will bless you, and make your name great, so that you will be a blessing. I will bless those who bless you, and whoever curses you I will curse; and in you all the families of the earth shall be blessed. (Gen. 12:2-3)

In all likelihood they would have expected their descendants to become a great and powerful nation, probably beginning in their lifetime. But years passed. Then decades. Still the initial heir of the promise had not even been conceived! Abraham and Sarah's pilgrimage took many twists and turns. Often they were tempted to doubt God's veracity (Gen. 17:17, 18:12). Yet finally the heir was born. God's promise was fulfilled—even if on a much lesser scale than they had hoped to see. The fulfillment of this promise stretches through the entire Bible. Sometimes it is fulfilled partially. Almost never is it fulfilled exactly as people expect. Yet as recent biblical scholars have noticed, much of biblical history takes place, so to speak, between promise and fulfillment. It is through these periods of waiting, striving, hoping and doubting that God's character and will become more fully known. In the course of carrying out those tasks to which God calls people, God is revealed.

This basic relationship between promise and fulfillment is quite different from the sort of literal biblical interpretation espoused by dispensationalism (Chaps. 6 and 9). According to dispensationalists, promises must be fulfilled in a literal way. Therefore, if an Old Testament passage promises something to "Israel," the nation Israel must experience its fulfillment. However, if it is the very nature of God's revelatory and saving work to move continually beyond the horizons of what had formerly been experienced and known, then one would expect fulfillments to often contain surprising dimensions which transcend the literal reading of promises. This does not mean, however, that fulfillments need have no relationship to the promises' literal features, so that anything whatsoever might be interpreted as a fulfillment. In order for a promise to "Israel" to be fulfilled in the Church, some appropriate historical continuity between the two must exist. The literal (or propositional) features of a promise mark out a broad range within which any valid fulfillment must fall. Nevertheless, while the fulfillment cannot contradict these literal paramaters of the promise, it can go well beyond them.[6]

God is also revealed at the end of many such journeys from promise to fulfillment. Yahweh becomes known especially when, after times of struggle and trial, he rescues and delivers his people.[7] Through his saving acts (such as the

---

[6] See esp. Chapter 12, Section I and Chapter 14, Section IV. Our overall critique of literal interpretation will be cumulative, emerging from the positive hermeneutic which we develop in many places, rather than being stated in detail at any one point.

[7] Rendtorff, in Pannenberg, pp. 30-33.

Exodus from Egypt) Yahweh's name and power become known to Israel and throughout all the earth.[8] Thus Israel, looking back to many such deliverances, can proclaim:

> O sing to the Lord a new song, for he has done marvelous things! His right hand and his holy arm have gotten him victory. The Lord has made known his victory, he has revealed his vindication in the sight of the nations. He has remembered his steadfast love and faithfulness to the house of Israel. All the ends of the earth have seen the victory of our God! (Ps. 98:1–3).

Notice that God's saving victory is the fulfillment of his promise: "he has remembered his steadfast love and faithfulness." Note also that it is God's own self-vindication. Yahweh not only saves his people; he also reveals his own faithfulness, goodness, and power. The above psalm, in fact, points forward to the final Judgment (vv. 7–9). From another angle, then, we can see that the consummation of God's eschatological activity will at the same time be the ultimate revelation of God. From this perspective it becomes all the more clear why revelation cannot be reduced to existential encounters with individuals. God's character and also the deepest meaning of human existence and history can become fully known only as God defeats all forces of evil and establishes justice and peace.

Recent Old Testament study has shown that several other themes thought to express a personalistic understanding of revelation relate more directly to historical vindication. The phrase "I am Yahweh," for instance, has been regarded as Yahweh's "self-representation" in situations of direct personal encounter. It is more likely, however, that this formula is an abbreviation of such phrases as "I am Yahweh, who has brought you out of the land of Egypt" (Exod. 20:2); or "I am Yahweh, and beside me there is no savior" (Isa. 43:11), which express God's unique saving power. Very frequently this phrase occurs at the end of a prediction or promise: when God has judged or saved his people, then they shall know "that I am the Lord."[9]

References to God's "glory" have also been thought to support a personalistic view of revelation. When Yahweh descends upon Sinai in a cloud of glory, God seems to be directly present for communication with an individual, much as Rudolf Otto said (Exod. 24:15–18; cf. 16:7, 10; 40:34–38). In other passages, however, not only the place of encounter but also "the whole earth," is full of God's glory (Isa. 6:3). In still others, "glory" is an eschatological theme. The triumph of God's righteousness will be the manifestation of God's glory (Ps. 97:6). When "the glory of Yahweh will be revealed...all flesh will see it together" (Isa. 40:5). Indeed all God's activities and promises are moving towards

---

[8] Exod. 9:16; Deut. 3:24; Ps. 77:14-15, 106:8-12, etc.

[9] Rendtorff, pp. 38-45. Among the numerous examples of the future usage of this phrase are Exod. 7:17, 14:18; 1 Kings 20:13, 28; Ezek. 39:28; Isa. 45:3, 6, 49:23, 26.

the time when "the earth will be filled with the knowledge of the glory of Yahweh, as the waters cover the sea."[10]

According to the biblical writings, then, even when God reveals himself in a highly personal way, these encounters point towards and have to do with history. God is revealed through promises and through the long walk of faithfulness that stretches between promise and fulfillment. God is revealed through saving acts and will be most fully revealed in the final eschatological judgment and self-vindication towards which they point. Said otherwise; the biblical God is meaningfully known only as he proves himself in the arena of conflicting historical forces. In our human, historical world, many gods and many ideologies make claims to ultimate truth. Experiences often seem to belie the claims of Yahweh and of his Christ. The true God makes himself known only as he proves himself in the face of these contrary forces and experiences, only by overcoming their opposition. Consequently this God will not be fully revealed until all opposing forces are put "in subjection under his feet" (1 Cor. 15:27).

This then, in outline, is how historical revelation is presented in Scripture. Most of these themes were rediscovered by the biblical theology movement. By themselves however, they do not fully resolve systematic theology's questions. For the biblical theology movement was never clear as to how the biblical narratives related to the actual historical world in which we live. What was the real locus of such a revelation? Was it certain spatio-temporal "events" (such as the crossing of the Reed Sea) lying behind the biblical text and perhaps accessible to historical science? If so, the appropriateness of the biblical writers' interpretations of these events could be measured and perhaps discarded by reference to them. Or did revelation lie in the writers' interpretation? For if it did then perhaps the question of whether the events occurred as they are reported could be disregarded. And if so, one need not worry about how present or future revelation might affect the course of nature and history.

The biblical theology movement never dispelled this confusion "as to whether the element of revelation...lay in the text, in some positivity behind the text, or in a combination of text and event or mode of consciousness."[11] Langdon Gilkey critiqued the "biblical theologians" even more severely. According to him they actually held a purely naturalistic view of historical events. Yet God's "mighty acts" were mighty for the biblical writers largely because they were thought to have interrupted any such historical sequence. Thus Gilkey concluded "biblical theology's" emphasis on revelation in history was so much rhetoric. The movement never really asked what "God's mighty acts"

[10] Hab. 2:14, cf. Isa. 11:9 and Rendtorff, pp. 33-37.

[11] Childs, p. 52.

might mean in light of modern views of history.[12] Whether or not Gilkey was entirely fair to the biblical theology movement, he raised issues that systematic theology must face. In the following section we must probe into the relationship between "event" and "interpretation." Then in Section III we must ask how the largely special and ancient revelatory history presented in Scripture relates to God's more general and contemporary historical activity.

II. Revelation as Personal and Historical

In Chapter 10 we concurred with several features of the personal view of revelation: Revelation proceeds from the divine initiative; it is an event; it calls one to decision. Nevertheless we wondered whether this perspective's sharp distinction between persons and things isolated revelation from history and from modern life. The present chapter has confirmed the inadequacy of the person/thing dichotomy. Can we now suggest a better way of affirming those valid emphases of the personal view?

A. Revelation as Divinely Initiated

Proponents of the personal view insist that revelation is neither a product of human reasoning nor of human moral, aesthetic, or historical experience. It is disclosure of the divine will, which takes place when, where, as God chooses, and on which we are wholly dependent for meaningful knowledge of God.

The historical perspective also stresses the divine initiative. God announces the promises (whose contents take humans by surprise) when, where, and as he chooses. Similarly the fulfillments of these promises usually occur in unforseen ways. They contain elements that humans did not anticipate. In particular, Yahweh's acts of salvation and self-vindication often involve rescue from otherwise hopeless situations, and these acts often provide occasion for wonder and awe.[13]

In the personal view, however, revelation can be so lacking in content that it may not be clear that one is truly encountered by an Other. One may find it hard to distinguish between what God is really doing and saying and one's own moods and wishes (p. 192 above).

But in its historical dimension, revelation is associated with a definite content. A promise is specific. Fulfillments are particular events with definite features. In these ways, historical revelations have specific characteristics which

---

[12] "Cosmology, Ontology, and the Travail of Biblical Language," *Journal of Religion* 41 (1961), pp. 194-205. James Barr critiqued various views of revelation as historical in much the same way. See esp. *Old and New in Interpretation* (London: SCM, 1966), pp. 65-102. For a good overview of these issues, see Dulles, *Models of Revelation*, pp. 56-67.

[13] Thus Moltmann argues that in this historical view of revelation "The presupposition for the knowledge of God is the revealing of God by God"—a standard neo-orthodox way of describing revelation (*Theology of Hope*, p. 116).

mark them as realities standing over against their recipients. Unlike purely personal revelations, they give concrete shape to what God is saying and doing.

Nevertheless the concreteness which characterizes promises and fulfillments also points beyond itself to God's initiative. A promise, though it makes a specific claim, is "open." It points towards the future. God can legitimately fulfill it in a number of ways. A fulfillment, even though it is a specific event (or group of events), often comes as a surprise. It usually contrasts sharply with the way events seemed to be moving, and in this way points to distinct character and purposes of the One who brought it to pass. Moreover, fulfillments, like promises, point beyond themselves. They prefigure and intensify hope for the fulfillment of all God's promises at the final revelation of Jesus Christ.

In these ways, revelation as historical is "open" to and points beyond itself to the One who initiates and transcends it. Yet its concreteness tells us by whom we are encountered and, at least within broad outlines, to what we are called. For revelation's historical characteristics mark out a broad range of possibilities within which we may expect God to act. They paint an anticipatory sketch, a vision, sufficient to enable us to strive towards and wait for God's future in hope. For we cannot live by hope if the future is an unknowable blank. Yet neither can we if the future is wholly closed. But promises and fulfillments are both definite and open.

B. Revelation as Event

The personal view insists that revelation is an occurrence, an activity. It is transforming interpersonal communication and communion. It creates new situations. It is not the mere unveiling of information which one can disregard.

Revelation as historical also involves events. Promises and fulfillments of promises demand responses. A promise is no mere prediction which one might ignore. It is God's personal word of hope, encouragement, and comfort. It transforms one's existence by giving one a new purpose, and bestowing upon one a new resolve. To ignore or reject a promise is to refuse to hope, to turn away from God's personal challenge and pledge. Similarly, a fulfillment is not an isolated historical occurrence. It is the manifestation, the actualization, of God's faithfulness and love. It creates a new situation in which God's people henceforth dwell.

In the personal view, however, revelatory events are often so distinct and discontinuous that they can fail to transform individuals or situations over the long run. Events are so distinct from interpretations that they may not carry any long-range significance.

But if revelation occurs as, and between, promise and fulfillment, then revelatory events are interrelated by patterns of continuity. And in these patterns, event and interpretation are inseparably intertwined. For a fulfillment cannot be recognized without recalling the words of a promise, and cannot be communicated verbally without linking the two together.

Now promises and fulfillments are linked mainly by propositions (sentences which affirm or deny the connection between a subject and a predicate). To be sure, other forms of language are involved in the process. Imperatives, exclamations, expressions of praise, thanks, and awe—these often pulsate through biblical texts when promises or fulfillments are in view. But since promises and fulfillments have concrete historical references, even if these are often very broad, much of the language which conveys them is propositional. Now without such propositional formulation, historical events could be neither promises nor fulfillments in the first place.[14] Propositional statements do not merely interpret non-cognitive encounters in very secondary, perhaps erroneous ways. These interpretations are part and parcel of the revelations themselves. Further, since promises and fulfillments keep pointing beyond themselves towards ever greater, farther-reaching fulfillments, these ever expanding revelations could not be revelations without constantly expanding propositional interpretations.

At the same time, however, while propositions ascribe certain definite features to promises and fulfillments, they do not exhaustively describe them. As Chapter 12 will show, propositions interpret God's acts in general terms. They mark out a broad range of possibilities within which God's acts can be legitimately described and reinterpreted.

Therefore like the promises and fulfillments themselves, their propositional interpretations are open. They point beyond the events towards the God who initiated them and towards God's future acts. Yet propositions also form the contours of those sketches and visions of God's acts that mark them as coming from him, and which give them enough definiteness and enough openness to arouse and sustain hope.

We have seen how such interpretations are found in those recitals which lengthen as biblical history develops (Chap. 1). Now we can see that these recitals, and not merely the events on which they were based, must be regarded as revelation. For without these recitals the significance of events incorporated into them would not have been perceived, nor could later events have been recognized as part of the revelatory stream. (And, of course, later events could not have been incorporated had not the propositions in which these recitals were formulated been open.) We also observed that what some call event and interpretation were intertwined in the early kerygma (Chap. 2). Now we see why they cannot rightly be separated. The kerygmatic events are revelatory events of the highest order. Yet as isolated events they could not be revelation. They are revelatory only because they they fulfill, and at the same time illumine the significance of, the ancient promises. The kerygmatic events are re-

---

[14] Cf. Barr, p. 77: "it is entirely as true to say that in the Old Testament revelation is by verbal communication as to say that it is by acts in history.... When we speak of the highly 'personal' nature of the Old Testament God, it is very largely upon this verbal character of his communication with man that we are relying. The acts of God are meaningful because they are set within the frame of verbal communication."

velatory only because they are interpreted in this way. But this means that interpretation is as integral a component of revelation as is event.

C. Revelation as Call to Decision

The personal view insists that revelation comes as a challenge, a demand, an offer which calls for decision. We can truly know God only by opening ourselves and orienting our lives in a manner which co-responds to God's active self-disclosure.

Historical revelation also demands response. Believing a promise is not merely assenting mentally to what it predicts. Instead one must launch out in the direction where it leads, struggling against those aspects of present reality that seem to belie the hope it arouses. In the course of such a pilgrimage we come to know better the person who leads us. Similarly, to believe in a fulfillment is not merely to recognize its continuity with a promise. To believe is to enter joyously into the state of affairs that comes into being, receiving the fulfillment as a gift from the One who promised it, and entering into fellowship with him by means of it.

In the personal view, however, the challenges which confronts one in each revelatory encounter can be quite different. They can be so highly individual that only I can recognize them. Thereby they can be restricted to very personal areas of each individual's life. In this way revelation can have very little influence on the broader issues of modern life. It may not call anyone to deal with issues of poverty, oppression and war that threaten to overwhelm us all.

God's biblical promises and fulfillments, however, call individuals and groups to broad historic tasks. Of course the challenge of such tasks is highly personal; they involve decision and risk. Yet God normally calls us to participate in something he is doing on history's broad stage. One is not merely challenged to make an internal decision; we are called to decide for or against, to help promote or retard, some social and historical process already or just about to be set in motion.

Yet like God's promises and the propositions which interpret them, these calls to decision are open. To be sure, they point us towards some definite task(s), towards some concrete form(s) of involvement in broader streams of events. Nonetheless they do not prescribe one's future course of action in detail. One needs to continually remain open to the shifting contours of the situation and to God's further revealing activity, activity which ultimately points towards the eschatological revelation of Jesus Christ.

From another angle, then, we see that revelation cannot be personal in a way that separates it from social, historical, or physical reality with thing-like features. Biblical revelations often convey God's desire for social reform, God's commentary on political and historical trends; they often affect (or promise to affect) the physical world. Thereby they provide us with wide ranges of vision, within which we can begin to discern God's will in the world at large today.

D. Summary

We have not sought to champion the merits of the historical view over against the personal view of revelation. Rather, we have insisted that the valid emphases of the latter cannot be adequately expressed without recognizing that God's personal revelation is also historical. Revelation is fully personal only when it is also historical, and it is truly historical only when it is also personal. (And, as we have begun to show, it cannot be fully either unless it is also propositional.) This conclusion corresponds with a major claim of both theories: that Jesus Christ is revelation's focal point.

For the personal view, God is most fully revealed when he comes to us as Jesus Christ. But Christ's incarnation and return are themselves historical acts with thing-like features, and he himself is an historical person with such features. For the historical view, Old Testament revelation points towards Jesus' coming and all revelation flows towards his return. Yet, as we insisted in Chapter 9, these events are not simply conclusions to a general historical program but personal acts of judgment, salvation and love.

III. "General" Revelation Through History

In beginning from the Bible's "special" history, we have seen that revelation affects reality's social and physical dimensions, and calls people to activity in these spheres. Since all this history points towards the eschatological consummation, revelation today, as in biblical times, still exhibits these features. So far, however, our concrete understanding of how this history operates has come from the ancient biblical records. But having examined them, systematic theology still has not completed its task. For it must ask, more specifically, just how revelation is to be discerned in our modern context. In particular, we must ask whether any connections exist between Scripture's special revelation and other more general ways in which God might be known through historical experience. To determine this, we will examine three current proposals as to the nature of such connections. Then we will evaluate these proposals critically.

A. Contemporary Theories

1. *Revelation as Universal History.* In Wolfhart Pannenberg's theology, most of the biblical material just mentioned plays a significant role. Nevertheless, Pannenberg insists, modern people cannot simply accept the claims of the Bible or of any religious tradition; all such claims must be tested by certain criteria.[15]

---

[15] Pannenberg believes that hellenistic people followed such a process in converting to Christianity: They tested the Christian missionaries' truth-claims by criteria developed in their own philosophy. (*Revelation as History*, pp. 134-135, 140, 149; see also his essay in Robinson and Cobb, *Theology as History* [New York: Harper, 1967], pp. 106-09.)

Pannenberg outlines criteria for determining whether a religion speaks authen-
tically about God, and about the end of history. God, must be that reality
which brings about unity in the stream of historical events and in the universe
as a whole:

> Unity is the most comprehensive characteristic of being....Everything that is,
> and everything conceivable, is by its very existence or conception 'one.' The quest
> for the ultimate unity which integrates and thus unifies everything is the question
> reaching for God....the way we must test any concept of God is by asking whether
> it can account for the unity of all reality. If an idea of God fails that test, it...is,
> therefore, not a true concept of God.[16]

Amid the competing claims of all religions, therefore, the true God will be
the one who is working towards the unity of history and of humanity. Now according to Christianity this unity has "already" been achieved by Jesus' work
which brings salvation to all nations. However, the truth of this claim depends
on the credibility of eschatological notions such as the resurrection. Are there
criteria for evaluating the likelihood of such an event? Pannenberg affirms on
the basis of modern science and philosophy that humans are always striving to
transcend their present situations in search of a future goal which they can
never attain in this life. This goal then can only be attained by resurrection beyond death.[17]

Having validated the biblical notions of God, eschatology, and revelation,
Pannenberg draws theological conclusions from the scriptural material somewhat like our own. It is crucial to notice, however, that he does not move directly from biblical assertions to systematic conclusions. Pannenberg first seeks
to establish, by general rational criteria, the extent to which biblical views are
valid for our day.

If Pannenberg's criteria are correct, where would one expect God to be working and thus revealing himself, today? Presumably, wherever people are transcending their present situations to build new futures, or wherever human
groups are moving towards greater unity. Pannenberg's approach connects biblical history with such movements in all cultures, past and present.

2. *Revelation through the Evolution of Consciousness.* Theologians other than
Pannenberg have regarded human beings as essentially "open towards the future." According to many current anthropologies, human beings, (individually
and collectively) are becoming increasingly conscious of themselves and of

---

[16] *Theology and the Kingdom of God* (Philadelphia: Westminster, 1969), p. 62.

[17] *What is Man?* (Philadelphia: Fortress, 1970); for a briefer account, see *Jesus: God
and Man* (Philadelphia: Westminster, 1968), pp. 82-88.

their creative capacities. We are moving together towards a world increasingly shaped by human creativity.[18]

According to this view, however, revelation is not uniquely focused through one stream of historical events. In fact, revelation is not so much an external (objective) occurrence as it is the enhancement of the (subjective) development of consciousness. According to Teilhard de Chardin:

> God never reveals himself from outside, by intrusion, but *from within*, by stimulation and enrichment of the human psychic current, the sound of his voice being made recognizable by the fullness and coherence it contributes to our individual and collective being.[19]

Moreover, God is not really an object of revelation. God is, as it were, the ultimate horizon, the all-embracing reality within which this process occurs. Revelation does not present us with new information which we must integrate with other historical or scientific knowledge. As Tillich also said, revelation is a perception of the meaning of things, of a new context within which things we already know take on different significance. The biblical accounts of revelatory historical occurrences, then, are important not because they tell of particular events with specific features. Instead, their interpretations are of greatest significance. These provide powerful symbols which can elucidate the meaning of human existence and can thus channel and reshape our experience. Accordingly the main function of propositions which seek to express revelation's meaning is not to refer to external events or spiritual realities. It is to stimulate human consciousness.

This view, then, is somewhat similar to the personal view which we have called revelation "through ontological shock." It differs in that its revelatory episodes need not be dramatic encounters with the *mysterium tremendum et fascinans*. In fact revelation tends to occur more subliminally, as an undercurrent or accompanying theme of one's growing self-awareness. Moreover, although revelation is not closely connected with specific historical events, it accompanies the historical and social development of the human race. In this way it reminds one of liberal theology. Many proponents of this perspective, however, are Roman Catholics. At least since Thomas Aquinas, Catholic theology has usually seen all humans as tending, though often confusedly and indirectly, towards the Good, known through natural theology. In modern times not only individuals but also the race can be envisioned as moving in this direction, illuminated by a general historical revelation.

If this general understanding of revelation is correct, where would one expect

---

[18] Such a view is expressed, e.g., in Gregory Baum, Man Becoming (New York: Herder & Herder, 1970); Leslie Dewart, The Future of Belief (New York: Herder & Herder, 1966); and Ray Hart, Unfinished Man and the Imagination (New York: Herder & Herder, 1968). For a good overview, see Avery Dulles, Models of Revelation, (Garden City, N.Y.: Doubleday, 1983), pp. 98-114.

[19] Christianity and Evolution (New York: Harcourt Brace Jovanovich, 1971), p. 143.

God to be working and thus revealing himself today? Presumably among those individuals, groups, and movements where people are moving towards greater self-awareness, and where their creativity is being enhanced. Such persons, however, would not necessarily adhere to explicit Christian beliefs, nor would such movements necessarily be guided by scriptural criteria. One would not expect to discern God's presence in any direct way among them. For God would be the general, largely subliminal "horizon" within which they operate.

3. *Revelation through Group Histories.* Although few liberation theologians have worked explicitly with revelation, the preceding perspective seems somewhat compatible with common liberation themes. Liberation theology stresses "conscientization": the process whereby oppressed peoples become aware of their own human potentialities and of the way in which social arrangements have repressed them (see Chap. 4). Accordingly, God's activity can be discerned in all forces which heighten this self-consciousness. In particular, liberation theologians stress that the historical experiences of their specific group, which have been oppressed, can be rich sources for understanding humanity and God. Much effort goes into seeking to articulate "women's experience," or "the experience of the poor," etc. In the past, such experiences have seldom attained formal literary expression. Yet they promise to provide rich resources for theologizing. Liberation theologies sometimes utilize such experiences as sources of revelation. They might be called special, since they are available and understandable to specific groups. Yet they have at least this in common with "general" revelation as traditionally understood: They are accessible to many with no specific Christian commitment.

James Cone, for instance, lists black experience, black history and black culture among the sources for his theology. For Cone, God's

> revelation comes to us in and through the cultural situation of the oppressed. His Word is our word; his existence, our existence. This is the meaning of black culture and its relation to divine revelation. Black culture, then, is God's way of acting in America, his participation in black liberation.[20]

It is difficult to tell exactly what Cone means by "black." At times it seems to be "an ontological symbol" for oppression in America, which afflicts some without black skin.[21] Occasionally, however, black experience seems available only to those of black physiognomy and culture.[22] It is also difficult to tell

---

[20] *A Black Theology of Liberation* (Philadelphia: Lippincott, 1970), p. 62. For a discussion of the same issues from the standpoint of feminist theology, see Rosemary Ruether, *Sexism and God-Talk* (Boston: Beacon, 1983), pp. 12-46.

[21] Ibid., pp. 27-28, 32, 217-18.

[22] "The black experience is possible only for black people. It means having natural hair cuts, wearing African dashikis and dancing to the sound of Johnny Lee Hooker or B. B. King, knowing that no matter how hard whitey tries, there can be no real duplication of black soul" (Ibid., p. 57).

whether black experience is the indispensible traditional vantage point, through which alone God's transcendent revelation can be rightly perceived; or whether black experience is the primary norm that determines which of the biblical events and interpretations are to be regarded as revelation.

In any case revelation for Cone is "God making himself known to man through a historical act of human liberation." As in the Old and New Testaments, revelation is neither mere personal encounter nor the imparting of information. It is an act of salvation: God makes himself known by establishing justice and delivering his people. As was often true in Israel's history, "to know God is to know what he is doing in human history on behalf of the oppressed of the land."[23] As Cone puts it "God's revelation means liberation."[24] Accordingly, certain events in biblical history (especially the Exodus and the history of Jesus) have great paradigmatic value for Cone. At times he appears to say that black experience can be critiqued according to these norms.[25]

If this understanding of revelation be correct, where would one expect God to be working and thus revealing himself today? Presumably among all movements and experiences that enhance the self-consciousness and work towards the social liberation of a given oppressed group. Some persons involved would be Christians, and would be gaining deeper insight into Scripture through such processes. But some with no Christian commitment, and some quite hostile to Christianity, would also be participating. These experiences and movements, further, would not necessarily be moving towards human unity. Quite often, the dawning awareness of a group consciousness accentuates its distinctness from and even its opposition to other groups.

B. Evaluation

The view of revelation which we began constructing in Section II was based on what we have called "special revelation through history." Now we must evaluate the more "general" theories just described. In proceeding we must keep two things in mind. First, since God's revelatory activity moves towards the universal consummation, we must acknowledge the possibility of finding it in many places. Second, however, we have noticed that the biblical God proves himself, reveals himself, in conflict with competing claims to truth. We must then be ready to reject assertions which contradict the biblical history of revelation.

In Chapter 10, we never fully evaluated what we called "revelation through ontological shock. Since it has similarities with "revelation through the evolution of consciousness" as presented in this chapter, we may usefully begin with the former.

1. *Revelation as "Ontological Shock."* All the critiques which were made ear-

---

[23] Ibid., p. 64; cf. *God of the Oppressed*, pp. 62-87.

[24] Ibid., p. 91; cf. p. 94.

[25] Especially *God of the Oppressed?* pp. 81-83.

lier about revelation as personal encounter apply to this view. Tillich stresses even more strongly than Brunner and Bultmann that revelation has no specific object. God is not present as a person, even though recipients of revelation usually describe God (symbolically) in that way. We do not wish to deny that some individuals might vividly experience the reality of Being overcoming non-being. But since being is not characterized by any distinguishing features, such events are open to extremely broad, even contradictory, interpretations. Whatever calls to decision one hears can be shaped by numerous subjective factors. Since such encounters involve no specific references to the natural, social, or historical realms, one's responses might be highly idiosyncratic. Or since criteria for evaluating responses are lacking, one might arbitrarily follow a line of conduct, radical or conservative, socialist or capitalistic—suggested by the immediate cultural context.

Again, we do not deny that God might sometimes be revealed as Tillich says. But we are arguing that this cannot be revelation's fundamental form. If it were, the revelations we find in Scripture—with their specific content, their interpretive interrelations, their implications for action—would be merely symbolic and secondary expressions of revelation. Their specificity would belong merely to the situations in which they were once received and not to the revelations themselves.

The concrete, objective features of biblical revelation, however, mark out the contours within which authentic fulfillments of God's promises (and any further promises) will occur. If these contours are disregarded, then individual or cultural subjectivity can determine what revelation is and what it means. But then these unusual experiences—profound, astounding, and significant as they might be—would not necessarily be revelations of the God who is directing all history towards the fulfillment of what he once promised. They might even be opposed to his historical work. Consequently the biblical history of promise and fulfillment, whose events and interpretations outline a framework within which further revelation will occur, must provide criteria for assessing the validity and implications of any contemporary encounter with Being.

2. *Revelation through the Evolution of Consciousness.* Theories of this sort are more historically oriented than the preceding type. Yet they affirm perhaps even less about any concrete form or object(s) of revelation. For some the human faith which responds to revelation is more concrete and directly known than revelation itself. For faith, which occurs along with the developing growth of consciousness, can be directly described. But revelation and its Source are known only indirectly and by inference from such faith-experiences.[26]

These theories, then, have difficulty in speaking of revelation as divinely initiated. Of course the illumination and enhancement of consciousness some-

---

[26] See J.P. Mackey, "The Theology of Faith: A Bibliographical Survey (and more)," *Horizons* 2 (1975), pp. 207-37 (esp. p. 235); and *Problems in Religious Faith* (Dublin: Helicon, 1972), p. 191; cf. Otto's criticism of Schleiermacher (p. 188)

how come from beyond. Yet one is primarily aware of the activity and growth of one's own self-awareness and creative potential. Much as for Schleiermacher, divine influence tends to be sensed indirectly in a subliminal manner rather than apprehended directly. For these theories also, revelation has neither propositional nor historical content. Accordingly decisions as to what counts as revelation, what it means, and how it is to be applied will be determined by one's theory of consciousness' development. The divine initiative will not define, illumine, define and energize what is truly human so much as one's theory of the human will define what is divine.

So understood, such "revelations" may fall outside God's historic activity in fulfillment of his promises. They may even support ideologies and movements which deify some merely human notion of what is ultimately true and good. God, of course, may and does reveal himself in ways that enhance human development. But Scripture's concrete revelatory history often challenges current notions of what is truly human. Only this history and the propositions which articulate it can mark out criteria for deciding which experiences come from the true God, and which do not.

Much as in the case of revelation through "ontological shock," God may well be revealed in many ways which enhance human consciousness. Yet these enhance enhancements cannot be revelation's fundamental form by which the biblical history of the promise is judged.

3. *Revelation as Universal History.* As presented by Pannenberg, this perspective grants an important role to Biblical history. It utilizes promise and fulfillment much as we do. We are indebted to it. Nevertheless the claim of this promise-fulfillment network to be true revelation is judged by criteria developed outside it. And so we can ask whether these criteria do not also critique and thus distort the shape of revelation developed within that history itself. Pannenberg insists, largely on philosophical grounds, that the true God must be working towards the unity of humanity and the cosmos. This is true, of course, of the God of the Bible. But how does this God work towards unity? Biblical history shows that this occurs in a surprisingly paradoxical way: by focusing his redemptive work through a particular people. At times this group appears to be a ridiculously small remnant. Very often it is persecuted and in sharp conflict with the world.

But given Pannenberg's approach, one's attention towards history may be directed more by the general criterion of universality than by this paradox of Scripture's special history. Thereby one may miss the extent to which God's work today occurs among smaller, persecuted groups outside history's apparent mainstream. One may overestimate the extent to which God is active among broad, popular movements which apparently are promoting human unity. But if God often supports minority causes, one may be found opposing God. Once again, though less so than in the two previous theories, criteria other than those provided by God's history of promise can decide what revelation is and how one is to apply it. Of course, God often does work through movements which promote human unity. Yet such trends themselves cannot be revelation's fundamental form by which biblical claims to revelation are judged.

4. *Revelation through Group Histories.* Rather than finding God too broadly active in history, such theories may confine God's work too narrowly. Nonetheless, rather than quickly criticizing, those working out of western theology's mainstream need to carefully consider the ways in which the experiences of blacks, women, and Hispanics may be revelatory. Biblical revelation often came to people who were minorities, and in situations of oppression. Therefore, although such revelations pointed openly beyond any specific situation, they are often best understood by others in similar situations. If revelation is not only communication of content, but is also transforming event and call to decision, revelation is most likely to occur today where situations are most open to these divine activities.

Liberation theologians, also insist that the experiences of their own groups, experiences which can dispose them to hear God's revelation, have seldom received articulate expression. "Black experience," "women's experience," etc., have been regarded as less legitimate forms of human awareness. Consequently, as liberation theologians insist, there is great need to bring such forms of awareness to explicit conscious attention and to discern how God might be heard through them.

In this respect we strongly favor an emphasis on the role that group histories may play in revelation. In this way discussions of revelation, pursued for so long within the university, can be more centered in the life of the churches. But insofar as a group's history or experience in general (e.g., the experiences that belong distinctively to all women by virtue of being female) provide notions of what revelation is and what it means—notions that conflict with biblical history—to that extent we cannot adopt it. Of course, God often does work through such movements. Yet no particular history of liberation itself can be revelation's fundamental form by which the biblical history of the promise is judged.

5. *Summary.* We have not denied that God can be revealed through "ontological shock," through consciousness' evolution, or through universal or group histories. Indeed God reveals himself through all these means. But we have argued that God's authentic revelations will be consistent with the biblical history of promise and fulfillment. Consequently we have denied that revelation of any other kind can provide ultimate norms for deciding what revelation is and what it means. Our concern has not been to judge the flow of history according to standards promulgated in a book or in a series of ecclesiastical pronouncements. Rather it has been to discern, amid the many interweaving and conflicting historical streams, where God is truly active. Our concern has not been primarily that of scholars to define the source of "right doctrine." It has been more nearly that of Churches seeking to find the proper starting point from which to pursue "right action." Since all true revelation flows towards the final revelation of Jesus Christ, the question of revelation is primarily one of how we are to walk with God through the "already" and towards the "not yet."

CHAPTER TWELVE

Revelation as Propositional

I n approaching revelation, we have decided not to restrict ourselves to its objects or contents. For when the God who draws all history towards its consummation reveals anything, these contents serve to challenge, to shatter, to heal, to comfort, to energize individuals, and to impel the whole creation towards its destiny. Were we to separate revelation's objective contents from the subjective illumination by which their significance is actualized, we would have to postpone discussing revelation's significance for the living Church. Instead, in seeking to develop a systematic theology to strengthen and guide the Church, our doctrine of revelation has been designed from the beginning to answer the urgent, broad question, How is God known? as asked by active, inquiring Christian communities.

Nevertheless the last two chapters have shown that, dynamic and subjectively active as revelation is, it is also propositional. Propositions give revelation shape, patterning, direction. Through propositions revelation is focused into concrete claims, challenges, visions. Thereby God's dynamism resists being dissipated or distorted by human subjectivity and guides action into definite and effective (even if broad) channels. Propositions are so integral to this process that without them personal encounters and historical events would not be revelation. Propositions are not mere packages in which revelation is contained; they form an integral dimension of revelation itself.

According to Protestant tradition revelatory propositions are found exclusively in the Bible. Roman Catholic theology, which historically has ascribed authority to both Scripture and tradition, has recently emphasized the priority of the former. Accordingly this chapter will deal with the Bible (while the next will deal with tradition).

I. The Canonical Context

The propositional dimension determines that revelation is concrete and specific. By means of its propositions, revelation flows within definite channels. Yet, we also said in Chapter 11, revelatory propositions are flexible and open. But how can they be both definite and open? How can they both concretize and open up truth?

The recent discipline of "canon criticism," or "canonical criticism," provides some clues.[1] The Latin word *canon* meant a measuring line, or ruler. In theology, *canon* refers to the collection of writings that the Church has regarded as authoritative Scripture (for Protestants, the Old and New Testaments; Catholics include the Apocrypha). Recently certain biblical scholars have emphasized *canon* as the proper framework for reading and interpreting Scripture. Canonical criticism has sought to move beyond the historical-critical reading of the Bible. Historical criticism seeks to reconstruct the original context and meaning of biblical texts. It seeks to distinguish among the contributions of later editors or redactors and often to "peel them away" to get back to some primitive text with a fairly definite, limited meaning. While canonical critics regard such efforts as indispensable, they argue that exegesis and interpretation should not stop there. To regard a biblical passage merely as an ancient text that once spoke to a specific context in a certain way is to abstract one particular dimension of Scripture from its full, living reality.[2]

Canonical critics argue that biblical interpretation should proceed from a vantage point which fully appreciates how Scripture actually functions. The Bible is a living document. It has and still does enliven and shape the lives of religious communities. It remains alive not primarily because it conveys information about ancient religions but because it continues to lay claim on people's lives. How can the interpreter grasp whatever it is that enables these ancient texts to take on life today? Canonical critics argue that these texts did not perish along with most of antiquity because they came to be regarded as

---

[1] In studying the biblical literature, James Sanders emphasizes the process by which it eventually came to be regarded as canon. For the study of this emphasis he prefers the term "canon*ical* criticism" *(Canon and Community,* [Philadelphia: Fortress, 1984], p. 18). Brevard Childs emphasizes the completed canon as the standpoint "from which the Bible is to be read as Sacred Scripture." Thus he prefers the term "*canon* criticism," fearing that "canon*ical* criticism" implies that "the concern with canon is viewed as another historical-critical technique which can take its place alongside of source criticism, form criticism, rhetorical criticism and the like." ("The Canonical Shape of Prophetic Literature," *Interpretation* 32, p. 54). For Child's view see also *Introduction to the Old Testament as Scripture* (Philadelphia: Fortress, 1979), pp. 27-83; and *Biblical Theology in Crisis,* pp. 91-219. For our purposes, we need not take sides in this debate. Hence, we shall refer to this new approach as "canonical criticism."

[2] "Critical method...is incapable of either raising or answering the full range of questions which the church is constrained to direct to its Scripture" *(Biblical Theology in Crisis,* p. 141; cf. p. 147; Sanders, pp. 23, 38-39).

"canonical." That is, they came to be heard not just as specific utterances, reports, poems, etc. (whose significance was limited to a particular place and time) but as authoritative expressions of God's continuing will. They attained this status by being included within a living complex of sacred writings.

Yet as they attained this status, their shape changed. Various texts were rewritten, joined together, and related to others in such a way that they took on additional dimensions of meaning. Their full meaning can now be discovered only by exploring all these interrelationships. And it is by recovering this canonical meaning that the interpreter gains insight into Scripture's living, effective character.

How can one explore this "canonical shape"? According to Brevard Childs, interpretation should begin with the the final shape of each book (or group of books). James Sanders, however, gives more attention to the process by which various texts attained canonicity. According to Sanders, all texts and books eventually included in the canon manifest both "stability" and "adaptability."[3] "Stability" means that they referred to some definite event and made some specific claim. But if this were the only function of such texts, they would never have been canonized. They became canonical only because later generations regarded the event or claim which they conveyed as "adaptable," as carrying a relevance which extended beyond their setting as having a range of meaning which illuminated contexts other than their own.

Canonical criticism, then, studies the processes through which various texts and books came to have their present shape and function within the canon. To be sure, the histories of many such units are obscure. They can be reconstructed only in highly conjectural fashion. Nevertheless others clearly passed through a wide range of "resignification." Yahweh's promise that Abram and Sarai would become "a great nation" through whom "all the families of the earth shall be blessed" (Gen. 12: 2–3) is a good example. Later passages in

---

[3] Sanders, pp. 22-24. Sanders stresses the ongoing nature of the canonical process. Religious communities and individuals recall and restate traditional texts to answer "essential and existential questions of *identity* and *lifestyle*" (p. 28). And even when some "final form" of the text is acknowledged, "numerous hermeneutical techniques" are soon applied "to crack it open once more and derive needed value from it." Consequently, Sanders places less emphasis than Childs on "that passing moment when the final form is achieved" (p. 25). Childs feels that by locating "the heart of the canonical process...in Israel's search for identity," Sanders "replaces a theocentric understanding of divine revelation with an existential history." However, "Israel did not testify to its own self-understanding, but by means of a canon bore witness to the divine source of its life" (*Introduction to the Old Testament as Scripture*, p. 59). Accordingly, Childs focus more on the final, normative canon. In fairness to Sanders, however, we note that he often insists that Scripture basically conveys "God's story." In any case, since Childs generally supports Sanders' "broadening the definition of canon to cover a process extending throughout Israel's history," our brief description characterizes both views, even though the terms "stability" and "adaptability" are Sanders' (Childs, p. 57).

Genesis expand on its meaning: the land involved will be Canaan (Gen. 17:8); it will not be possessed by Ishmael, though he will father another great nation (Gen. 17:20); their descendants will not really possess Canaan for another four hundred years (Gen. 15:13-16), etc. We have seen how the expansion of this promise—and all the attendant dynamics of hoping and waiting, rejoicing and doubting—lies at the heart of God's historical revelation. Finally, in the New Testament, Paul tells us that the ultimate heir promised in Genesis 12:3 was Christ (Gal. 3:6) while Hebrews declares that the country they sought was really a heavenly one (Heb. 11:13-16).

By tracing the historical elaboration of such passages, the original text's "adaptability," its range of resignification, can be illuminated. Yet also can its "stability," those points of reference which remain firm throughout. Often this process of resignification will flow in the direction from promise towards fulfillment.

Moreover, the broader significations of a text often emerge through a process of conflict with various other understandings of God and of the cosmos. Sanders, for instance, shows that Israel and its neighbors shared certain beliefs about reality. But a study of the biblical texts in which such common beliefs are expressed determines that the writers constantly reinterpreted events in light of Israel's experience with Yahweh. Their full meaning is to be discovered not by identifying some original, specific signification, perhaps compatible with Canaanite religion, but by tracing the way in which other dimensions of meaning unfold as Yahweh triumphs over Baal.[4]

Canonical criticism, then, can help systematic theology articulate the movement of revelation as historical. It can help theology avoid explaining biblical history's "real" flow by extraneous categories: the evolution of consciousness, history as closed causal continuum, universal history, etc. For "the study of the canonical shape of the literature is an attempt to do justice to the nature of Israel's unique history."[5]

Canonical criticism can also help theology understand how biblical propositions can be both specific and open. It shows that propositions make concrete, definite assertions, but the meanings of those which became canonical cannot be restricted to one single signification. For if they had only a single meaning, they would never have been recognized as having a significance transcending their original situation. This insight helps exegesis and theology guard against two opposite errors. First, it shows that one can rarely speak of *the* meaning of a proposition or text, if this means that each text can mean only one thing. Instead, biblical propositions themselves have a certain range of meanings. On the other hand, this range is circumscribed. It is connected with (and therefore

---

[4] Sanders, pp. 52-57. Sanders traces four way in which Israel adapted wisdom from other cultures they depolytheized, monotheized, Yahwized and Israelitized it (pp. 56-57).

[5] Childs, *Introduction to the Old Testament as Scripture*, p. 71; cf. p. 76.

limited by) the proposition's original meaning. It cannot mean whatever contemporary interpreters might wish. This is how propositions structure revelation so that it flows within definite channels, yet channels that are yet open towards God, the world, and the future.

The search for a biblical proposition's meaning and truth, then, involves a search for the range of meanings it can legitimately bear. This search must take two contexts into account. The first is that of the entire canon. The total meaning of a text can seldom be determined by historical and grammatical analysis of its particular contents alone. Scripture must interpret Scripture. Only within the context of all other propositions and texts to which it points and which point to it can its range of meaning be determined. This intra-biblical range of meaning, however, could be determined by biblical theology alone. Systematic theology must ask an additional question: whether, and in what sense, biblical propositions might be true. For even should a certain biblical proposition harmonize perfectly with all others, this coherence could be a mere literary one. Systematic theology must ask how all these interrelated biblical assertions correspond with reality as it is known by other means.

Our discussion of revelation's propositions, then, having first considered their function and their meaning, must move on to the issue of their truth. This issue has come to the fore in the heated disputes over the authority of Scripture.

II. The Total Truthfulness of Scripture

In recent decades, discussions of biblical authority have been most intense in "evangelical" circles. Within these, many have sought to emphasize biblical authority by insisting on "inerrancy"; namely, that the entire Bible, in the original manuscripts, is wholly free from error. Expositions of this position usually devote much space to defending it. This happens, first, because inerrancy is a very comprehensive claim, and is challenged by various possible contradictions and errors. It happens, second, because "in-errancy" is a negative term. It asserts that something is *not* true of the Bible: that it does not contain a single error. Asserting so comprehensive a claim in this manner almost invites objectors to begin looking for errors. Defenders seem to become responsible for explaining every possible obscurity in all sixty-six biblical books.

Perhaps the emotion often aroused by such debates could be somewhat stablized, and central issues distinguished from peripheral ones, by first emphasizing what is true of Scripture, rather than what is not. Most participants in such discussions, whatever their view on in-errancy, are concerned to affirm that the Bible speaks truly.[6] Let us then propose, or adduce, the following affirmation: "the Bible is wholly truthful in all that it affirms." Let us first see what positive meaning this affirmation might have (Section A and B). Then only afterwards, let us inquire as to its implications concerning possible errors (Section C). Finally, let us determine how well this affirmation might meet the criteria for theological doctrines (Section III; cf. Chap. 3).

A. The Biblical Notion of Truth

In the Old Testament, a true word or a truthful person is one on whom someone can depend or rely. Words and persons prove themselves to be reliable, enduring, steadfast over the course of time. Thus the words for truth and truthfulness are often translated as "faithfulness."[7] The Old Testament notion of truth, then, is related to revelation's historical dimension. We have observed that God reveals himself by predicting, claiming, or promising something which later comes to pass. When someone's word does come to pass or when they act in accordance with an earlier commitment or promise, the Old Testament calls the state of affairs or the person "true."

Since it is usually the efforts, the promises, and the character of persons that prove to be true, truth also has a personal dimension. In the Old Testament, however, human persons seldom prove to be reliable or true. Humans usually turn aside from commitments and break promises. Yet over against this, Yahweh brings his promises to pass. Consequently the resulting "true" states of affairs are the outflow, the expression of Yahweh's truthful character. This truthfulness stands over against human untruth, challenging and exposing it. Yet being grounded in God's faithful, reliable character, it also gives rise to hope. Finally, God's truth is conveyed through specific events and words. Israel is often asked to trust God on the basis of Yahweh's signs (Exod. 4:31), words (Gen. 15:6, Josh. 3:5), or delivering acts (Isa. 43:7). Words which accurately de-

---

[6] According to Paul Feinberg, "the key concept both in the Scriptures and in the minds of those who use the term [inerrancy] is truthfulness....the positive side of the negative idea is that if the Bible is *inerrant*, it is *wholly true*." Consequently, "If some better word can be found, then let us use it." Feinberg, however, prefers to retain inerrancy and define it in terms of truthfulness: "Inerrancy means that when all the facts are known, the Scriptures in their original autographs and properly interpreted will be shown to be wholly true in everything that they affirm, whether that has to do with doctrine or morality or with the social, physical or life sciences." (The Meaning of Inerrancy, in Norman Geisler, ed., Inerrancy ([Grand Rapids: Zondervan, 1981], p. 293). Millard Erickson also defines inerrancy by emphasizing truthfulness: "The Bible, when correctly interpreted in light of the level to which culture and the means of communication had developed at the time it was written, and in view of purposes for which it was given, is fully truthful in all that it affirms" (*Christian Theology*, Vol. I, pp. 233-34).

[7] The main nouns are 'emeth and 'emunah. See TDOT 1, pp. 292-323; TDNT 1, pp. 232-38 for what follows.

scribe God's commands, promises, or acts are true. Truth then, like revelation, has a propositional dimension too.

In the New Testament truth also has an historical dimension. Christ came "to show God's truthfulness, in order to confirm the promises given to the patriarchs" (Rom. 15:8). In Jesus Christ, God's faithfulness and truth triumph over human faithlessness and lies.[8] Truth, moreover, is largely a matter of action. As liberation theologians have also stressed,[9] truth is largely what one does (John 3:21, 1 John 1:6-8, Eph. 4:21-25, 1 Pet. 1:22). And Christians now can do the truth because as John especially emphasizes they are "of" the truth (1 John 3:18-19). They are "of" the truth because the Truth itself—God as Son, Spirit, and Father—actually dwells in them and they in God.[10] Or as both Paul and James express it, truth is God's saving, recreating activity.[11] Truth, therefore, is also deeply personal. Finally, even in New Testament times, sharp conflict still raged over what the truth really was. Assertion of truth by clear propositions became an important weapon in this conflict (Gal. 2:5, 14; 2 Cor. 4:2, 6:7-8; 2 Tim. 2:18). Truth was known and expressed by specific assertions.[12]

The above outline provides a very incomplete sketch of the key biblical terms usually translated as "truth." Yet it is enough to show that, were theology to organize its discussion of biblical revelation around this term, it would move along much the same lines as we have followed in the last few chapters. Scripture's truth would consist largely in its broad claims to present amid the claims of other forces and gods, the One who truly guides all things towards the goal that he has declared. Scripture's truth would also consist largely in its capacity to bring us into communion with the One who challenges, encourages, and transforms us by his presence. And finally, Scripture's truth would consist in the veracity of its propositions.

Let us notice, however, that in the first and second of these dimensions, the Bible itself would be "true" in a somewhat indirect sense. Scripture's capacity to bring us into personal communion with God cannot be a property residing solely in its written words. For these words present God to us only when utilized by the Spirit to that end. Similarly God's historical truthfulness is a dynamic process which will be fully established only at the consummation. This full historical and eschatological truthfulness cannot reside solely in the Bible's words as such. Instead, Scripture's truth consists in its capacity to point

---

[8] John 1:14, 17, 8:26; Rom. 3:3-8; 1 Cor. 1:20; 1 John 2:8; Rev. 3:14, 19:11-16.

[9] Miguez-Bonino, *Christians and Marxists*, pp. 35-38.

[10] 1 John 5:20; the relationships between Father and Son are frequently spoken of in terms of truth (John 7:18, 28; 8:13-16, 26), as are those of Son and Spirit (John 14:17, 15:26, 16:13; 1 John 5:7).

[11] 2 Tim. 2:10-12, Gal. 1:5-6, 1 Tim. 2:4, James 1:18.

[12] 2 Tim. 2:15, Heb. 10:26, John 4:31, 10:41, 19:35-36, 21:24.

us towards truthfulness and bring us into it. When theology consults the Bible to help establish its concept of truth, it finds that the Bible points beyond itself. Truth, like revelation, is fundamentally a divine activity in which Scripture plays an indispensible role. But the Bible's truth, like that of revelatory encounters, events, and propositions, lies not only within itself, but in its openness, its pointing towards something greater, and thereby in its capacity to be utilized by the One who is Greater.

Nevertheless this pointing would not be possible unless truth could be more directly ascribed to the propositions of the Bible. For God's claims to guide history involve specific assertions about what will occur. Similarly truthful relationships and actions exhibit certain identifiable, describable characteristics and are incompatible with others. The truth or falsity of God's revelation, then is intrinsically bound up with the truth or falsity of certain propositions.

B. Total Truthfulness

But even though biblical truthfulness includes that of propositions, ought we to affirm that this applies to every biblical proposition? If so, on what basis might we affirm this? In this section we shall examine the manner in which inerrantists have usually sought to establish this, and determine the extent to which we can or cannot follow it.

Inerrantists have often supported such a claim in deductive fashion.[13] Sometimes their reasoning has proceeded from general premises such as "God is true" and "all the words of Scripture are words of God"; these seem to entail the conclusion that all the words of Scripture are true. At other times, certain biblical passages have served as premises from which the truthfulness of all biblical propositions is deduced. In his classical affirmation of inerrancy, Benjamin Warfield began by exegeting three texts:

Second Timothy 3:16 declares that "All Scripture is inspired by God." Warfield argued that the word translated "inspired by God," *theopneustos*, means "God-breathed." This means "that the Scriptures are a Divine product....The 'breath of God' is in Scripture just the symbol of His almighty power, the bearer of His creative word....God's breath is the irresistible outflow of his power."[14]

Second Peter 1:21 is often translated as saying that "men moved (*pheromenoi*) by the Holy Spirit spoke from God." According to Warfield, however, *pheromenoi* meant that the Spirit was "bearing" the biblical writers. That is, the meaning here

---

[13] Harold Lindsell, "The Infallible Word," *Christianity Today*, August 25, 1972, p. 11; R. C. Sproul, "The Case for Inerrancy: a Methodological Analysis" in James Montgomery, ed., *God's Inerrant Word* (Minneapolis: Bethany, 1974), p. 274.

[14] "The Biblical Idea of Inspiration" in *Revelation and Inspiration* (New York: Oxford, 1927), p. 79.

is not to be confounded with guiding, or directing, or controlling, or even lead-ing in the full sense of that word....what is 'borne' is taken up by the 'bearer,' and conveyed by the 'bearer's' power, not its own, to the 'bearer's' goal, not its own. The men who spoke from god are here declared, therefore, to have been taken up by the Holy Spirit and brought by His power to the goal of His own choosing.[15]

Finally in John 10:34–35, Jesus based his argument against his opponents on a single word ("gods") in Psalm 82:6 and on the assumption that "the Scrip-ture cannot be broken." Since Jesus here appealed to one of the Old Testa-ment's "most casual clauses—more than that, the very form of its expression in one of its most casual clauses," Warfield concluded that "the indefectible au-thority of Scripture" extends to its specific words.[16]

In his classic presentation Warfield began by analyzing or unpacking biblical propositions, and thereby establishing that Scripture is God's direct expression and that this characteristic extends to all its words. If one also assumes, as an-other premise for deduction, that this characteristic is incompatible with error, the Bible's inerrancy seems to have already been established.

But how much do such general biblical propositions really tell us about the specific character of scriptural truth? How precisely do they help us define no-tions of truth and error? By themselves, not very precisely. Unless one assumes that the very notion of divine truth excludes anything that might be called in any way an error, biblical texts such as those above tell us little about how God's truth is actually conveyed through Scripture. To attain a more precise notion of what biblical truth is like, we must investigate much more closely the ways in which Scripture actually speaks. Warfield, however, did just this. Al-though his classic article apparently began with a deductive sort of proof, most of it investigated biblical phenomena in more inductive fashion.

Warfield, like many of his followers, focused on Jesus Christ as the center to-wards which all the biblical writings point. Jesus' words and deeds form "the fundamental revelation"[17] Now Jesus, it is argued, regarded all Scripture as au-thoritative and without error. Further, acknowledging Christ as Lord involves adhering to what he taught. Inerrancy, then, is christologically based. It is an implication of one's commitment to Christ.

Although we cannot rehearse such arguments in full, we regard them as fun-damentally sound. Jesus announced that God's kingdom was "at hand" in ful-fillment of the Old Testament promise (Mark 1:15). But this claim, we shall

[15] Ibid, p. 83.

[16] Ibid., p. 86; for a recent and somewhat different reading of these passages, see Paul Achtemeier, The Inspiration of Scripture (Philadelphia: Westminster, 1980), pp. 106-14.

[17] Pinnock, Biblical Revelation, p. 63. Since this classical exposition of the case for inerrancy, Pinnock's approach has changed marked, even though still attributes a limited usefulness to the term. See esp. The Scripture Principle (Harper: San Fran-cisco, 1984).

see, was hotly disputed (Chap. 15). To support it, Jesus often insisted that events in his lifetime, especially those whose significance was unclear, or which seemed to contradict his claims, occurred in fulfillment of the Scriptures.[18] These Scriptures were so conclusively authoritative for Christ that he often justified his actions and authenticated his claims by referring to them with the simple formula: "It is written."[19]

Consider such an instance. When asked by the Pharisees why Moses made provisions for divorce (cf. Deut. 24:1–4), Jesus answered that divorce was not God's original intention: "He who made them from the beginning...said 'For this reason a man shall leave his father and mother and be joined to his wife, and the two shall become one' " (Matt. 19:4–5). Here Jesus quoted Genesis 2:24, which does not designate God as the speaker. Jesus, however, quoted these words as if they were God's. This is one indication, as Warfield noted, that for Christ the words of Scripture were the words of God.[20]

Even in Warfield's day, however, some argued that many such passages expressed not Jesus' attitude but those of the gospel writers. Yet regardless of how critics distribute the relevant passages between Jesus and the evangelists, no significant difference between their general attitudes towards the Old Testament can be discerned. In fact few people of any theological persuasion would claim that Jesus and the gospel writers held any view different than the one common to Jews in their time: that all the Old Testament words are God's.[21] The other New Testament writers also explained Christ's life, death, and resurrection as the fulfillment of the Scriptures.[22] The events of their own time were similarly understood.[23] As with Jesus, references to the Old Testament were frequently introduced with the simple "it is written."[24] Warfield argued that the New Testament's frequent use of the term "the Scriptures (ta graphe)" indicates that all its writers shared the common ancient notion of a body of writings divinely authoritative in all its parts.[25] Moreover the various New Testament writers, like Jesus, often refer to the words of Scripture, no matter who their hu-

---

[18] Mark 9:12-13, 12:10-12 and par., 14:48-49 and par.; Luke 24:25-26, 46-47; John 12:14-16, 13:18-19, 17:12.

[19] Matt. 4:4, 7, 10; 11:10; 21:13; 26:31 and pars.

[20] Warfield, p. 89: Genesis 2:24 "can be treated as a declaration of God's only on the hypothesis that all Scripture is a declaration of God's."

[21] See Richard Longenecker, Biblical Exegesis in the Apostolic Period (Grand Rapids: Eerdmans, 1975), pp. 19-50. For a discussion of the significance of this, see Pinnock, The Scripture Principle, pp. 29-60.

[22] Acts 1:16, 8:27-35, 17:2-3, 26:22-23; 1 Cor. 15:3-4, etc.

[23] Rom. 8:36, 9:22-23, 11:8, 15:9, 21; 2 Cor. 4:13, etc.

[24] Rom. 1:17, 3:4, 10, 11:26, 14:11; 1 Cor. 1:19, 2:9, 3:19-20, 15:45; Gal. 3:10, 13, 4:27, etc.

[25] Revelation and Inspiration, pp. 93-96, 115-168, 335-94.

man author or speaker may have been, as words of God.[26]

Although we cannot rehearse it in more detail, we regard this argumentation as fundamentally sound. Jesus and the New Testament writers consistently regarded the Old Testament's words as God's words. Anyone who affirms the full Lordship of Christ and the general reliability of Scripture, then, cannot simply dismiss any biblical passage as containing obvious errors.[27] On the contrary, one's initial assumption must be, like that of Jesus and the New Testament writers, that every biblical proposition is wholly truthful in all that it affirms.

Yet despite the general soundness of this conclusion, Warfield and many other inerrantists provide little help in defining this truthfulness more precisely. They seldom investigate in detail exactly how the New Testament writers utilized the Old. But careful examination shows that Old Testament passages were used in many different ways: sometimes precisely quoted, sometimes loosely paraphrased, sometimes interpreted quite differently from that which their original author seems to have intended.[28] As the Old Testament texts, caught up in the trajectory moving from promise to fulfillment, became incorporated in new canonical contexts, their range of significantion often altered.

[26] Paul, for instance, wrote that "the Scripture, foreseeing that God would justify the Gentiles by faith, preached the gospel beforehand to Abraham" (Gal. 3:8; cf. Rom. 9:17). In Hebrews 1:5-13, "God" is identified as the speaker. Yet in the following Old Testament passages quoted, God was the original speaker in only three (Ps. 2:7 and 2 Sam. 7:14, quoted in Heb. 1:5; Ps. 110:1, quoted in Heb. 1:13). In two others, God is not the speaker (Deut. 32:43 LXX, quoted in Heb. 1:6; Ps. 104:4, quoted in Heb. 1:7). In the remaining two, God does not speak, but is addressed (Ps. 45:6-7, quoted in Heb. 1:8-9; Ps. 102:24-27, quoted in Heb. 1:10-12). See Warfield, pp. 92-93, 283-334.

[27] So far this classical argument, precisely speaking, has established the total truthfulness of the Old Testament. Later New Testament authors, however, twice estimated the writings of the New Testament in the same way. First Timothy 5:18 quotes statements from both Deut. 25:4 and Luke 10:7 as "Scripture"; 2 Peter 3:16 designates Paul's writings in general as Scripture. The total truthfulness of the New Testament, however, is based on the broader sort of phenomena indicated by Warfield:

"The New Testament writers...do not for an instant imagine themselves as ministers of a new covenant, less in possession of the Spirit of God than the ministers of the old covenant....They prosecute their work...in full confidence that they speak "by the Holy Spirit" (1 Pet. 1:12), to whom they attribute both the matter and form of their teaching (1 Cor. 2:13). They, therefore, speak with the utmost assurance of their teaching (Gal. 1:7, 8); and they issue commands with the completest authority (1 Thess. 4:2, 14; 2 Thess. 3:6, 12), making it, indeed, the test of whether one has the Spirit of God that he should recognize what they demand as the commandments of God (1 Cor. 14:37)" (p. 109).

[28] For a detailed discussion, see Longenecker's entire book; also Pinnock, *The Scripture Principle*, pp. 36-45.

Consider once again, for instance, Jesus' interpretation of the Mosaic divorce regulations. Although Warfield emphasized that Jesus quoted the words of Genesis as those of God, he did not say what Jesus' use of them did to the words of Moses. If the Mosaic regulations were only temporary concessions granted due to "hardness of heart" (Matt. 19:8), how can they also be regarded as words of God? Obviously, not in an eternal and straightforward sense. They can be true only as expressions of God's will for a limited historical and cultural context. In other words, even this passage emphasized by inerrantists shows that in order to learn exactly what kind of truth Scripture conveys, one must carefully study the ways in which biblical writers use other Scriptures.

C. A Definition of Error

Despite disagreements on many issues, proponents and critics of inerrancy agree that theological definitons of truth and error should be based on research of this kind.[29] Yet much more needs to be done in this area, and general agreement on its results will be slow in coming (if it comes at all). Further, much of the work will belong to biblical rather than systematic theology. Nonetheless, even as biblical investigation proceeds, Christians will be studying Scripture and seeking to discern God's revelation by means of it. In the meantime, then, can theology propose any rule for handling and interpreting the propositional truthfulness found within it?

The above notion of biblical truthfullness implies a notion of error. For no truth-claim can be meaningful if it is not falsifiable; in other words, if it is compatible with every possible state of affairs. Our affirmation that "the Bible is wholly true in all that it affirms," then, entails that the Bible, in all it affirms, is "inerrant." Our discussion will make little connection with the current debate unless we can clarify what it would mean for us.

"The Bible is inerrant" would mean, first, that when properly interpreted, it will not point us towards ultimate commitment to any force or power which is not really guiding history. It would mean, second, that the Bible, when properly interpreted, will not lead us toward relationships or activities inconsistent with personal communion with God. Third, it would mean that no biblical proposition describing historical forces, relationships, activities, or anything else is false in what it intends to affirm. Biblical inerrancy then has to do with more than propositions. It refers in part to Scripture's capacity, when utilized by the Spirit, to guard us from false orientations and improper conduct. However, the truth or falsity of its propositions is relevant even to these features. For Scripture's claims as to who is, or is not, guiding history (and as to what relationships and activities are or are not proper)—these are expressed largely through propositions.

---

[29] See James Dunn, "The Inspiration and Authority of Scripture" (a reply to Roger Nicole), *The Churchman*, Vol. 98, No. 3 (1984), pp. 209-10; Achtemeier, pp. 76-93, 124-36, Pinnock, pp. 175-96; Feinberg, pp. 297-302; Geisler, pp. 142-44.

Moreover, none of these claims can be meaningfully stated unless theology can show what they mean in light of other, contemporary notions of falsity and truth. For as we observed in Chapter 11, many of God's claims have to do with the natural and historical realms, not merely with a religious or existential sphere. The truth or falsity of many biblical propositions, then, has to do not only with their coherence with other propositions within the canon but with their correspondence to what actually happens in nature, history, and human behavior.

For these reasons our theological notion of truth must entail a notion of error which applies to propositions. Further it must show how biblical propositions could be judged as truthful or errant in relationship to other kind of truth.

Due to our incomplete understanding of the ways in which propositional truth and falsity function in Scripture, any definition of error proposed at this time may need further refinement in light of subsequent data. Nonetheless, in light of the data we do have, we propose, or adduce, the following definition: A biblical proposition is erroneous if it absolutely contradicts any other biblical proposition or any well-established proposition about any other kind of truth.

Notice that this definition, although it affirms one quite definite feature of biblical propositions, is in other respects very open. Inerrancy, as we define it, says nothing positively about how biblical truth must be conveyed. It does not necessitate that every biblical writer deal with things in a way which modern people would consider the clearest and most adequate; some themes might be handled in ways which seem quite fragmentary, unclear, or overly general to us. In fact our definition is quite able to account for the wide variety among canonical writings. It leaves room for different authors to express things from different vantage points and in different forms of language. It leaves room for one author to pick up a theme or even a quotation from another and to discover strikingly new dimensions of meaning in it.

Moreover, our affirmation plays a somewhat different theological role than it does for many inerrantists, and than it did for many Protestant orthodox theologians. For them, biblical propositions function as premises from which theological doctrines are deduced. The inerrancy of these premises must be affirmed in order to safeguard the entire theological enterprise. For if the premises of a deductive system be uncertain, all its conclusions lose their main support. For us, Scripture's propositional truths play a more modest role. We could affirm that God is revealed through Scripture (personally, historically, and even propositionally) even if we believed that certain of its propositions were false. Nevertheless, even while full propositional truthfulness is not at the foundation of our theological method, we feel that it plays a significant, even if subordinate, role. Accordingly, for guidance amid the rich diversity of the canonical writings, our definition insists on one rule: Never interpret any one biblical proposition so that it comes into flat contradiction with any other proposition either from the Bible or from any other well-established source of truth. Shades of meaning, levels of meaning, variety of emphases and expression—our definition is open to the richness of such phenomena in Scripture. But it insists that this variety does not reach the point where some propositions must be considered as true and others clearly and irretrievably false.

III. Objections to the Total Truthfulness of Scripture

But is our definition of propositional error really an implication of the biblical notion of truthfulness? Even though it is more general than what most inerrantists have in mind, it may still be open to an objection raised against standard presentations of inerrancy: that it is an arbitrary standard forced upon the ancient biblical texts. In face, since our view of total biblical truthfulness entails the assertion that Scripture is inerrant, our position might be subject to several criticisms leveled against common inerrancy arguments. By considering several of these, we can better define the position we are adducing and argue for its cogency.

A. Apparent Errors

Outside evangelical circles, most theologians and biblical scholars simply assume that the Bible contains many errors. This supposition can be supported by various passages which seem to involve contradictions.[30] This straightforward, and often unexamined, assumption forms a common and widespread objection to total biblical truthfulness.

To be sure, when such "problem passages" are simply listed one after another, they seem quite numerous and apparently destructive of our theory. Nevertheless, when one considers the lengthy history over which the Bible was written, the wide diversity of themes, perspectives, and literary genre which fill its pages, then it seems surprising that so few can be found.[31] Many apparent errors can be plausibly explained. Scripture's total propositional truthfulness has more inductive evidence in its favor than is usually acknowledged.

On the other hand, given the limitations of our knowledge, not all apparent errors can be fully resolved. As all scholarly inerrantists acknowledge, Scripture's total truthfulness will never be supported by complete and indubitable inductive evidence this side of the eschaton. Does this mean that no assertion of propositional inerrancy whatever can be valid? Not if other factors besides inductive support are crucial for establishing this theological doctrine. We shall examine some of these in the next section.

---

[30] See Stephen Davis, *The Debate about the Bible* (Philadelphia: Westminster, 1977), pp. 95-107; Dewey Beegle, *Scripture, Tradition and Infallibility* (Grand Rapids: Eerdmans, 1973), pp. 175-95.

[31] For a good discussion, see Pinnock, *The Scripture Principle*, pp. 85-129.

B. Ambiguity

How do inerrantists handle texts which contain possible errors? Often, by defining "error" in such a way that the assertion in question no longer can be called erroneous. To take a simple example: Jesus called the mustard seed "the smallest of all the seeds on earth" (Mark 4:31). Yet modern botany knows of smaller seeds. Jesus, then, seems to have made an error. What do inerrantists do with such a passage? Often, they will insist (much as we have) that the Bible is wholly truthful only "in all that it *affirms*." In this particular case, they will argue, Jesus was not intending to teach botany; he was merely pointing to the smallest thing his hearers knew; therefore, considered in light of what he intended to affirm, his statement was not in error.

Probably most people would not raise great objections to this particular explanation, which we have used as a simple illustration. But hopefully it clarifies the kind of procedure that inerrantists often use: when an error seems to be found, the definition of error is shifted. But, critics complain, when definitions keep getting revised like this, they die "the death of a thousand qualifications." When "truth" or "error" are repeatedly redefined, they become too ambiguous to mean anything.[32]

Some who raise such objections, however, are not fully aware of the nature of theological doctrines. They sometimes expect theological concepts and assertions to be perfect mirror images of certain states of affairs, and thus to be wholly disproved whenever they fail to correspond to reality at any single point. In Chapter 3, however, we pointed out that theological doctrines employ various models and statements to account for wide ranges of data. Their suitability cannot be judged solely by their applicability, by how exactly they mirror certain data, but other complex criteria (coherence, consistency, adequacy) must also be employed. Consequently, when a certain concept fails to fit exactly with certain data, it is not immediately discarded. Instead, theologians, like many scientists, first seek to revise the concept to better account for the data.

Such revising need not be a way of hanging on to one's theory despite the unwelcome reality of the facts. On the contrary, it is precisely through such revising that the reality under investigation can become better known and more adequately expressed. Accordingly, if revising one's concepts of "truth" or "error" in light of difficult passages leads to a deeper understanding of biblical truthfulness, these concepts will not become ambiguous and useless, but all the more profound.

The possibility that our definition of propositional error might need to be refined in light of further data, then, does not discredit it. Neither does the fact that, given our present knowledge, a few passages seem to assert contradictions. Of course, such possible contradictions point to weakness in our theory,

---

[32] Pinnock, "Three Views of the Bible in Contemporary Theology" in Jack Rogers, ed., *Biblical Authority* (Waco, Tx.: Word, 1977), pp. 64-65.

which cannot yet fully account for them. Nevertheless, we recall that any theory or model adduced in theology must be evaluated by four criteria, and that none will satisfy all four perfectly. Consequently, in deciding whether to adopt any such theory, one should not ask: "Is it perfect?" but: "Does it do a better job than any other?"

What other conceptualities then, might render the relevant data better than our own? One popular view regards the Bible as "infallible," in matters of faith and practice, but as occasionally errant in matters of history, geography, and science. This theory has the apparent advantage of distinguishing between matters with which Scripture is centrally concerned (faith and practice) and those which are peripheral (dates, places, and outmoded cosmologies).[33]

However if revelation and biblical truthfulness are themselves historical and cosmic in scope, no such broad distinction does justice to Scripture. The central doctrines of Christianity—incarnation, resurrection, consummation, etc.—involve far-reaching affirmations about time and space. Only a highly personalistic understanding of revelation, which separates the realm of "persons" from that of "things" (Chap. 10), can make the very broad distinctions in terms of which this "infallibility" theory is usually stated. To be sure, advocates of "infallibility" may merely wish to distinguish historical, geographical, and scientific minutiae from the core of revelatory truth. But if this is their basic intent, they must construct categories far more subtly nuanced than "faith," "practice," "history," "geography," and "science" for identifying what truly are minutiae.

Another popular approach distinguishes what is truly Christian from what is merely cultural. Surely all theologians and exegetes must make some such distincton. For biblical writers record many time-bound customs which they do not intend to affirm. Such a distinction has perhaps been employed most convincingly, and with the most significant implications for biblical authority, by Paul Jewett. Jewett seeks to explain why Paul, who generally affirmed the role of women in the Church (cf. Gal. 3:28), sometimes seemed to deny this (cf. 1 Cor. 14:34–35, 1 Tim. 2:12–15). Jewett attributes the first perspective to Paul when he is speaking wholly as a Christian apostle; the second reflects Paul as still conditioned by his Jewish, pharisaical outlook. The latter affirmations are erroneous and thus devoid of contemporary authority.[34] Jewett's detailed argument can impress readers so long as they focus on concerns relating to women.

---

[33] Davis argues that in this way "the Bible is infallible but not inerrant" (p.230). See also Daniel Fuller, "Benjamin Warfield's View of Faith and History," Bulletin of the Evangelical Theological Society 11 (1968), pp. 75-83. Inerrantists often respond that any view which regards the Bible as errant in matters where its veracity can be checked (history, geography, and science) and then asks one to accept its inerrancy in matters which cannot be checked (faith and practice) seems highly inconsistent and unconvincing.

[34] Man as Male and Female (Grand Rapids: Eerdmans, 1975.)

Problems arise, however, when one asks how broadly this distinction be-tween Paul the apostle and Paul the pharisee can be extended. The Pharisees, after all, believed in the bodily resurrection of the dead, whereas the Saducees did not (cf. Acts 23:6–9). When we hear Paul affirming the bodily resurrection, then, is it merely Paul the pharisee who speaks? Should we seek to distinguish behind this crudely physical, time-bound view a more spiritual and truly au-thoritative understanding emanating from Paul the apostle?[35] Or if, on the other hand, some Pauline expressions concerning women are overly condi-tioned by his pharasaic background whereas those concerning the resurrection are not, how shall we determine where this undesirable influence begins and ends? Much like the distinction between "faith" and "history, science, geogra-phy," this one needs much refining if it is to adequately distinguish what Scrip-ture truly affirms from what is merely cultural.

To clarify our preference for inerrancy, understood as an implication of bibli-cal truthfulness, let us see how it and these other two theories measure up to the four criteria for theological doctrines. Our theory well satisfies the require-ment of *coherence*: that connections among major theological concepts should be clear. We have defined truthfulness, in connection with the major catego-ries we have used to describe revelation. Our theory however, meets the crite-rion of *consistency* less well. Even though we propose to keep on refining the nuances of our theory in light of biblical data, our doing so gives rise to some unclarity in its usage. Our concept of truthfulness is quite *applicable* to certain important data. It well describes the often-expressed attitude of Jesus and the New Testament writers to Old Testament Scripture. Yet it is less *adequate* to ex-plain the entire range of phenomena (possible contradictions, etc.) relevant to this issue.

The total truthfulness of Scripture, then, is not a perfect theory. Perhaps a better one could be found. But could it be provided by the above distinctions between "faith and practice" and "history, geography, and science"? or be-tween the truly Christian and the culturally conditioned? We find neither of these broad distinctions of categories coherent. When one seeks to relate, say, the distinction between "faith" and "history" to, say, the work of Christ, the latter reality cannot be divided into these two, or into similar, spheres. When one endeavors to apply the distinction between a Christian core and a Phari-saic husk to the resurrection, similar problems arise. For much the same rea-

---

[35] Historical analysis of biblical texts can lead one to regard nearly all their distinc-tive emphases as belonging merely to the culture in which they were written. Karl Barth once noted that, according to a liberal scholar (Paul Wernle), the following views of Paul were mere historical "relics": "Pauline 'depreciation' of the earthly life of Jesus—Christ the Son of God—redemption by the blood of Christ—Adam and Christ—Paul's use of the Old Testament—his so-called 'Baptismal-Sacramentalism'—the Double Predestination—his attitudes to secular authority." But how, exclaimed Barth, could one possibly understand what Paul intended to say if one regarded all these points as irrelevant to his main message? (*Epistle to the Romans*, p. 12.)

sons, it is extremely hard to employ such concepts with consistency.

Somewhat like total truthfulness, these distinctions are applicable to certain kinds of data. In some passages focusing on issues of "faith and practice," biblical writers probably do not intend to affirm the accuracy of incidental historical or geographical minutiae. In many texts the cultural practices recorded are not what the writer intends to teach. Our theory also accounts for such phenomena, however by limiting the Bible's truthfulness to "all that it affirms." However due to the intertwining of faith and history, Christ and culture, etc. in so many biblical texts, the broad distinctions stressed by these two views are not adequate for dealing with broad ranges of biblical material.

In conclusion: since total biblical truthfulness which entails that no biblical proposition flatly contradicts any other true proportion, satisfies the criteria for theological theories significantly better than the alternatives, we prefer to retain this theory and keep on revising it in light of further data rather than scrapping it for another one.

C. Circular Reasoning

Arguments for inerrancy are often accused of being circular. That is, they often seem to begin with Scripture passages (2 Tim. 3:16, 2 Pet. 1:21, etc.) which function as premises, and then conclude that the Bible is wholly truthful because these passages say so. Do not such arguments assume that those biblical premises are true before they even begin? In other words, do they not simply assume the truth of their conclusion, and thus not really established it at all? Our own procedure might be accused of a similar flaw. We have often said that biblical truthfulness must be defined in such a way that the relationship between biblical propositions and those found in other fields is clarified. Yet we seem to have derived our main concepts solely from Scripture, and have not yet shown how its truth-claims compare with others.

In answer, let us recall that we have never established any doctrine on the basis of criteria generally acknowledged outside the "circle of faith." As an activity of the living Church, our theology assumes the kerygma's basic truth, and seeks to probe and articulate its implications. Our efforts to understand revelation's propositional dimension in greater detail already assume its general veracity. Properly speaking, our argument is not seeking to "prove" our theory by reference to some neutral, commonly acknowledged criteria. Instead, it seeks to show in depth what affirmation of Scripture's general reliability and commitment to Christ's Lordship really imply.

One thing they imply is that biblical truthfulness cannot be limited to some existential realm of "faith and practice" divorced from realms like "history, science, and geography" known through other fields of study. We have argued that eschatology and revelation have to do with the entire cosmos. One implication of total biblical truthfulness, then, is that no biblical proposition should ever be interpreted as in flat contradiction to a true proposition from any other field of knowledge.

Given limitations of space, we can only affirm *that* such a principle holds. We cannot investigate the numerous complex and intriguing questions as to *how* it might operate in relationship to the claims of various fields of knowledge. We can indicate, however, that this principle is very general. Just as it allows for great diversity of perspective, emphasis, and linguistic form among various biblical writings, so it makes room for great differences between biblical and modern scientific forms of expression. It can consider the possibility, for instance, that ancient writers were not always concerned to report dates and events with the strict accuracy that modern historians desire. Or that some biblical affirmations concerning the physical universe were expressed in partically poetic form, all the details of which need not be taken literally. The insistence that biblical and other kinds of affirmation not conflict need not mean that these affirmations are always expressed in the same kind of language.

This broad principle of propositional truthfulness need not lead to artificial, unnatural interpretation either of Scripture or of modern fields of study. For neither religion nor science are best served when one wholly adopts the truth-claims of the other, and suppresses certain of its own affirmations because the other field seems to demand it. The principle that a biblical affirmation should never be interpreted as flatly contradictory to scientific truth can demand that both fields participate in creative dialogue. It can help theology reconsider and refine its grasp of the true import of Scripture, and can help science consider how ultimate and/or provisional are its various methods and claims.

D. Stifles Interpretation

These considerations lead to perhaps the most vocal objections raised against inerrantists. These objections are practical ones. When one passage seems to contradict another (or a truth known by other means), inerrantists sometimes rush to harmonize them. But this often involves closing one's eyes to "the most self-evident character of the text."[36] The insistence that one assertion not contradict another seems to put blinders on a person. Accordingly, opponents often insist that one can be truly open to the claims of particular texts only if the possibility of errors is acknowledged.

We have insisted that every proposition and text has a certain range of adaptability; thus it can be compatible with others which initially seem quite different. Nevertheless, although we allow for numerous ways of explaining relationships among propositions, we have insisted that no text or proposition be interpreted in flat contradiction to another. Might this limit still stifle a truly unbiased hearing of biblical texts?

On the contrary, as long as we are alive to diversity of perspectives and linguistic forms within and beyond the canon, the limit which we propose can help unlock the meaning of apparently contradictory affirmations. For if two

[36] Dunn, p. 211.

texts or propositions are absolutely contradictory, then at least one must be entirely false. And once a textual propsition is regarded as indisputably false, it loses its ability to reveal new things: to challenge, to shake us up, to present God afresh.

Much that appears erroneous in Scripture is due to our own lack of understanding. If, however, one is committed to keep on wrestling with apparent discrepancies, then new insights as to how Scripture speaks and conveys truth can be obtained. As Karl Barth said when writing his commentary on Romans:

> The commentator is thus presented with a clear "Either-Or". The question is whether or not he is to place himself in a relation to his author of utter loyalty. Is he to read him, determined to follow him to the very last word, wholly aware of what he is doing, and assuming that the author also knew what he was doing?...Anything short of utter loyalty means a commentary ON Paul's Epistle to the Romans, not a commentary so far as is possible WITH him—even to his last word. True exegesis involves, of course, much sweat and many groans....[the interpreter] will, moreover, always be willing to assume that, when he fails to understand, the blame is his and not Paul's....I cannot, for my part, think it possible for an interpreter honestly to reproduce the meaning of any author unless he dares to accept the condition of utter loyalty.[37]

Such continuous wrestling, however, is the opposite of an easy and premature harmonizing of texts. If we approach Scripture with both an appreciation of its variety and a commitment to its total truthfulness, certain questions may refuse to resolve themselves for a long time. Yet this attitude, rather than being an escape from difficulties, can open up a space for the personal God to speak. It can allow God to reveal far deeper correspondences among biblical affirmations than we could at first perceive.

Maintaining that the Bible is wholly truthful in all that it affirms, then, can be a good way to ensure that exegetes and theologians deal with all the biblical material, including passages which seem unclear, irrelevant, and counter to our way of thinking. It can be a good way of ensuring that all of Scripture be heard as God's Word and retain its capacity to be "living and active, sharper than any two-edged sword, piercing to the division of soul and spirit, of joints and marrow, and discerning the thoughts and intentions of the heart." (Heb. 4:12).

---

[37] *Epistle to the Romans*, pp. 17-18. Barth continued: "I have never attempted to conceal the fact that my manner of interpretation has certain affinities with the old doctrine of Verbal Inspiration. As expounded by Calvin, the doctrine seems to me at least worthy of careful consideration....Is there any way of penetrating the heart of a document—of any document!—except on the assumption that its spirit will speak to our spirit through the actual written words?" (p.18) But although Barth's own exegetical method, in his Romans commentary and in his later writings, often displayed such loyalty to the very words of biblical texts, he cannot be called a consistent proponent of verbal inspiration. (See Klaus Runia, *Karl Barth's Doctrine of Holy Scripture* [Grand Rapids: Eerdmans, 1962]).

If instead of persisting in this commitment to let all Scripture speak God's truth to us, we close off certain passages as erroneous, we will likely be judging and partially silencing God's revelation by means of modern criteria of truth and error.

Suggestions for Further Reading

Achtemeier, Paul. *The Inspiration of Scripture*. Philadelphia: Westminster, 1980.
Barr, James. *Holy Scripture: Canon, Authority, Criticism*. Philadelphia: Westminster, 1983.
———. *The Scope and Authority of the Bible*. Philadelphia: Westminster, 1981.
Beegle, Dewey. *Scripture, Tradition and Infallibility*. Grand Rapids: Eerdmans, 1973.
Berkouwer, C. G. *Holy Scripture*. Grand Rapids: Eerdmans, 1975.
Boice, James., *et al.* *The Foundation of Biblical Authority*. Grand Rapids: Zondervan, 1978.
Davis, Stephen. *The Debate About the Bible*. Philadelphia: Westminster, 1977.
Fuller, Daniel. "Benjamin Warfield's View of Faith and History," *Bulletin of the Evangelical Theological Society* 2 (1968), pp. 75-83.
Longenecker, Richard. *Biblical Exegesis in the Apostolic Period*. Grand Rapids; Eerdmans, 1975.
McKim, Donald, ed. *The Authoritative Word*. Grand Rapids: Eerdmans, 1983.
Montgomery, John, ed. *God's Inerrant Word*. Minneapolis: Bethany, 1974.
Nicole, Roger and Michaels, J. Ramsey, eds. *Inerrancy and Common Sense*. Grand Rapids: Baker, 1980.
Pinnock, Clark. *The Scripture Principle*. San Francisco: Harper, 1984.
Preus, Robert. *The Inspiration of Scripture: A Study of the Theology of the 17th Century Lutheran Dogmaticians*. Edinburgh: Oliver & Boyd, 1955.
Rogers, Jack, ed. *Biblical Authority* Waco, Tx.: Word, 1978.
Rogers, Jack and McKim, Donald. *The Authority and Interpretation of the Bible*. New York: Harper, 1980.
Runia, Klaus. *Karl Barth's Doctrine of Holy Scripture*, Grand Rapids: Eerdmans, 1962.
Warfield, Benjamin. *The Inspiration and Authority of the Bible*. Philadelphia: Presbyterian & Reformed, 1948.
———. *Revelation and Inspiration*. Toronto: Oxford, 1927.
Woodbridge, John. *Biblical Authority: A Critique of the Rogers/McKim Proposal*. Grand, Rapids: Zondervan, 1982.
Youngblood, Ronald. ed., *Evangelicals and Inerrancy*. Nashville: Nelson, 1984.

CHAPTER THIRTEEN

Special and General Revelation

The three preceding chapters have shown that special revelation is, first of all, specific. In Christianity revelation is neither a generalized communication from God nor a general awareness of the divine. Revelation occurs in specific personal encounters which call, challenge, and comfort. It occurs in particular historical events in the lives of particular peoples. It is expressed in propositions which make definite assertions.

At the same time, revelation is "open-textured." Personal encounters are not private, self-enclosed experiences; they open one up towards God, towards others, and towards historic tasks. Revelatory historical events are not merely uncanny, isolated theophanies; they concretize God's historical purposes, fulfilling and extending what has happened before, promising and straining towards what is to come. And revelatory propositions are not narrow, iron-bound assertions; they interpret and thus open up the significance of encounters and events, linking them together and increasing the power of their flow. Chiefly through its historical continuity and its propositional articulation, the revelatory stream is channeled, as it were, within certain banks. Or to change the image, special revelation occurs within a certain framework. Numerous encounters, events, and assertions are included within it. But they all fall within a certain range.

So conceived, revelation is not merely a deposit consisting of objective contents. Revelation consists not merely of past events, nor of the inscripturated

Word of God. Revelation is also an activity of God's Spirit, bringing challenge, judgment, and life by means of these things. In order to apprehend the unity of this full-orbed reality, we have chosen not to restrict the term "revelation" to its objective dimension and to later discuss the manner in which the Spirit brings "illumination." We have wanted to focus on the intertwined modalities by which both Spirit and written Word, both God himself and truths about God, can be known by today's active, inquiring Church.

Nevertheless our account of these intertwinings may still be incomplete. For we have not been very specific as to how the Bible and the past history recorded in it come alive in the present. Does the Spirit simply pick up what happened and was written in ancient times and drop it directly, as it were, into the present? Or do important connecting links exist, about which any adequate theology of revelation should speak? Roman Catholicism, along with Eastern Orthodoxy, has long maintained that they do. Not only Scripture but also Church tradition is a source of revelation for these communions. Tradition is clearly historical. Since decisions of popes and councils have been declared authoritative, it is also propositional. Finally, since the Spirit is the ultimate subject of tradition,[1] it is also personal.

Since it is claimed that the three major dimensions of revelation are operative in tradition, a consideration of this topic can help tie together all that we have said about special revelation so far. Then having attained clarity as to what is distinctive about revelation in the Christian sense, we can consider comprehensively a theme we have dropped since the end of Chapter 11: the possibility of general revelation.

I. Tradition

In response to Protestant claims that Scripture alone was the source of religious authority, Roman Catholicism crystallized many of its teachings on tradition at the Council of Trent (1545–63). Most Protestants, along with most Catholics, understood the Council to mean that the fullness of the gospel could not be found in Scripture alone, and that it therefore had to be supplemented and interpreted by teachings of the Roman magisterium. Tradition, as both sides tended to see it, was a body of authoritative propositions in addition to those found in the Bible. Protestants objected that these propositions not only added to but often critiqued and distorted what the Scriptures said.

[1] Yves Congar, *The Meaning of Tradition* (New York: Hawthorn, 1964), pp. 51-58. (The following page references in our text are to this work.) For an interesting dialogue between Catholics and evangelical Protestants on the role of tradition in theology, see the articles by Clark Pinnock, Avery Dulles, and David Wells respectively in the *TSF Bulletin* 6/1, pp. 2-5; 6/3, pp. 6-8; and 6/5, pp. 5-6.

A. The Modern Catholic Position

Since at least the mid-nineteenth century, however, many Catholics have begun to view tradition in a somewhat different manner.[2] Yves Congar, for instance, points out that tradition, in its broadest sense, means the entire process
of handing on a religious faith. This process of transmitting the remembrance
of earlier events, of basic teachings, of rituals and ethical norms and customs,
goes back to the earliest roots of the Judeo-Christian heritage. In this broad
sense tradition includes not only the teachings but the whole atmosphere of a
religious faith: those moods evoked in its worship, those attitudes, life-styles,
and patterns of relationship which shape the lives of its members at the deepest levels. All Christian groups today are rooted in tradition in this sense.

Like many modern Catholics, Congar asserts that the entire normative apostolic teaching can be found in Scripture.[3] He can say that

> The Holy Scriptures have an absolute value which Tradition has not...they are
> the supreme guide to which any other [norm] there may be are subjected. If Tradi-
> tion or the Magisterium claimed to teach something contradicting the Holy Scrip-
> tures, it would certainly be false, and the faithful ought to reject it.[4]

Nevertheless, Congar also argues that Scripture's living authority cannot reside in its bare words alone, as he understands Protestant orthodoxy to main-

[2] For a good overview, see Congar, *The Meaning of Tradition* (New York: Macmillan,
1966), pp. 189-221. The notion of "living tradition," in contrast to that of tradition
as the transmission of authoritative teaching, was first fully developed by the "Tü-
bingen school," particularly in the work of Johann Moehler (1796–1838). It was
furthered in the Catholic "modernist" movement around the beginning of this
century.

[3] See Karl Rahner, *Foundations of Christian Faith* (New York: Seabury, 1978), pp. 369-
78; see the discussion in C. G. Berkouwer, *The Second Vatican Council and the New
Catholicism* (Grand Rapids: Eerdmans, 1965), pp. 89-111. Vatican II, however, still
insisted that "it is not from sacred Scripture alone that the Church draws her certainty about everything which has been revealed." (Walter Abbot, ed., *The Documents of Vatican II* [New York: Guild, 1966] p. 117.)

[4] Pp. 94-95; in the words omitted from the above quotation, however, Congar cau-
tions that the Scriptures are not "the absolute rule of every other norm, like the
Protestant scriptural principle." We shall seek to unfold the exact distinctions involved here as we proceed.

tain.[5] Instead the written Word is "a kind of sacrament: a grace-bearing sign that effectively realizes communion with God, and salvation, when it is used in the right conditions" (p. 86). An essential condition is that the Bible be heard within the context of the living Church.

Phrased otherwise, Congar speaks of two stages of revelation. The first is that of delivery, when revelation was originally given to the Church "as something unique, accomplished once and for all." The second is that of transmission. Throughout this stage the Spirit is continually actualizing the Word in the Church, so that this stage "is also filled with the active presence of what God has accomplished once and for all at the time of the prophets, of Christ and of the apostles" (pp. 48-49).

So far we can largely agree with this modern Catholic perspective. It helps explain concretely how the Bible participates in God's continuing historical and personal revelatory work. Perhaps by often speaking of God's personal revelation as challenging, calling, rebuking, etc., we have given the impression that personal revelation always breaks in unexpectedly and "vertically, from above." Now we can more fully appreciate that revelation often comes alive because the teaching, the worship, the whole process of character formation carried on in the Church attunes people to what God wants to say. The Catholic perspective helps keep us from regarding the role of the Bible in too isolated a way, the work of the Spirit in too individualistic a way.

Yet despite this general apprecation we have not yet examined carefully what modern Catholicism says about tradition's authority. Since this has formed the major point of controversy between Catholics and Protestants, let us consider it carefully.

B. The Authority of Tradition in Catholicism

Although tradition in the broadest sense includes the transmission of the Church's essential faith and life, traditions in the narrower sense "are decisions which become norms under certain conditions" (p. 118). Congar stresses that the Church's leaders are generally quite reluctant to articulate the faith so precisely. Nevertheless situations arise when the College of Bishops, united to the Pope as to its head, finds it necessary "to 'define' the traditional belief...in the form of a 'dogma,' that is, a formula which is taken as a norm, and is legally binding" (p.65). Such formulations reflect, on one hand, the creativity appro-

---

[5] According to Protestant orthodoxy, Congar asserts, "Scripture possesses by itself and in itself, that is, without needing the addition of any other principle, the qualities of a real sacrament of salvation....It possesses authority, making it recognized and developing it unaided; it possesses efficacy, being the principal—and for some the sole—means of Grace; it is clear, explaining itself without help and needing nothing besides itself to make known God's thoughts" (pp. 87-88). For the views of Protestant orthodox theologians themselves, see Heppe, pp. 21-41; Schmid, pp. 50-80.

priate to the transmitting channel. Yet Congar emphasizes that the Magisterium seeks primarily to recognize and then to submit itself to the apostolic truth which it articulates (pp. 68-69).

What grounds exist for speaking of an authoritative Tradition in addition to Scripture? Catholics point out that the New Testament writers themselves referred to unwritten traditions which they had passed down and which they regarded as authoritative.[6] This fact indicates that a certain fullness of the gospel was communicated to the apostles; they expressed some aspects of it in writing, but others they did not. Yet since such traditions came from the apostles, Catholics argue that they have the same binding quality as the apostolic writings and continue to be authoritative for the Church today. Therefore, if need arises, the Church can also put them in writing.

Further, Catholics argue that the writings we do have are "fragmentary and occasional"; they do not provide sufficient guidance on certain important issues (pp. 37, 69). The best example of this is the canon of the New Testament itself. In order for the Church to be rightly guided, it must know which writings are authoritative and which are not. Yet no New Testament book contains a list of such writings. The list was decided upon by the Church itself. Hence the Church played an authoritative role even in deciding what the biblical norm should be (pp. 102-05; cf. p. 36).

Yet even though Catholics refer to tradition as "apostolic," they acknowledge that many of its precise features do not go back to the apostles themselves. For, according to Congar, when a living subject receives something, that subject "necessarily puts something of himself into what he receives" (p. 105). Thus the general, unwritten apostolic directives were articulated in more precise form by those who received this tradition. In this way the Spirit transformed the channel of transmission "into a sort of source with regard to what it transmits."[7]

The real differences between the historic Catholic and Protestant perspectives might be most vividly apprehended by glancing at those features of Catholicism that are thought to be revealed by tradition. For Congar the Eucharist is at the heart of Catholicism. Yet since the New Testament contains only "a small number of verses" on this theme,

> the faith of the Churches in this absolutely central mystery depends directly on the oral teachings of the apostles, on the example of their celebration of it and on the eucharistic reality itself, placed in the heart of the communities as an unfailing fountain of truth, much more than on the Gospel *texts* (p. 97; cf. pp. 24-25).

[6] 1 Thess. 4:1-2; 2 Thess. 2:13-14; 1 Cor. 11:2; cf. John 20:30, 21:25.

[7] Congar, p. 114; thus during the "Golden Age of the Fathers" (the mid-fourth to the mid-fifth centuries), when the Catholic church and tradition began to take on definitive shape, the fact that something was universally known and accepted sufficed to render it apostolic, whether or not it could be traced back to the apostles (pp. 40-41, 134-39).

Elsewhere, Congar lists certain details of Church liturgical practice (pp. 39. 125-32) and of Church structure (pp. 25-26). In addition, he stresses that

> such inner realities as those founded on a sense of God's presence, activity and exactingness in the creature he sanctifies: the Marian mystery, the religious life (monachism), the dignity of consecrated virginity, the eucharistic presence—are re-alities that concern the religious relationship in its inmost truth; they are in no way secondary, but intimate and almost secret (p. 118).

C. Response

We appreciate the general Catholic emphasis on tradition, but we generally support the following Protestant objections to its role as a propositional, revela-tory authority.

Although the apostles clearly handed down traditions which they did not commit to writing, it is not at all clear that they intended them to be of con-tinuing authority. The apostles certainly said, commanded, and probably even wrote much that was relevant for their own times but which would have be-come outmoded after several generations. Moreover even if they did intend some of their traditions to be enduringly normative, Protestants have doubted that we can know what they were. Since Roman Catholics acknowledge that many traditions do not go back to the apostles in anything like their precise form, how shall we distinguish those which may truly reflect their spirit from those which do not? We are especially wary of the fact that much of the tradi-tion took on definitive shape during "the golden age of the Fathers"; between the mid-fourth and the mid-fifth centuries (pp. 134-39). By this time Christian-ity had been transformed from a frequently persecuted, largely counter-cultural movement to the favored religion of the Roman Empire. It began to support and be supported by, the social, political, and military endeavors of the State. It became more and more the religion of the *status quo* and less and less a reli-gion which challenged it. This is hardly to say that God did not continue to reveal himself through Church tradition during that time. But to discern where and how this occurred one needs criteria derived from elsewhere, not those formed largely within this context.

Is there merit to the argument that the Church of this time designated the limits of the canon? It is true, of course, that these exact limits were specified by the Council of Constantinople in 381. Since we have insisted on reading the Bible within the canonical context, we can hardly overlook this fact. But does it mean that the Church in some authoritative way decided, or defined, or established the canon itself? Careful reading of the history of canonization shows that very few books not now in the canon were ever seriously considered for inclusion.[8] It also shows that the canonicity of only a few of those included was ever doubted.[9] When a disputed book was or was not considered canonical, the reasons were usually obvious: Most often, books eventually excluded were considered for a time because they were thought to be apostolic; similarly, those eventually included were doubted for a time because they were not thought to be apostolic.

The history of canonization, (which we must skim over far too swiftly) leads to the conclusion that the Church, rather than itself creating or defining the canon, more or less recognized it. It recognized that certain writings had continued, over the course of many decades, to speak with an authority that transcended and grounded the Church itself. This history, of course, indicates that the biblical writings did not suddenly fall from heaven with seals of authority engraved upon them. Scripture was committed to writing and continued to function within the Church. Nevertheless the history of canonization gives no warrant for supposing that tradition can ever become an authoritative norm for theology.

The strongest argument against such an authoritative role is that some doctrines uniquely rooted in tradition not only supplement New Testament teachings but at points contradict them. This is so not only with incidental teachings but with some which writers like Congar find at the heart of Catholicism, those concerning sacraments and Church structure in particular. The Catholic teaching on the eucharist, for instance, not only goes well beyond the New Testament data but serves to shape one's understanding of worship, of the priesthood, and of the communion with Christ in very decisive ways. Accordingly, we cannot regard biblical teachings on such matters as undesirably "fragmentary and occasional." This "fragmentary" nature raises an authoritative barrier against such developments. Of course we recognize that, in order to celebrate the sacraments and structure churches, traditions which supplement the New Testament data must be developed. God can reveal himself personally

---

[8] There are about thirteen major listings of canonical New Testament writings before AD 381. (We include Irenaeus, the Muratorian Canon [190], Tertullian, Clement of Alexandria, Origen, Codex Claromontanus [280], Methodius, Eusebius, Codex Siniaticus [340], Cyril of Jerusalem, the Synod of Laodoceia [365], Athanatius, and Gregory Nazianzus.) Of the books considered in any way for inclusion in the New Testament canon, the Shepherd of Hermas appears on four of these lists. The Apocalypse of Peter appears on three, the Epistle of Barnabas on two, and no other book appears more than once.

[9] Of the twenty-seven books in our present New Testament, the canonicity of only eight was questioned in any way on any of the lists mentioned above. Only two books (Hebrews and Revelation) were omitted from two of these lists and only four were omitted from one (James, 1 and 2 Peter, and 3 John are all missing from the Muratorian Canon). No book was recorded as having doubtful canonical status on any more than four lists (2 Peter and 3 John were questioned four times). Doubt as to apostolic authorship can explain almost all these omissions and questions.

and historically through such traditions. Yet no such historical tradition can provide authoritative propositions by which those of Scripture may be critiqued and judged.

Unfortunately we can substantiate our claims about sacraments and structure only in another context (Vol. II, Chaps. 9, 13–14). However, we can perhaps justify them in part in light of some distinctions already familiar to us. Congar writes that:

> The Protestants want a Church ceaselessly renewing herself by a dramatic and precarious confrontation with the Word of God. Together with the Fathers we see the Church as the continuous communication, through space and time, of the mystical community born from the Lord's institution and Pentecost (pp. 104-05).

Elsewhere, he similarly says,

> the Protestant starts from the Word of God, as the principle from which his religion reaches him, and in practical terms from the sacred *Text*, considered as being the Word of God, while the Catholic starts from the reality of Christianity itself which reaches him in and by the Church, ever since the apostles (p. 117).

From our early chapters we have insisted that the Church, and hence theology, exists at the intersection of kerygma and context. We misconstrue the nature of the Church, and thus of theology, if we overlook either one. Nevertheless we have also insisted that a certain relationship exists between them. The Church is called into being by the kerygma; it continues to truly be the Church only as long as the kerygma critiques and renews it. In other words our theology has been essentially kerygmatic: We have emphasized the sharp difference between the divine perspective on reality and the ways in which human beings, even within the Church, normally understand God, the world, and themselves. In our treatment of revelation, this kerygmatic emphasis has been evident particularly in our notions of revelation as God's personal call to radical decision and of historical revelation as God's unexpected promise, often fulfilled in ways which surprise us.

For these reasons we cannot regard any Church teaching which goes well beyond what Scripture teaches, and which promotes to the center of faith elements which Scripture leaves largely undeveloped, as equally authoritative with the Bible. We believe in the continuous existence of the Church from Pentecost on, but not necessarily in the "continuous communication" of authoritative teachings which attained no recognized propositional form for centuries.

D. Conclusions

In speaking of revelation as historical and personal, if we overlook the function of tradition, then our understanding of revelation will be quite incomplete. We might well leave the impression that the Spirit simply picks up the written Word from the first century and drops it, unmediated, into our own.

We would overlook the important fact that special revelation normally occurs within Christian communities shaped by all those sociological, doctrinal, and affective characteristics that constitute tradition. Tradition may well distort God's revelation in certain ways. Yet (as we said in Chap. 3) we finite humans always begin to perceive revelation through the particular lens or angle of vision that tradition provides.

Important practical implications follow. It is mistaken, for instance, to assume that the Bible, the wholly truthful written Word, will normally communicate God's full revelatory will and presence simply by being read in isolation. Important as individual Scripture reading is, the Bible is intended to come fully alive amid worshipping, fellowshipping, missionary communities. It leads people not merely to individual experiences or cognitive insights but also into just such communities.

Essential as it is to revelation's dynamics, tradition nonetheless adds no content to revelation's propositional truth. Revelation, like theology, has various sources; but Scripture is its only propositional norm (cf. pp. 54-55 above). Scripture alone marks out the range within which authentic revelation occurs.

II. Discerning God's Revelation

Where, amid the cacophany of experiences, events, and writings which claim to express the ultimate truth about things, can the Church discern the true revelation of God? How can we know that what purports to be revelation really is such? This is the question with which we began our study of revelation. We can now begin to give some broad answers.

At the beginning of this chapter, we summarized special revelation's fundamental characteristics. Special revelation is, first of all, specific; it is grounded in particular encounters, events and propositions. These specific occurrences and assertions, second, are open-textured; they point toward each other and towards God. Finally as patterned by these specific, open-textured events and statements, authentic revelation falls within a certain framework or range.

The second of these characteristics, open-texturing, is especially important in helping one discern whether claims to revelation are authentic. It means, essentially, that authentic revelations cannot be isolated and enclosed within themselves. For instance, is a deeply moving personal encounter with an apparently Wholly Other reality a revelation of the true God? One fundamental test for answering this question is this: Does, or did, this encounter point beyond itself, towards the broader sweep of history and towards the God who is guiding all things unto their consummation? (In other words, is the dominantly personal character of this revelation connected with an historical dimension?) The second fundamental criterion: Does this manifestation of the Wholly Other point towards, and is it consistent with, the propositional claims about God's acts and character found in Holy Scripture? (In other words, is its personal character connected with a propositional one?) Of course this openness, or interconnectedness, of the personal dimension of such a revelation with historical and propositional ones need not be explicit. An encounter with a "Wholly Other" might well be quite overwhelming. As it occurs it might neither bring to mind God's past dealings nor call one to specific future tasks (although most biblical records of these encounters contain such elements). Neither need biblical passages run through one's mind.

Nevertheless it is important that such personal encounters be implicitly linked with revelation's historical and propositional dimensions. As time goes by one may legitimately ask: How did, or does, that past experience link up with what I have experienced before, and what is happening to me now? Towards what kind of involvements with current and future events is it drawing me? Similarly one can also ask: How does that experience relate to what Scripture says about God and human destiny; about what is good and right and true?

If in answer to such questions no connections can be discerned, that past experience, whatever it was, has remained self-enclosed; it has not opened one up towards God, towards God's historical movement, and towards God's written Word. On the other hand, such an experience could have opened one up towards historical forces quite different than those guided by the biblical God or towards verbal interpretations of reality at variance with those of Scripture. But if so, that experience has been a revelation of something else. Astounding, overwhelming, even practically significant as such encounters may be, they are not, simply by virtue of these characteristics, revelations of the true God. They are moving experiences of a quite different sort—or else revelations of other forces still contending with God for ultimate control of history.

Apparent revelations which are chiefly historical or personal in character may be evaluated in similar ways. Is a certain historical event a revelation of God? One needs to ask whether it points openly, even if only implicitly, towards God's past acts and their future consummation. One also needs to ask whether this event makes an (at least implicit) personal claim. Does God call, challenge, comfort, or rebuke one through it? Finally, does its significance, when propositionally expressed, fall within the framework of meaning outlined by biblical propositions? Is a certain proposition a revelation of God? If it is not found in Scripture, it might accurately express or help communicate revelation. But as indicated in our discussion of tradition, only the propositions of the Bible can, in the direct sense, be revelation. Yet even they are not fully revelatory if they are simply comprehended as cognitive assertions. No matter how correct their content, they are not actually revelations of God if they do not (at least implicitly) point us towards God's personal presence and call. Moreover they are not revelations if they do not (at least implicitly) open out towards God's past and future historical activity.

In summary, it is when specific encounters, events, and propositions are open-textured—when they point beyond themselves and bring one into contact with history and/or Scripture and/or God's personal address—that they are truly revelatory. Revelation, so understood, is always moving, always personally challenging, always overflowing any event or formulation. Yet at the same time, by virtue of the other specific features of revelation to which any one occurrence or statement points, the dynamic movement of authentic revelation always occurs within a certain framework.

However, since this pointing of any true revelation towards others is often implicit, the authenticity of many alleged revelations can be discerned only through the passage of time. Did a particular encounter, event, or proposition really come from God? Often we can be sure only if its significance eventually links up with that of other dimensions of revelation; if it eventually proves to be revelatory. Yet this test need not be due to the imperfection of a revelatory event. For the Biblical God reveals himself through conflict with opposing claims and forces. Revelation itself is one dimension of God's broader historical working, which brings truth, righteousness, and peace to their final triumph at the *eschaton*.

As today's Church sets out with God on this path towards the consummation, revelation, chiefly in its past-historical and propositional dimensions, gives it a framework within which to perceive and to act. Yet the frequent need for waiting to discern the revelatory significance of statements and events keeps the Church continually open to God and to the world.

III. From Special to General Revelation

According to the above account, events and statements can be called revelation only if they are (at least implicitly) three-dimensional; if they possess, or are interconnected with, revelation's personal, historical, and propositional dimensions. But what, then, of apparent revelations where only one, or even two, dimensions are present? What about a biblical proposition by itself or such a proposition which accurately reports an historical event? What about a deep personal experience or such an experience which accords with a biblical proposition? Are none of these phenomena revelatory, even though they are characterized by one or two dimensions of revelation?

If we insist that they are not, we seem to be denying revelation's objectivity. Consider a biblical proposition which apparently does not come alive personally to anyone, or an historic act of God which nobody apparently recognizes. If these are not revelation until they confront somebody personally, must we say that God has not truly revealed himself in them? Do they depend on human response in order to become revelation? If so, then God's revelation does not seem to possess reality or objectivity in and of itself. On the other hand, consider personal experiences of, say, "ontological shock." If they do not lead one into contact with God's particular historic work and/or its propositional expression, can we be sure that God was in no way present in them? If so, then our three-dimensional view of revelation seems to also deny the subjective, as well as the reality of much that might well be called revelation.

Our reason for insisting on revelation's tri-dimensionality is this: Even though many phenomena characterized by one or two of these dimensions may in some sense be from God, humans can respond to them in a way greatly at variance with the divine intention. Consider biblical propositions, even those which truthfully articulate revelatory historical events. Unless such propositions become vehicles of God's personal address, they can lead away from God instead of towards him. If one simply assents to a biblical proposition, no matter how profoundly true its content may be, without hearing the claim of the God to which it points, one will remain distant from God. Further, one can resist God precisely by assenting to more and more such propositions. One may learn a great deal about the Bible or theology, may affirm their truth on a merely intellectual level, and even teach others to affirm it, but all the while use precisely these seemingly earnest affirmations to shield oneself from the awareness that one has not really responded, at the deepest levels, to the personal claims and presence of God.

Or consider personal encounters, even those whose meaning can be expressed by biblical propositions. Unless they point one towards God's historic activity, one can remain distant from active, concrete fellowship with God. What is more, one can resist God precisely by experiencing more and more such encounters. One can focus existence increasingly around them and even lead others to share them, but all the while use this preoccupation to avoid following God into the concrete realities of contemporary historical life.

The above examples (which we could multiply by considering all combinations of revelatory dimensions) clarify an important feature of revelatory truth. Apprehending God's truth is not merely a matter of apprehending various aspects of it in such a way that the more one apprehends, the more truly is God revealed. Whether or not revelation truly occurs has much to do with the context within which certain items of truth are perceived and with the use which one makes of this knowledge. If one correctly apprehends a certain truth about God, say the truth of a biblical proposition, but does not grasp its openness towards and interconnectedness with those personal and historical dimensions within which alone it has its true revelatory significance, that truth will not lead one towards God. In other words, if this truth is not perceived within the proper context, and if one does not make proper use of it, then one will be apprehending it in a different context and making a different use of it. And all other such contexts and uses will lead one, in greater or lesser degree, away from God.

Our attempts to synthesize what we have said about special revelation are leading us towards an understanding of truth somewhat different than the usual common-sense notion. Most people think of "truth" as a matter of correspondence: If particular beliefs or statements correctly represent a reality which is largely "out there" or external to one, then they are true. According to this common-sense notion, the more items of truth one comes to know, the more fully do one's thoughts and one's life come into accord with whatever is ultimately true.

The view of truth which we are presenting, however, indicates that although one can acknowledge many true statements, one's overall life can be, in the full biblical sense of the term, in error (Chap. 12 above). For truth is not just a matter of the correspondence of one's beliefs to reality; more importantly, it is a matter of their coherence with other beliefs and actions. Truth is not just a matter of individual, specific beliefs; it has to do with the way in which these beliefs are interrelated with others (the context within which they function) and of the way in which they operate in one's behavior (their use). The ultimate truth of any one belief cannot be determined in isolation from the overall complex of beliefs in which they find their ultimate meaning. And neither, as liberation theologians insist, can it be determined apart from its actual function in praxis.

This, then, is why we have insisted that special revelation must be three-dimensional: because only when particular truths about God are apprehended within the context of all three dimensions do they point adequately towards the divine reality. If only one or two dimensions are present, they can be apprehended in quite different contexts and used in quite different ways. Nevertheless, the question raised at the beginning of this section has not yet been answered. Even if, say, a biblical proposition or a religious encounter can be apprehended and used in a way that leads away from God, do we want to say that God was not revealed in them in any sense? We do not wish to say this. It appears, then, that we must make some distinction between kinds of revelation.

To indicate the sort of distinction we wish to emphasize, we introduce the terms "integrating" and "fragmentary" revelation. Integrating revelation includes (at least implicitly) all three revelatory dimensions. The term indicates that any such revelation points and draws one towards the fullness of God's revelatory activity and thus can integrate one's awareness and activity into this stream. Fragmentary revelation involves only one or two of the revelatory dimensions. The term indicates that, by itself, such a revelation might possibly direct one towards God's full revelatory activity; yet it could well be interpreted and used in an opposite way.[10] Unusual though this way of speaking about special revelation is, it leads directly to the issue of general revelation. For general revelation, as the term is commonly understood, is partial and fragmentary in character. Some theological traditions, however, affirm it as a stepping-stone towards God's fuller revelation, while others argue that it leads in the opposite way.

IV. General Revelation

General revelation is revelation of the true God which is available to people whether or not they have responded to, or whether they have even heard of the special revelation focusing on Jesus Christ.

---

[10] An integrating revelation, however, can also be rejected. Yet since God decisively approaches one in such an encounter, and has to be definitively rejected, it will be much harder to integrate the truth so apprehended into an alien context.

A. Divergence in Theological Tradition

According to traditional Roman Catholicism, sufficient general revelation is available to construct a natural theology. Natural theology is usually understood to be the reflective, philosophical elaboration of a more intuitive, spontaneous awareness of certain theological truths possessed by all humans.[11] We have pictured natural theology as the lower level of the Thomistic theological system (Chap. 4 above). By means of this lower level revelation, one apprehends certain general truths (such as God's existence) which are then supplemented by truths of the higher level of special revelation (such as God's triune nature).

Protestants, however, have traditionally been critical of this Catholic affirmation that, beginning with reason and general human experience, one can begin moving upwards towards God's special revelation. To some like Karl Barth, it seemed to imply that humans, through their unaided efforts, could begin establishing a saving relationship with a God fashioned after the concepts of the human mind. For these reasons Barth sharply rejected all talk of general revelation and natural theology (Chap. 5 above). Barth's position, however, seems to have been more extreme than the traditional Protestant one. John Calvin, for instance, affirmed the existence of general revelation. Yet he insisted that although all people know of God in this way, such knowledge cannot lead to salvation (Chap. 5).

Where shall we position ourselves amid these understandings of the relationship of general and special revelation? Since we have begun our overall theologizing from the standpoint of the kerygma and have resisted starting from the general philosophical perspective of any context, we must investigate general revelation from the standpoint of what we have already said about special revelation. Traditionally, general revelation has been thought to be available through two main sources: through awareness of the natural world and through one's moral nature, or conscience. We will work towards our own view as we examine these two possible sources.

B. Revelation through Nature

Traditionally, natural theologians have been impressed by the large amount of harmony and order discernible in the natural world. The teleological argument for God's existence has maintained that order and design can only be the products of an intelligent, purposeful mind; therefore, the design in the uni-

---

[11] For an interesting discussion of this "primordial" approach to God, see Jacques Maritain, *Approaches to God* (New York: Macmillan, 1954), esp. pp. 17-26.

verse proves the existence of an intelligent, purposeful God.[12] Critics, and even proponents, of the teleological argument have pointed out that such a Designer need not have all the attributes traditionally ascribed to God. The argument by itself cannot prove that the Designer also was the Creator of the matter that he so skillfully arranged. Neither need the Designer be omnipotent. Nor can the argument tell us whether the Designer possesses "moral attributes" such as goodness, justice, and love.[13]

We assume that this argument is a philosophical elaboration of intuitions which many people sense spontaneously. Beginning, however, from the standpoint of special revelation, what value and validity can we find in it?

Many Old Testament writers found evidence of Yahweh's creative and sustaining power in the order and harmony of nature. Isaiah declares that the God who created the heavens and established the earth "did not create it a chaos, he formed it to be inhabited" (Isa. 45:18). Jeremiah praises the God who "placed the sand as the bound for the sea, a perpetual barrier which it cannot pass; though the waves toss, they cannot prevail; though they roar, they cannot pass over it!" (Jer. 5:22, cf. 31:35–36). The order and regularity of nature impresses the Psalmists (e.g., Ps. 104:10–23), as does the power which brought it into being (104:5–9), and creation's moment-by-moment dependence on that power (104:27–30). Closely examined, however, passages such as these express a fuller apprehension of God than does the teleological argument. The teleological argument focuses on nature's order and regularity alone. Nature runs so perfectly that the continual presence and activity of the Designer is hardly necessary. Perhaps the Designer is ensconced somewhere above the clouds, serenely contemplating the perfection of his product. Or perhaps the Designer has simply left it and gone off somewhere else.

But for Old Testament writers, nature's regularity is a manifestation of God's primordial and continuing power. Creation itself is often depicted as a mighty struggle, as a conquest of the powers of chaos and destruction (Job 38:4–11; Ps. 74:14–17; Isa. 51:9, etc.). In the passages recently cited, Yahweh is depicted not as more-or-less leaving nature to run itself but as continually sustaining life and holding back disintegration by means of his power. In the overall Old Testament perspective, nature is not a virtually autonomous mechanism, operating according to its own unbreakable laws. It is a realm continually sustained

---

[12] Although the teleological argument can be found in Greek philosophy, it was developed in detail during the Enlightenment, when natural science was rapidly discovering new evidences of design. It's classic expression is William Paley's *Natural Theology* (Philadelphia: Woodward, 1831), esp. Chaps. 1-3. (Space prevents us from considering various forms of the cosmological argument.)

[13] This was a main claim of history's sharpest critique of the teleological argument, David Hume's *Dialogues Concerning Natural Religion* (New York: Hafner, 1948 [originally published in 1779]), Parts V, X, XI. Paley, however, sought to derive God's goodness from this argument (chap. 26).

by Yahweh and therefore open for unique, unusual displays of his power.

If this is roughly the way that God's presence in nature is apprehended in the Old Testament, nature's order and design is only one aspect of it. In fact, spontaneous inferences or philosophical arguments which focus only on this design and move from it to a cosmos wholly regulated by unbreakable laws arrive at a Designer quite different from the biblical God. Such unalterable design would not evidence the continuing presence of Yahweh's power. It would be evidence of Yahweh's absence from, or limitation by, or imprisonment within, a self-sufficient mechanism. (Twentieth-century science, however, suggests a worldview more adequate to the Bible; a natural realm generally ruled by regular patterns but "open" in various ways to something beyond [Chaps. 6 and 8 above].)

But while the Old Testament perceives God's reality in both nature's regularity and in its openness to Yahweh's superior power, it says little about how generally available to all people these perceptions are. Most texts dealing with these themes have been significantly shaped by Israel's own historical experience with Yahweh. To be sure, the Psalmist declares that:

> The heavens are telling the glory of God;
> and the firmament proclaims his handiwork.
> Day to day pours forth speech,
> and night to night declares knowledge.
> There is no speech, nor are there words;
> their voice is not heard;
> yet their voice goes out through all the earth,
> and their words to the end of the world (Ps. 19:1-4).

Nonetheless the Old Testament gives us little help in knowing just what kind of revelation is involved and what saving function, if any, it has. In the New Testament, however, as God's special revelation is carried to all nations, we get a bit more help in understanding how general revelation might function. Three passages are especially significant.

Towards the beginning of his Roman epistle, Paul affirms that

> what can be known about God is plain to [humanity], because God has shown it to them. Ever since the creation of the world his invisible nature, namely, his eternal power and deity, has been clearly perceived in the things that are made. So they are without excuse; for although they knew God they did not honor him as God or give thanks to him, but they became futile in their thinking, and senseless minds were darkened (Rom. 1:19–21).

Notice several features of this passage. First, what all people know about God through the created order is not necessarily his rational character as Designer, but his "eternal power and deity." As in the Old Testament, nature witnesses primarily to God's power. Second, notice that the sin or error spoken of consists in the response which people make to God's revelation. They do not use or apply it properly: it does not lead them to honor or thank God. Third, notice that humans have not lost all knowledge of God: "what can be known about God" still "is plain to them." To be sure, their minds have been "dark-ened." The awareness that remains is probably confused and distorted. Never-theless Paul insists that human beings in general still do know God through nature. There is a "general revelation" of this sort. Fourth, however, notice that such revelation does not lead to salvation. The only function of general revelation mentioned in this passage is, as Calvin also stressed, to leave people "without excuse."

Acts 14, however, records a more positive function of general revelation. When the inhabitants of Lystra begin worshipping Barnabas and Paul as incar-nations of Zeus and Hermes, Paul cries out:

> Why are you doing this? We are also people of like nature with you, and bring you good news, that you should turn from these things to a living God who made the heaven and the earth and the sea and all that is in them. In past generations he allowed all the nations to walk in their own ways; yet he did not leave himself with-out witness, for he did good and gave you from heaven rains and fruitful seasons, satisfying your hearts with good and gladness (Acts 14:15–17).

In this passage it is nature's regularity which gives evidence of God. This reg-ularity gives witness not chiefly to God's power, nor even to his character as Designer, but to a moral characteristic: God's goodness. We do not hear that this general revelation can bring salvation. However, it can be used to critique some false religious notions and to set the stage for presentation of the keryg-ma.

In Acts 17 Paul speaks with the Athenian philosophers. Since the Atheni-ans have built an altar "To an unknown God," Paul proclaims "that which you worship as unknown" (Acts 17:23). Notice the phrase. Paul affirms that they do, in some sense, worship the true God—even though this God remains un-known. Throughout his speech, much as in Lystra, Paul assumes that his hearers have some general awareness of God. Some features of this awareness have been expressed by Greek thinkers whom Paul quotes (17:28). He uses this general revelation to critique pagan religions and to set the stage for the ke-rygma. Nevertheless when Paul utters the fundamental proclamation about Jesus' resurrection, his coming judgment, and the need for repentance, most of the philosophers laugh (17:30–32). Despite whatever continuity between gen-eral and special revelation Paul may have drawn on, the discontinuity seems far more pronounced.

C. Revelation through Conscience

In contrast to animals, human beings possess notions of right and wrong. Even though many often do not live according to what they believe is right, important distinctions of this sort can be found in all cultures. Some of hu-manity's most noble representatives, non-Christians and Christians alike, have felt that it was better to suffer, even to die, than to do what is wrong.

According to the moral argument for God's existence, our notion of the right

includes the conviction that those who follow it should find happiness.[14] In
this world, however, those who do what is right often suffer, while those who
do what is wrong are often rewarded. Why, then, do some people continue to
live and die for what conscience tells them is right, and why do so many more
feel that they ought to be doing so? The moral argument answers: because conscience tells us that the universe, ultimately, is governed by what is just and
right. Conscience assures us that even though the righteous suffer and the
wicked prosper in the present, all things will balance out in eternity. In other
words our moral sense of right and wrong assures us, usually in an instinctive,
non-intellectual way, that there is a God who will ultimately reward the righteous and punish the wicked. Only on this assumption that right and justice are
at the heart of the universe is it possible to live a truly moral life.

Assuming that this argument is a philosophical elaboration of what many
people sense spontaneously, what can special revelation tell us about such a
general moral sense? While the Old Testament emphasizes the distinctiveness
of Israel's moral and social laws (e.g., Deut. 4:6–8) and often depicts the Gentiles as far from knowledge of God, it sometimes intimates that other nations
know of and are judged by Yahweh's standards (e.g., Gen. 20:1–11, Amos 1:3—
2:7). Some moral admonitions found in Proverbs and other wisdom literature
are very like those current in other nations.

Towards the beginning of Romans, which deals with how the Gentiles know
God, Paul affirms that

> When Gentiles who have not the law do by nature what the law requires, they
> are a law to themselves, even though they do not have the law. They show that
> what the law requires is written on their hearts, while their conscience also bears
> witness and their conflicting thoughts accuse or perhaps excuse them on that Day
> when...God judges people's secrets by Christ Jesus (Rom. 2:14–16).

This text seems to go further than those speaking of revelation through nature. If some might be "excused" at the Judgment for following the law "written on their heart" alone, perhaps general revelation can lead to salvation. Yet
even if this be possible, the New Testament as a whole gives little ground for
thinking that it happens often. Conscience seldom clearly reflects God's will.
Its hearing is often clouded by sin. The conscience can be weak (1 Cor. 8:7–
12), "seared" (1 Tim. 4:2), defiled (Tit. 1:15) or evil (Heb. 10:22). Accordingly
purification and strengthening of the conscience is a chief feature of the salvation process (Tit. 1:15, Heb. 9:14).

D. Conclusions

Is any revelation of the true God available to all people, whether or not they
have responded to, or even heard of, the special revelation focusing on Jesus

[14] Immanuel Kant, *Critique of Practical Reason* (Indianapolis: Bobbs-Merrill, 1956
[originally published in 1788]), Part I, Book II, Chapter 2.

Christ? In contrast to the extreme position of Karl Barth, the biblical texts which we have examined clearly say, Yes.

They are less clear, however, as to what general revelation might tell anyone about God. Perhaps different individuals apprehend different things by means of this source. From the natural world most people seem to get some sense of God's ordering, sustaining, and perhaps inbreaking power, and perhaps also of God's providential care. Through conscience people know something of God's moral demands. In some individuals conscience might ring clearly enough to help them fulfill these demands. In most, however, conscience seems so damaged that it dims or distorts God's voice.

Acts 14 and 17 show that certain truths of general revelation can be presented so as to critique false religion and set the stage for the kerygma. Acts 17, however, suggests that general revelation does not provide a stable, well-articulated lower level on which an upper level of special revelation may be securely balanced and constructed. In general, although Scripture affirms that those who have not submitted to special revelation do know God, it offers only fragmentary indications as to what they might know. Yet since all people do know God, perhaps systematic theology (even a kerygmatic one) can ask whether the contents of general revelation might be spelled out by a natural theology. Space constrains us to limit our considerations to the teleological and moral arguments for God's existence.

Both arguments, in our view, affirm things that are true about God. God is a rational Designer. God also governs the universe in accordance with moral law. Might these arguments, then, lead one to the true God? We give the same answer that we gave for "fragmentary" special revelation: It depends on the overall context in which they function and the use to which they are put. By itself, as we showed above, the teleological argument could easily lead to a cosmic mind withdrawn from its universe. In fact the more this argument stresses how intricate and widespread design is, the further it could lead one from the ever-sustaining Creator who is so dynamically related to his works that he is able to affect their operations at any moment. Similarly the moral argument, by itself, could lead, and often has led to the notion of an inflexible legalist who governs the universe without compassion or mercy. No theistic argument, in fact, can lead to more than a few of the revealed attributes of God. And because of this, taken by itself, each one presents a distorted and one-sided view of the Deity.

Does this mean, as Barth insisted, that dealing with theological issues beginning from general revelation will always lead one in a false direction? Again, it depends on the context and the use of such arguments. To those who doubt whether God exists at all, examining the widespread design in the universe or the foundations of moral conviction can show that God's existence is a plausible hypothesis. The major arguments of natural theology, we might say, provide significant models by means of which large ranges of important data may be organized. Rational argument can show that such models are meaningful (often, in our view, superior) alternatives for understanding the modern world over against those offered by other religious and non-religious explanations.

However, much like fragmentary revelation, the overall function of such arguments can lead in opposite ways. For people willing to orient their entire lives around whatever truth they find, the arguments of natural theology could form part of a process leading away from their original life-orientation and world view, and towards God's full, integrating revelation. But others might, for instance, stop at belief in a moral Governor, using it to support certain norms that might conflict with God's revealed character, thereby opposing the true God.

What about modern scientific and social theories? Are they part of general revelation too? Our answer is much the same. Certain scientific and social insights stated in a fairly direct, non-theoretical way are quite compatible with Christian truth. Take, for instance, Marxism. Considered individually, certain Marxist insights into personal and social behavior are profound. But Marxism as a system explains them in a materialistic and atheistic way. What, then, should today's Church make of certain longings for economic equality and justice which Marxists support? Is God speaking in some way through them? It depends on the overall context in which these longings are apprehended and the use to which one puts them. If they are channelled to help establish, by whatever means necessary, a proletarian dictatorship that will seek to stamp out religion then the Church cannot align itself with—and must in some way oppose—those working towards this end. But these longings also can sensitize people to God's concern for poor, to his hatred of the evil of conditions which perpetuate poverty, and to his concern to set things right.

In this way, such general social longings (or elements of social or scientific theories) can form part of general revelation. Interpreted in the second context above and heard within the Church guided by Scripture and seeking to discern God's historical will, they can become channels for God's integrating revelation, just as can tradition and those forms of general personal and historical revelation we discussed in Chapter 11. Like these other two channels, modern theories do not add to revelation's propositional content. They are means by which God's personal and historical will, which flows within the banks marked out by biblical history and its propositional interpretation, is concretely made known.

Of the classical positions on general revelation, ours comes closest to Calvin's.[15] Calvin argued that humankind was incurably religious and was always dealing with God, yet in a way that could not, of itself, bring salvation. We have attempted to account for such a paradox by distinguishing between fragmentary and integrating revelation. Fragmentary revelation, whether through general revelation or through one or two of special revelation's dimensions, is God's true revelation. Yet apart from God's full, integrating revelation, it can be interpreted and used in ways which lead away from God.

---

[15] For a modern discussion from this perspective, see C. G. Berkouwer, *General Revelation* (Grand Rapids: Eerdmans, 1955).

Indeed Scripture suggests that by itself, given humanity's deep and sinful rebellion, it always (or almost always) does. Calvin's verdict that general revelation alone cannot save, but simply leaves us "without excuse," seems wholly (or very largely) true. Nevertheless Romans 2:14-16 leaves open the possibility that the law written on the heart might lead towards salvation in ways we do not suspect.

Perhaps these conclusions seem uncomfortably inconclusive. Our investigation, however, has led to the broader issue of how salvation reaches non-Christians. We will attain more precise conclusions only by exploring the Church's mission in depth (Vol. II, Chap. 12).

V. Revelation: Summary

Throughout our chapters on revelation, as in those on eschatology, we have sought to discern the proper balance between objective and subjective factors. Rather than starting with an objective content (for which some would reserve the title revelation) and later examining the process of its subjective illumination, we began with the full reality of God's self-presentation to the living Church. We then discovered that such special revelation involves the communication of certain contents (historical events and propositions), but as brought alive through God's personal address. Revelation in the full (or special or integrating) sense occurs only where all three dimensions—personal, historical, and propositional—are at least implicitly present.

We also acknowledged, however, that God is often revealed in some way through an encounter, an event, or an assertion alone. God can even be revealed through nature, through conscience, through Church tradition, through general forms of personal and historical revelation, and through contemporary discoveries and theories and events. In all these cases, however, revelation is only fragmentary: the glimmers of divine truth visible through these means can be interpreted and used in ways which oppose God's integrating revelation. They participate in the latter only when drawn into the framework measured by historical and propositional revelation and brought to life by God's personal address. It is not always immediately clear whether a certain encounter, event, proposition, or other sort of truth is truly revelatory. For integrating revelation is ultimately eschatological—flowing towards the final "revelation of Jesus Christ." As it walks towards the consummation the Church which wishes to hear God's voice must often test various claims that God is speaking. It must patiently probe Scripture, ponder its current context, and spend time in prayer. Through this watchful waiting it becomes more open to the God who guides all things towards their fulfillment and whose true revelation proves itself amid the struggle of contending claims and forces.

Finally we have said that revelation in all its dimensions points towards Jesus Christ. Revelatory history and its propositional interpretation flow towards Jesus' life, death, and resurrection, and direct one's gaze towards his parousia. When God addresses us personally it is with "the face of Jesus Christ" (2 Cor.

4:5). Yet when probed in depth, history, the written Word, and the living Word become alive to us by means of the Holy Spirit.

Suggestions for Further Reading

Berkouwer, C. G. *General Revelation*. Grand Rapids: Eerdmans, 1955.

Bruce, F. F. *Tradition: Old and New*. Grand Rapids: Zondervan, 1970.

Compenhausen, Hans. *The Formation of the Christian Bible*. Philadelphia: Fortress, 1972.

Congar, Yves. *Tradition and Traditions*. New York: Macmillan, 1966.

Demorest, Bruce. *General Revelation*. Grand Rapids: Zondervan, 1981.

Hanson, R. C. P. *Tradition in the Early Church*. London: SCM, 1962.

Jenkins, Daniel. *Tradition, Freedom and the Spirit*. Philadelphia: Westminster, 1951.

Mackey, J. P. *Tradition and Change in the Church*. Dayton: Pflaum, 1968.

CHAPTER FOURTEEN

Approaches to Christology

As a theological system develops, it does not move in linear fashion; from one relatively distinct topic to another, and then another, each lying next to each other on a straight line. We might better say that systematic theology moves in a deepening spiral. The system begins with one topic (say, eschatology), and moves downward to the next (say, revelation) as a means of exploring the first in depth. As the second area is explored, reflection spirals back upward to comment on the first from a different, more profound perspective. Then in order to grasp both areas in even greater depth, the system spirals downward again to a third topic and upwards again to consider the first two areas from this new perspective. And so the system goes.

We have shown how all dimensions of revelation point beyond themselves and ultimately towards the eschatological "revelation of Jesus Christ." That is, study of revelation has led us upwards again towards eschatology but with a deepened grasp of how our entire personal, historical, propositional (and general) awareness of God moves us towards it. We have seen that revelation is itself a dimension of God's historical and eschatological saving work. At the same time we have become more deeply aware that revelation in all its dimensions points towards Jesus Christ. All biblical history and the propositions which interpret it point towards or present us with the life, death, resurrection, and return of Christ. To be sure, that history, those propositions, and Jesus himself come alive to us personally through the Holy Spirit. Yet the Spirit, said Jesus, "will not speak on his own authority, but whatever he hears he will speak, and he will declare to you the things that are to come. He will glorify me, for he will take what is mine and declare it to you" (John 16:13-14).

The eschatological revelation, then, is not simply an unusual event. It is the climax of a comprehensive divine work. And if we wish to apprehend it even more profoundly, we must focus directly on this work itself. Of course Father, Son, and Spirit share in this work. But at its center stands the Son, through whom divine reality is focused and in whom divine and human reality most definitively meet. Jesus Christ reveals not only God to us but also that human mystery that we are ourselves, yet his work, we shall see, includes much more than revelation.

Traditionally, systematic theology has divided discussion of Christ (Christology) into two main phases: his Person and his Work. Christ's Person, in turn, has often been discussed in two locations. First, towards the beginning of most systems, under the doctrine of God, it has been customary to argue that the Son is divine.[1] His relation to other members of the trinity are discussed in this context. The concepts of "divine" and "Person" applied to the Son has usually been developed in connection with a preceding natural theology and/or from biblical texts which apparently describe God's nature apart from extensive consideration of God's historical acts. Following their doctrine of God, traditional systems turn to Creation, and then to Anthropology, which focuses largely on "the Fall" and sin of humankind. Consideration of sin leads to a discussion of salvation (Soteriology). Here the Person of Christ emerges again (either preceding Soteriology or as its first main division). This time traditional systems deal with the question of how this divine Person could also be human.[2]

Christ's deity, its relationship to his humanity, and his place amid the Trinity, are surely among the most difficult topics ever approached by finite minds. Traditional discussions are filled with complex distinctions among such refined concepts as "being," "essence," "nature," "person," and their Greek and Latin equivalents. Considerable academic training is required for participation. Only after the issue of Christ's Person is settled do traditional theologies move on to what he did and does, to his Work.[3] Since the Reformation, Protestant systems have often subdivided this into his activity as Prophet, Priest, and King. Jesus' priestly work on behalf of human sin, however, has absorbed most of the attention (cf. Chap. 5). Since this overall approach begins with Christ's deity and one then moves to his humanity and his earthly work, it has often been called Christology "from above."

[1] E.g., Calvin, Institutes, pp. 129-41; Hodge, Systematic Theology, Vol. I, pp. 483-521. Aquinas, SCG, Book IV, Chaps. 1-14; ST I, QQ 27-43.

[2] Calvin, pp. 464-93; Hodge, Vol. II, pp. 378-454. Aquinas, SCG, Book IV, Chaps. 27-49; ST III, QQ 1-26.

[3] Calvin, pp. 482-534; Hodge, Vol. II, pp. 455-638. Aquinas, ST III, QQ 31-59 (in SCG, Book IV, Aquinas virtually omits the topic, moving almost directly from Christ's divine-human character to the sacraments).

I. General Considerations

A. The Order of Treatment

We have recently argued that all true knowledge of God, all integrating revelation, involves personal encounter. Nevertheless as we indicated in Chapter
6, clear intellectual apprehension of God's character, or Person, usually develops slowly through time as one experiences more of God's acts, or works.
We also indicated that biblical revelation itself moves generally from God's
specific works to fuller and fuller understanding of his person. Accordingly, in
contrast to the traditional systematic order, we propose to begin with Christ's
Work before we deal directly with his Person. This general approach can be
called Christology "from below." Our procedure hardly indicates that we consider the divine nature unimportant or inaccessible. Quite the contrary; the divine reality, in its inmost essence, is the Source of everything with which
theology deals. At their deepest levels, revelation and salvation involve the
opening up, the accessibility, of this reality itself (Vol. II, Chaps 16–17). We
postpone discussion of divine reality precisely because it is the most important
and profound of all theological topics. We dare not approach this mystery until
we have learned as much as possible about God's historically accessible, and
therefore more easily understandable, acts.

Accordingly we close Volume I by considering the Work of Jesus Christ. Having gazed towards the End of all things (Chaps. 6–9), then having asked how
God is revealed in the present (Chaps. 10–13), we now cast our reflections
backwards to the center of of God's historical work, considered as fulfillment of
his earlier promise. We will proceed chronologically through Jesus' life, death,
and resurrection. The latter, we shall find, was more a work of Father and Spirit
than of the Son; through it, the divine dimensions of this work will begin to
emerge more fully. Nevertheless we will not focus directly on the divine nature
until we have considered all aspects of the divine work, at the end of Volume II
(Chaps. 15–18).

Even though we wish to approach Jesus in a somewhat untraditional way, we
will find our questions and our attempts at answers shaped (whether we like it
or not) by the way in which various traditions have viewed him. Consequently
rather than seeking to reflect on Christ's work without benefit of previous research, we devote this chapter to an overview of major Christological traditions and to charting our own course among them.

B. Paradox

Many have found Jesus to be a savior and an example, a companion and a
friend. Yet when they have considered and experienced him in depth, many
have also found him a riddle. Not only was he both divine and human but
Jesus was the healer who suffered, the miracle-worker who was weak, the king

who was a servant, the giver of life who died. Since we will approach Jesus from the standpoint of his history, the extraordinary contrasts between various phases of his Work (e.g., between his arrival as messianic King and his God-forsaken death) may prove as significant as the much discussed contrast in his Person (between his divine and human natures). Since such vast contrasts characterize Jesus, theological theories often lay disproportionate weight on one side or another. Accordingly many Christologies can be helpfully understood as diverse models, each of which emphasizes one side of things, but which may not do justice to others. To be sure, general theological criteria (Chap. 3) will show that some Christologies are quite superior to others. Still, it will be helpful to ask whether some are not so much contradictory as they are complementary approaches to the paradoxical mystery of Christ.

We can appreciate the complementary elements in some Christologies if we think of them as answers to certain pressing questions. We have noticed that theology itself arises largely from questions which grip Christians: how their faith is to be lived and understood amid their own context. Therefore, if Christians in different times and places have arrived at different theological answers, this may have been partly because their questions were different in the first place. Let us then treat the major approaches to Christology as answers to different kinds of questions. Many Christologies can be roughly classified as can theological systems in general: as kerygmatic or contextual.

II. Kerygmatic Approaches to Christ

As our first few chapters occasionally noted, in the ancient and medieval western world the realm of the divine, the supernatural, was real and significant. This atmosphere also pervaded Reformation times. Since the Enlightenment, however, the divine has become increasingly unreal to most people, while the human realm has become far more real and significant. It would be expected, then, that Christ's deity and his otherness and distinctness from us would be most emphasized in earlier periods.

A. Patristic Christology

Why did Christ come? For many of the early Fathers the answer was that we might "become partakers of the divine nature" (2 Pet. 1:4). In Christ, God became what we are (human) in order that we might become what he is (divine). Down to the present the Greek and Oriental Orthodox churches understand salavation primarily in this way: as divinization.[5] But let us look not only at the

[5] See Athanatius, "On the Incarnation of the Word" in Edward Hardy, ed. *The Christology of the Later Fathers* (Philadelphia: Westminster, 1954), esp. Chaps. 1-20; Pelikan, *The Emergence of the Catholic Tradition*, pp. 232-43 and *The Spirit of Eastern Christendom*, pp. 10-16. For a recent Greek Orthodox statement, see Georgios Mantzaridis, *The Deification of Man* (Crestwood, N.Y.: St. Vladimir's, 1984).

patristic answer: Christ became human that humans might become divine. Let us also ask why this was stressed. In what way was the human situation understood, how were human needs and fears and longings experienced so that this kind of salvation became their solution? What questions were most people in the first several Christian centuries asking, so that divinization became the most common answer?

If participation in the divine nature is desired above all else, something about human nature must be experienced as undesirable, feared, or at least very incomplete. For most people in the first few Christian centuries, human existence seemed to be permeated by decay (or "corruption") and death. Most people shared the common Greek world view: All physical reality, by its very nature, is subject to pain, disease, disintegration and death. Human existence, at least insofar as it is bodily, cannot not come into contact with the divine. For the divine is entirely immaterial. Humans can contact the divine only through their soul in an intellectual, or mystical way.

Patristic theologians, of course, emphasized that physical matter could not be wholly alien to God, for God had created it. And so salvation of the person must involve salvation of the body. Nevertheless human life as they experienced it (especially the body) still seemed imprisoned in the toils of corruption and death. Accordingly the chief question with which they approached the revelation of Christ was, How can our entire human nature be saved from corruption and mortality? How can we attain incorruption and immortality in union with God?

Because it was elaborated largely in response to this profound question, patristic Christology (the patristic answer) emphasized certain features of Christ's work in certain ways.[6] The incarnation became the focal point. For it was here that the incorruptible, immortal divine nature became indissolubly united to corruptible, mortal human nature. Furthermore, the Fathers understood the human nature involved to be not just that of Jesus of Nazareth; it was a common, trans-personal reality which all people share and in which we all participate. The incarnation, therefore, was the point at which divine nature began to permeate and revitalize humanity as a whole. This permeation by, or participation in, divine nature touches individuals as they hear Christ's teachings and follow his example. Yet it is often communicated most effectively through the sacraments and through mystical contemplation.

Given this understanding of salvation, it became important for patristic Christology to insist that Jesus Christ was fully divine. For had the divine nature not fully joined itself with ours, we could not be divinized. It also became important to insist that Jesus Christ was fully human. For had God not taken

---

[6] The themes we sketch were more strongly emphasized by the Alexandrian school (e.g., by Clement [ca. 150-215] and Cyril ca. 370-444 of Alexandria) and less so by the Antiochene school (e.g. by Theodore of Mosupestia [ca. 350-428]) and Nestorius (ca. 381-481). The Eastern churches have tended to follow Alexandrian Christology, while western Christology has been more influenced by Antiochene tendencies.

on a full human nature, all that we are (including our bodies) could not be saved. Consequently patristic Christology struggled to establish the full deity of Christ (affirmed at Nicea in 325) and its relationship with his full humanity (articulated at Chalcedon in 451). Through the centuries the Eastern churches, which have most consistently retained the patristic notion of salvation, have stressed the role of the Son's divinity in taking on and elevating his humanity. Western theologians, however, (especially Protestants) have challenged the patristic emphasis. Divinization seems to imply that humans actually become God. The crucial distinctions between the finite and the infinite, between creature and creator, seem to be denied.

In the nineteenth century, liberal Church historians criticized divinization in another way. The Fathers, they argued, conceived the divine nature rather crudely, as a sort of spiritual substance. Thus they thought of salvation as an almost physical transformation.[7] Liberal theologians, however, conceived salvation largely in moral terms; a union not of human and divine natures but of human and divine wills. Consequently they tended to severely critique, even to ignore, the Eastern and patristic notion of salvation.[8]

But this liberal critique of the Fathers has itself been critiqued. Emil Brunner argued that the liberals themselves had ceased to believe in any spiritual reality beyond the physical. That is why they interpreted patristic statements about divine nature, or substance, or about divinization as evidence of a crude, quasi-physical outlook. Because of this view, the liberals could not appreciate the extent to which the Fathers emphasized moral action or the will.[9] Others have pointed out that while Western theology has emphasized precise rational definitions and distinctions, that of the Fathers and their Eastern heirs is more mystical.[10] If certain of their statements about divinization are taken literally, they do seem to say that humans actually become God. Yet they are intended to point to mystical experiences of divine presence with which westerners often are unfamiliar.

---

[7] For a brief statement of this approach, see Adolph Harnack, *Outlines of the History of Dogma* (Boston: Beacon, 1957), pp. 235-41; *History of Dogma* (New York: Russell and Russell, 1958), Vol. III, pp. 163-77.

[8] Albrecht Ritschl derided the patristic notion for conceiving salvation on "the analogy of a *chemical process of nature,* while the human nature which undergoes it is regarded only as a *natural unit*," and therefore omitted it from his massive historical study of soteriology (*A Critical History of the Christian Doctrine of Justification and Reconciliation* [Edinburgh: Edmonston and Douglas, 1872], p. 8).

[9] Emil Brunner, *The Mediator* (Philadelphia: Westminster, 1957), pp. 249-64. Gustav Aulen also challenged the liberal interpretation of patristic soteriology (*Christus Victor* [New York: Macmillan, 1960], pp. 22-25).

[10] "We do not in the Christian West move easily among such kaleidoscopic forms of theological or spiritual understanding. We like our doctrinal concepts clear-cut, even at the expense of a certain shallowness." (H.E.W. Turner, *The Patristic Doctrine of Redemption* [London: Mowbray, 1952], p. 95.)

B. Reformed Christologies

1. *John Calvin.* Since patristic Christology generally regarded the human situation as hopeless apart from Christ's intervention; it can be called kerygmatic. John Calvin also regarded humans apart from Christ as helpless, but for somewhat different reasons. For the Fathers, humans were estranged from God largely because of the opposition between their natures: Humans were corruptible and mortal, the divine was the reverse. For Calvin estrangement was due more nearly to an opposition between wills. The gulf between God and humanity was due more prominently to sin, understood in moral or legal terms, than to corruption, understood as something ontological.

Accordingly the question to which Reformed Christology became an answer was, How can we who have transgressed God's commands be saved from God's wrath? How can we attain a positive relationship with God? Calvin, who sought to derive theology simply from Scripture and not from philosophical speculation into ultimate reasons and causes, asserted that there was no "absolute necessity" for Christ's coming. Rather the Son's taking on flesh stemmed from God's good pleasure, "from a heavenly decree."[11] Nevertheless Calvin occasionally spoke as if Christ's coming and his character could be deduced from the nature of sin. First, "Since our iniquities...had completely estranged us from the Kingdom of Heaven, no man, unless he belonged to God, could serve as the intermediary to restore peace" (p. 464). So the redeemer must be divine. But in order "that his divinity and our human nature might by mutual connection grow together," he must be human. 'Otherwise the nearness would not have been near enough, nor the affinity sufficiently firm, for us to hope that God might dwell in us" (pp. 465-66).

Notice that the first quotation above stresses the moral, or legal, dilemma which Calvin regarded as the primary reason for the incarnation. The second quotation, however, speaks of divine and human natures growing together, much as did the Fathers. Although we can distinguish between a moral emphasis in Calvin (and among Protestants) and an ontological one in the Fathers (and in eastern Christianity), we must not separate them as sharply as did the liberal critics of Patristic theology. Indeed Calvin sometimes echoes the Fathers: "Who could have done this had not the self-same Son of God become the Son of man, and had not so taken what was ours as to impart what was his to us, and to make what was his by nature ours by grace?" (p. 465) In fact, Calvin, like all original thinkers, expressed the reasons for Christ's coming in a

---

[11] Calvin, *Institutes*, p. 464. (The following page numbers in our text are to this work.) Charles Hodge explained the reasons for Christ's coming in explicit deductive fashion (*Systematic Theology*, Vol. II, pp. 455-57). To make the union of deity and humanity in Christ plausible, Hodge first used introspection and philosophical definitions to show that "We have...the same knowledge of the essence of God as we have of the substance of the soul" (Vol. I., p. 367). He then argued that the union of deity and humanity was analogous to that of body and soul (p. 378).

variety of ways. He sometimes envisioned the evil that binds humanity as a group of hostile forces. Therefore, the Redeemer had

> to swallow up death. Who but the Life could do this? It was his task to conquer sin. Who but the very Righteousness could do this? It was his task to rout the powers of world and air. Who but a power higher than world and air could do this? (p. 466)

Primarily, however, Calvin insists that Christ had to remedy our disobedience and

> counter it with obedience, satisfy God's judgment, and pay the penalties for sin. Accordingly, our Lord came forth as true man...to present our flesh as the price of satisfaction to God's righteous judgment and, in the same flesh, to pay the penalty that we had deserved (p. 466).

Whereas patristic Christology emphasized the incarnation, Reformed theology's understanding of humankind's dilemma led it to emphasize Jesus' death. Even though Calvin was the first to subdivide Christ's work into prophetic, kingly, and priestly functions, he focused very largely on the last (Chap. 5 above). Calvin acknowledged that Jesus exercised this priestly function throughout "the whole course of his obedience....from the time when he took on the form of the servant." Nevertheless Calvin insisted that "to develop the way of salvation more accurately, Scripture ascribes this as peculiar and proper to Christ's death" (p. 507).

2. *Karl Barth* would probably be suspicious of our search for questions to which his Christology would be an answer. As we have learned, Barth denied that any genuine theological knowledge was available apart from God's personal revelation in Christ (Chaps. 5, 10, 13). Consequently one cannot speak of a general sense of estrangement from God through corruption or through disobedience, to which Christology provides the answer. According to Barth, "Even the fact that he is a sinner cannot be known from man himself. It is rather the result of knowing Jesus Christ; in His light we see the light and in this light our own darkness."[12]

Barth, of course, is classically Reformed in regarding humans as so estranged from God that only God's initiative in Christ can bridge the gap. He conceives this estrangement so radically, however, that Christ is necessary not only for salvation but also for any genuine knowledge of God and of the human situation. Christology, then, tends to function as the very center and starting point of Barth's entire theology. (Despite the structure of his *Dogmatics*, which begins with the doctrine of God, Barth's emphasis suggests that one might start theological reflection with the divine-human reality of Christ.)

Like Calvin, Barth emphasizes that Jesus bore God's wrath against sin, thereby overcoming our otherwise unbridgeable alienation from God.[13] Yet

[12] *Dogmatics in Outline* (New York: Harper, 1957), p. 69.

[13] Ibid., pp. 104-07; *Church Dogmatics*, Vol. IV, Part 1, pp. 211-83.

Jesus revealed our sin not only by bearing God's wrath. In addition, his life of obedience to God provided the norm—against which we fall short—as to what we human beings should be. To show how Jesus provides this norm, however, Barth had to concentrate on more than Christ's priestly function performed primarily on the cross. Barth emphasized Jesus' roles as prophet and king.[14] Barth linked Jesus' performance of these functions to the Old Testament, showing how Jesus fulfilled three tasks originally assigned to Israel.

C. Conclusions

Throughout the centuries many have valued Jesus primarily because he provides them with salvation from a situation which they find desperate. He rescues them from it and places them in an otherwise unattainable relationship with God. When this apprehension of Christ receives theological articulation, its proponents seek primarily to explain and defend the way in which Jesus, as divine, provides this salvation. Kerygmatic Christologies, generally speaking, are answers to the urgent question, What must I do to be saved? even if that question had not been formulated prior to the experience of salvation. Since they focus on Christ's deity, they are usually Christologies "from above."

III. Contextual Approaches to Christ

As the modern world developed, the divine realm appeared less and less real to most people. The earthly, human realm became more real and important. People became less concerned about being delivered from the corruption and sin of the world and more concerned about living meaningful lives within it. Understandably the key questions with which most people approached Christ changed. People now wondered whether Jesus could help one attain full, significant human living. Christological reflection tended increasingly to begin by considering Christ's human nature "from below."

A. Liberal Christologies

1. *Friedrich Schleiermacher.* How can theology explain the significance of Christ to modern people who see little relationship between him and their everyday living? One way is to describe some kind of experience(s) which everyone presumably shares and to show how Christ can be relevantly related to it. Although Schleiermacher began *The Christian Faith* with the doctrine of God, following good systematic tradition, he prefaced this with an introduction largely devoted to describing religious "feeling."[15]

Human conscious awareness, Schleiermacher said, moves between two poles. Indeed the whole process of human maturation is a movement from one towards the other. At one pole is a "confused animal grade." Today we might

[14] Ibid., pp. 72-81; *Church Dogmatics*, Vol. IV, Part 1, pp. 164-74.

[15] *The Christian Faith*, pp. 5-31. Cf. Chap. 4 (the following page numbers in our text are to this work).

call it a continuous "stream of consciousness" where perceptions, impressions, and moods come and go without particular order or meaning. At this pole everything appears disconnected. Different feelings, objects, values, and persons seem oppposed. Insofar as this "confused animal grade" prevails, we are swayed by whatever moods come along. At the other pole of consciousness is the "feeling of absolute dependence." This feeling is a sense of the unity and harmony of all things. It is always undivided and unchanging. The origin, or "whence," of this feeling, says Schleiermacher, is what Christians call "God."

Each person's self-consciousness lies between these two poles. Since the consciousness of absolute dependence (or "God-consciousness") is wholly unchanging, indivdual self-consciousness could never merge entirely with it (for then one would lose all self-consciousness and cease to be a person). So the goal of human experience is not to become identical with higher self-consciousness. It is, rather, to bring all elements of one's personality, including the lower pole of consciousness, into harmony with it. Schleiermacher writes that when this higher self-consciousness prevails,

> This means an easy progress of that higher life, and bears, by comparison, the stamp of joy. And as the disappearance of the higher consciousness...would mean a diminution of life, so whenever it emerges *with difficulty*, this...can only be felt as an inhibition of the higher life (p. 24).

In other words our self-conscious feelings are of two main sorts: pleasant when our particular experiences are in harmony with the feeling of absolute dependence; unpleasant when the impulses and disharmony of the confused animal grade prevails. When the pleasant predominates, our actions and thoughts flow in coherent patterns. We experience solidarity with other persons. Our human potential becomes actualized. But when the unpleasant grade predominates, our lower impulses and the demands of each moment divide and disperse out thoughts and actions. We feel divided from and opposed to other persons. We fail to actualize our uniquely human potential.

In this introduction to his theological system, Schleiermacher has sketched what he thinks it means to be fully human. He thinks that if his readers, non-Christian and Christian, will reflect carefully on their own experiences, they will agree with his analysis. Hopefully, then, he has found a point of contact in terms of which to make Christian beliefs intelligible to an audience which might well regard them as very strange.

Schleiermacher continues to build his bridge by claiming that what everyone experiences as unpleasant and pleasant states of consciousness, Christianity calls "the Antithesis of Sin and Grace" (pp. 259-64). Sin, in other words, can be defined neither as bondage to corruption, nor as transgression of God's law, but as "everything...that has arrested the free development of God-consciousness" (p. 271). A sinful condition exists when one's God-consciousness is dominated by one's lower consciousness. And even though everyone aspires towards the higher consciousness, Schleiermacher argues that the lower is always more powerful (pp. 282-93).

Now Schleiermacher can bring in Jesus. For the dominance of the lower consciousness could be overcome if one's God-consciousness could receive enough strength to reverse things. And this is precisely what Jesus can do. For, alone among all who ever existed, Christ's every act was completely dominated by a consciousness of absolute dependence. And the strength of his God-consciousness can make so powerful an impression on people today that their own God-consciousness can begin to gain ascendancy over their lower consciousness. For Schleiermacher, then, Jesus brings redemption by means of the impression which his consciousness of absolute dependence makes on ours. This impression is communicated to the individual by

> the picture of Christ, which exists in the [Church] as at once a corporate act and a corporate possession, the impression of the sinless perfection of Jesus, which becomes for him at the same time the perfect consciousness of sin and removal of the misery (p. 364).

Notice that Jesus reveals God to us by revealing what humanity (as directed by God-consciousness) should be like. And it is this revelation of what we ought to be that brings us (as Barth also said) to repentance, to "the perfect consciousness of sin." The powerful revelatory picture of Jesus is primarily the gospel portrait of his life. For Schleiermacher's Christology, then, emphasis falls neither on Christ's incarnation nor on his death or resurrection, but on his life. The impression of Jesus recorded in the Gospels, however, reaches people by means of the Church: a continuous historical body of those who have been revitalized by the impulse proceding from Jesus and passing on to others. Schleiermacher's Christology, then, is concerned not only with Christ's impact on individuals but with the collective impact which he, through the community of redeemed individuals, makes on society. Indeed, Schleiermacher envisioned all of history, with the Church at its center, as moving towards the moral and social perfection of the kingdom of God.[16]

Finally let us notice that God-consciousness provides the key to Christ's deity. For Schleiermacher theological doctrines are simply "accounts of the Christian religious affections set forth in speech" (p. 76). Theology cannot say what God is like apart from our experience. It cannot describe relationships among the trinitarian persons, nor how one of them became incarnate. Christ's deity, then, could only consist in "the constant potency of his God-consciousness, which was a veritable existence of God in him" (p. 385). Christ was divine through being fully directed by, or filled with, the divine.

2. *Albrecht Ritschl.* About fifty years after Schleiermacher, Ritschl was seeking to explain Jesus' significance to people somewhat less concerned with individual self-fulfillment and somewhat more concerned about contributing to

---

[16] "In the realm of Christianity the consciousness of God is always related to the totality of active states in the idea of a Kingdom of God....In Christianity all pain and joy are religious only in so far as they are related to activity in the Kingdom of God." (Ibid., p. 43; cf. pp. 723-26.)

the heady technological and social progress of Western society. Many were already understanding the significance of this "progress" in ethical terms.

Even before Schleiermacher, Immanuel Kant had argued that human beings, because they possess reason, have intrinsic value. They are infinitely more valuable than irrational natural creatures. (Roots of the sharp existential distinction between persons and things can be found here.) Moral law, therefore, instructs us to regard individuals as ends in themselves, and never as means to someone else's ends. Kant spoke of an ideal social order, a "Kingdom of Ends." Here everyone would be treated as intrinsically valuable; no one would exist primarily to gratify someone else's desires.[17] Kant also argued, in good Enlightenment terms, that human society would inevitably evolve towards this kingdom. The natural world would provide obstacles to this development, both through the egoistic sensuous impulses of each person's body and through the sheer resistance of nature to the building of civilization. Yet the collective power of scientific and moral reason would gradually subdue the material world.[18]

Ritschl envisioned Christian faith as an ellipse with two foci. One was justification. In good Protestant fashion, he insisted that people never progress in Christian living unless they are convinced that they have been accepted by God and forgiven.[19] Justification, however, leads one to be concerned about the second focus in the Christian ellipse: reconciliation with others and with all of God's creation.

In explicating Reconciliation, Ritschl utilized Kant to make Christianity comprehensible to his contemporaries. Like Schleiermacher, Ritschl felt that theology could not deal directly with realities which lay beyond our present world. We have already seen how eternal life for him referred to the this-worldly value of persons as those destined to conquer nature (Chap. 9). Ritschl also noticed that Kant's "Kingdom of Ends" sounded remarkably like the kingdom of God that was the chief goal of Jesus' ministry. The way lay open, then, to understanding Christ's work as that which enables modern people to fulfill the ethical and cultural mandate to build a technological civilzation characterized by personal and social freedom.

Schleiermacher had argued that all humans should be guided by God-consciousness but in fact are not. Ritschl now argued that all humans should be dedicated to the moral task of bringing God's kingdom (which Schleiermacher also had mentioned) but in fact do not. For Schleiermacher Jesus was the first

[17] "Foundations of the Metaphysics of Morals," in A. I. Melden, *Ethical Theories*, 2nd ed. (Englewood Cliffs, N.J.: Prentice-Hall, 1967 [originally published in 1797]), pp. 347-51.

[18] *On History* (New York: Bobbs-Merrill, 1963), pp. 11-26.

[19] *The Christian Doctrine of Justification and Reconciliation*, pp. 35-38. (The following page numbers in our text are to this work.) Ritschl insisted that this religious emphasis made his theology more than a mere ethical system.

to be wholly God-conscious; his saving work consisted in his enabling others to be so. For Ritschl Jesus was the first to be wholly dedicated to bringing God's Kingdom; his saving work consisted in his enabling us to do so: "Only through the impulse and direction we receive from him" can we successfully embark on the task that he did (p. 387).

Schleiermacher had explained Christ's deity as "the constant potency of his God-consciousness," through which God's redemptive intentions were actualized in people and which was therefore "a veritable existence of God in him." Similarly, Ritschl affirmed of Jesus that

> as the Founder of the Kingdom of God in the world, in other words, as the Bearer of God's ethical lordship over men...He is that being in the world in Whose self-end God makes effective and manifest after an original manner His own eternal self-end, Whose whole activity, therefore, in discharge of His vocation, forms the material of that complete revelation of God which is present in Him, in Whom, in short, the Word of God is a human person (p. 461).

In general, liberal Christologies can be seen as answers to modern questions of how people can attain full, significant personal and social lives. To respond to these questions, they focus primarily on the life of Jesus Christ.

B. Liberation Christologies

Throughout the Christian era many oppressed persons have found in Jesus a fellow sufferer and a friend. In most cases, however, they experienced Jesus as a source of comfort who enabled them to endure their oppression. The established churches usually taught them that faith in Christ did not lead to changing things in this life; Christ would reward them in the life beyond. In recent decades, however, many oppressed peoples have become much more aware of the undesirability of their situation. Many press for sweeping social changes here and now. But how ought such changes to come about? What might a better world look like? In light of these questions, liberation Christologies have sought to provide some answers.

For liberation theologians, Jesus' main purpose was to bring God's kingdom. Like Ritschl they understand the kingdom primarily as a social reality. Like him they regard it as something for which people in all times and places long. For Ritschl it was synonomous with the "Kingdom of Ends" towards which moral reason guides us; for many liberation theologians, it is "the realization of a fundamental utopia of the human heart."[20] Liberation theologians, however, contrast God's kingdom more sharply with the present situation than Ritschl

---

[20] "In humankind there is a principle of hope that generates great happiness and utopian visions. This is attested to by all cultures and civilizations." In announcing the kingdom, Jesus announced that the fulfillment of these visions was "close at hand." (Leonardo Boff, *Jesus Christ Liberator* [Maryknoll, N.Y.: Orbis, 1978], pp. 50-51; cf. Jon Sobrino, *Christology at the Crossroads* [Maryknoll: Orbis, 1976], pp. 43-44, 246.)

did. According to Leonardo Boff, it is "a total, global, structural transfiguration and revolution."[21] Jon Sobrino insists that God's activity can only be envisioned as the *overcoming* of a negative situation. God's action does not simply affirm the positive aspect of human existence. Rather, it affirms it through *negation*—which is to say, through a liberation.[22] For Jesus sin was "the rejection of God's kingdom which is drawing near in grace."[23] Consequently acceptance or rejection of Jesus cannot be separated from acceptance or rejection of the kingdom he brings.[24]

Because the kingdom is so central, liberation Christologies, like liberal ones, emphasize Jesus' life, in which he brought God's kingdom through preaching, teaching, and example. Sometimes these Christologies represent the content of his message as little different from that of common-sense morality. According to Boff, Jesus

> draws his doctrine from the common experiences that all live and can verify. His listeners understand immediately....Christ did not come to bring a new morality, different from the one people already had. He brings to light that which people always knew or ought to have known, but because of their alienation were unable to see, comprehend, and formulate.[25]

Christ sought primarily, as it were, to give people back to themselves: to enable them to use their own common sense and moral ability to guide their lives, unclouded by the distortions of the religious and social systems which had trapped them. Due to the opposition of these systems, however, Jesus' life was caught up in a struggle which led directly to his death. Because they stress this conflict, liberation Christologies usually place more emphasis on Jesus' death and resurrection than do liberal ones.

For Reformed Christologies Jesus died bearing the wrath of God which we justly deserve. But for most liberation Christologies Jesus is put to death by his social and religious opponents, and he bears the rejection and shame that they unjustly inflict upon him. Since many oppressed people experience rejection and death at the hands of the authorities, liberation theologians stress that on the cross Jesus shared their pain and abandonment. By this empathy with us, "Jesus opened up a new possibility for human existence, i.e., an existence of faith with absolute meaning, even when confronted with the absurd."[26]

By itself, however, Jesus' death would have been the defeat of the dawning kingdom. For this reason his resurrection is also essential to his saving work.

---

[21] Boff, p. 53.

[22] Sobrino, p. 47, cf. pp. 50-67.

[23] Ibid., p. 51.

[24] Ibid., p. 108; Boff, pp. 53, 114.

[25] Boff, pp. 82-83.

[26] Ibid. p. 119; cf. Sobrino, pp. 227-28.

Through his resurrection, Jesus' teaching about the kingdom and his claims were vindicated.[27] The resurrection, therefore, is "the central nucleus of the Christian faith." Because of it, "we know that life and meaningless death now have meaning. A door was opened for us to an absolute future and an ineradicable hope penetrated the human heart."[28]

Liberation theologians, however, stress that Christ's life, death and resurrection benefit only those who open themselves to God's kingdom. "The only way to get to know Jesus is to follow after him in one's own real life; to try to identify oneself with his own historical concerns; and to try to fashion his kingdom in our midst. In other words, only through Christian praxis is it possible for us to draw close to Jesus."[29] Finally, for liberation Christologies as for liberal ones, Christ's deity usually consists in his perfect openness or obedience to God rather than in his being a pre-existent divine person. Sobrino and Boff understand this openness as process: "The more Jesus existed in God, the more God resided in him. The more the man-Jesus dwelled in God, the more he was divinized."[30] Thus Christ's deity itself can be explained by the notion so central to patristic Christology: divinization. For many, however, Christ's uniqueness consisted not in his being divine at the incarnation but in his being the first to complete the process of divinization.[31]

C. Conclusions

Over the last few centuries more and more people have wrestled with what it means to be fully human. Many have come to value Jesus because he enables them to develop their individual potential, or to direct them and their fellows towards a better society, or to do all these things through liberating them from oppressive social forces. When this apprehension of Christ receives theological articulation, its proponents focus on Jesus "from below," on the way in which Jesus, as human, teaches us, impresses us, liberates us, and sets us an example. Contextual Christologies, generally speaking, are answers to the question, How can I, and how can we all, become fully human?

IV. Christ as Fulfillment of the Promise

The questions which kerygmatic and contextual theologians have put to the mystery of Jesus Christ are no doubt valid. Jesus surely came to deliver humankind from many evils. He certainly helps Christians actualize their human potential. But are there other, perhaps equally valid questions which Christians

---

[27] Sobrino, p. 265; Boff, p. 130.

[28] Boff, p. 121.

[29] Sobrino, p. xiii; cf. pp. xxiv, 275; Boff, pp. 180, 245, 291.

[30] Boff, p. 197; "Thus we can say that Jesus becomes the Son of God rather than that he simply is the Son of God" (Sobrino, p. 105).

[31] See Sobrino, pp. xxiv, 104-08, 338-40; Boff, pp. 17-20, 194-205.

might raise about Christ? Might there be others equally appropriate, or perhaps more appropriate, to our situation today? And might other lines of questioning be at least as close to the Bible's own approach? To sharpen and broaden our sensitivity to the questions that might be asked about Christ, let us ponder: What questions would those who first encountered Jesus ask? From what standpoint would they seek to apprehend and evaluate his significance? By the first century, Palestine had long been under foreign rule. Now the mighty Roman Empire threatened to suffocate Israel's distinct religion and perhaps her very existence. Yet the atmosphere tingled with Messianic expectation. Long ago Yahweh had promised to deliver Israel from all enemies and bless all nations through her. When Jesus appeared, then, the most urgent question would have been, Is this, at last, the one to fulfill the promise? Can this finally be the Messiah?[32] Our exploration of revelation's historical dimension indicated that biblical history was guided by a promise (Chap. 11). To understand more clearly how Jesus' contemporaries evaluated him, let us consider more precisely

A. The Nature of the Promise

Originally, we remember, God promised Abram and Sarai that their descendants would become a great nation, that God would bless or curse all who blessed or cursed them, and that all the families of the earth would be blessed through them (Gen. 12:2–3). The content of this Promise may be called the kingdom of God: the establishment of God's rule over a people called to live in especially close fellowship with him and in obedience to his rule.[33] Yahweh's covenant with Israel showed that it was not only religious but also social and ethical in character. Israelites were to regard each other as sisters and brothers. Special concern was to be shown the poor and the unfortunate (Exod. 23:6–11; Lev. 19:9–10; Deut. 15:7–11, 24:10–22). In contrast to surrounding nations, who revered their rulers and the rich, no Israelite was to amass great political power or wealth (Leviticus 25, Deut. 17:14–20, 1 Sam. 8:10–18).

Throughout its history Israel oftened tended to regard the promise as pertaining only to itself. Accordingly when they first settled in Canaan, when the Davidic monarchy flourished, or when they returned from Babylonian exile, many thought that the promise had been wholly fulfilled. The Old Testament increasingly emphasized, however, that all nations were included in its scope. Yet while the promise broadened to include all nations, it narrowed in another respect. In times of apparent fulfillment many Israelites turned aside from Yahweh's laws; in times of despair, many turned aside from hope. Those who kept clinging to the promise tended to become an increasingly smaller remnant. In

---

[32] Matt. 11:2-5, 16:13-14; John 1:19-22, 7:11-12. In *The Crucified God*, pp. 98-107, Moltmann suggests this is the basic question for Christology. The organization of our chapter was suggested originally by that of his (pp. 98-111).

[33] John Bright, *The Kingdom of God* (New York: Abingdon, 1959), pp. 17-30. Our following remarks on the kingdom are supported by Bright's detailed historical study.

a society which strayed further from Yahweh's covenant, this remnant tended to be persecuted, poor, and scorned.[34]

At the same time the promise deepened. In light of Israel's repeated failures, the obstacles to the kingdom's coming appeared to be lodged in ever deeper recesses of the human heart. The promise would reach fulfillment only when God made a "new covenant," writing it on hearts (Jer. 31:31-33; cf. Ezek. 36:26-27, 37:14).

B. The Dynamics of the Promise

In Chapter 11 we said that God is often revealed between promise and fulfillment. Let us briefly expand on this. In the Old Testament many promises were fulfilled only in part, after some delay, and somewhat differently than people expected. This partial divergence between promise and fulfillment allowed for at least three kinds of response.

First, those who regarded some past or partial fulfillment (such as the establishment of David's monarchy) as the final, complete actualization of Yahweh's promise, forget its universal dimension; they ceased walking towards it, and expected God to conserve and protect themselves and the nation, whether or not their conduct was consistent with the covenant. Second, especially during a long, difficult course of waiting for fulfillment, one might turn aside in despair. We remember how Abraham and Sarah were tempted to do so. Such journeys of hope, of course, offer numerous situations in which God may become better known. But precisely because they offer possibilities for real choices and real doubt, they also allow one to turn aside. Finally, experiences of partial or postponed fulfillment can arouse desire for the greater fulfillment which lies beyond:

> The God who is recognized in his promises remains superior to any fulfillment that can be experienced, because in every fulfillment the promise and what is still contained in it does not yet become wholly congruent with reality and thus there always remains an overspill....Every experience of fulfillment...ultimately contains a disappointment. Man's hopes and longings stretch further than any fulfillment that can be conceived or experienced. However limited the promises may be, once we have caught in them a whiff of the future, we remain restless and urgent, seeking and searching beyond all experiences of fulfillment.[35]

For those who thus respond, the ultimate object of hope is not any promise but the One who promises. Thus through times of waiting and doubt, they cling to Yahweh, remembering his past love and faithfulness (Psalm 74, 77, etc.). When promises are fulfilled differently than they had anticipated, they are not wholly confused; eventually, at least, they rejoice in the unexpected creativity of God. When promises are only partially fulfilled, they do not cease

[34] Isa. 10:2, 14:30, 26:6, 32:7, 41:17; Jer. 22:16; Pss. 9:18, 12:5, 37:14, 40:17, 70:5, 72:4-13, 74:21, 82:3-4.

[35] Moltmann, *Theology of Hope*, pp. 105-06.

hoping; that concrete fulfillment bestows "a whiff of the future," drawing them on towards the kingdom. Nevertheless even for such persons, postponed, unexpected, or partial fulfillment can give rise to real doubts.

C. The Promise in Jesus' Day and Today

Israelites in the first century had good reason to struggle with doubt. Even at its Davidic heights, their nation had been relatively insignificant on a world scale. And now, over four centuries after their return from exile, they had long been occupied by foreign powers. Evil persons and nations continually triumphed, seemingly unopposed. The righteous continued to suffer, frequently without redress. Thus many Israelites despaired and capitulated to their conquerers. Others became Zealots and fought desperate battles of resistance. Still others sought to obey every iota of the Law, hoping thereby to win Yahweh's favor. Yet century followed century. Yahweh seemed to be absent. The gods of Greece and Rome, and the armies and rulers who worshipped them, seemed to govern the universe.

And so the faithful (and the doubters) raised the burning question of God's cosmic power. Could Yahweh really deliver tiny Judah? Was Yahweh stronger than the gods of Rome? Ultimately, this question was one of cosmic justice. Did God really care for the righteous, the poor, the needy? Did God care that the lies, the oppression, the violence of the unrighteous triumphed? Would Yahweh ever remember his promises to his remnant? Would Yahweh—could Yahweh—ever vindicate them?

During the centuries immediately preceding Jesus, these questions took on cosmic proportions. Since the righteous died so often without being vindicated, how could Yahweh fulfill his promise unless he raised them and judged their persecutors after death? Stimulated by such questions, belief in the resurrection and last judgment of all humanity became widespread. Since the world was so firmly in the grip of powers opposed to God, how could Yahweh set things right unless he shook heaven and earth, unless he transformed the natural as well as the social realm? The cry for Yahweh's saving deliverance became a longing for salvation beyond the gates of death and to the furthest reaches of the universe.[36]

As we stressed in discussing eschatology, questions like these still burn today (cf. pp. 144-45). Two thousand years have passed. Poverty, injustice, and war are still horrifyingly widespread. For every person who doubts God's existence for intellectual reasons, many more probably question it for ethical ones. In a world where millions perish from famine while others overeat, where social and ethnic hatreds grow worse and worse, where enough weapons exist to annihilate us all many times over, who can really believe in a God of justice and compassion? Even those who search for God in a very private, existential man-

[36] Ibid., pp. 133-38.

ner are often (subconsciously) horrified by the increasingly dire trend of social and international life.

D. Conclusions

The question underlying kerygmatic Christologies—How can I be saved from a desperate situation?—was alive in New Testament times and is so today. Nevertheless those who heard and saw Jesus were seldom most concerned about deliverance from physical corruption or from God's wrath in a general sense. They were more concerned with deliverance from concrete religious and social oppression. Most people today also recognize humanity's situation as desperate. Yet they are searching mostly for from liberation from social and personal conflicts.

The question underlying contextual Christologies—How can I find human fulfillment?—was alive in New Testament times and is so today. Nevertheless those who heard and saw Jesus were seldom concerned with self-actualization in a humanistic sense. They were mostly concerned with the concrete obedience consistent with the establishment of God's kingdom. Most people today are concerned about self-actualization. Yet this search becomes distorted when separated from broader issues of social justice.

For these reasons we consider the questions concerning God's righteousness—Is God just? Will God vindicate those who suffer and judge those who oppress? Does God care?—the best one in light of which to articulate our own Christological answers. The kerygmatic and contextual questions are certainly valid. We shall seek to answer them also as we proceed. Nevertheless we shall expound their significance from the vantage point of these broader, cosmic questions about the righteousness of God.

Suggestions for Further Reading

Brunner, Emil. *The Mediator.* Philadelphia: Westminster, 1957 (originally published in 1927).

Boff, Leonardo. *Jesus Christ, Liberator.* Maryknoll, N.Y.: Orbis, 1976.

Cobb, John. *Christ in a Pluralustic Age.* Philadelphia: Westminster, 1975.

Green, Michael, ed. *The Truth of God Incarnate.* Grand Rapids: Eerdmans, 1978.

Griffin, David. *A Process Christology.* Philadelphia: Westminster, 1973.

Groff, Warren. *Christ, the Hope of the Future.* Grand Rapids: Eerdmans, 1971.

Helwig, Monika. *Jesus, The Compassion of God.* Wilmington, Del.: Glazier, 1983.

Henry, Carl, ed. *Jesus of Nazareth: Savior and Lord.* Grand Rapids: Eerdmans, 1966.

Hick, John, ed. *The Myth of God Incarnate.* Philadelphia: Westminster, 1977.

Kasper, Walter. *Jesus the Christ.* New York: Paulist, 1976.

Mantzaridis, Georgios. *The Deification of Man*. Crestwood, N.Y.: St. Vladimir's, 1984.

McDonald, H.D. *Jesus: Human and Divine*. Grand Rapids: Zondervan, 1968.

Pittinger, Norman. *Christology Reconsidered*. London: SCM, 1970.

———. *The Word Incarnate*. New York: Harper, 1959.

Robinson, John A.T. *The Human Face of God*. Philadelphia: Westminster, 1979.

Schooneberg, Piet. *The Christ*. New York: Herder, 1970.

Sobrino, Jon. *Christology at the Crossroads*. Maryknoll, N.Y.: Orbis, 1978.

Turner, H.E.W. *The Patristic Doctrine of Redemption*. London: Mowbray, 1952.

CHAPTER FIFTEEN

The Life of Jesus Christ

In our attempt to penetrate and unfold the significance of Christian faith, we have sought to begin from the center of biblical revelation, from the early kerygma. This kerygma, proclaimed the life, death, and resurrection of Jesus Christ and eagerly anticipated his return. The kerygma looked backward toward Jesus' earthly history and forward toward the consummation of his reign. For early Christian communities the present was filled with a worshipful sense of Christ's presence through the Spirit, with close fellowship and with continuous witness to God's acts and God's presence. Given the intensity of their experience and the power of their hope, early Christians might well have supposed that the new age had fully dawned, that God's purposes were fully consummated, that past history was now irrelevant. In their joyous communion with the exalted "Christ of faith," "the Jesus of history" might have faded into the background.

But as we have seen (Chap. 7 above), this intense sense of the "already" of God's kingdom was gradually balanced by a realization that it was "not yet" consummated. Although Jesus had won the decisive battle, victory still coexisted with struggle, joy with persecution. Paul and others began stressing that the risen Christ was one and the same with the crucified Jesus (esp. 1 Cor. 1:18—2:5, Gal. 3:1, 4:12–14). To worship and serve him was not merely to bask in his spiritual presence; it was also walking—and suffering—in the way he had walked.

Christian life today, we have argued, exists amidst this same tension of the "already" and the "not yet." It is not fully lived or understood unless victory and struggle, success and (temporary) defeat are (at least at significant times) intertwined. They form a mysterious but deeply real unity. Likewise Jesus Christ is not fully known, nor do our lives conform to his will, unless his exaltation and suffering are grasped together. Perhaps apprehending the unity among these vastly different aspects of his work will prove as essential to understanding him as will fathoming the unity of his divine and human natures.[1]

Largely to connect the risen Christ with the earthly Jesus were the gospels written. Though some account of Jesus' life often accompanied the earliest preaching,[2] Paul's first epistles (our oldest New Testament writings) focus on Christ's death, resurrection, and return. The writing of the gospels reflect the early Church's growing awareness that it was crucial to ground these events firmly in Jesus' earthly history (cf. Luke 1:1-4).

In this volume's final chapters, we will seek to re-present the process we have just described. We too have begun with the eschatological expectation of the earliest Christians. We too have gradually realized that the revelation of Jesus Christ to which we look forward can be adequately understood only by looking backward (Chap. 11). And that backward look has already shown us that Jesus' history cannot be rightly apprehended in isolation but only as the fulfillment of the history of Israel.

At last then, having briefly traced the nature and dynamics of the Old Testament promise (Chap. 14), we come to Jesus himself. How shall we begin fathoming the immeasurably deep and highly paradoxical mysteries of his work? By means of what models, under what headings, shall we seek, at least provisionally, to arrange the different events, sayings, and "redactional" presentations which inform us about him?

I. The Ministry of Jesus

We remember that Protestant systematics have traditionally subdivided Christ's work into the offices of prophet, priest, and king. This schema might provide a balanced, comprehensive articulation of his activity. Even though Christ's priestly work vastly overshadowed the other offices in the Protestant tradition,[3] Karl Barth employed them to present Jesus as the fulfillment of those functions originally assigned to Israel (Chap. 14).

However the virtually unanimous verdict of biblical studies in this century

[1] Although traditional theology focused on the relationship between Christ's natures, it sometimes dealt with the former relationship by speaking of Christ's humiliation and exaltation (e.g., Heppe, pp. 488-509; Schmid, pp. 367-407; Hodge, *Systematic Theology*, Vol. II, pp. 610-38).

[2] According to Dodd, Acts 10:34-43 sketches the outline of the common early apostolic preaching (pp. 27-28). Careful reading of Paul's letters shows that he also knew a fair amount about Jesus' earthly ministry, and that this was not irrelevant to his Christology (see A. M. Hunter, *Paul and his Predecessors* [London: SCM, 1940], pp. 10-13; *The Gospel According to Paul* [Philadelphia: Westminster, 1966], pp. 76-88).

[3] For a criticism of Protestant orthodoxy's usual handling of the three offices, see A. Ritschl, *The Christian Doctrine of Justification and Reconciliaiton*, pp. 428-34.

suggests a more comprehensive vantage point. Scholars of all theological orientations have agreed that Jesus regarded his own mission as the bringing of the kingdom of God.[4] This phrase or an equivalent term appears some fifty-two times in Matthew, forty-one in Luke, and fourteen in Mark. Jesus' message (like John the Baptist's) is frequently summarized by this phrase.[5] When Jesus sends his disciples to preach and heal, their message is the same (Matt. 10:7; Luke 9:2, 10:9–11, cf. 9:60). Jesus' parables usually have the kingdom for their theme (Mark 4; Matt. 13, 20–25; Luke 13-14). With Jesus' coming, God's kingdom struck a mighty blow against Satan's (Mark 3:22-27 and par; cf. Luke 4:5–8). Rather than beginning with distinct features of Christ's work (such as his offices) and gradually synthesizing them, we propose beginning with his central theme and gradually distinguishing its various aspects.

A. What Is the Kingdom of God?

While scholars agree that the kingdom was central for Jesus, they disagree as to what kind of kingdom it was. In the Old Testament and for Jesus' contemporaries, God's kingdom was not only a religious but also a social reality. Liberal and liberation Christologies emphasize the social dimension (Chap. 14).

Reformation and orthodox Protestantism, however, interpreted Jesus' relationship to the Old Testament differently. According to their hermeneutic Israel's repeated transgressions of the covenant's social prescriptions revealed that the real issue was not a social one. These transgressions revealed the deep sinfulness of the human heart. Accordingly Jesus came to effect not external, social change but inward, personal repentance. The kingdom which he brought was really heavenly and spiritual, not earthly and social.[6] Recently existential interpreters have revived this general line of approach.

Jesus heralds his ministry by exclaiming: "The time is fulfilled, and the Kingdom of God is at hand; repent and believe the good news!" (Mark 1:15; cf. Matt. 4:17). The Greek word *eggiken*, translated "is at hand," is the perfect passive form of the verb "to bring near" (*eggizo*). God's kingdom, then, "has already been brought near." When something has been brought near, is it fully here? Or is it not quite here?

Such oscillation in meaning characterizes not only this key word but the per-

---

[4] For the original advocacy of this perspective see Johannes Weiss, *Jesus' Proclamation of the Kingdom* (Philadelphia: Westminster, 1971) and Albert Schweitzer, *The Quest of the Historical Jesus* (New York: Macmillan, 1959), pp. 330-43. (These works were originally published in 1892 and 1906 respectively.)

[5] Matt. 3:2; 4:17, 27; 9:35; Mark 1:15; Luke 4:43, 8:1. We regard "kingdom of God" and "kingdom of heaven" as equivalent terms. Cf. p. 157, note 6.

[6] On Calvin see p. 83; for Luther's views, see Paul Althaus, *The Ethics of Martin Luther* (Philadelphia: Fortress, 1972), pp. 43-82. See also Heppe, pp. 481-87; Schmid, pp. 370-76; Hodge, pp. 596-609. These views will be discussed more fully in Vol. II, Chap. 1.

spective of the Synoptic Gospels in general. The awesome power of Jesus' healing, exorcising, teaching, and preaching suggest that God's kingdom "already" was present. Proponents of "realized" eschatology argue that it was.[7] Yet opposition to Jesus grows rapidly; his course becomes marked by suffering and death. Proponents of "consistent" eschatology argue that God's kingdom was "not yet" present in Jesus' ministry.[8]

B. The Existential Interpretation

Rudolf Bultmann reconciled these emphases in his own way. He agreed with "consistent" eschatology that God's kingdom always remained future for Jesus; it never really came. Nevertheless Bultmann insisted that Jesus' proclamation of it encountered hearers vividly with the urgent demands of God (much as "realized" eschatology stressed). Crucial to this way of reconciling these emphases was Bultmann's "demythologized" interpretation of Jesus' kingdom message itself. According to Bultmann, Jesus held a radically apocalyptic (discontinuous) view of God's kingdom (Chap. 6). Unlike the Old Testament prophetic perspective, Jesus did not forsee the kingdom as the (continuous) culmination of Yahweh's social and historical promises to Israel. Instead it was a wholly other (discontinuous), heavenly reality which would suddenly break into history. This end of history, which was never "realized" in Jesus' ministry, was "not the completion of history but its breaking-off."[9] Consequently, God's kingdom could not be "an ideal which realizes itself in human history; we cannot speak of its founding, its building, its completion."[10]

But if this be so, how can we understand Jesus' teachings which apparently deal with social and ethical matters? Bultmann's interpretation of these teachings parallels his interpretation of Jesus' eschatology. To be sure, Jesus' proclamation contained some specific eschatological notions: struggle with Satan, final judgment, other events to occur before the end.[11] But Bultmann insists that these are just imaginative, mythological pictures. Modern people must delve behind them to recover their underlying intent: to bring individuals face to face with God's urgent demands on their lives. Similarly Jesus' ethical teachings mentioned specific issues: living without extra food and clothing,

[7] C. H. Dodd's *The Parables of the Kingdom* (New York: Scribners', 1961) is the classic statement of "realized eschatology." Dodd bases his case on Luke 10:9-11, 23-24 and par; Luke 11:20, 11:31-32 = Matt. 12:41-42; Luke 12:18-30, 16:16; Matt. 11:2-11 and 12:28.

[8] Both Weiss and Schweitzer espoused "consistent eschatology." For a discussion of "realized" versus "consistent" eschatology, see Ladd, *The Presence of the Future*, pp. 3-42.

[9] Bultmann, *History and Eschatology*, p. 30.

[10] Bultmann, *Jesus and the Word*, p. 38.

[11] Bultmann rightly points out that Jesus went into much less detail on such matters than did most apocalypticists of his day (Ibid., pp. 39-42).

giving one's possessions to the poor, etc. Yet Bultmann argues that true moral-ity cannot spring from following general rules but only from encountering and obeying God in particular situations.[12] (For general rules are things, whereas encounters involve only persons: cf. Chap. 10.) Accordingly, Bultmann insists, Jesus was not teaching specific ethical principles any more than he was endors-ing specific eschatological mythology. Modern people must penetrate the un-derlying intent of his teaching: By giving examples of the sort of radical behavior that God might require, Jesus sought to bring individuals face to face with God's urgent demands.

According to Bultmann, then, Jesus gave no specific teachings on issues like wealth or property: "From the gospels we learn nothing at all about the eco-nomic situation in Palestine."[13] Of course Jesus did demand that everyone who followed him "must have the strength and freedom to renounce his posses-sions" (cf. Mark 10:17-31). Yet Bultmann insists that "everyone has to decide for himself" whether and to what extent one's posessions constitute a barrier to the kingdom.[14]

In an effort to correct Bultmann in certain ways, Gunther Bornkamm, a neo-Bultmannian, observed that Jesus reached out especially to those "on the fringes of society, men who because of fate, guilt or prevailing prejudice are looked upon as marked men, as outcasts": the sick, demoniacs, lepers, women, children, and tax collectors.[15] Bornkamm notices that Jesus showed special concern for the poor. Yet, Bornkamm argues, the poor designates not chiefly the economically poor, but those who "in their lives and in their attitude...are beggars before God." Moreover Jesus' Beatitudes concerning the poor, the mourners, the hungry, and the thirsty, do not refer chiefly to social groups. In-stead they "are embraced in one idea, that God wills to be with us...in as manifold and individual a way as our needs are manifold and individual."[16]

Bultmann also insisted that Jesus was not concerned with social or political questions. Anticipating the abrupt end of everything earthly, Jesus saw no need to deal with such issues. Yet even had his eschatological anticipation not been so urgent, Jesus would still have left political decisions to individuals in their concrete situations.[17] Bornkamm concurs: "Not a word does [Jesus] say ei-ther to confirm or renew the national hopes of his people."[18]

Existential interpretation, then, can eliminate the social aspects of Jesus'

[12] Ibid., pp. 83-89. In such encounters, "man is trusted and expected to see for himself what God commands. God's requirements are intrinsically intelligible" (77).

[13] Ibid., p. 105.

[14] Ibid., p. 99.

[15] *Jesus of Nazareth* (New York: Harper, 1960), pp. 79-80.

[16] Ibid., pp. 76-77.

[17] *Jesus and the Word*, pp. 93, 107-08.

[18] *Jesus of Nazareth*, p. 66; cf. pp. 121, 123.

kingdom proclamation by regarding it essentially as the urgent, personal revelation and claim of God. God and the fulness of his reign, as "consistent" eschatology argued, always remain future. Yet, as "realized" eschatology stressed,
God's demands already affect the present.[19] However since such encounters always involve persons and not things, general ethical or social teachings cannot
belong to the core of Jesus' kingdom message. What teachings one finds in the
gospels must be *ad hoc* illustrations of what the ever-future reign of God might
perhaps involve.

II. The Great Reversal

Existential theologians do not agree with liberal and liberation theologians
that Jesus' kingdom message has direct social implications. But they all agree
that Jesus' kingdom involved a surprising reversal. For centuries the wicked
had triumphed while the righteous suffered (see Chap. 14). The Gentiles ruled
while Judah was squelched. Israel's longing for God's kingdom intensified, expecting that the righteous remnant would be delivered while sinners would be
punished. Surely the kingdom's coming would reverse the existing order of
things.

Jesus did indeed bring the great eschatological reversal. But not in the form
in which it was normally expected. For those who regarded themselves as righteous, as good Jews, and those who were wealthy expected God's kingdom to
come to them. They were rudely stunned when Jesus offered it to sinners, to
Gentiles, and to the poor. We can determine who were these "poor" only by
examining Jesus' ministry in detail. We must remember, however, that whether
their poverty was either social or spiritual or some combination of the two,
these persons were the highly unexpected recipients of God's surprising grace.

A. The Kingdom and the Gentiles

Often in Old Testament times many Israelites identified the fulfillment of
God's promise with the good fortunes of their nation. By Jesus' day, in contrast,
those who sought to become the righteous remnant often distinguished themselves sharply from the nation as a whole. Nevertheless they often separated
themselves even more widely from Gentiles. Caught up in the heightened eschatological sense of conflict between good and evil, they expected the coming of God's kingdom to involve destruction for most, if not all Gentiles.

Scholars debate to what extent (or even whether) Jesus sought to reach Gentiles. On at least one occasion Jesus restricted his disciples' mission to Israelites
(Matt. 10:5-6, cf. v. 23). In those few instances when Jesus healed Gentiles, it

---

[19] Unlike Bultmann, Bornkamm can speak of God's reign being present in Jesus
himself (Ibid., pp. 62-63, 74, 92-93, 169-70, 200; see Ladd, pp. 35-36).

was they who sought him out and displayed exceptional faith.[20] Bultmann and Bornkamm argue that Jesus did not seek to reach Gentiles.[21] On the other hand when increasing opposition pressured Jesus out of Galilee, he worked in regions populated largely by Gentiles (Mark 3:7–8, 7:24—8:27 and par). It is difficult to argue that Jesus ministered only to Jews in these regions. For Galilee itself had a very mixed population, and he encountered Gentiles even there (Matt. 8:5, cf. Luke 17:11-19).

But even if the nature and extent of Christ's actual mission be debated, his message not only extends salvation to the Gentiles but regards them in some ways as favored. Jesus wholly "detaches the nationalistic idea of revenge from the hope of redemption."[22] He not only rebukes negative attitudes towards Samaritans (Luke 9:51–56), but uses them as examples which put Israelites to shame (Luke 10:25-37, 17:18, cf. John 4:4–44). He expects the Ninevites, the Queen of Sheba, the inhabitants of Tyre and Sidon and even those of Sodom and Gomorrah to rise for final judgment and to shame many Israelites.[23]

Jesus reverses the traditional eschatological hope even more explicitly: "I tell you, many will come from east and west and sit at table with Abraham, Isaac, and Jacob in the Kingdom of heaven, while the sons of the Kingdom will be thrown into the outer darkness!" (Matt. 8:11–12 and par). As Joachim Jeremias has noted, "no Jewish scholar and no Jewish apocalypticist had ever dared to utter such a thing."[24] Here Jesus envisions Gentiles as full participants, many of them replacing Israelites, in the coming Messianic banquet. Beginning from this vantage point one can see that Gentiles are included in an additional host of eschatological images.[25] In conclusion, the kingdom of God,

> this central conception of [Jesus'] proclamation, *includes the Gentile world*....the incorporation of the Gentiles in the Kingdom...was expected and announced by

[20] The healings of the centurion's servant (Matt. 8:5-13 and par) and the Syro-Phonecian woman's daughter (Matt. 15:21-28 and par), take place at a distance: Jesus does not enter their dwellings. Jesus at first refuses the woman's plea, saying, "I was sent only to the lost sheep of the house of Israel" (Matt. 15:24). The Gadarene demoniac, who was probably a Gentile, also approaches Jesus unexpectedly (Mark 5:1-20 and par). For the argument that he limited his own and his disciples' ministry to Israel, see Joachim Jeremias, *Jesus' Promise to the Nations*, pp. 11-39.

[21] *Jesus and the Word*, p. 40; *Jesus of Nazareth*, p. 78.

[22] Jeremias, p. 43.

[23] Matt. 12:41-42 and par, Matt. 11:22 and par (cf. Luke 4:26-27), Matt. 10:15 and par.

[24] Ibid., p. 51; cf. Mark 12:1-12 and par.

[25] Jeremias lists the Temple of the New Age, the City of God, the River of Life, the Inheritance and the Joy of the New Age, and the Angelic summons to it (pp. 65-70).

Jesus as God's *eschatological act of power, as the great final manifestation of God's free grace.*[26]

But if Jews and Gentiles were to be incorporated in God's kingdom in any way while on this earth, this incorporation would necessarily involve sweeping social changes for both. In Christ's day one's personal identity was deeply tied to membership in a national or ethnic group. Jews and Gentiles were deeply divided not only by emotional hatreds but by deeply ingrained traditions, customs, and forms of social life. Any kind of fellowship including them both would have to have a novel social character.

B. The Kingdom and the Poor

By "Gentiles," Jesus meant people with specific ethnic and social characteristics. What about "the poor"? By this term, did Jesus mean primarily those who "in their lives and in their attitude...are beggars before God"? Or those of an economic and social class?

Gunther Bornkamm acknowledges that in the Psalms and much later Jewish literature, "the poor" originally meant those who were economically poor but faithful to Yahweh. Eventually, however, this term was extended to those who suffered for their faithfulness. By New Testament times it could also denote those who were pious, regardless of economic situation.[27] Such a meaning may be found in Matthew's rendering of Jesus' first Beatitude: "Blessed are the poor *in spirit*" (Matt. 5:3). In contrast with Luke's "Blessed are you poor" (6:20), Matthew seems to spiritualize poverty. As for the economically poor, both Matthew and Mark report Jesus' apparent downplaying of their needs in saying "you always have the poor with you" (Mark 14:7, Matt. 26:11). From such data it has been argued that the first two gospels reflect little concern with economic poverty.[28]

Such considerations, however, are overly narrow in two respects. First they focus on analysis of a single term when Jesus' whole perspective on wealth and its place in God's kingdom must be considered. Second they pay too little attention to Luke, who was clearly concerned about poverty and wealth. On the other hand liberal and liberation theologians have often placed too much emphasis on Luke, exalting the model provided by his particular "redaction" to

---

[26] Ibid., p. 70.

[27] *Jesus of Nazareth*, pp. 76-77.

[28] *TWNT* VI, pp. 902-04; this interpretation of Mark 14:7 has been rejected in many standard commentaries; e.g., C. E. B. Cranfield, *St. Mark* (Oxford: University, 1959); Frederick Grant in the *The Interpreter's Bible*, Vol. VII (Nashville: Abingdon, 1951); and William Lane, *The Gospel According to Mark* (Grand Rapids: Eerdmans, 1974).

undue systematic importance.[29] We can extend our own investigation more widely by examining what the Synoptic Gospels broadly and commonly affirm about wealth and poverty. We shall consider Luke's particular emphasis only after we have done this.

1. *Jesus' Own Poverty.* The Synoptic Gospels represent Jesus as belonging to the masses of the common people. In a land subjugated and heavily taxed by Rome, few such people were even moderately well off. Jesus took up the life of a travelling Rabbi, one of a group even poorer than most.[30] Those who followed him found it not only existentially challenging but also physically difficult: "Foxes have holes, and birds of the air have nests; but the Son of Man has nowhere to lay his head" (Matt. 8:20). When this is recognized, incidents like plucking grain on the Sabbath take on new meaning: Jesus was not only contesting legalism, but also grabbing a meal as did the poor.[31]

Jesus' parables reflect deep acquaintance with the common people and their way of life. In particular, many reflect a setting where land was controlled by wealthy absentee landlords, and Jewish farmers had been reduced to near serfdom under harsh overseers.[32] Jesus was especially sensitive to widows, who were thoroughly vulnerable to exploitation. He castigated scribes who enjoyed prestigious social position but who, by foreclosing on property when the male owner died, "devour [ed] widows' houses" (Matt. 12:38–40). Jesus sharply contrasted rich people who made splendid temple offerings with a widow who, with two small coins, gave "everything she had, her whole living" (Mark 12:41–42).

To be sure, Jesus did not deliver a lecture series on economic theory. But Bultmann is surely wrong in claiming that "from the gospels we learn nothing at all about the economic situation in Palestine." Nevertheless all this might be fairly incidental to Jesus' kingdom ministry. We must examine whether his words and actions were more intentionally directed to issues of poverty and wealth.

2. *Jesus on Wealth.* Jesus' remarks on riches are strongly and uniformly nega-

[29] This is a weakness of John H. Yoder's generally insightful *Politics of Jesus* (Grand Rapids: Eerdmans, 1972). Instead of merely asserting that "any other Gospel text could equally have been used" (p. 24), Yoder might well have acknowledged, as did Walter Rauschenbusch, that Luke was "The socialist among the evangelists." (*Christianity and the Social Crisis* [New York: Macmillan, 1907], p. 82).

[30] Richard Batey, *Jesus and the Poor* (New York: Harper, 1972), p. 7; Joachim Jeremias, *Jerusalem in the Time of Jesus*, 3rd ed., (Philadelphia: Fortress, 1969), p. 115.

[31] Mark 2:23-28 and par in light of Deut. 23:25; cf. Matt. 11:12-14 and par.

[32] Matt. 5:25-26, 18:23-25, 24:48-49, 25:14-19; see Yoder, pp. 66-74. Several recent studies on the sociology of Palestine in Jesus' day support our general thesis and illustrate it in detail. See esp. Sean Freyne, *Galilee from Alexander the Great to Hadrian* (Wilmington, De.: Glazier, 1980); John Gager, *Kingdom and Community: the Social World of Early Christianity* (Englewood Cliffs, N.J.: Prentice-Hall, 1975; and Gerd Theissen, *Sociology of Early Palestinian Christianity* (Philadelphia: Fortress, 1977).

tive. In light of the kingdom which calls everyone to radical decision, Jesus insists: "No one can serve two masters; for either he will hate one and love the other, or he will be devoted to one and despise the other. You cannot serve God and mammon" (Matt. 6:24). He draws an equally sharp distinction between laying up treasures on earth and in heaven (Matt. 6:19–21). For "delight in riches" will choke the seed of the Kingdom (Mark 4:19 and par).

In contrast, a clear sign of the kingdom's dawning is that the poor receive new hope (Matt. 11:4–5). Moreover ultimate admission to the kingdom will depend on one's service to the hungry, the thirsty, the stranger, the naked, the sick, and the imprisoned (Matt. 25:31–46).

However Christ's main concern was neither to condemn wealth nor extol the poor. It was to call all to a joyous way of life which, confident in God's care, ceases to be anxious about material things:

> Consider the lillies of the field, how they grow; they neither toil nor spin; yet I tell you, even Solomon in all his glory was not arrayed like one of these....Therefore be not anxious, saying 'What shall we eat?' or 'What shall we wear?' For...your heavenly Father knows that you need them all. But seek first his Kingdom, and his righteousness, and all these things shall be yours as well (Matt. 6:28–33).

Freed from these anxieties, the lifestyle of the kingdom includes giving to all in need, even to those who seize one's possessions (Matt. 5:40–42). Accordingly many whom Jesus called left their occupations, whether honest ones like fishing (Mark 1:16–17 and par) or despicable ones like tax collecting (Mark 2:14 and par). When they went on missions they took "no bread, no bag, no money in their belts" (Mark 6:8–9).

Against this background Jesus' command that the "rich young ruler" give all his goods to the poor (Mark 10:21–28 and par) hardly seems like unusual advice. Jesus simply asked him to do what all his followers had. And though many have sought to restrict his command to this special case, Jesus immediately added that "It is easier for a camel to go through the eye of a needle than for a rich man to enter the Kingdom of God!" At this the disciples were "exceedingly astonished, and said to him, 'Then who can be saved!?' " For they shared the common opinion that riches are a sign of divine blessing; the wealthy must be among God's most favored. But this episode ends in a reversal: The rich man turns away from the kingdom, which now belongs to the disciples, who have left everything for it.

When we extend our research beyond a single term like "the poor," we see that Jesus did far more than select occasional poor persons as symbols of existential poverty. He taught broad, reversed attitudes towards possessions, attitudes central to the kingdom he was bringing. This is clear from Matthew and Mark alone. It becomes even clearer in one particular gospel.

3. *The Lucan Emphasis.* Luke fills out the picture of Jesus as a man of the common people. Jesus was born in a barn. The offering which his parents made for him, a pair of birds, was the one allowed for those who "cannot afford a lamb" (Luke 2:24, Lev. 12:18). Luke's prologue prophesies sweeping economic and so-

cial changes (Luke 1:51-53, 71-73). When the crowds ask John the Baptist how to prepare for all this, he replies:

> "Whoever has two coats, let him share with him who has none; and he who has food, let him do likewise." Tax collectors also came to be baptized, and said to him, "Teacher, what shall we do?" And he said to them, "Collect no more than is appointed you." Soldiers also asked him....And he said to them, "Rob no one by violence or false accusation, and be content with your wages"(Luke 3:11-14).

Subsequently, as even Gunther Bornkamm recognizes, Jesus announces and summarizes his mission as the fulfillment of Isaiah 61:

> The Spirit of the Lord is upon me, because he has annointed me to preach good new to the poor. He has sent me to proclaim release to the captives and recovering of sight to the blind, to set at liberty those who are oppressed, to proclaim the acceptable year of the Lord.[33]

When we remember that Matthew and Mark announce and summarize Jesus' message as "Repent, for the Kingdom of Heaven is at hand!" (Matt. 4:17, Mark 1:14-15), the above text appears to give a good indicate how Luke understands Jesus' kingdom ministry.[34] Shortly thereafter (Luke 6:20-25), Jesus pronounces the Lucan Beatitudes in terms which anticipate a wide-ranging social reversal:

> Blessed are you poor, for yours is the Kingdom of God. Blessed are you that hunger now, for you shall be satisfied. Blessed are you that weep now, for you shall laugh....But woe to you that are rich, for you have received your consolation. Woe to you that are full now, for you shall hunger. Woe to you that laugh now, for you shall mourn and weep.

As liberation theologians have noticed, these words sound similar to the Marxist notion of class reversal. What follows, however, is hardly a situation where oppressed and oppressor merely exchange places. Luke 6:27-38 envisions a way of life where everyone loves enemies, forgives others, gives to those who ask (even to those who steal), and lends without expecting return. As in Matthew and Mark, no mere readjustment of class divisions but the dawning of an entirely new social reality, is at the core of this reversal.

Like Matthew (22:2-10), Luke presents Jesus' kingdom call as an invitation

---

[33] Luke 4:18-19. Bornkamm, p. 75.

[34] John H. Yoder argues that "the acceptable year of the Lord" refers to the year of the Jubilee (cf. Lev. 25). Jesus, then, is announcing that a permanent Jubilee of redressing economic inequities has come. If this be so, the familiar words of "The Lord's prayer"—"forgive us our debts as we forgive our debtors" (Matt. 6:12, Luke 11:4)—could refer to the cancelling of cash debts (*Politics of Jesus*, pp. 36-40, 64-67). Joachim Jeremias notes that Jesus' quotation stops just before the words "the day of vengeance of our God" (Isa. 61:2); Jesus, then, is proclaiming the fulfillment of Israel's hopes without including God's judgment on the Gentiles, a chief reason for his hearers' anger (Luke 4:24-29; Jeremias, pp. 44-45).

to a banquet. But Luke places it in a context where Jesus, observing the desire of invited guests for seats of honor, advises his followers to avoid such scrambles for prestige (Luke 14:7–11, cf. Matt. 23:6–12). He encourages them, in giving banquets, to invite neither their kinfolk nor the rich, but "the poor, the mained, the lame, the blind" (Luke 14:12–13). Then follows the parable of the Great Banquet. The invitees excuse their absence—two of the three to examine new property—so the host invites "the poor and maimed and blind and lame" (Luke 14:15–24).

As in Matthew and Mark, but in greater detail, Luke presents Jesus' special sensitivity to the socially and economically unfortunate. He is especially concerned about widows (Luke 2:37, 4:25–26, 7:12–15, 18:1–8) and beggars (Luke 16:19-31). Jesus told of a prosperous farmer who built bigger barns, telling himself "take your ease, eat, drink and be merry," but that night he suddenly died. Such is the fate "of one who lays up treasure for himself, and is not rich towards God." Then follows Jesus' appeal to cease worrying about food and clothing, much as in Matthew, except that Jesus tells all his disciples to "sell your possessions, and give alms" (Luke 12:16–34, cf. Matt. 6:25–33). The story of Zacchaeus depicts a proper response to the kingdom. For him repentance included the vow: "half of my goods I give to the poor; and if I have defrauded anyone of anything, I restore it fourfold" (Luke 19:8).

4. *Conclusions*. Although Luke describes Jesus' approach to poverty and wealth in more detail than Matthew and Mark, he expands on a theme central also for them. In all three gospels Jesus does not merely select occasional poor persons as symbols of existential poverty. He insists that the dawning kingdom demands sweeping economic reversals. To be sure, Jesus does not crudely and simplistically condemn mere possession of wealth. He is concerned about serving mammon, about "delight in riches." Accordingly many interpreters (including Rudolf Bultmann) argue that, so long as one's inner attitude is sound, it does not matter how much one possesses.

Yet Jesus' frequent and uniform condemnation of riches challenges such separations of an inner, existential realm from outward economic and social ones. For if rich and poor were to be incorporated in God's kingdom in any way while on this earth, the attitudes of sharing and freedom from anxiety would hardly be possible if some possessed vastly greater wealth than others. Large economic differences would perpetuate large social and cultural differences. Any kingdom fellowship incorporating rich and poor would require sweeping social changes for both.

C. The Kingdom, Women, and Men

According to many women's liberation theologians, numerous biblical writings bear the undesirable imprint of the partriarchal culture from which they come. Most such theologians, however, find Jesus' attitude and ministry very affirmative of women.[35] We have noticed Jesus' sensitivity not only towards individuals who happened to be widows, but also to their problems as a social and economic group. Widows experienced in extreme fashion many restrictions common to women as a whole. In contemporary Israelite society, wives could often be easily divorced, sometimes for not being pretty enough, for failing to bear children, or even for being poor cooks. Yet women had few ways to divorce their husbands. This led to economic dependence and insecurity, since property was held almost exclusively by men. A woman's testimony was usually not accepted in courts of law. Women normally went about veiled. In many quarters they dared not speak to men in public. Women took no leadership in public worship. Many rabbis seldom spoke to women and would never take them as disciples.[36]

The situation of a typical woman in Jesus' day, then, would hardly stem from her personal character or history alone. Economically she was almost entirely dependent on her husband or father. Religiously her privileges and responsibilities were quite limited. As an extreme but by no means unique rabbinic declaration put it: "Praised be God that he has not created me a gentile! Praised be God that he has not create me a woman! Praise be God that he has not created me an ignorant man!"[37]

Much as Jesus' words and actions breathe a sensitivity to the problems of the poor, so do they to the concerns of women. Jesus often used feminine images and examples; he never represented women negatively.[38]

Unlike the rabbis, Jesus spoke extensively with women. In perhaps the Synoptics' most profound dialogue (Matt. 15:21–28), most extensive healing scene (Mark 5:25—34 and par), and most graphic depiction of the reversal of the "righteous" and sinners (Luke 7:36–50), a woman is the central character. In a society where a woman's role consisted in domestic service, Jesus reproved Martha of Bethany, who was busily preparing a meal, and affirmed her sister Mary who was—contrary to rabbinical custom—absorbing his teaching (Luke 10:38–42; cf. John 4, 11:1–37). Jesus also rejected the notion that a woman's worth came primarily through childbearing. When a woman cried out

---

[35] See Virginia Mollenkott, *Women, Men and the Bible* (Nashville: Abingdon, 1977), pp. 10-21; Leonard Swidler, *Biblical Affirmations of Women* (Philadelphia: Westminster, 1979), pp. 161-290; Mary Evans, *Women and Men in the Bible* (Greenwood, S.C.: Attic, 1983), pp. 44-60; James Hurley, *Man and Woman in Biblical Perspective* (Grand Rapids: Zondervan, 1981), pp. 79-114; Elizabeth Schuessler Fiorenza, *In Memory of Her* (New York: Crossroad, 1983), pp. 118-54.

[36] Evans, pp. 33-38; Hurley, pp. 58-74.

[37] *Tosephta Berakhoth*, 7, 8; quoted in Swidler, p. 155.

[38] Swidler, p. 164. Jesus could use a woman to represent God (Luke 15:8-10) and portrayed his own love for Jerusalem as that of a hen for her chicks (Matt. 23:37 = Luke 13:34-35). Sometimes the same point is made first in language which one sex could best grasp, immediately followed by language most appropriate to the other (e.g., Matt. 13:31-32; see Swidler, pp. 252-53).

"Blessed is the womb that bore you, and the breasts that you sucked!" Jesus returned, "Blessed rather are those who hear the word of God and keep it!" (Luke 11:27–28). Moreover, whereas contemporary laws regarded a wife's unfaithfulness more severely than a husband's, Jesus put them on the same plane (Matt. 10:10-12). Again unlike these laws, he disallowed husbands to divorce their wives on any other grounds Mark 10:10–12. Upon hearing this insistence on marital equality, Jesus' male disciples wondered whether marriage would be worth the trouble (Matt. 19:9–10)!

Also in sharp contrast with rabbinic practice, women were among Jesus' regular followers.[39] Sometimes women perceived the significance of events more clearly than men. For example, when confusion reigns about the meaning of Jesus' final days, a woman anoints him for burial (Mark 14:6 and par). As Jesus is captured and crucified, his male disciples flee, but the women stand by.[40] They prepare him for burial. In a society where a woman's testimony was seldom legally valid, they first witness his resurrection (Mark 16:1–8 and par)— only to be scornfully dismissed by the men (Luke 24:11)!

Jesus' valuation of women's domestic, maternal, marital, and religious roles are indications of the new sense of identity to which God's kingdom was calling everyone. Among Israelites family ties and roles defined the contours of everyone's existence. Yet when Jesus' own family once came seeking him, he looked upon the crowd he was teaching and uttered the unthinkable: "Here are my mother and my brothers! Whoever does the will of God is my brother, and sister, and mother!" (Mark 10:28-30). The disciples who, in contrast to the rich young ruler, had left all their property to follow Jesus, had also often left "brothers, sisters, father, mother, children" (Mark 10:28–30 and par). For Jesus often warned them that the call to God's Kingdom could tear even these relationships asunder:

> Do not suppose that I have come to bring peace to the earth; it is not peace that I have come to bring, but a sword. For I have come to set a man against his father, a daughter against her mother, a daughter-in-law against her mother-in-law.... Anyone who prefers father or mother to me is not worthy of me. Anyone who prefers son or daughter to me is not worthy of me (Matt. 10:34-38, cf. Luke 12:51-53, 14:26-27).

Jesus, of course, was hardly seeking to destroy all family relationships. But he was portraying the call of God's kingdom as so all-encompassing that even this most basic framework of personal identity and social existence could be (and often would be) deeply shaken by it.

When we realize that the kingdom disrupted not only Israel's external differ-

---

[39] Mark 15:40-41 and par, Luke 8:1-3; see also Fiorenza, pp. 140-51.

[40] Mark 15:40-41 and par. In a society where men were regarded as more important than women, the male disciples were in greater danger. Nevertheless the women were at least as faithful to Jesus as his male followers at this point.

entiation from Gentiles, not only its internal differentiations among rich and poor, but shook even its internal rootage in family structures, then we can no longer suppose that the kingdom's claim could be a merely existential one. God's kingdom challenged the most basic social relationships in Israel's existence, and promised to renew her total life and that of all humankind. Consequently, if women and men were to be incorporated into God's kingdom while on this earth, their new relationships would involve sweeping social changes for both.

III. The Kingdom and the Demonic

Jesus fulfilled Yahweh's ancient promise, and answered the intensifying cry for God's righteousness, by bringing a Kingdom which reversed many contemporary relationships. In the view of those who thought themselves righteous, the kingdom which Jesus was bringing was hardly reversing things as they had anticipated. Clearly so sweeping an alteration of their existence would arouse fierce opposition. But at its deepest, most theological level, in what did this opposition consist? In all four Gospels Jesus' ministry involves sustained struggle with demonic forces.

With the rise of biblical criticism, however, it was thought that if any features of the Gospels needed "demythologizing," it certainly would be these. Nonetheless, the totalitarian regimes, the genocide, and widespread destruction of World War II pushed many to reconsider. Once again it seemed plausible that humanity might be influenced in uncanny ways by massive irrational, malevolent forces. As similar phenomena continue to operate in today's apocalyptic atmosphere, theology must once again ask what reality these dark powers might have.[41]

A. Demonic Opposition to Jesus

When Jesus was baptized, the Holy Spirit descended and a voice from heaven proclaimed, "Thou art my beloved Son, with whom I am well pleased" (Mark 1:11 and par). These words, which would again be echoed at Jesus' transfiguration (Mark 9:7 and par, 2 Peter 2:17) recalled Yahweh's call to his Ser-

---

[41] Neo-Bultmannian treatments, which deny that Jesus' ministry had significant social implications, generally acknowledge the pervasiveness of the demonic in the Gospels (Bultmann, p. 28; Bornkamm, pp. 65-68). Nevertheless they deny that such realities have much meaning for the present (Bornkamm, p. 67). According to Ernst Käsemann, Jesus emphasized God's sole lordship over creation (*Jesus Means Freedom* [Philadelphia: Fortress, 1969], p. 25-26). If he struggled with the demonic in any way, it was more in the sense of destroying an illusion than of fighting anything real. Jesus "was conscious of being sent, not to fight the devil, but to minister to man" (*Essays on New Testament Themes* [London: SCM, 1964], p. 40; cf. Bultmann, pp. 56, 141, 155-56; and Ernst Fuchs, *Studies in the Historical Jesus* [London: SCM, 1964], pp. 52-53.)

vant.[42] Jesus' baptism, then, was in part a comissioning to exercise his messi-anic role according to the pattern of the Servant.[43] Immediately, however, the Spirit drove Jesus into the wilderness to confront Satan (Mark 1:12 and par). These temptations were not merely tests of his personal fortitude. They were proposals as to how he might exercise and validate his kingly mission.[44] In chal-lenging Jesus to turn stones into bread, Satan proposed that he prove himself Messiah chiefly by providing for the physical needs of people . The challenge to jump from the temple proposed that he do so by spectacular signs. Satan's request that Jesus worship him proposed that he acknowledge the Devil as the world's real ruler.

Jesus rejected all of these as the main means of bringing God's kingdom in favor of the servant pattern. Then the Spirit led him back to Galilee (Luke 4:14, cf. 18). Very soon he was assualted by a demonaic who shrieked, "What have you to do with us, Jesus of Nazareth? Have you come to destroy us? I know who you are: the Holy One of God!" (Mark 1:24, Luke 4:34). This episode fol-lows a pattern familiar in the Synoptics. It is initiated by a challenge, which identifies Jesus by specific titles (cf. Mark 5:7 and par); Jesus then sternly re-bukes the demons (cf. Mark 9:25 and par) and commands them to silence be-cause they know him (Mark 1:34, 3:12; Luke 4:35, 41).

These commands to silence were consistent with Jesus' servant pattern. Mat-thew explains why Jesus ordered those whom he healed "not to make him known" (Matt. 12:16) by identifying him as the fulfillment of the entire pas-sage from which his baptismal affirmation came:

> Behold my servant whom I have chosen, my beloved in whom my soul is pleased. I will put my Spirit upon him, and he shall proclaim justice to the Gentiles. He will not wrangle or cry aloud, nor will any one hear his voice in the streets; he will not break a bruised reed or quench a smoldering wick, till he brings justice to victory; and in his name will the Gentiles hope (Matt. 12:18–21; cf. Isa. 42:1–4).

[42] The "servant songs" are found in Isa. 42:1-7, 49:1-13, 50:4-9 and 52:13—53:12. For a thorough discussion of this theme, see Christopher North, *The Suffering Ser-vant in Deutero-Isaiah*, 2nd. ed. (Oxford: University, 1963).

[43] Joachim Jeremias, *TWNT* V, pp. 700-02. In *Jesus and the Servant* (London: SPCK, 1959), Morna Hooker argues that these baptismal words do not clearly recall Isaiah 42 (pp. 68-73), and that the New Testament seldom regards Jesus as Isaiah's servant. Her argument concerning the baptism, however, fails to consider Matt. 12:28-31. In general, she will acknowledge the influence of this Isaianic theme only where it can be proven that a passage "could only have come" from a particular servant passage (p. 62). She thus attempts to dispose of possible references one by one, failing to account for the cumulative weight of texts which point to Isaiah's servant with high probability. In support of the importance of the servant motif, see Jeremias, pp. 677-717 and C. H. Dodd, *According to the Scriptures* (London: Nisbet, 1952), pp. 88-96.

[44] We follow the general approach of Yoder, pp. 30-34; for an adequate understanding of the temptation stories it is not necessary to suppose that Satan spoke audibly or appeared visibly. Jesus may simply have felt definite suggestions forming in his mind, yet recognized that they originated from a source beyond him.

Exorcisms occur frequently throughout the Synoptics. Often they are mentioned along with preaching, teaching, and healing as signs that God's kingdom truly is at hand.[45] At the end, however, Satan incites Judas to betray Jesus (Luke 22:3, cf. John 13:2, 27). John regards Jesus' final days as his climactic struggle with "the ruler of this world" (John 12:31, 14:30, 16:11; cf. Luke 22:53).

But what meaning can theology find in this language about the demonic? Is it simply vivid imagery for powerful psychophysical forces which first-century people did not understand? This possibility is strengthened by the fact that exorcisms are often described much as are healings. Both are effected by an authoritative command. In his first account of each, Luke places "rebuking" a fever directly between two episodes of "rebuking" demons (Luke 4:35–41). Cures are sometimes described in terms appropriate to exorcism.[46] Like exorcisms, healings are often followed by injunctions to remain silent (Mark 1:44 and par, 5:43 and par). Perhaps, then, theology should translate synoptic language about the demonic into psychosomatic terminology.

B. Religious Opposition to Jesus

Descriptions of the demonic, however, are also similar to descriptions of Christ's conflicts with human opponents. These opponents usually initiate debate with a sharp, accusing question. Jesus usually responds with a brief, definitive reply. He seldom undertakes sustained argument. Most often, Jesus legitimates his actions and his claims by reference to the newness and uniqueness of the situation which he is bringing about. For instance, when asked why his disciples do not fast, Jesus simply asserts: (1) the Bridegroom is here; (2) new wine cannot be contained in old wineskins [Mark 2:18-22 and par]. Much of Christ's "teaching" is of this sort.[47]

On the whole, Jesus' teaching and his actions are more closely intertwined than one might first think. Not only are teaching, healing, and exorcisms of-

[45] In addition to the texts cited above, see Mark 1:39 = Matt. 4:23-24; Mark 3:14-15 = Matt. 10:1; Mark 6:7, 12-13; Luke 7:19-23, 8:1-2, 9:1-2, cf. 17-19.

[46] Mark 7:34-35, Luke 13:10-16. Notice also the use of the word "scourge (mastix)" in Mark 3:10; 5:29, 34 (James Kallas, The Significance of the Synoptic Miracles [London: S.P.C.K., 1961], p. 79); also the term "cast out" in the healing of Mark 1:43 (Ernest Best, The Temptation and the Passion [Cambridge: University, 1965], p. 34; James Robinson, The Problem of History in Mark? [London: SCM, 1957], p. 40.) For much of what we say on Jesus' healings and debates, see Robinson, pp. 33-42.

[47] Cf. Robinson, pp. 43-53. Other such debates are found in Mark 2:6- 11, 16-17, 24-28; 12:18-27. Similar are those occasions where Jesus answers first with a counter-question and then with the definitive reply (Mark 10:2-9, 11:27-33, 12:13-17). Jesus also answers those who are not opponents in a similar way (Mark 3:31-35; 6:2-3; 7:17-23; 9:38-40; 10:13-16, 17-22; 13:1-2; 14:3-9); however, some passages listed by Robinson do not fit his categories well: Mark 3:2-5; 7:5-15; 8:11-12, 27-30, 31-33; 10:35-41.

ten mentioned together in summaries of Jesus' kingdom ministry. Jesus' exorcising power also can be called "teaching" (Mark 1:21–27, cf. Luke 4:31–36),
as can his expelling money-changers from the temple (Mark 11:15–18). Both
Jesus' wisdom and his mighty works produce a unified impression (Mark 6:2–5
and par). Preaching about Jesus (Mark 1:45, 7:36) or the word about him (Luke
5:15), can report his healing work. Jesus heals both through words and through
actions, such as touch. In short,

> the authority of Jesus' teaching resides not in its force of logic or the originality
> and profundity of its contents, but rather in a power inherent in him as Son of God
> and bearer of the Spirit, a power which is revealed by the efficacy of his word.
> When he speaks, God acts; in casting out a demon, in healing a paralytic, in forgiv-
> ing sin, in addressing his people at worship.[48]

In the Gospels, then, demonic resistance to God's kingdom is intertwined
not only with that presented by illness but also with that raised by Jesus' religious opponents. Much as Satan challenged Jesus to validate his mission by
jumping down from the temple, so the Pharisees tempt Jesus, asking for a sign
from heaven (Mark 8:11–12 and par; John 2:18, 6:30). This conflict with Israel's religious leaders comes to a head when they insist that his power to cast out
demons comes from the Prince of Demons (Matt. 12:22–32 and par). Jesus' reply shows that his exorcisms are not mere isolated psychosomatic healings.
They are evidence that a major battle has been won: The Devil has already
been bound; through the power of the Spirit, "the Kingdom of God has come
upon you!" He then warns his opponents that those who blaspheme God's
Spirit can never be forgiven.[49]

Through the centuries, Christians have understood "blaspheming the
Spirit" in various ways. In this context, however, its meaning is plain. It is to
suppose that the reality and power of God's kingdom are those of the Devil.
Those who do this, however, place themselves in total opposition to God's
kingdom. According to this text, then, Jesus' religious opponents have become
direct agents of Satan and his kingdom in its conflict with the kingdom of
God. (Of course they have not actually become the Devil. Perhaps Christ's
strong words imply a warning, alerting them to the alliance they have made).

Increasing demonic opposition to Jesus, however, does not only press upon

---

[48] Robinson, p. 50.

[49] According to John, Jesus' religious opponents also accuse him of being demoni-
cally empowered (John 7:19-20, 10:19-21) and he counters that they themselves are
under the devil's dominion (8:44-48). John's gospel can also be understood as a
continuing trial with his religious enemies. See esp. A. E. Harvey, *Jesus on Trial*
(Richmond: Knox, 1977).

Jesus and his followers from without.[50] It also operates by intensifying human weakness from within. As Jesus turns towards Jerusalem, he asks his followers who he is. When Peter replies that he is the Christ, Jesus immediately foretells his coming sufferings. Horrified, Peter insists that the Messiah could never undergo this. But Jesus shocks him with the rebuke: "Get behind me Satan! For you are not on the side of God, but of humans" (Mark 8:27–33 and par)!

Scholars agree that Peter rejected Jesus' predictions because he, and probably all Jesus' followers, expected the Messiah to be a victorious warrior.[51] They were ultimately motivated by the longing for one who would subdue their enemies by force, and place them in positions of safety, power, and prestige. Nothing prepared them for Jesus' announcement that Messiahship would involve suffering. But here Jesus vehemently denounces this conventional expectation and those who support it as "Satan."

Much as in the wilderness temptations, Jesus is defining his mission in contradiction to usual notions of how one wields kingly power. Much as in his showdown with the Pharisees, he forges astonishingly close links between those who misinterpret the fundamental thrust of his mission and Satan.

Jesus' disciples, however, utterly fail to understand how his messianic mission can be consistent with his humility and suffering (Mark 9:30–32, 10:32–34 and par). As they approach Jerusalem, they begin arguing as to who should have the most prestigous positions in the kingdom. Jesus identifies their desires with those of Gentile rulers, who relish and abuse such positions of power. He contrasts sharply with the servant-like behavior of his true followers, whose model is to be the one who "came not to be served, but to serve, and to give his life a ransom for many" (Mark 10:35–44). This saying echoes Isaiah 53,

---

[50] As opposition intensifies, Jesus' teachings warn that the way of the kingdom will involve persecution. Satan will snatch away many "seeds" of the kingdom (Mark 4:15 and par). The Evil One will continue to promote conflict until the Judgment, when "the righteous" will finally be separated from "the evil ones" (Matt. 13:25, 28, 49). The "Sermon on the Mount," the source of so much teaching on God's kingdom, envisions existence in conflict with evil. Jesus' followers must pray to be delivered from the "temptation" of the Evil One (Matt. 6:13). Those who live for Jesus will be called "evil" (Matt. 5:11, Luke 6:22), much as he was associated with the Prince of Demons. Yet one should respond to evil ones with straightforward speech, love, and intercessory prayer (Matt. 5:37, 39, 44). Here again we see that Jesus' teachings cannot be separated from the overall framework of conflict with the demonic.

[51] E.g., Oscar Cullmann, *Peter*, 2nd ed. (London: SCM, 1966) pp. 22-23. For similarities and differences between Jesus and the Zealots, see Cullmann, *Jesus and the Revolutionaries* (New York: Harper, 1970); Moltmann, *The Crucified God*, pp. 138-45.

once again indicating that the servant pattern is at the root of Jesus' approach to kingship.[52]

In these passages, a linkeage begins to appear between Satanic forces and the disciples' human weaknesses, which prove to be very like the attitudes and practices those political forces opposing Jesus and the way of his kingdom.

C. Political Opposition to Jesus

From a general, impartial historical standpoint, one would expect that any-one regarded as the Messiah in Jesus' day would have political aims. Even Bult-mann and Bornkamm describe the volatile political climate of his times.[53] Most Jews deeply resented Roman rule. Zealot campaigns, often led by one calling himself Messiah, frequently burst forth to dislodge it. Given this tense atmosphere, the Romans could hardly help regarding Jesus as another political threat. Despite this, many claim, like Bornkamm, that "Jesus' message has nothing in common with such religio-political movements."[54] Most such scholars notice (rightly) that Jesus' movement was quite different from any other political movement of his day. They then seem to assume that it could not have been political in any sense. However, we have argued that since Jesus sought to incorporate Jews and Gentile, rich and poor, men and women, into his kingdom, it would take a social form contrasting sharply with the political structures of his time. Along with its other surprising features, then, God's kingdom involved a novel conception and actualization of "political" exis-tence.[55] Its novelty was certain to conflict with the guardians of the old order.

While the Synoptics forge close links between Jesus' demonic and religious opposition, his political opposition hovers more covertly in the background. Nevertheless, its threatening shadow darkens his entire course. Matthew viv-idly recounts how Jesus' birth threatened Herod and how only repeated super-natural aid rescued the infant from his political foes (Matt. 2:1-3, 12, 14, 20, 22). Luke's prologue abounds in phrases which would hardly be understood apolitically: He will reign on David's throne "and of his kingdom there will be no end"; he will save us "from our enemies and from the hand of all who hate us" (Luke 1:31-32, 71, cf. 52, 74, etc.).

Later another Herod beheaded John the Baptist, who had rebuked him not

---

[52] Jeremias, TWNT V, esp. p. 710; The Eucharistic Words of Jesus (New York: Macmil-lan, 1955), pp. 118-35, 142-52; Eduard Lohse, Martyrer und Gottesknecht (Göttingen: Vandenhoeck & Rupprecht, 1965), pp. 118-21.

[53] Bultmann, pp. 16-26; Bornkamm, pp. 27-52. Bultmann concludes that "there can be no doubt that Jesus like other agitators died on the cross as a Messianic prophet" (p. 26; cf. pp. 28, 124).

[54] P. 44; cf. pp. 45-46, 66, 153-54, 164.

[55] Cf. Yoder, pp. 111-13 (cf. p. 50, note 36, p. 63).

in any purely religious way but "for all the evil things that Herod had done"[56] (Luke 3:19). When Jesus heard of John's death, he wisely retreated from public view (Matt. 14:13). Yet when Herod learned of Jesus, he was sufficiently struck by the similarity between the two, to conjecture that Jesus was John raised from the dead (Mark 5:14, Matt. 14:2). So Herod desired to cross-examine him (Luke 9:7).

Given the increasingly tense situation that builds as Jesus nears Jerusalem, he would surely have disclaimed all political intentions, were this his aim. Yet he deliberately adopts the messianic symbolism of entering Jerusalem on a donkey. Jesus accepts acclamation as Israel's king (Mark 11:1–10 and par), explicitly rebuffing suggestions of its inappropriateness (Matt. 21:15–16 and par), and prompting Israel's leaders to fear that "the Romans will come and destroy both our holy place and our nation" (John 11:48).

Closer examination shows that this political opposition was interlinked with Jesus' religious and demonic opposition. Mark records that Jesus' religious opponents allied themselves with Herod from early on (Mark 3:16, 8:15, 12:13; cf. Matt. 22:16). Luke corroborates this by recounting how Herod's Pharisaic allies threatened Jesus. Yet Jesus, undaunted, scorned Herod, as did the Zealots, as "that fox" (Luke 13:31–33). During Jesus' last few days the demonic again explicitly entered the scene. Satan took over Judas. How? By directing him to Israel's religious authorities (Luke 22:2–3, John 13:2, 27). In the garden of Gethsemane Jesus urged his disciples to pray "that you may not enter into temptation" (Mark 14:38 and par). What specific trial awaited them? The approach of the temple guards, before whom they all fled (Mark 14:47 and par). Fear of them could provoke armed resistance, which some initially attempted, or flight, to which they all eventually succumbed. Jesus called this the hour of the triumph of his opponents and the hour of "the power of darkness" (Luke 22:53).

In Gethsemane Jesus also wrestled mightily again with temptation. He begged his Father that his cup of suffering might pass (Mark 14:35–36 and par). But how might Christ have avoided the fate to which his way of exercising kingship was bringing him? Very possibly, by beginning to wage, even now, the Messianic war against the Romans.[57] Even now his Father could send 72,000 angel warriors (Matt. 26:53)! The demonic temptation to exercise his kingship in the expected political way, initiated in the wilderness and renewed at Peter's confession, rushed in as the urgent choice between life and death. Yet Jesus held firm: "Put your sword back into its place," he admonished a disciple, "for all who take the sword will perish by the sword" (Matt. 26:52).

---

[56] Luke 3:19. Herod's marriage to his brother's wife, for which John especially rebuked him, was a political as well as a personal ethical matter (Yoder). Later Jesus contrasted John with those "clothed in soft raiment...who are gorgeously appareled and live in luxury." (Luke 7:25, cf. Matt. 11:18; cf. Mark 1:6 = Matt. 3:4).

[57] Yoder, pp. 53-57; Cullmann, pp. 39-50.

The Gospels identify Jesus' religious opponents as the chief advocates of his death. Nevertheless crucifixion was a distinctly Roman punishment, designed by its barbarity and its public character to terrorize all who dared think of opposing the Empire.[58] Pilate's capitulation to Sanhedrin pressure despite his better judgment and Sanhedrin collusion with a power they normally despised to preserve their social position (John 19:15, etc.) formed an invincible linkage of religious and political power. And through their combined voices Jesus must have once again heard the Tempter who confronted him in the wilderness: "If you are the king of the Jews, save yourself!" the Roman soldiers shouted (Luke 23:37). "So also the chief priests, with the scribes and the elders, mocked him saying...'He is the King of Israel; let him come down now from the cross, and we will believe in him!' " (Matt. 27:41-42).

D. Conclusions

As Jon Sobrino insisted, "God's action does not simply affirm the positive aspect of human existence." Especially in the coming of Jesus' kingdom, "God's action can only be envisioned as the overcoming of a negative situation...through a liberaton" (p. 248). What was that negative force which opposed Jesus' kingdom? By tracing the interlinkings among its demonic, religious, and political dimensions, we have sought to show that the first can neither be dismissed as "mythology" nor reduced to the psychosomatic. Throughout Jesus' ministry, Satanic opposition operated not only through distinctively demonic activity but also through religious and political forces.

This does not mean that religious or political activity can be wholly reduced to the demonic. Each area possesses its relatively distinct character. Nevertheless we have seen how demonic forces, by playing on the deepest roots of human fear and human longing for security and power, managed to utilize religious and political forces for their own ends. God's kingdom, with its religious and social dimensions, clearly opposed the religious and social systems of Jesus' day. Yet at its deepest levels, its struggle was with the kingdom of Satan.

IV. Dimensions of God's Kingdom

So far we have been mainly concerned to show how God's kingdom is a social reality. Yet we have just seen that its significance extends beyond what we normally think of as social, into religious, or spiritual, dimensions. We shall better apprehend the kingdom's full significance by considering its impact on two additional realms: the outer world of nature and the inner world of the human heart.

A. The Physical Dimension

Many modern people find it easiest to understand the gospel miracle stories, like its tales of the demonic, in a "demythologized" sense. Accounts of Jesus'

---

[58] Martin Hengel, *Crucifixion* (Philadelphia: Fortress, 1977), pp. 22-63).

signs and wonders, which seem hard to believe if understood as descriptive statements, might still carry meaning if regarded as ancient, picturesque ways of
depicting the impact he made. Miracle stories seem designed to heighten, in a
naive way, the awe and wonder of this impression.

We remember, however, how Jesus began his ministry by rejecting Satan's
suggestions that he seek to impress people by such means. When crowds flock
after him because of his miracles, Jesus moves on (Mark 1:36-38, John 6:14–
15). He urges those whom he heals to refrain from sensational publicity. Yet
many are unable to resist, and soon the spectacular gossip hinders his free
movement (Mark 1:44–45). Although the Gospels report Jesus performing numerous miracles, they also record his deep concern lest, precisely by being understood as marvelous displays of power, they detract from the deeper
significance of his mission.[59] Whatever the meaning of the gospel miracles may
be, then, they cannot be spectacular devices to heighten the impression which
Jesus wished to make.

Their significance emerges when we reconsider (cf. Chap. 14) Israel's situation during the centuries before Christ. As tiny Judah increasingly succumbed
to foreign domination, and as the righteous continued to suffer without redress, Israel's eschatological hope had become increasingly cosmic in scope.
Liberation of Judah seemed impossible lest earth, heaven, and the evil powers
be shaken. Yahweh's justice would be mocked unless the suffering righteous
would rise, bodily, from the dead.

Today we also must ask whether God could fully reign unless the natural order be affected. Despite the control over nature which modern technology has
gained, millions still suffer from natural disasters like hurricanes, earthquakes,
droughts. Despite the progress of medical science, many diseases are still
largely beyond our control. Could God's justice be fully present in a world
where such things would still sweep countless people away in infancy or youth?
Or (as we argued in Chap. 9) is it more likely that the eschaton will affect all
dimensions of the cosmos?

Jesus' miracles help answer these questions. They indicate that God's kingdom is affecting not only all of society but all dimensions of the cosmos. They
proclaim that the God who is beginning to reign is also the Creator—not only
of humanity's existential and social life but of its physical life and environment
as well. Of course the miracles' specific character tells us even more. Jesus'

---

[59] This is the theme of the "messianic secret" emphasized by Mark. Jesus enjoins
silence after performing miracles (Mark 1:45, 5:43, 7:36, and 8:26); after exorcisms
(Mark 1:25, 34; 3:12); after revelations to his passion (Mark 8:30, 9:9); and with-
draws secretly from the crowds (Mark 7:24, 9:30). Whereas the originator of the
"messianic secret" thesis, Wilhelm Wrede (1901), regarded this theme as the construction of the early Church, many others have found it intrinsic to the essence of
Jesus' ministry, and therefore historical (e.g., Cranfield, pp. 66-67, 78-79, 83-84, 157-
58). In Chap. 17, Sec. III, we shall argue that this "secrecy" was related to the
servant manner of Jesus' ministry, and also to his "deception" of Satan.

feedings underline God's concern for the hungry. His healings indicate the holistic nature of the salvation he brings. Yet they all point to a power which governs all spheres of reality.

B. The Personal Dimension

At the beginning of this chapter we noticed that Protestants have traditionally thought that Jesus came primarily to deal with the inner, existential problem of sin. Israel's repeated failure to actualize God's kingdom had shown that the real barriers to it lay in the human heart (e.g., Jer. 17:9-10, 31:31-34). Consequently Jesus' radical social and ethical commands should be interpreted not as actual prescriptions for behavior, but as means of confronting us with God's awesome holiness and thus with our own need for repentance and inward salvation. Because many people regard this position as the "biblical" one, and suppose that only "liberals" who allegedly disregard Scripture speak of Jesus' social message, we have spent many pages examining what the Gospels really teach.

Does our emphasis on the social character of Jesus' ministry mean that he bypassed the inner realm of the heart? Not at all. Against the external legalism of his religious opponents, Jesus emphasized that real evil comes "from within, out of the heart" (Mark 7:20-23). Jesus insisted that murder is rooted in hatred, adultery in lust, and was concerned above all with the roots of these things (Matt. 5:21-30). Humanity's deep sinfulness, however, is nowhere revealed more vividly than in the overall course of Jesus' ministry. When God's kingdom definitively arrives, not only do Israel's leaders hand him over to death, not only do the world's political powers do away with him, not only do the crowds desert him, but his closest followers continually misunderstand him and his mission, and they too forsake him at the end. As Karl Barth stressed, the sinfulness of the human heart could not be more graphically portrayed than in humanity's rejection of Christ.

In dealing with Jesus' life, theology's question cannot be whether he came to deal with sin. Obviously he did. The question, rather, is: what kind of sin did Jesus come to deal with? The centrality of the kingdom and its social character show that sin is not only personal rejection of God but also of the way of life which God commands. Therefore sin is also against one's fellow human beings. It shows that sin consists not only in the inner rebellion of the heart but also in the outward allegiance to social and religious powers. Sin is not only turning away from God, but turning towards other relationships, values, and actions.

The disciples' responses to Jesus will help illuminate some features of this sinful turning. Although they opposed the religious power of Israel's leaders and the political power of the Romans, they hoped that Jesus would conquer these by utilizing power of the same essential sort. Like their opponents these disciples were ultimately motivated by the same drive for power, security, and status. The notion of a Messiah who would conquer through suffering, through exposure to insecurity, and through humility, was as incomprehensible to them as it was to their enemies. At bottom, it was through these deep-seated longings of their hearts, and through their deep-seated fear of suffering, insecurity, and humility, that Jesus' disciples (like his religious and political opponents) became vehicles for the activity of Satan.

This longing for power, security, and status deeply pervaded those dominant classes whose position Jesus came to reverse. Many of the religious leaders who opposed him also regarded themselves as "righteous" Israelites, better than the masses of Jews and than Gentiles. The religious institutions and observances which they upheld gave them positions of security, status, and power in Israelite society. Wealth also conferred many of the same privileges, and males tended to hang on to their superior position over women for many of the same reasons. In contrast, Jesus' concern for Gentiles, the poor, and women—for those exposed to suffering, insecurity, and humiliation—corresponded to the servant-like attitude which guided his ministry.

Although we cannot fully describe the nature of sin until we examine the Old Testament and the rest of the New (Vol. II, Chap. 6), the Gospels show us that these inner desires and fears block the coming of God's kingdom and provide the means for Satan to extend his. God's kingdom cannot come unless it transforms these deep-seated sins of the heart.

These considerations raise one final question. Since the kingdom comes as especially good news for Gentiles, the poor, and women, are individuals in these groups exempt from God's judgment against sin? Does sin characterize only the dominant groups? Is sin so closely identified with social behavior that the kingdom's coming is primarily a reversal of social classes, as some liberation theologies apparently suggest?

No. For in the end, people of all classes forsook Jesus. The same fear of suffering, insecurity, and humiliation motivated them all. Furthermore, Jesus' call to the kingdom involves a call to repentance. As the good news of God's grace, this call is issued to everyone in every class. However, to those whose sense of personal worth and religious well-being was tied up with being wealthy, being Israelite, or being male, such a message sounds like extremely bad news. For it means surrendering that which gives them their sense of identity and security (through being better than others) and it means sharing life on an equal basis with those on whom they had looked down. On the other hand, for those who have been at the bottom of the heap and have much less to lose, a kingdom where they are welcomed despite their poverty, race, or sex sounds like much better news. This, then, is the sense in which the poor and other classes are especially favored by God: not that belonging to these groups is of itself good; not that they have no need to repent; but that their circumstances tend to make them more open to the radical transformations of the dawning kingdom.

Suggestions for Further Reading

Brandon, S.F.G. *Jesus and the Zealots.* Manchester: University, 1967.

Cullmann, Oscar. *Jesus and the Revolutionaries.* New York: Harper, 1970.

Edwards, George. *Jesus and the Politics of Violence.* New York: Harper, 1972.

Evans, Mary. *Woman in the Bible.* Greenwood, S.C.: Attic, 1983.

Gager, John. *Kingdom and Community: The Social World of Early Christianity.* Englewood Cliffs, N.J.: Prentice-Hall, 1975.

Hengel, Martin. *Christ and Power.* Philadelphia: Fortress, 1977.

———. *Property and Riches in the Early Church.* Philadelphia: Fortress, 1974.

———. *Victory over Violence: Jesus and the Revolutionists.* Philadelphia: Fortress, 1973.

Kähler, Martin. *The So-Called Historical Jesus and the Historic Biblical Christ.* Philadelphia: Fortress, 1964 (originally published in 1896).

Marshall, I. Howard. *I Believe in the Historical Jesus.* Grand Rapids: Eerdmans, 1977.

Mollenhott, Virginia. *Women, Men and the Bible.* Nashville: Abingdon: 1977.

Robinson, James. *A New Quest of the Historical Jesus.* Naperville, Ill.: Allenson, 1959.

———. *The Problem of History in Mark.* London: SCM, 1957.

Schleiermacher, Friedrich. *The Life of Jesus.* Philadelphia: Fortress, 1975 (originally published in 1832).

Schüssler Fiorenza, Elizabeth. *In Memory of Her: A Feminist Reconstruction of Christian Origins.* New York: Crossroads, 1983.

Sloan, Robert. *The Favorable Year of the Lord: A Study of Jubilary Theology in the Gospel of Luke.* Austin, Tx.: Scholars, 1977.

Swidler, Leonard. *Biblical Affirmations of Women.* Philadelphia: Westminster, 1979.

Trocmé, Andre. *Jesus and the Nonviolent Revolution.* Scottdale, Pa.: Herald, 1973.

Theissen, Gerd. *Sociology of Early Palestinian Christianity.* Philadelphia: Fortress, 1978.

Yoder, John. *The Politics of Jesus.* Grand Rapids: Eerdmans, 1972.

CHAPTER SIXTEEN

Perspectives on the Death of Jesus Christ

The life of Jesus Christ cannot be separated from his death. Jesus did not die from accident, illness, or old age. He died because of the way he lived. Because Jesus, guided by the Spirit, lived in uncompromising fidelity to God his Father and to his kingdom and because the dawning of that kingdom aroused fierce opposition from the beginning, Jesus' ministry was characterized by conflict throughout. It was this escalating opposition—religious, political, and, at bottom, demonic—which eventually put him to death. Systematic theology, therefore cannot separate the reasons why Jesus died from the reasons why he lived, or the meaning of his death from the meaning of his life.

Throughout its history, however, theology has generally focused much more attention on Christ's death than on any other phase of his "Work." Symptomatic of this focus is the way the term "atonement" (which technically means at-one-ment, and can thus refer to all phases of Christ's activity) is usually used to refer chiefly to his death. Discussion of the atonement has often been detailed and not infrequently heated. It has illuminated, or at least highly influenced, the way in which everyone reads the basic biblical texts on this subject.

For this reason, in developing our own synthetic understanding of the work of Jesus Christ, we must again allow the lenses of theological tradition to help focus our gaze. In this Chapter three major historical models will aid us. Each will be related to one of the major approaches to Christology outlined in Chapter 14. As we consider each we will find ourselves not concentrating narrowly on a particular approach to the cross but moving progressively towards linking Jesus' life and death together.

I. The Substitutionary (Objective) Model

According to kerygmatic Christologies, humanity is in a desperate situation from which Christ alone can rescue it. Kerygmatic Christologies are designed above all to answer the urgent question, "What must I do to be saved?" (Chap. 14 above). Especially for early Reformed theology and Protestant orthodoxy, humanity's situation was desperate because each person was considered a sinner and thus under the penalty of God's wrath. Unless this wrath could be turned aside, each individual would spend eternity in hell.

The substitutionary theory of Christ's work, which seeks to explain how he turned God's wrath aside, is often called "objective" because it seeks to explain condemnation and redemption as actual relationships between God and humankind as a whole, which exist whether or not any individual acknowledges such relationships. Christ's saving work was primarily directed towards altering this relationship, not people's "subjective" feelings or character. Christ first of all transformed the objective cosmic situation; as a result of this, humans can be subjectively changed.

A. The Model in History

Substitutionary interpretations of Christ's work can be found since the Fathers. During the Church's first millennium, however, the so-called "Christus Victor" motif probably provided the dominant way of articulating Christ's work.[1] This approach depicted Jesus as conquering the Devil and other dark powers. So crude and fantastic was the imagery in which it was sometimes expressed that, according to many historical theologians, no consistently formulated theological model of the atonement existed until nearly A.D. 1200.[2]

1. *Anselm of Canterbury.* During the eleventh century, western Christians with some education were becoming less content to believe things simply because traditional authority had taught them and were searching for reasons for their faith. In response, Anselm (1033–1109) often insisted that faith must come first; reason's proper function lies in exploring the significance of what one already believes. Anselm beautifully confessed that

> I do not endeavor, O Lord, to penetrate thy sublimity, for in no wise do I compare my understanding with that; but I long to understand in some degree thy truth, which my heart believes and loves. For I do not seek to understand that I may be-

---

[1] For the first 400 years, see J. N. D. Kelly, *Early Christian Doctrines*, rev. ed. (San Francisco: Harper, 1960), pp. 163-88, 375-400.

[2] E.g., Albrecht Ritschl, *A Critical History of the Christian Doctrine of Justification and Reconciliation* (Edinburgh: Edmonston and Douglas, 1872), pp. 19-34.

lieve, but I believe in order to understand. For this I also believe—that unless I believed, I should not understand.[3]

Anselm's approach of "faith seeking understanding" is often contrasted with that of Thomas Aquinas, who allegedly sought first to understand in order that he might believe. But whatever Anselm's personal route from faith to reason may have been, when he introduced the two books that make up his famous contribution to Christology, *Cur Deus Homo?* (Why did God Become Human?), he explained that

> The first...leaving Christ out of view (as if nothing had ever been known of him)...proves, by absolute reasons, the impossibility that any man should be saved without him. Again, in the second book, likewise, as if nothing were known of Christ, it is moreover shown by plain reasoning and fact that...all things were to take place which we hold in regard to Christ.[4]

At the end of these efforts, Anselm's discussion partner, Boso, concludes that he now sees

> the truth of all that is contained in the Old and New Testament. For, in proving that God became man by necessity, leaving out what was taken from the Bible...you convince both Jews and Pagans by the mere force of reason...so no one can dissent from anything contained in these books (pp. 287-88).

Now why did Anselm feel that Christology's central affirmations needed independent support from reason? What features of the biblical account of Christ seemed unconvincing to rational people of his day? Primarily it was the claim "that God, who is omnipotent, should have assumed the littleness and weakness of human nature" (p. 180); that the eternal, unchanging Deity could have become a baby, and later endured "fatigue, hunger, thirst, stripes and crucifixion among thieves" (p. 182). Rational people also found difficulty with the "Christus Victor" motif: the popular view that God entered into a mighty struggle with Satan and won only at the cost of his life. For if God must struggle so, is not God pretty weak? Or, if God did not have to but did so anyway, is

[3] *Proslogion* in *St. Anselm: Basic Writings* (La Salle, Il.: Open Court, 1962), p. 7.

[4] Anselm, *Cur Deus Homo?* in *Basic Writings*, pp. 177-178. (The following page numbers in our text are to this work.) In developing his famous "ontological argument" in the *Proslogion*, Anselm reported that he had been looking for "a single argument which would require no other for its proof than itself alone; and alone would suffice to demonstrate that God truly exists...and whatever else we believe regarding the divine Being" (Ibid., p. 1). Similarly he wrote his *Monologion* "in order that nothing in Scripture should be urged on the authority of Scripture itself, but that whatever the conclusion of independent investigation should declare to be true, should...be briefly enforced by the cogency of reason" (Ibid., p. 35). Karl Barth, however, argued that Anselm began theologizing from faith, not reason, and sought to develop his own methodology along similar lines (*Anselm: Fides Quarens Intellectum* [Cleveland: World, 1962]).

not God stupid (p. 185)? Christian beliefs conflict so sharply with a rational understanding of God's power and wisdom that reasonable people will not accept the biblical story of Christ's work "unless it be proved that He could not otherwise have saved man" (p. 186); that is, unless "the death of the Son can be proved reasonable and necessary" (p. 200).

Anselm seeks to demonstrate the rational necessity of Christ's suffering by defining sin in a manner which is apparently clear apart from biblical teachings. Sin, briefly, is "not to render God his due" (p. 200). And what, more precisely, is his due? That "every wish of a rational creature should be subject to the will of God." Anything less "robs God of His honor" (p. 202).

When we consider that God is the supreme governor of the universe, the seriousness of sin becomes apparent. For it "is not fitting for God to pass over anything in His Kingdom undischarged" (p. 203). For this reason, all "justice to man is regulated by law."[5] And this means, despite Boso's protest, that God cannot simply "put away sins by compassion alone, without any payment of the honor taken away from him" (p. 203). Given this rational understanding of God's justice, Anselm asks Boso: What if someone should say to you, " 'Look thither!' and God on the other hand, should say 'It is not my will that you should look.'?" Suppose that "it were necessary either that the whole universe...should perish...or else that you should do so small a thing against the will of God?" Boso protests, but finally concedes: "I ought not to oppose the will of God even to preserve the whole creation" (p. 229).

Gradually Anselm pushes Boso into a corner. Because it is so important that the Law-giver's honor be maintained, those who rob God of it must either pay back what they owe or else be punished. But all have sinned. Everyone owes God a debt. And whatever anyone might give to God—"Repentance, a broken and contrite heart, self-denial, various bodily sufferings, pity in giving and forgiving, and obedience"—they owe to God anyway. So there is no way for anyone to pay the debt. Boso admits that Anselm's arguments "would drive me to despair, were it not for the consolation of faith" (p. 230). On this note, Book I of *Cur Deus Homo?* ends. In Book II Anselm begins working out of this jam. From an apparently rational consideration of divine and human nature, he defines the goal of human existence: to freely love and choose God, the supreme Good, and to enjoy eternal communion with him (p. 240). Further, since God has planned that some human creatures should attain this, "it is necessary for

---

[5] Ibid., p. 204. Moreover, the "supreme justice, which maintains God's honor in the arrangement of things...is nothing else but God himself" (p. 206). In saying that sin violates God's honor, Anselm does not primarily mean that God is personally offended. In Anselm's day, "honor" was "something objective, social in its nature, and the guarantee of social stability." (R. W. Southern, *Saint Anselm and His Biographers* [Cambridge, England: University, 1963], p. 98.) It consisted largely in the social obligations which a person lower on the feudal heirarchy owed to one higher up. To dishonor someone was to fail to meet these obligations, and often, in consequence, to lose one's property, position and livelihood.

him to perfect in human nature what he has begun" (p. 242); otherwise, it would "seem that God...was unable to accomplish his design" (p. 238).

Accordingly when Adam and Eve were placed on earth, they were given the task of overcoming all temptations, including Satan's, and growing toward this perfection. But of course they failed, as has the entire race ever since. And our collective sin against God's honor is so great that humanity's goal cannot be attained "except the price paid to God for the sin of man be something greater than all the universe besides God" (p. 244).

The situation is this: On one hand, humanity must overcome Satan and maintain complete obedience towards God. But fallen humanity cannot do this. On the other hand, full satisfaction must be made for our sin. But we cannot do this either. With these premises in place, Anselm is ready to deduce the master stroke of *Cur Deus Homo?* Since humans cannot pay the price for sin, "none but God can make this satisfaction." But since humanity was originally given the task of obeying God and overcoming Satan, "none but a man ought to do this" (p. 245). Consequently none but a God-man can carry out this task.

Now since it is necessary that this task be completed (otherwise God's purposes would fail), Anselm feels he has answered the challenge of the intellectuals of his day. He has shown, "leaving out what was taken from the Bible...[and only] by the mere force of reason," why it was necessary for God to become incarnate, to struggle and suffer. And he has shown why the God-man struggled with Satan: not because God had to do so, but because as human he had to fulfill the task assigned to our race.

Nevertheless Anselm carefully insists that, although his divine nature conferred infinite value on his work, Christ's actual growth, struggle, and death were, strictly speaking, carried on in his human nature alone. For instance Christ did not really increase in wisdom but "deported himself as if it were so" (p. 195). In general Anselm reassured his readers, "When we speak of God enduring any humiliation or infirmity, we do not refer to the majesty of that nature, which cannot suffer; but to the feebleness of the human constitution which he assumed" (p. 190).

So conceived Christ's work was "substitutionary" in two main senses. First, his death paid the penalty for our sin. Second, the obedience exercised throughout his life earned the reward of eternal life. However, since the Son, who already has everything, needs no such reward, he bestowed it on those for whom he died (pp. 283–86). Jesus, in other words, both paid the penalty of eternal death and merited the reward of eternal life "in our place"—in a substitutionary way.

2. *Observations.* Notice that this model need make no reference to the specific features of Christ's life. In passing, Anselm does acknowledge that Jesus' sufferings set an example: that we "should never turn aside from the holiness due to God on account of personal sacrifice" (280). Nevertheless we hear almost nothing about Jesus' approach to Gentiles, the poor, women, to the demonic—about all the concrete emphases of his kingdom ministry. To be sure, the substitutionary theory insists that Jesus' life was one of complete obedience

to God. Yet where Jesus lived (in Judah), when he lived (during the Roman empire), and specifically how he lived are irrelevant to the theory. This tendency continued in the slight emphasis given Christ's kingly and prophetic offices in early Reformed and Protestant orthodox Christology.

Second, Christ's resurrection has little importance for this model. When Jesus has merited heaven for us by his life and saved us from hell by his death, his work is completed. Of course substitutionary theorists believe that Jesus rose from the dead. But this has little direct relevance to his work. As is true of kerygmatic Christologies in general, the substitutionary model focuses mostly on Jesus' death.

Third, this model fits in smoothly (although not necessarily) with a socio-political conservatism. Overwhelming stress falls on God's character as universal law giver. Nothing is worse that the slightest transgression of his commands. Proponents of substitution have often assumed that society ought ideally to be governed by fixed, divinely sanctioned and rigidly enforced laws.[6]

Fourth, we underline again the rational character of this theory. If one accepts its foundational definitions of God's justice, God's purpose, and of human sin, the rest follows deductively with compelling, obvious clarity. No doubt the popularity of this model over many centuries owes something to its simple, clear-cut character. However if the Bible be the norm and primary source of our theology, we must ask to what extent and where we can find

B. The Model in Scripture

When they turn to the Old Testament, proponents of substitution emphasize the sacrifices. Ritual animal sacrifices begin with the offerer laying hands on the victim's head. This act is thought to signify that the animal is "dying in the worshipper's place as his substitute."[7] Sacrificial blood is thought to function primarily as evidence that this penalty has been paid.[8] Such a sacrifice is called an expiation, the offering of something which compensates for the injury done to the divine human relationship and thereby restores it. Read in light of this theory, the Old Testament witnesses primarily to God's holiness, to Israel's repeated sinfulness, and to the divine wrath which this frequently calls forth. The Old Testament increasingly portrays a widening gulf between God and humanity which will have to be bridged in some definitive, objective way.

The gospels seldom present Christ's work in an explicitly substitutionary way. Yet two texts seem to do so. In Mark 10:45 (Matt. 20:28, cf. 1 Tim. 2:6), Jesus says that he gives his life "a ransom for many." The word for ransom, *lu-*

---

[6] On Anselm's own conservative approach to social issues, particularly while he was Archbishop of Canterbury, see Southern, pp. 122-93.

[7] Gordon Wenham, *Leviticus* (Grand Rapids: Eerdmans, 1979), p. 62.

[8] Leon Morris, *The Apostolic Preaching of the Cross*, 3rd ed. (Grand Rapids: Eerdmans, 1965), pp. 112-28.

tron, can mean payment or price. Second, at the last supper Christ speaks of his blood as "poured out for many" (Mark 14:24 and par). This use of "for" (in Greek: *peri* or, more often, *huper*) seems to be the same as that found elsewhere in the New Testament to speak of substitutionary sacrifices.

The epistle to the Hebrews speaks of sacrifices "for sins" as a technical term for the Old Testament "sin offering" (Heb. 10:6, 8; 13:11) and frequently uses the Greek prepositions meaning "for" in this general sense.[9] John explicitly calls Jesus an expiation, "for our sins" (1 John 2:2, 4:10).[10] Paul often makes brief references to Christ's death "for" us, assuming that the meaning of this phrase is already familiar to his readers (1 Thess. 5:10, 1 Cor. 8:11, Rom. 14:15). In one place Paul explains its significance in some detail: "For us," God made Christ "to be sin who knew no sin, so that in him we might become the righteousness of God" (2 Cor. 5:21). Perhaps the phrase "to be sin" means that Jesus became "a sin offering." In any case it seems that Christ has become identified with our sin, and his righteousness has become ours in a direct, substitutionary way.

Seeing how widespread and apparently familiar was this notion, it is not surprising that it appears in the earliest kerygma. Paul summarized the gospel which antedated even him as follows:

> that Christ died for our sins in accordance with the scriptures, that he was buried, that he was raised on the third day in accordance with the scriptures, and that he appeared to Cephas and then to the twelve (1 Cor. 15:3–5).

Substitutionary advocates often make much of another explicitly sacrificial term. The word *hilasmos* means an expiatory sacrifice.[11] We have seen that John applies it to Jesus twice (1 John 2:2, 4:10). Hebrews uses the related verb in a central passage on Christ's work: "Therefore (Christ) had to be made like his brethren in every respect, so that he might become a merciful and faithful high priest in the service of God, to make expiation (or propitiation) for the sins of

[9] See *peri* in Heb. 5:3; 10:18, 26; cf. *huper* in 5:1, 7:27, 10:12. When Paul says that God sent his son "for sin" (*peri hamartias*: Rom. 8:3), he may mean that Jesus was sent "as a sin-offering."

[10] The word is *hilasmos*, which we shall shortly consider in more detail. John often speaks of Jesus "laying down his life for...," which may have much the same meaning (John 10:11, 15; 15:12–13, 37-38; 1 John 3:16, 4:9–11). (Cf. note 32 below.)

[11] Some substitutionary theorists argue that *hilasmos* is better translated "propitiation." Whereas "expiation" is a more general term, and can indicate a wide range of offerings which restore a broken relationship, a "propitiation" is offered for the distinct purpose of quelling the wrath of the offended god (see Morris' extended discussion, pp. 144-78). C. H. Dodd argued that this notion is sub-Christian (*The Bible and the Greeks* [London: Hodder & Stoughton, 1935], pp. 82-95). He was challenged at length by Roger Nicole ("C. H. Dodd and the Doctrine of Propitiation," *Westminster Theological Journal* 17 [1955], pp. 117-57.)

the people" (Heb. 2:17). Paul uses an almost synonymous noun in a very significant passage, usually translated as follows:

> Since all have sinned and fall short of the glory of God, they are justified by his
> grace as a gift, through the redemption which is in Christ Jesus, whom God put for-
> ward as an expiation by his blood, to be received by faith (Rom. 3:23–25).

The sacrificial and substitutionary meaning of this passage seems to be
heightened by its use of the term "blood." Hebrews frequently speaks of the
saving efficacy of Christ's work as a function of his sacrificially shed blood.[12]
Substitutionary theorists often find this meaning when blood is mentioned
elsewhere,[13] and when Christ is designated by other terms, such as "lamb," or
"passover," which often convey a sacrificial meaning.[14]

Finally advocates of the substitutionary model stress texts which speak of a
price, or of purchasing. We noticed that Jesus spoke of giving his own life as a
ransom (*lutron,* Mark 10:45). In the Romans 3:23–25 passage redemption (*apolutrosis*) comes from the same Greek stem; "blood" might be the redemption
"price."[15] "Redemption" could carry the same meaning elsewhere.[16] Revelation
5:9 praises the Lamb who "by thy blood did purchase for God" people from all
human groups (cf. Rev. 14:3-5, 2 Pet. 2:1). Paul twice briefly reminds the
Corinthians, of something with which they were quite familiar, that they
"were bought with a price" (1 Cor. 6:20, 7:23). He uses a related word to emphasize, in a manner that sounds quite substitutionary, that "Christ redeemed
us from the curse of the Law, having become a curse for us" (Gal. 3:13; cf. 4:5).

In summary, substitutionary advocates tend to emphasize texts (1) affirming
that Christ died "for us (you)" or "for our (your) sins"; (2) containing sacrifical
terminology like "expiation," "blood" and "lamb"; and (3) containing the terminology of purchasing or price. Some of these terms and passages, however,
may be open to interpretation in other ways. We shall see this as we examine
the next two perspectives on the death of Jesus Christ.

II. The Moral Influence (Subjective) Model

Contextual Christologies, like kerygmatic ones, seek to explain how Christ
bridged the gap between God and humanity. Yet the two approaches conceive
this gap in very different ways. For many kerygmatic Christologies, it is an unbridgeable, objective gulf constituted by God's wrath and the penalty which it

---

[12] Heb. 9:12, 10:19, 12:24, etc.

[13] Acts 20:28; Rom. 5:9; Eph. 1:7; 1 John 5:8; Rev. 1:5, 5:9; etc.

[14] John 1:29, 36; 1 Cor. 5:7; Heb. 11:28; 1 Pet. 1:18-19; Rev. 5:9; etc.

[15] So Charles Hodge, *Commentary on the Epistle to the Romans* (Philadelphia: Clax-
ton, 1864), p. 142.

[16] Esp. Eph. 1:7, Col. 1:14; Heb. 9:12, 15. For such an interpretation of almost all
redemption terminology in the Old and New Testaments, see Morris, pp. 11-64.

demands. For contextual Christologies, however, humans are more or less distant from God due to their relative lack of God-consciousness and moral development. Consequently contextual Christologies are designed to answer the urgent practical question, "How can I, and how can we all, become fully human?" (Chap. 14).

The moral influence theory of Christ's work is often called "subjective" because it focuses on the way in which Jesus enhances our religious and moral development. It is through this "subjective" transformation of human character that any "objective" estrangement from God is overcome.

A. The Model in History

Shortly after Anselm, Peter Abelard (1079–1142) argued that Christ's cross is not so much a propitiation of God's wrath as it is a demonstration of God's love. This model, however, seldom provided an influential explanation of Christ's death until the nineteenth century. We have seen that Friedrich Schleiermacher concentrated far more on Jesus' life than on his death. Nonetheless Schleiermacher argued that the impression which Christ's God-consciousness makes on us is heightened when we see that not even his sufferings, which climaxed on the cross, could diminish it. Futhermore "in His suffering unto death, occasioned by his steadfastness, there is manifested to us an absolutely self-denying love" which makes vivid to us "the way in which God was in Him to reconcile the world to Himself."[17] Similarly Albrecht Ritschl argued that the supreme test and evidence of Christ's commitment to God's kingdom consisted in his perseverance in this vocation unto death; thereby he also revealed a love which nothing could destroy.[18] However this approach to Christ's death, emphasizing his moral influence, was developed in greater detail in the United States.

1. *Horace Bushnell.* This American pastor (1802–1876) was searching for a position between the traditional Reformed orthodoxy and the newly rising Unitarianism of his own day. He sought to affirm classical doctrines, supporting them with copious biblical quotations, but to interpret them in a manner consistent with the latest scientific perspectives. Bushnell designated his own position with the term "vicarious sacrifice" (a common label for the substitutionary theory) yet interpreted it as an expression of a universal moral law, much as a liberal like Ritschl might do. The principle of vicarious suffering, Bushnell argued, is a characteristic of active love. For it is universally true that any

> good being is...ready, just according to his goodness, to act vicariously in behalf of any bad, or miserable being, whose condition he is able to restore....it is the nature of love, universally, to insert itself into the miseries, and take upon its feeling

---

[17] *The Christian Faith,* p. 458; cf. p. 436.

[18] *The Christian Doctrine of Justification and Reconciliation,* pp. 448-53.

the burden of others....Love is a principle essentially vicarious in its own nature, identifying the subject with others, and taking on itself the burden of their evils.[19]

How does this love operate? Like any moral power, it

> works only by inducement; that is, by impressions, or attractions that may be re-
> sisted....But where it wins consent, or faith, it is...transforming the subject all
> through, in the deepest secrets of impulse; creating, as it were, new possibilities of
> character, new springs of liberty in good....bearing the soul up out of its thralldom
> and weak self-endeavor, to be a man newborn, ranging in God's freedom, and con-
> sciously glorious sonship (p. 403–04).

Much as Schleiermacher said, Christ's work consists chiefly in those impressions of him which transform us in this way. For Bushnell, however, it is not so much Jesus' (human) God-consciousness which moves us as it is the vicarious love of God himself. Anselm had held that the divine nature itself cannot suffer. But Bushnell insists that, since God acts according to the law of vicarious suffering,

> the burdens of love must be upon him. He must bear the lot of his enemies, and
> even the wrongs of his enemies. In pity, in patience, in sacrifice, in all kinds of holy
> concern, he must take them on his heart, and be afflicted for them as well as by
> them (p. 226).

Christ came above all to share our human lot, and thereby to express God's love. Although this was the chief theme of his ministry, it impressed and attracted people most powerfully through his death:

> Christ...takes us first, on the side of natural feeling, showing his compassions
> there, passing before us visaged in sorrow, groaning in distressful concern for us, dy-
> ing even the bitterest conceivable death, because the love he bears to us cannot let
> go of us. In a word we see him entered so deeply into our lot, that we are softened
> and drawn by him, and even begin to want him entered more deeply, that we may
> feel him more constrainingly. In this way a great point is turned in our recovery. Our
> heart is engaged before it is broken. We like the Friend before we love the Saviour
> (p. 154; cf. 160).

Bushnell feels that such an impression was opposite of that made by the substitutionary emphasis on God's judgment and wrath, from which one "recoils painfully, shivers with dread, and turns away" (p. 154). But does this mean—as critics of the moral influence theory often charge—that Bushnell's God could only love and forgive and could never penalize or establish justice? If not, it

---

[19] *The Vicarious Sacrifice*, Vol. I, (New York: Scribner's: 1903; originally published in 1877), pp. 41-42. (The following page numbers in our text are to this work.) Even God is, in a sense, under this law of love. For God "does not make the law of love, or impose it upon us by his own mere will. It is with him as an eternal, necessary, immutable law, existing in logical order before his will, and commanding, in the right of its own excellence, his will and life" (308; cf. p. 235).

would seem that Bushnell's God, unlike Anselm's, could not really govern the universe.

Bushnell insists that God governs things not only through the law of vicarious love but also through justice. In order to curb the effects of sin, God instituted natural and civil laws (pp. 255-57). These recompense wrongdoing with appropriate penalties. Yet in so doing they have other effects. Laws against sin increase one's sense of how evil sin is. Laws and their harsh penalties intensify people's longing for a better situation.[20] Throughout history, Bushnell argues, God has been working through both kinds of laws: The law of love arouses humanity's higher moral feelings, while laws of justice curb our lower nature and negatively reinforce these higher aspirations (pp. 273-74). Bushnell, in fact, has sought to transform God's justice from a standard expressing God's highest demands and pressing down on us vertically, as it were, from above and to identify it with the horizontal network of natural and civil laws through which sin is repressed and punished. Interpreted in this way, justice is not an eternal expression of God's inmost character. It is a general name for the complex of sometimes highly imperfect statutes and legal procedures through which history and society are regulated in a rough way. In their negative functions, they comprise the operation of God's judgment.

By means of this interpretation, Bushnell (much like Schleiermacher[21]) can speak of Jesus as bearing God's justice, or wrath. Moved by vicarious love to share our lot, Christ came into our world where sin's death-dealing effects, including the sometimes brutal operation of civil punishments, affected everyone. Living wholly by vicarious love he inevitably came to be opposed by "the hell of the world's corporate evil, to be wounded and galled by the world's malice, and bear the burden of the world's undoing" (p. 193). And continuing to live by love amid "the great river of retributive causes where we were drowning" (p. 389, cf. 203), Jesus too eventually drowned. This is the way that he bore, vicariously, the wrath of God which we deserve.

2. *Observations.* Bushnell felt that the substitutionary theory separated Jesus' death too widely from his life. To remedy this he showed how Christ's consistent exercise of vicarious love amidst a hostile world, as expressed in his specific words and deeds (pp. 129-230), led to his death. Nevertheless, like Anselm, Bushnell tended to regard the cross as the culmination of Jesus' saving work and gave his resurrection relatively little attention. Bushnell also felt that substitutionary advocates separated Jesus' death too widely from the lives of Christians. Substitutionists regarded it, he felt, as an extraordinary, divine act, wholly unlike anything we could ever do. Bushnell, however, insisted that the

[20] This was Bushnell's interpretation of the popular Protestant notion, originally emphasized by Martin Luther, that before people are ready to appropriate the forgiveness offered in the gospel, they must be brought to a knowledge of sin through the law (cf. Vol. II, Chap. 1).

[21] *The Christian Faith,* pp. 341-52.

saving significance of the cross consists precisely in its capacity to move us to live according to the same vicarious law of love. Consequently he had extremely harsh words for the substitutionary model:

> What shall we think of any theologic doctrine or dictum, that makes a blank space at the very heart of the gospel...which breaks down the fact of community between Christ and his disciples....The supreme art of the devil never invented a...theft more nearly amounting to the stealing of the cross itself, than the filching away thus, from the followers of Christ, the conviction that they are thoroughly to partake of the sacrifice of their master.[22]

Nevertheless Bushnell and Anselm are similar in significant ways. Despite his emphasis on feeling Bushnell also sought to portray Christ's saving death as the necessary result of rational, universal laws. Once one affirms Anselm's premises concerning God's purpose, God's honor, and human sin, Christ's incarnation and the cross inevitably follow. Once one accepts Bushnell's premises that vicarious love always takes on the sufferings of those less fortunate and that God's actions are guided by vicarious love, the same consequences follow. Astounding and unique as Christ's loving sacrifice may appear, Bushnell interpreted it (much as Ritschl did God's kingdom) as the outworking of a universal moral process. And like Ritschl he felt that Christ's influence had deeply permeated, and would continue to permeate western society:

> It penetrates more and more visibly our sentiments, opinions, laws, sciences, inventions, modes of commerce, modes of society, advancing, as it were, by the slow measured step of centuries, to a complete dominion over the race....If in some particular century the gospel seems to suffer a wave of retrocession, it is only gathering power for another great advance (pp. 211-12; cf. 302).

B. The Model in Scripture

Moral influence theorists usually regard the emphasis on sacrifices as representing a lower stage of Old Testament religion. Neither on a conservative reading, which regards most sacrificial literature as early, nor on a critical one, which places it in a late, degenerative period, is the sacrificial emphasis the high point of Old Testament revelation. Moral influence proponents point out that sacrifice was sometimes sharply criticized by the prophets.[23]

Some such scholars maintain that sacrifices were primarily gifts to Yahweh. In higher stages of Old Testament religion the meaning of sacrifice was spiritualized: the inner attitudes of gratitude and praise, rather than the outer sacrifi-

---

[22] P. 122; this criticism is overdone. Substitutionary theorists can consistently regard Christ's death as the climax of his human obedience—something that we all owe to God—and thus as something of a model.

[23] Amos 5:21-24; Hos. 6:6; Mic. 6:6-8; Jer. 6:20, 7:22-23, 14:12.

cial gifts themselves, came to be seen as the truly important thing.[24] This attitude reached its highest point in Yahweh's mysterious Servant (Isa. 52:13–53:12), who gives his entire life "for the glory of God and for the benefit of his fellow-men."[25] And in the New Testament sacrificial terms are frequently metaphors for giving oneself to others and to God.[26]

According to other scholars sacrifices were offered chiefly to effect communion with God. This communion could occur through consuming the flesh of the sacrificed animal, as at Passover (Exod. 12:8–11), following the institution of the covenant (Exod. 24:9–11), or in all "peace offerings" (Lev. 7:14–18). Moreover the victim's life, which was contained in its blood (Lev. 17:11), was released through sacrifice.[27] Although Israelites did not consume this blood, its application could cleanse diseased persons (Lev. 14–15) and cultic priests and objects (Exodus 29). In these ways sacrifices could bring Israel into participation in the living holiness of Yahweh. In the New Testament the loaf and cup which commemorate Christ's death are also "participation" in his body and blood (1 Cor. 10:16–17; cf. John 6:32–58).[28]

We can hardly begin to fathom all the rich meanings of sacrifice here. But we can see that sacrificial descriptions of Christ's death need not necessarily be taken as substitutionary interpretations of his work. Sacrifice has many other dimensions of meaning.

More positively, when moral influence advocates read the Old Testament, they stress the social dimensions of Yahweh's covenant and the ethical and social emphases of the prophets. When they read the Gospels, they find Jesus renewing the message of the prophets and proclaiming (as we also stressed) the dawning of God's kingdom. They focus on the kingdom as the culmination of God's loving purpose and emphasize texts speaking of God's forgiving love and grace. They argue that this message of love can be found in numerous passages,

---

[24] As evidently indicated, e.g., by Psalms in which sacrificial terminology is used metaphorically to describe attitudes of thanksgiving: Pss. 50:9-12; 69:30-31; 107:22; 116:17-18, etc. See George B. Gray, *Sacrifice in the Old Testament* (Oxford: Clarendon, 1925).

[25] W. O. E. Oesterly, *Sacrifices in Ancient Israel* (London: Hodder and Stoughton, 1937), p. 232. cf. H. H. Rowley, *The Meaning of Sacrifice in the Old Testament* (Manchester: University, 1950), pp. 110-14.

[26] E.g., Rom. 12:1, 15:26; Eph. 5:2; Phil. 2:17; Heb. 13:15-16; 1 Pet. 2:5, 9; Rev. 1:6.

[27] The classic expression of the "life theory" of sacrifice is W. Robertson Smith, *The Religion of the Semites* (New York: Meridian, 1956). It can probably explain less than Smith claimed for it, since he argued largely from parallels with other Semitic religions which centered around consuming sacrificial blood, whereas Israel forbade this. For a vigorous rejection of the "life theory's" more general understanding of blood, see Morris, pp. 112-28.

[28] See E. O. James, *Sacrifice and Sacrament* (New York: Barnes and Noble, 1962), pp. 74, 119, 126-28.

whereas an explicit substitutionary emphasis appears, as we saw, in no more than two (Mark 10:45, 14:24 and par). Sometimes, however, they overlook Jesus' proclamation of judgment.

When they turn to the remainder of the New Testament, moral influence proponents point out that some terms which substitutionists stress appear fairly seldom. "Expiation" words, for instance, appear eight times in the New Testament; "ransom" occurs only in Mark 10:45 (= Matt. 20:28).[29] But words from the stem for "love (agape)" appear over 250 times. Moral influence advocates usually acknowledge that the substitutionary model is present in the New Testament. Yet the relative infrequency of key terms which express it, and their customary occurrence in brief formulae, suggest that it was an early understanding which later was superseded or at least suplemented.[30] Examination of some overall contexts in which such terms and formulae occur seems to support this.

Consider, for instance the "expiation" word group. John's characterization of Jesus by means of it occurs in the following context:

> In this the love of God was made manifest among us, that God sent his only Son into the world, so that we might live through him. In this is love, not that we loved God but that God loved us and sent his Son to be the expiation for our sins. Beloved, if God so loved us, we also ought to love one another (1 John 4:9–11).

Similarly after Paul has affirmed that God put forth Jesus "as an expiation by his blood," he explains that "This was to show God's righteousness, because in his divine forbearance he had passed over former sins; it was to prove at the present time that he himself is righteous and that he justifies" (Rom. 3:24–26). Whatever the full meaning of these two important passages, they insist that Jesus' sacrificial death serves to manifest God's love and righteousness. It exerts a powerful influence.[31]

The early affirmation that Christ died "for us (you)" or "for our (your) sins" also takes on broad meaning in various New Testament contexts. In Mark 10:45 Jesus spoke of "giving" his life a ransom "for many." Later, Paul finds this self-giving to be a life bestowing expression of Jesus' own love, in which he now

---

[29] However, lutroomai appears 3 times; lutrosis, 3 times; lutrotes, once; and apolutrosis ("redemption"), 10 times. agorazo ("buy") is used 5 times in connection with Christ's work, and eksagorazo, twice. Not all these uses, though, necessarily favor a substitutionary interpretation.

[30] For a classic expression of the conflict in Paul between his allegedly earlier, cultic views and his later, more thoroughly Christian understanding, see Otto Pfleiderer, Paulinism, (London: Williams and Norgate, 1877), Vol. I. pp. 91-117.

[31] Hebrews 2:17 may also link emphases found in the substitutionary and moral influence models when it says that Jesus was made like us "that he might become a merciful and faithful high priest in the service of God, to make expiation for the sins of the people." In 1 John 2:2, however, the substitutionary emphasis seems to predominate.

participates: "I have been crucified with Christ. It is no longer I who live, but Christ who lives in me; and the life I now live in the flesh I live by the faithfulness of the Son of God who loved me and gave himself for me."[32] For Paul God's love was manifested precisely in the fact that "while we were yet sinners, Christ died for us." One good human being will scarcely ever die for another. Yet Christ died "while we were enemies" of God! Knowing that he loved us this much, we can be entirely confident that "we shall be saved by his life" (Rom. 5:8–10). Or, as Paul triumphantly asserts:

> If God is for us, who is against us? He who did not spare his own Son but gave him up for us all, will he not also give us all things with him?...Who shall separate us from the love of Christ?...I am sure that neither death, nor life, nor angels, nor principalities, nor things present, nor things to come, nor powers, nor height, nor depth, nor anything else in all creation, will be able to separate us from the love of God in Christ Jesus our Lord! (Rom. 8:31–39).

To determine precisely the scope of the moral influence model in Scripture, we would have to survey all passages which speak of Christ's work as the manifestation and actualization of God's love, God's grace, etc. But this is enough to indicate that even some texts which speak of Jesus' sacrificial death "for us" might perhaps be interpreted by means of this model.

III. The Christus Victor Model

The Christus Victor model, like the substitutionary model, envisions humanity in a desperate situation from which Christ alone can rescue it. As is true of kerygmatic Christologies in general, the Christus Victor motif functions largely to answer the question "What must I do to be saved?" Yet the force from which one seeks deliverance, to be exact, is neither God's wrath nor human sin understood in legal terms but the bondage imposed by evil powers. Since this bondage exists independently of whether individuals recognize or acknowledge it, it may be called objective, as can most features of Christ's saving work which overcome it.

A. The Model in History

We have already learned that this motif provided the chief understanding of Christ's work until the time of Anselm. Anselm rejected its dramatic imagery for a rational theory which could prove that Christ's incarnation, suffering, and struggle with Satan were necessary. Although Christus Victor imagery long lingered in popular piety, most theologians shared Anselm's perspective. Generally speaking, the substitutionary model reigned until the nineteenth century, when the newly arising moral influence theory engaged it in heated

---

[32] Gal. 2:20 (for our translation of *pistis* as "faithfulness," see Vol. II, Chap. 7). John's similar phrase, that Jesus "lays down his life for...," also expresses the supreme example of self-giving love, which Jesus' disciples are to follow (John 15:12-13, 1 John 3:16; cf. note 10).

polemic. So sharply drawn were the battle lines between these two models that most people assumed that they were the only serious theological options.

We have seen how, during the 1930s and '40s, New Testament scholars began taking the presence of the demonic in Scripture more seriously. Current events were suggesting that such phenomena, long dismissed as mythological, might be more real than enlightened modern people had thought (Chap. 15). During this time the Swedish historical theologian Gustav Aulen argued that the Christus Victor motif, rather than being a crude, pictorial expression of a long-gone era, in fact constituted a third, fully theological explication of Christ's saving work. In what follows we present, somewhat as Aulen did, a general overview of this model as developed during second to fifth centuries, with occasional references to theologians of that and later periods.

1. *The Source of Bondage.* What is that force from which humanity seeks deliverance? It might be called, as in the substitutionary model, human sin. For all humanity has turned away from God. Nevertheless for the Christus Victor motif this turning away was also a turning towards death and the Devil. As a result humanity is now under their power. Most adequately stated, then, humans seek deliverance not just from their sins (legally or morally considered) but from oppression by these powers. Humanity also yearns for deliverance from God's wrath and judgment. More precisely speaking, however, God exercises wrath primarily by turning humans over to the dominion of these powers. When people choose to follow Satan, God hands them over to Satan. This is God's judgment. God that is normally exercises wrath and judgment not directly but indirectly through the agency of the powers.

So conceived the relationship of these powers to humanity and God is exceedingly paradoxical. Consider first their dominion over humankind. On one hand it seems legitimate. For people have turned away from God and received their just deserts. Yet on the other hand the powers rule humankind in oppressive and unjust ways. Or consider God's relationship to the powers. Is God for or against them? On one hand God seems to be for them. For they are executors of divine judgment. On the other hand God seems to be against them. For Christ's saving work consists in defeating them. It is partly these difficult paradoxes and not only its dramatic and mythological character that have caused many to reject the Christus Victor motif in favor of the straightforward clarity of the substitutionary and moral influence approaches.

Moreover, modern people indeed have difficulty in comprehending what these powers might be. According to Justin Martyr and Origen (and also several writings of intertestamental times) many of them were deities, or forces behind the deities worshipped in pagan religions. These worked on humans subjectively by producing fear and anxiety which could be alleviated only by bondage to these religions.[33] Objectively, however, many of these were also gods of the state. They influenced rulers to maintain many abominable pagan

---

[33] Justin, *First Apology*, Chaps. 5, 14; *Second Apology*, Chap. 5; Origen, *De Principiis* (in *The Ante-Nicene Fathers*, Vol. 5), Book III, Chaps. 2-4.

practices and to persecute God's people.[34] Although Justin and Origen never directly identified evil powers with political rulers, they regarded these rulers as the concrete agents through which the demonic is often expressed.

After Christianity became Rome's favored religion, however, this socio-political understanding of the powers rapidly declined. Zealous Christians now seldom became martyrs, suffering from the clash between the kerygma and their social context; often they emigrated to the desert, where the powers waged war internally, through temptations against their souls. During the Reformation, Martin Luther revived Christus Victor imagery. Yet the Devil's work was limited largely to the conscience, where he tormented individuals with fear of judgment and hell.[35]

Regardless of how they understood the social and psychological activities of the powers, all Christus Victor proponents believed that a dark volitional agent, the Devil, was somehow behind it all. They also spoke of Sin—not merely as the sum of all individual sins, but as an active, collective force which enticed and pressured individuals towards sinful acts. The ultimate penalty towards which Satan and sin propelled everyone was death viewed not merely as the cessation of biological existence but as a cosmic force opposed to all manifestations of the life of God (cf. Chaps. 8–9), terrifying individuals with threats of ultimate futility, shame, and extinction. (The fact that the Fathers viewed death like this shows that not only did they regard salvation as liberation from mere physical decay and corruption but also from all forms of sin and moral evil.[36])

2. *The Character of Liberation.* How did Christ liberate creation from the powers? Whereas contextual Christologies focus on Christ's life and kerygmatic Christologies on his incarnation or his death, the Christus Victor motif conceives all these as episodes in a continuing conflict. Its highest point, however, was Jesus' resurrection, which completed his triumph over the powers and was "also the starting point for the new dispensation, for the gift of the Spirit" which continues this work in the Church.[37] To understand this more fully let us look briefly at each phase of Jesus' work.

As held by the Fathers, one main effect of Christ's saving work was to bring humankind into vital, participatory relationship with the divine (divinization: Chap. 14). This process began with the incarnation. Here a human person came into being who was not only in touch with the divine but also free from all penalties imposed by Death and other Powers. As this person grew towards

---

[34] Justin, *First Apology,* Chap. 5; *Second Apology,* Chaps. 1, 7-8, 10. Origen, *Contra Celsum* (Cambridge: University, 1965), Book I, Chap. 1; Book V, Chaps. 29-37; Book VIII, Chaps. 24-44. For the various strains in Origen's political outlook, see Gerard Caspary, *Politics and Exegesis* (Berkeley: University of California, 1979).

[35] See Aulen's account of Luther, esp. pp. 111-22.

[36] Aulen argues this on pp. 22-26; cf. p. 263 above.

[37] Aulen, pp. 31-32.

adulthood he, to use Justin's and Irenaeus' term, "recapitulated" all stages of human growth.[38] In Jesus, that is, a human being developed through all phases of growth, who was obedient to and thus in fellowship with God, just as Adam should have been. In particular, whereas Adam had succumbed to Satan's temptations and fallen away from God, Jesus resisted and remained in communion. For Irenaeus Jesus' wilderness temptations and his death on the cross formed the high points of this struggle.[39]

Underlying the idea of recapitulation is the notion that Adam and Eve were created as infants beginning a process of moral and spiritual growth.[40] This is not unlike the moral influence theory. For both models Jesus treads this path ahead of everyone else, stimulating us by his teaching and his example. In stressing that Jesus rendered God the obedience that Adam and everyone else owed, the Christus Victor model is like the substitutionary theory. The chief effect of this process, however, was more nearly the emergence of a new kind of human being than the acquiring of legal merit. Moreover this process was not complete until the resurrection. Then the human who had conquered even death arose, finally wholly freed from all penalties and influences of the Powers, as the firstfruits of a new human race to follow.[41]

When Christus Victor advocates began explaining Jesus' death, two particularly controversial notions often emerged. First, the notion of a ransom. Some Fathers, emphasizing that the Devil fittingly rules over humanity (since humans choose to obey him rather than God) and that God executes judgment through Satan, argued that there was a certain legality to this arrangement. Therefore if Satan were to be deprived of his rule over humanity, he would have to be offered some compensation, or ransom, in exchange. In place of those whom he rightly punished, Satan could require another of equal value to bear their punishment in a substitutionary way. Of course since the Devil was an executor of God's judgment, this ransom could be thought of as ultimately paid to God, but only indirectly; directly, it was paid to the Devil.[42] Other Fathers, however, stressed the Devil's cruel oppression of humanity and God's ultimate opposition to the evil powers. As Gregory of Nazianzus insisted: "It is not fitting that the devil, who is a robber, should receive a price in return for what he

---

[38] *Against Heresies*, Book II. Chap.22, (4); III. 22, (3).

[39] On the wilderness, see Ibid., V. 21, 2-3; Justin, *Dialogue with Trypho*, Chaps. 103, 125. On the cross, Irenaeus, V. 23, (2). By Jesus' humility, he recapitulated Adam's "pride of reason" (V. 21, [2]); his obedience recapitulated Adam's disobedience (V. 16, [3]). Mary's obedience also recapitulated the disobedience of Eve (III. 22, [4]; Justin, *Dialogue with Trypho*, Chap. 100).

[40] Ibid., II. 28, (1); III. 22, (3); IV. 37, (1, 6); 38. (1); 39, (1).

[41] Ibid., III. 19, (3).

[42] Aulen, p. 50.

had taken by violence, and a price of such value as the Son of God Himself."[43]

The second disputed notion, the "deception of the Devil," also sought to explain Christ's death in legal terms. According to this scheme the Devil could rightly inflict the death penalty on all other humans, for they had sinned. But when he sought to kill Christ, who had never sinned, he exceeded his legal jurisdiction. Thereby Satan himself came under God's judgment and was deprived of his power over humanity. This notion aroused objections, however, when its proponents sought to explain just why Satan attacked Christ. They argued that the Devil would never have done so had he known who Jesus really was. But in Jesus, God's Son appeared, as it were, "in disguise" and thereby tricked Satan into thinking that he could destroy him. Gregory of Nyssa explained this in a way that many (like Anselm) found crude and objectionable:

> Since the hostile power was not going to enter its relations with a God present unveiled, or endure His appearance in heavenly glory, therefore God, in order to render himself accessible to him who demanded a ransom for us, concealed himself under the veil of our nature, in order that, as happens with greedy fishes, together with the bait of the flesh the hook of the Godhead might also be swallowed, and so, through Life passing over into death, and the Light arising in the darkness, that which is opposed to Life and Light might be brought to nought.[44]

But however Christus Victor advocates explained the cross, God's triumph over Satan was incomplete until the resurrection. If in killing Christ, Satan overstepped his legal bounds, then this verdict was not rendered until God raised Christ, thereby declaring his innocence.

3. *Observations*. The Christus Victor motif interrelates Jesus' life, death, and resurrection more coherently than do our other two models. The conflicts of Jesus' earthly ministry can be understood as early phases of that struggle which climaxed at his death and resurrection. Like the moral influence theory, however, it emphasizes the role of Jesus' teachings and example in preparing the way for a new humanity, yet a humanity decisively brought to life only at his resurrection.

This model, however, appears considerably less rational than the other two. Attempts to explain its features as the necessary result of legal procedures seem inconsistent and sometimes unconvincing. It is difficult to know what meaning, if any, its proponents might ascribe to "the Devil" and other powers in the modern world. Does this "mythological terminology" mean, as theological tradition has long held, that the Christus Victor motif holds no real cognitive value? Finally this model has social implications, though their character is not immediately obvious, for only some of its proponents emphasized the powers' socio-politcal activity. Nonetheless, they all spoke of humans as participating in the risen, reigning Christ, who imparts new life to all the cosmos. Neverthe-

---

[43] Aulen's summary of Gregory's view (p. 50).

[44] "Address on Religious Instruction" in Hardy, ed., Chap. 24) as quoted in Aulen, p. 52.

less, even though Christ has broken the powers' sovereignty, their activity is still pervasive. This model pictures the Church as still engaged in hostile conflict, and not, like the moral influence model, as in the vanguard of progressive movements which are gradually reducing evil.

B. The Model in Scripture

Since the Christus Victor motif is seldom discussed in relationship to the Old Testament, we postpone our thoughts on this until the next chapter. When reading the Synoptics, Christus Victor proponents can point not only to Jesus' frequent encounters with demons but to the fact that his ministry begins with Satan's challenge in the wilderness (Matt. 4:1-11 and par), ends with similar taunting on the cross (Matt. 27:37-44 and par), and contains indications that a major struggle with the Devil is being waged all along (Matt. 12:22–32, 16:23 and par). Such a struggle is also central for John.[45]

The earliest kerygma proclaims Jesus' death "for our sins," not only in a general substitutionary way (1 Cor. 15:3), but as a liberation from evil forces: He "gave himself for our sins to deliver us from the present evil Age" (Gal. 1:3). It mentions that Jesus "went about doing good, and healing all who were oppressed by the devil" (Acts 10:38), yet that the Jerusalemites and their rulers delivered him to death "because they did not recognize him" (Acts 13:27). Jesus' resurrection is God's vindication over against those who slew him (Acts 3:13-15, 5:30-31, 13:27-30). In these and many other early kerygmatic phrases, Christ's resurrection is the high point of God's saving work (Rom. 1:4, 8:34, 10:9; cf. Chap. 18).

We have seen that the kerygma also emphasizes Christ's exaltation to God's right hand as Lord and coming Judge (Acts 2:33, 5:31, 10:41; Rom. 2:16, 8:34). We have argued that, from early on, "Lord" was not only an exclamation of personal adoration. The earliest confession, "Jesus Christ is Lord," included at least implicitly, the the subordination of all powers to him (Phil. 2:9-11, 1 Pet. 3:22, 1 Tim. 3:16).

Paul speaks of evil powers in at least four ways. He often refers to a single figure: "Satan," "the Devil," etc; he sees his ministry and the lives of his converts caught up in conflict with Satan and his agents.[46] Second, Paul speaks of

---

[45] 12:31, 13:27, 17:15. Though he tried, "the Ruler of this World" could find nothing to convict Jesus of (14:30). This Ruler was then judged by Jesus' resurrection (16:11). Jesus' discourse in John 8 closely connects Death and Sin (8:21, 24, 34) with the Devil (8:44-48), as does 1 John—especially 3:4-15 and 5:18-19. Further investigation would show that "Darkness" and "the World" in John also have a demonic character.

[46] 1 Thess. 2:18, 3:5; 2 Thess. 3:3; 1 Cor. 7:5; 2 Cor. 2:11, 4:4, 11:3, 13-14, 12:7; Rom. 16:20; Eph. 2:2-3, 6:10-20. For an overview on the role of the demonic in Paul, see James Kallas, *The Satanward View* (Philadelphia: Westminster, 1966) and C. A. Anderson Scott, *Christianity According to St. Paul* (Cambridge: University, 1937).

Christ's work as liberation from the forces behind pagan religions and philosophies.[47] Third, Paul uses terms which indicate rulership: "principalities," "dominions," "thrones," etc. Their close connection with political rulers appears when Paul says that "None of the rulers of this age" understood God's hidden wisdom, "for if they had, they would not have crucified the Lord of glory" (1 Cor. 2:6–9). By means of the cross and resurrection, however, Christ "disarmed the principalities and powers, and made a public example of them" (Col. 2:15). Jesus' resurrection raised him far above them (Eph. 1:20–22), and his reconciling work will affect them all.[48] In the present Christ is "destroying every rule and authority and power. For he must reign until he has put all his enemies under his feet" (1 Cor. 15:24–25; cf. 2 Thess. 2:3-11).

Finally, Paul speaks of generalized evil forces which oppose God. Among the enemies which Christ is conquering, "The last enemy to be destroyed is Death"; he goes on to say that "The sting of death is sin, and the power of sin is the law" (1 Cor. 15:26, 56). In Romans 5–8 Paul describes the contrast between the old age and the new as a contrast between the reign of sin and death on one hand and righteousness and life on the other (esp. Rom. 5:17, 21; 6:12–13). Sin works through a power called "the flesh" (Rom. 7:5, 18), which is opposed by God's Spirit (Rom. 8:3–9; cf. Gal. 5:16–18, 24; 6:8). Paul attributes a dynamism and a specificity to the working of these forces which goes beyond the language of mere metaphor. He ends this section affirming that no reality or power in the universe can separate us from Christ (8:37–39). In Romans 7 Paul includes "the law" in his panorama of evil forces. He does insist that, in and of itself and apart from the way it actually functions, the law is "holy and just and good" (7:12). Yet in its actual function the law increases the power of sin and the flesh. This teaching corresponds to what Paul says in 1 Corinthians 15:56, and in Galatians.[49] In Ephesians 2:14–16 and Colossians 2:14–15 he describes the law as something which Christ's work overcame.

Peter speaks of Christ's past work[50] and his readers' continuing trials (1 Pet.

---

[47] This is largely what he means by the "elemental spirits of the universe (*stoichea*)": Gal. 4:3-9, Col. 2:8, 18-23. Paul also regards pagan religions in general as forces opposing Christ: e.g., 1 Cor. 10:20-21, 2 Cor. 6:15-16, etc.

[48] Col. 1:13-20, Eph. 3:10. On the apparent contrast between destroying and reconciling these powers, see Vol. II, Chaps. 6 and 10.

[49] Paul parallels being "slaves to the elemental spirits of the universe (*stoicheia*)" and being "under the law" (Gal. 3:23, 4:1-5, 8-9). Historically, Martin Luther emphasized the hostile role of the law (Aulen, pp. 111-16).

[50] 1 Pet. 3:19-22; cf. 4:6. The "spirits" of verse 19 (cf. 2 Pet. 2:4) are evidently the fallen angels who became gods of ancient pagan civilizations. Whatever the exact results of Christ's preaching to them, the revealing of the gospel to even these arch-powers shook the primordial foundations of pagan society. In its context this witness of Christ provides a model for the readers' witness before the pagan rulers of their own day (3:15-16; see Bo Reicke, *The Epistles of James, Peter and Jude* [Garden City, N.Y.: Doubleday, 1964], pp. 109-11).

5:8) as struggles with demonic forces. Acts reports exorcisms similar to those performed by Jesus (Acts 5:16, 8:7, 16:18, 19:11) and conflicts between the gospel and pagan demonic forces (Acts 8:9-24, 13:6-12, 16:16-18, 19:13-19). Even though these dynamics are not as pervasive as in the Gospels, they have hardly disappeared (cf. also Acts 5:1-11, 26:17). Hebrews expresses the Christus Victor motif classically as follows:

> Since therefore the children share in flesh and blood, he himself likewise partook of the same nature, that through death he might destroy him who has the power of death, that is, the devil, and deliver all those who through fear of death were subject to lifelong bondage (Heb. 2:14-15).

This is the same passage which goes on to speak of Jesus being made "a merciful and faithful high priest in the service of God, to make expiation for the sins of the people" (Heb. 2:17). Elements of all three soteriological models seem to be present in this one text. Hebrews also speaks of Jesus as the "forerunner" or "pioneer" (Heb. 2:10, 12:2) of salvation in a way congenial with the notion of recapitulation (2:18, 3:14, 4:15, 5:7-9).

Finally, continuing conflict between Christ's people and demonic forces runs throughout the Revelation. Here the political and religious character of the latter is obvious (esp. Revelation 13, 17-18). In our next chapter (and in Vol. II, Chap. 6) we can begin elaborating some of these complex themes. For now we notice that the notion of Christ's work as conquest of evil powers occurs frequently in the Synoptic Gospels, John, Paul, and Revelation; it appears in almost all other New Testament books.

CHAPTER SEVENTEEN

The Meaning of the Death of Jesus Christ

After examining three major understandings of Christ's death, it has become quite apparent that the meaning of his death cannot be separated from that of his life. For the moral influence model, the cross has meaning as the climactic expression of that vicarious love which Jesus manifested throughout his ministry. For the Christus Victor model, Christ's death forms one episode in a struggle with evil forces begun in his incarnation and ministry and climaxed in his resurrection. Although the substitutionary model regards Christ's cross as making complete payment for sin, it does not limit Jesus' saving work to his death. For salvation also includes bestowal of eternal life; and this can occur only because Jesus merited it throughout the course of his obedient life. Accordingly, as we seek to penetrate the meaning of Jesus' death in this chapter, we will find ourselves constantly integrating material from Chapter 15 with various themes and passages discussed in Chapter 16. Moreover, our findings will frequently point forward toward Christ's resurrection, where the meaning of his death will be definitively actualized and revealed.

This chapter will heighten our appreciation of the role of models in theological thinking. We have seen that each of the three models just discussed is "applicable" to some of the biblical data. Consequently, their ardent defenders have extended their range, to make them "adequate" explanations for all the biblical data (cf. Chap. 3). However, as we bring forward, or adduce, each of them, we shall find that none is fully adequate. This will force us to resist the synthetic tendency of the human mind to explain everything in terms of one comprehensive theory. Instead, we shall seek to determine what combinations and interrelations of these models best illuminate the data we find in Scripture. We shall seek to clarify these interrelations as fully as the data allows. Yet we shall also have to stop where the data leaves off, and to allow for incompleteness and paradox where the Scriptures do.

I. The Main Purpose of Jesus' Saving Work

As we begin adducing these models, let us ask if theology can identify a major goal of Jesus' work, an overall purpose for which he lived, died and rose?

Chapter 15 argued that it was the kingdom of God, that is, God's unobstructed reign over all dimensions of the cosmos. Much of Chapter 15 showed in what ways this involves human social relationships. Yet we also indicated that the coming of the kingdom began the transformation of the natural world. Further, it involved the subjugation of all cosmic spiritual powers. And it penetrated the deep religious and existential depths of the human heart. The coming of God's kingdom demanded that all individuals and social structures open themselves to the dawning of the *eschaton*, to the surprising "reversed" fulfillment of God's ancient promise. In answer to the burning question of when and how Yahweh would save his people, Jesus announced that this sort of kingdom was "at hand."

Jesus, however, could not save anyone *for* God's kingdom without also saving them *from* those forces which opposed it. What were these? They included natural phenomena (illness, storms, etc.). But primarily, they were spiritual in character. Chapter 15 traced the way in which these forces opposed Christ not only through psycho-physical "possession," but chiefly through the religious and political structures which finally killed him.

We observed, moreover, that the same demonic impetus which pervaded these structures affected all his contemporaries, even and perhaps especially his disciples. For they too were ultimately motivated by the longing for a conquering Messiah. They hoped for one who would subjugate their enemies by force and guarantee them safety and status. It was this fundamental drive for power, security, and prestige—and the corresponding fear of suffering, insecurity, and humiliation—that also impelled those dominant classes ("righteous" Jews, the wealthy, males, Israel's religious leaders and Romans) whose ways God's kingdom threatened to reverse. Ultimately, all Jesus' contemporaries succumbed to these fears and distanced themselves from the radical repentant openness that the dawning kingdom demanded. They proved to be in bondage to the impulses dominating the religious movements and social structures which opposed Christ.

The coming of God's kingdom, then, was so sharply opposed by evil powers that it could not have definitively arrived unless these powers had been defeated. This indicates that, whatever exact use we may make of our soteriological models, the Christus Victor model will prove applicable to at least some of the biblical data. Accordingly, we propose to adduce this model first, to see how much of the meaning of Christ's work, and especially of his death, it can illumine. Yet as we proceed, we will doubtless be interrelating it with the substitutionary and moral influence models.

As we begin, we remember that this model has seldom been used in systematic theology, partly due to its highly paradoxical nature. In particular, we remember that it presents God as on one had sanctioning the powers' work (insofar as they execute his judgment on humankind), and on the other as opposing it (insofar as they cruelly oppress humankind). This paradox has made clear understanding of this model so difficult that we shall have to view Christ's death from two very different angles in light of it: first, we shall ask how he bore God's judgment; second, we shall ask how his death liberated us from the power's.

II. How Did Christ Bear God's Judgment?

According to the substitutionary model, we remember, sin is punished by the justice and wrath of God bearing down upon each individual vertically, as it were. On each individual it inflicts the legal penalty of eternal condemnation. Jesus bore sins by enduring an amount of punishment that could be considered legally equivalent to that which was due all sinners. Nevertheless substitutionists say little about how this divine justice operates in concrete historical life.

Moral influence theorists seek to remedy this by interpreting these realities in horizontal, socio-historical terms. For them, sinful acts bring about their own punishment; they elicit evil effects and responses, which make necessary the State with its coercive and penal actions. For moral influence advocates, this retributive network of sin and evil is itself God's judgment on the world. God exercises judgment indirectly. Jesus bore this judgment by entering this network and by experiencing what it inflicted on anyone who sought to live wholly by love.

According to the Christus Victor model, God also exercises judgment indirectly, by handing sinners over to the consequences of their actions. Yet this model speaks mostly of God delivering sinners to the dominion of evil forces: sin, death, the Devil, etc. Nevertheless is it possible that these have something in common with the socio-political forces emphasized by moral influence advocates? Historical theology's verdict is mixed. Before the reign of Constantine, some Fathers understood the powers in socio-political ways. After this, however, the powers were usually interpreted in spiritual terms. To answer, we must turn to Scripture.

A. Sin and Judgment in the Old Testament

This issue has rarely been investigated with help from the Christus Victor motif. In Old Testament history, sin consisted primarily in idolatry, in turning from Yahweh to worship other gods.[1] However idolatry was not, as we might think today, an exclusively religious sin. The pagan gods were the special guardians of the pagan nations themselves. They were invoked to ensure the prosperity of national agricultural and commercial life, the smooth functioning of social life, and to grant military protection and victory. These gods supported, represented, and embodied the social, cultural, and political values of their societies.[2]

By turning to other national gods, therefore, Israel turned away not only from the religious commands of Yahweh's covenant but from its social ones as well. Idolatry meant not only preference for another religious cult but for the whole way of ethical and cultural behavior which accompanied foreign cults. It meant asking the gods of Egypt, Canaan, and Assyria, etc., for economic prosperity and military protection in exchange for adopting the moral and social way of life which they represented.

How was such sin punished in the Old Testament? Occasionally, God's wrath was exercised in a rather direct way; through a plague (Numb. 16:41–50, 25:1–13,) or a famine (2 Sam. 21:1–9) aroused by a particular transgression.[3] Most often, however, Yahweh executed judgment by handing Israel over to its enemies. According to the passage which summarizes the theme of Judges, Israel often forsook Yahweh, "who had brought them out of the land of Egypt; they went after other gods, from among the gods of the peoples who were round about them, and bowed down to them." In response, Yahweh "gave them over to plunderers, who plundered them; and he sold them into the power of their enemies round about." Nevertheless, when the Israelites cried out, God "was moved to pity by their groaning because of those who afflicted and oppressed them." In answer, Yahweh "raised up judges, who saved them out of the power of those who plundered them" (Judg. 2:11–19).

This passage, which could well summarize most of Israel's history, corresponds remarkably with the Christus Victor model. Notice that Israel's punishment was just from one perspective: Israel worshiped the gods of the nations and was handed over to the power of these nations. From another angle, however, it was unjust: these nations cruelly "afflicted and oppressed them." Notice, moreover, that these nations were, in one way, God's agents: they

---

[1] This is acknowledged by so firm an advocate of the substitutionary model as Leon Morris, *Apostolic Preaching*, p. 150.

[2] For a detailed discussion of the functions of the gods of Mesopotamia and Egypt, see Henri Frankfort, *Kingship and the Gods* (Chicago: University, 1948). For a comparison of societies ruled by these gods and Israel, see Frankfort, *et. al.*, *The Intellectual Adventure of Ancient Man* (Chicago: University, 1946), and also our fuller discussion in Vol. II, Chap. 6.

[3] Walther Eichrodt, *Theology of the Old Testament* (Philadelphia: Westminster, 1961), pp. 261–62). (Such plagues and famines, however, must also have been, at least in part, the result of "natural" causes.)

executed Yahweh's judgment. Ultimately, however Yahweh opposed them, and raised up saviors to liberate his people.

Those who object to the paradoxes of the Christus Victor model, or to the notion that God's judgment is often exercised indirectly, have seldom noticed how closely these paradoxes mirror what we find in the Old Testament. Repeatedly through the prophets Yahweh says, "I" will punish or destroy you. Yet who carries out the actual destruction? It is usually the armies of Moab, Assyria, Bablyon, etc. Once we recognize, further, that the gods whom Israel worshipped were the ultimate forces behind the economic, social, and military might of these nations, we perceive that they were the functional realities for which late Old Testament, intertestamental, and New Testament authors developed the specific terminology of "principalities" and "powers." The Old Testament's fundamental understanding of sin and its punishment, therefore, is largely in line with the Christus Victor model.

This understanding of the powers correspond with what we learned about Jesus' ministry. In the Old Testament, a given nation's gods were not exhaustively identical with its religious or political leaders; the gods were the ultimate forces of which the latter were agents. In the Gospels neither Israel's nor Rome's leaders were themselves demonic powers; yet they were the chief agents of the kingdom of Satan. Our survey of other New Testament writings yielded similar results. The spiritual "thrones, dominions, principalities, and rulers" clearly impacted the social and political lives of the nations.

B. Sin and Judgment at the Cross

In light of this biblical data, and in light of our account of Jesus' ministry (Chap. 15) we may conclude that Jesus bore God's judgment by suffering under those religious, political, and demonic forces which were the agents of God's wrath in his own day. This does not contradict the assertion of the substitutionary model that Jesus bore God's wrath. But it clarifies *how* this occurred. We can say, along with the moral influence model, that Jesus suffered under the corporate network of sin and evil regulated in part by the State. The American "social gospel" theologian Walter Rauschenbusch, a proponent of moral influence, identified six concrete social forces which put Jesus to death: religious bigotry, graft and political power, judicial corruption, mob spirit, militarism, and class contempt.[4]

Jesus, then, bore God's wrath when his religious and political opponents persecuted and put him to death. Precisely speaking, it was the cruel wrath of the powers which he bore directly. Jesus bore God's wrath only indirectly. For although God hands people over to the powers to acute his judgment, God's attitude towards sin and sinners is very different from theirs. The wrath which Jesus bore on the cross is not best pictured as being poured out vertically, as it

---

[4] *A Theology for the Social Gospel* (New York: Abingdon, 1917), pp. 244-58. Rauschenbusch was significantly influenced by Schleiermacher, Bushnell, and Ritschl.

were, by an angry Father directly upon an agonizing Son. Such imagery, sometimes suggested by the substitutionary model, might draw one to love the Son,
who identifies with our pain; yet one might still approach with trembling the
Father, who remains remote and just barely appeased. This entire picture, however, runs counter to the profound unity of obedience and love with his Father
which undergirded Jesus' life (Mark 1:11 and par, 8:7 and par; John 5:19, 30).
But if the Father executed judgment by handing over the Son, for good reasons, to the cruel forces of evil, then the Father's own attitude would be one of
continuing love, and even of sorrow and grief. We will explore this further in
Section IV below.

For now, the moral influence model can help us understand another aspect
of Christ's death: that he not only bore God's judgment but also bore our sins.
Although certain religious and political leaders instigated Jesus' crucifixion,
we have seen (Chap. 15) that all of Jesus' contemporaries participated by ac-
quiescing to them, by fleeing, or by ignoring what was happening. Rauschenbusch showed how this complicity in Jesus' death extends much more widely:

> We are linked in a solidarity of evil and guilt with all who have done the same
> before us, and all who will do the same after us. In so far then as we, by our con-
> scious actions or passive consent, have repeated the sins which killed Jesus, we have
> made ourselves guilty of his death. If those who actually killed him stood before us,
> we could not wholly condemn them, but would have to range ourselves with them
> as men of their own kind.[5]

The substitutionary model stresses that the sin which humankind commits
was somehow transferred to and borne by Christ. Yet it has difficulty in explaining how so unusual a transference took place. The moral influence model
can make that link plain. The sin which Christ bore was precisely that which
his contemporaries committed by putting him to death, and in which the rest
of humanity is involved by participating in a universal solidarity of sin. Jesus
did not bear these sins in an

> artificial sense, but in their impact on his own body and soul. He had not con-
> tributed to them, as we have, and yet they were laid upon him. They were not only
> the sins of Caiaphas, Pilate, or Judas, but the social sin of all mankind, to which all
> who ever lived have contributed, and under which all who ever lived have suffered.[6]

---

[5] Ibid, p. 259; "These public evils so pervade the social life of humanity in all times
and places that no one can share the common life of our race without coming
under the effects of these collective sins. He will either sin by consenting in them,
or will suffer by resisting them. Jesus did not in any real sense bear the sin of some
ancient Briton who beat up his wife in B.C. 56, or of some mountaineer in Tennessee who got drunk in A.D. 1917. But he did in a very real sense bear the weight of
the public sins of organized society, and they are in turn causally connected with all
private sins" (p. 247).

[6] Ibid., p. 258.

The moral influence model, then, can help show concretely not only how Jesus bore God's judgment but also how he bore our sins. Nevertheless, if theology reduces Christ's bearing of judgment and sin entirely to his bearing of social opposition, then the character and power of sin, and thus of Christ's redeeming work, will be partially and superficially understood. To apprehend sin's true depth, theology must add that social behavior is permeated by demonic forces, to which humans are bound through their longing for security, status, and power, and their fear of humiliation, insecurity and suffering.[7] On the cross, then, Jesus also bore the dreadful wrath of these powers. We will consider this deeper dimension in Section IV.

C. A Ransom

In emphasizing that salvation cannot occur unless someone bears the weight of divine judgment and of human sin in our place, substitutionary theorists have said that a "ransom price" at least equivalent to the penalty for human sin must be paid to God.[8] According to some Christus Victor advocates, the devil had the right to inflict the death penalty on all who sinned. He would not give up this power over human lives unless he were offered a life at least as valuable in exchange. However, since Satan inflicts this penalty as God's agent, one can also speak of this ransom price as payable ultimately, though indirectly, to God. Are such notions simply mythological and artificial? Or do can they help illumine, the historical process of atonement?

The preceding analysis of how Christ bore judgment and sin indicates that the notion of a ransom says at least the following. When people sin, they ensnare themselves inextricably in a network of evil and its penalties, governed ultimately by forces opposed to God so that those imprisoned within it are shut off from God's saving activity. This imprisonment, which ends in eternal death, is the penalty for their sin. Given this situation, how might they be saved? Only if God would enter into this network dominated by the powers and begin operating savingly from within. Yet entering this network means coming under the powers' dominion. It means becoming subject to the penalty of eternal death. Moreover, as Horace Bushnell noticed, God's saving activity was wholly pervaded by vicarious love. Now anyone who attempts to live by vicarious love amid such a network of sin will pay the ultimate penalty of death.

This, at least in large part, is the concrete, historical meaning behind the assertion that, for salvation to occur, a ransom of at least equivalent value to the penalties of the condemned must be paid. Its value lies in insisting that sin does have consequences. Sin really does bind humans in a situation from which they cannot free themselves. It is a way of saying that this network of sin

---

[7] Rauschenbusch himself reinterpreted the "super-personal forces of evil" wholly in sociological terms, rejecting any sort of supernatural demonic activity (Ibid., pp. 69–94).

[8] One the notion of equivalence, see footnote 18 below.

and evil is so constituted that anyone who enters it, even if it be someone not originally subject to it, would inevitably pay the penalty it imposes. It explains why God did not, as Anselm's friend Boso hoped, simply "put away sins by compassion alone." God did not because sin and its consequences are a terribly real feature of our historical cosmos, and their power could not be broken save by suffering under them.

III. How Did Christ Defeat the Powers?

The Christus Victor model paradoxically asserts both that God judges by means of the powers, and that God judges the powers. We have just considered the first half of this paradox. We have sought to explain how Jesus, in our place, bore the judgment which God, through the powers, inflicted upon him. Now we must seek to explain how the powers themselves were judged and defeated by Jesus in the same act. Since we must adduce a somewhat different combination of models to elucidate this, readers should not attempt to immediately synthesize what we say here with what we have just said. Although theological models must always be "consistent" with each other—at least in the sense of not being contradictory—they will not always be perfectly "coherent." That is, the major concepts of one model may not be fully translatable into those of another. Systematic theology seeks for coherence by indicating, as far as possible, how these different models are interrelated. But since it cannot always fully translate the meaning of different models into a common terminology, in some respects it must simply let them stand side by side.

A. Deceiving the Devil?

According to many versions of the Christus Victor motif, Jesus came in some sort of "disguise," and thereby "tricked" Satan into forfeiting his dominion. Does God really work through deceit? We remember the kerygma's affirmation that the Jerusalemites and their rulers killed Jesus "because they did not recognize him, nor understand the utterances of their prophets" (Acts 13:27). We remember Paul saying that the rulers of this age crucified Christ because they did not know "the secret and hidden wisdom of God" (1 Cor. 2:7). Then too, the Gospels present Jesus and his mission as being completely misunderstood, even by his closest followers. For Mark, their real significance was a "messianic secret."[9] Luke emphasizes the disciples' blindness to the way Jesus was fulfilling the Old Testament promise (e.g., Luke 24:13–27, 44–48). John portrays Jesus continually telling people who he is and people continually misunderstanding his words (John 2:18–22, 4:13–15, 6:32–52, 10:1–6, etc.). Clearly, then, a great discrepancy existed between who Jesus was and whom he was perceived to be. But what lay at the root of this? And what significance did it have in Jesus' conflict with his enemies?

[9] See Chapter 15, note 59 above.

We suggest that this discrepancy was rooted in the fundamental conflict between the popular messianic expectation of a conquering warrior-king, and the servant manner which Jesus adopted. We have argued that the former, which is rooted in the craving for power, prestige, and security, was at bottom demonic. Yet all Jesus' opponents were motivated by this craving. The Romans based their empire on favoritism for some groups, suppression of others, and the imposition of brutal force. Israel's religious leaders also pronounced some groups as closer to God, others as much more distant. Even Jesus' disciples craved positons of power (Mark 10:35–41 and par). And Jesus himself was strongly tempted by this satanic option.

But the kingdom of God, which promised to overcome all divisions between Jews and gentiles, rich and poor, male and female, involved the rejection of those distinctions fundamental to all other social and religious orders. Further, Jesus' servant activity involved the rejection of exercising rulership by force. In other words, Jesus' manner of bringing his kingdom sharply contradicted all other assumptions as to how power is attained and exercised. Now if these assumptions are at bottom demonic, and if Satan's entire thrust towards universal dominion is based on them, Satan and his allies would misunderstand Jesus and his intentions at least as badly as Jesus' own followers did.

In other words, the powers could be "deceived" not because Christ intentionally tricked them but because of their own assumptions about power and how it is exercised. When one claiming to bring God's kingdom angered the rich and the powerful, associated with the poor and the despised, and yet made no obvious call to arms, his enemies could only draw one of two conclusions: either Jesus was deceiving them, and was covertly preparing a popular uprising; or else he was simply a naive, idealistic fool, who imagined he could change the world through his words and deeds alone. But either way he posed a threat. The solution was obvious. Annihilate Jesus by force.

Satan and the powers, then, were deceived by Jesus. But not because he tricked them by appearing in some deceitful disguise. In Jesus, God came to humankind as he truly was: gracious, forgiving, seeking to win people by love and not by force. Christ's disguise was not, as Gregory of Nyssa said, his human nature, which hid his divine nature. It was his humble, servant manner, which most people suppose to be incompatible with deity, or with any kind of power that matters. Jesus' enemies, then, were deceived because they could not imagine that any actual kingdom, especially not one claiming to represent the ultimate deity, could possibly be established in this way.

The notion of deceiving the Devil, then, does refer to and can help illumine certain features of Jesus' life and death. But how did this deception lead to the powers' defeat? According to many proponents of the Christus Victor model, it resulted in Satan exceeding the "legal" scope of his authority, and thereby coming under God's judgment, which deprived him of this jurisdiction. Does Jesus' history give evidence that Christ's opponents brought judgment upon themselves in this way?

1. *Blood.* Both substitutionary and moral influence theorists, we have seen,

usually connect the meaning of this phenomenon with sacrifice (Chap. 16). For the former, blood provides evidence that a death penalty has been paid. For the latter, blood is the outpouring of the life which the sacrificer offers, to bring others into communion with him. But while blood doubtless has both meanings in connection with Christ's work at times, atonement theories have usually overlooked another very prominent one.

In the Old Testament, "blood" signifies death by violence in over half of its uses.[10] Beginning with the very first murder, such blood brought a curse upon whatever it touched; it "cried out" for Yahweh to avenge it (Gen. 4:10–11). Such blood, then, brought the one who shed it under God's judgment (Gen. 9:5–6; cf Rev. 6:10, 16:6). To be guilty was to have the murdered one's blood "upon one," or "upon one's head."

Shortly before his death, Jesus pronounced just such a judgment on his religious opponents. The religious leaders claimed (had they lived earlier) that they would not have shed "the blood of the prophets." Yet by killing him, Jesus insisted, there will come "upon" them "all the righteous blood shed on earth, from the blood of the innocent Abel....all this will come upon this generation!" Jesus was identifying his coming murder as the climax, the summing up, the recapitulation of all violent resistance against all God's righteous representatives throughout history.[11] Therefore, the guilt of all these previous acts would be included in the murder of Christ. By killing him, Jesus' opponents were bringing themselves under God's judgment for all these acts. When Pilate sought to declare himself "innocent of this righteous man's blood," the crowds cried out: "His blood be on us and on our children!" (Matt. 27:24–25). In this way, Jesus' religious opponents and the crowds in general openly declared their responsibility for his death. And by publicly seeking to divest himself of this responsibility, Pilate, the reprentative of Jesus' political opponents, ironically declared it also. By killing Jesus whose messianic character and function they did not recognize, these powers brought God's judgment upon themselves. Since this is the meaning of Jesus' "blood" in these passages, this may well, its meaning in other which ascribe salvation to the blood of Christ.

2. *The Kerygma.* Scholars have often noted that the early kerygma in Acts regards the cross as a judicial murder. But since these speeches express the cruci-

---

[10] So staunch a supporter of substitution as Leon Morris insists that the commonest use of "blood" in the Old Testament "is to denote death by violence, and...this use is found about twice as often as that to denote the blood of sacrifice" (p. 113).

[11] Matt. 23:29–36; cf. Luke 11:47-51; cf. Mark 12:1–12 and par. Just as Irenaeus spoke of Christ's obedience as "recapitulating" that of the entire race, so his death was "the recapitulation that should take place in his own person of the effusion of blood from the beginning...and that by means of Himself there should be a requisition of their blood" (*Against Heresies*, 14. 1). For Walter Rauschenbusch, Matthew 23 provided insight into the great linking "in a solidarity of evil and guilt" which unites the human race (p. 259). On the relationship between this notion and that of an "equivalent ransom," see footnote 18 below.

fixion's meaning in neither substitutionary nor moral influence terms, they usually assume that it has "no soteriological significance" here.[12] However, if such a death were considered as the decisive judgment of God's enemies, then—especially in connection with the kerygmatic announcement of resurrection as the vindication of God's Messiah—it would have deep soteriological meaning indeed. For Christ's death and resurrection together would mean that the dominion of the powers has been broken.

Expressions of such an understanding abound in Acts' early chapters. Israel's religious leaders understood the kerygma's proclamation as designed "to bring this man's blood upon us" (Acts 5:28). Indeed the kerygma of Christ's death is often an accusation of those who killed him (Acts 2:23, 3:13-15, 4:10). The early community also remembered Psalm 2: "The kings of the earth set themselves in array, and the rulers were gathered together, against the Lord and his Anointed." They discerned its fulfillment as follows: "truly in this city there were gathered together against thy hold Servant Jesus, whom thou didst anoint, both Herod and Pontius Pilate, with the Gentiles and the peoples of Israel" (Acts 4:27). Especially significant is the term "servant" (*pais*: Acts 3:13, 26; 4:30), a title which soon ceased with reference to Jesus. It indicates that very shortly after his death, Jesus was understood to be Isaiah's servant.

This came about very likely because in Isaiah's "servant songs," especially in 52:13—53:12, the earliest Christians were stunned to find a description of what they had just experienced. Much of Isaiah 52:13—52:12 expresses the confession of those whose eyes have suddenly been opened. Much as Jesus' significance was hidden from his contemporaries, so the servant's was obscured by his unlikely appearance and his fate.[13] Much as Israel participated, actively or passively, in Jesus' condemnation as a blasphemer, so the servant's contemporaries had "esteemed him stricken, smitten by God" (Isa. 53:4; cf. 3, 8).

Yet unexpectedly, like the converts in Acts, the servant's contemporaries were astonished at the outcome of events. For he was finally "exalted and lifted up" (52:13), much as Jesus was raised. A wholly unforseen reversal had occurred; it would startle nations and kings (49:7, 52:15). All this engendered an overwhelming awareness of sin and the heartfelt confession, "surely he has borne *our* griefs and carried *our* sorrows!" (53:4-6)—not unlike the repentance of those who "were cut to the heart" (Acts 2:37) when they realized their complicity in Jesus' death.

This early understanding of Christ's death yields two important results. First, the early community found Jesus' total ministry and fate foreshadowed in the servant. As indicated in Acts 8:32-33, where Philip began expounding the kerygma by beginning from Isaiah 53, the injustice of the servant's fate especially

---

[12] Eduard Schweizer, *Lordship and Discipleship* (Naperville, IL: Allenson, 1960), p. 33; cf. Hans Conzelmann, *The Theology of St. Luke* (Philadelphia: Fortress, 1961), p. 201.

[13] Isa. 42:2-3, 49:7; 50:6, 52:14; 53:2, 7.

impressed them.[14] They were struck (at first, stunned) by the contrast between the way their rulers (and, by complicity, they themselves) had evaluated Jesus and the real, deeply hidden nature of his character and mission. Once again, we find the Christus Victor motif of one coming in a disguise which draws his enemies into killing him; yet in that very act they bring judgment upon themselves. Second, in speaking of one who was made "an offering for sin" (Isa. 53:10) or who "bore the sin of many" (53:12), the servant songs pointed the way to understanding Jesus' death as a substitutionary sacrifice. Notice, however, that the sin which he bore, and for which he was sacrificed, was not just general dishonoring of God's law. It was concrete social resistance to God's servant, his mission of justice to the Gentiles, and his humble way. Consequently, although Acts does not depict Christ's death in substitutionary sacrificial terms (except perhaps in 20:28), its servant emphasis provides the source from which they could very early arise. The early kerygmatic speeches of Acts however, emphasize the broader framework within which substitution is an element: Christ's death as decisive judgment on the powers and, indeed, on all humanity.

B. Summary

The biblical data discussed above shows that Christ's murder by enemies who did not recognize his true character brought a hidden but very real divine judgment upon them. How closely does all this conform to the Christus Victor notion that because the powers exceeded the legal scope of their authority, God revoked their jurisdiction over humankind?

To speak of Christ's atoning work in legal terms like this is an attempt to stress its objectivity. In any objective model of Christ's work, alienation between God and humanity involves some state of affairs having a structure distinct from the subjective state of any or all humans. Before Christ's teaching or example can meaningfully affect our subjective alienation, this situation must be altered. The Christus Victor model is objective in that the powers' dominion constitutes a structure or barrier thick enough to separate humanity from God's salvation. We have seen that some Christus Victor proponents resist

---

[14] Morna Hooker will grant that Isaiah's servant theme has directly influenced the early Church's concept of salvation only where "the nature of the Servant's sufferings and of their atoning value" is present (p. 110; cf. Chap. 15, footnote 43). Since she cannot find these themes in Acts 8:32–35, she concludes that Isaiah 53 is used there only "as a proof-text of the necessity for Christ's passion, and not as a theological exposition of its meaning" (p. 114). Its presence merely shows "how the early church was ready to make use of any Scripture which was presented to her, in order to show how Christ's work had been foreshadowed there" (p. 113). Like many scholars, Hooker assumes that Christ's death is understood in a saving way only where substitutionary expressions are present; not recognizing the soteriological significance of themes consistent with the Christus Victor model, she assumes that Acts' early kerygma attaches no saving significance to the cross.

calling this dominion legal because (1) Its frequently unjust operation, and (2) God's ultimate opposition to it. Others, however, regard the power's dominion as legal because (1) It is the fitting penalty for human sin, and (2) God actually executes judgment by this means (Chap. 16).

Certainly the powers' dominion is not legal, or lawful, in the full sense of these words. There is no universal principle that would obligate God to deal justly with the powers. As Gregory Nazianzus insisted, the Devil operates by means of robbery and violence, and this lays no obligation on God to deal with Satan justly. Nonetheless, the powers' rule may be called "legitimate" in certain ways. As the situation which humans have chosen, it is an appropriate or legitimate kind of punishment. Further, in delivering over sinners to the fruits of their doings, God has clearly allowed the powers to rule them. The dynamics of sin and evil now operate within a certain system or structure which closes off humankind from God's saving presence. In order for salvation to occur, this objective structure, which God has allowed to operate, would have to be altered.

Now suppose God decided to alter this structure by depriving the powers of their dominion. The character of this demonic activity itself would not obligate him to deal justly with it. Nevertheless, we have seen that in this ultimate saving activity, God did not will to operate by coercion or force. Had Jesus exercised his ministry in this way, he would have adopted Satan's own methods! The notion of "legitimacy," then, is a way of saying that although God was not compelled to treat the powers justly, he chose to do so in a way that was consistent with the heart of his redeeming activity.[15] The notion that God deprived the powers of their jurisdiction by legal, or legitimate, means is a way of saying that God worked in a manner entirely consistent with his justice; and yet a manner which allowed his enemies, acting in a way consistent with their own deepest nature, to commit actions which so violated all justice that they were fittingly deprived of their rule over humanity.

This depriving of the powers was legitimate in another way. In general, God exercises judgment by handing violaters over to the fruits of their doings. The punishments which God imposes are not wholly arbitrary and unrelated to the corresponding sins but fitting consequences of them. In depriving the powers of their rule, then, God did not simply snatch their authority away. Instead, God allowed the powers to disqualify themselves. God allowed them to commit actions which violated all justice and true authority, and which manifested

---

[15] Cf. Irenaeus, V, Chap. 1 (1): "the Word of God, powerful in all things, and not defective with regard to his own justice, did righteously turn against that apostasy, and redeem from it His own property, not by violent means, as the [apostasy] has obtained dominion over us at the beginning, when it insatiably snatched away what was not its own, but by means of persuasion, as became a god of coursel, who does not use violent means to obtain what He desires." According to Aulen, "The Greek Fathers find the deepest reason for God's action in an inner, divine necessity, the necessity imposed by his love" (p. 45).

their unfitness to rule. Here again, the notion of legitimacy does not say that God was legally obligated to act in this way but that God chose to act in a consistent way.

This discussion of God's judgment of the powers yeilds significant insights into the character of legal explanations of the atonement. In this case, concepts of legality, or legitimacy, do not constitute universal, rational principles which any historical atoning process must follow. It is not as if reason could determine everything that must be involved in atonement, and that the historical details of how this came to pass are more or less irrelevant. Instead, it appears that the historical process of atonement first occurred. The notion of the devil's deception, including its legal concepts about jurisdiction,was one model that arose to explain it. This model, as explained here, can illuminate certain very profound features of Christ's saving work. It can show how certain of God's actions were consistent, fitting, or legitimate in relation to others. But when one seeks to press the central concepts of this model too far—in particular, if one argues that God's actions were not only "legitimate" in relation to each other but could also be deduced from some universal "legal" principles (such as that God had to treat all creatures, including Satan, with perfect justice)—then the claims of the model begin to contradict what is known of other realities. We will return to these issues in Section VI.

IV. For What Does Christ Save Us?

In discussing how Jesus bore God's judgment, how he bore our sins, and how he defeated the powers, we have been focusing on what he saves us *from*. We have been discussing those objective barriers which kept humankind from god's saving presence, and on how they were removed. Yet if the overall purpose of Christ's work was bringing the kingdom of God, theology must focus at least as much on what he saves us *for*. How did Jesus bring us into the kingdom, the rule, and the presence of God?

A. Jesus' Obedience

Despite their differences, all three models of Christ's death regard his obedience to God as central to his work. Paul summarizes Christ's work with this term (Rom. 5:19, Phil. 2:8) as does Hebrews (5:8–9). The substitutionary theory correctly stresses that Jesus rendered to God that obedience which all people owe but which no one else has performed. Nevertheless, this model normally makes the claim in too general a fashion. The specific ways in which Jesus obeyed God, and thus what concrete obedience really involved, can easily be lost from view.

By emphasizing Jesus' teaching and especially his example, the moral influence (and to some extent the Christus Victor) model(s) fill out the picture of what it means for a human to fully obey God. However, when moral influence theorists argue that Christ's saving work consists chiefly in the impression created by his example, they overlook the stark realism with which the Gospels portray his way to the cross.

Jesus' disciples, who were impressed by his teaching and example as directly as anyone could be, constantly misunderstood him and his mission. As the cross drew nearer, they shuddered and finally fled. His crucifixion made no impression on most of them. They were nowhere near it. As substitutionary theorists correctly stress, before Christ's climactic death could savingly impress anyone, a barrier of misunderstanding and alienation between God and humanity would have to be removed.

Many Christus Victor advocates stress that Jesus had to remove not only external, objective barriers between God and humanity. In addition, the internal, subjective alienation between God and humans was so deep that impressions of Jesus' life and death could not overcome it by themselves. Jesus also worked at a deeper level. He created a new, organic union between humanity and God. His obedience, that is, consisted in "recapitulation." This occurred in two main ways. First, by passing through all stages of growth in communion with God, Jesus joined a mature human nature to the divine. Through Jesus a unity of wills, and one of mutual feeling *sym-pathy* was formed.

Second, this recapitulating obedience had a negative side. Obeying God meant resisting the demonic at those points where Adam and humankind capitulated. How, in concrete terms, did Jesus accomplish this?

Chapter 15 showed Christ rejecting demonic suggestions as to how he might be the Messiah in the wilderness, at Peter's confession, in Gethsemane, and on the cross. Further, his response to his religious and political opponents fills out the picture of what such resistance involves. Jesus did not merely resist evil forces. He first approached them boldly proclaiming and living out God's kingdom. He spoke and did the truth, no matter what the danger or cost. When violently attacked by his enemies, however, Jesus never utilized their own methods in retaliation. He resisted those impulses towards violent acquisition of power, security, and status which motivated his opponents and ultimately all humanity. Instead, he lived his life according to the pattern of God's Servant. Through this kind of recapitulating obedience, Jesus established a human reality inwardly free from demonic dominion and its penalties, and in close communion with God.

B. Jesus' Abandonment

Nevertheless, this human so profoundly joined to God had to pass through the terror of the cross. Jesus' enemies attacked and put him to death. We have seen how, in bearing their judgment, he also bore God's judgment; for God judges by delivering over sinners into the hands of the powers. We have also stressed, however, that this judgment cannot be wholly explained in historical and sociological terms, helpful as they are at a certain level. In order to grasp the full significance of the cross, we must remember that those social forces which killed Christ were ultimately motivated by greater, mysterious powers which sought to cut off all humanity from God and his kingdom.

Chapter 15 showed that they do so by playing upon human desires for powers, security, and status, which are intertwined with human fears of suffering, insecurity, and humiliation. But suffering, insecurity, and humiliation are fearful (and therefore power, security, and status are appealing) because people, deep down, fear death (cf. Heb. 2:14–15). Not death simply as the cessation of biological existence, but Death as ultimate banishment from the Life of God (Chaps. 8 and 9); Death as the ultimate futility, as the threat that everything for which we are created will never be attained, that existence will never be anything but a ceaseless, senseless round of disease, failure, disappointment, and pain.

Now religious and political forces in service of these powers operate by promising their adherents powers, status, and prestige, and by inflicting suffering, insecurity, and humiliation on those who oppose them. And the more powerful a religious or political force is, the more forcefully can it, through these means, expose one to the ultimate power of Death. If Israel's leaders had someone put to death, most Israelites would regard that person as definitively cursed by God (cf. Gal. 3:13). And perhaps no more effective means than Roman crucifixion has been devised for injecting physical torture with public dishonor and shame.[16]

On the cross, then, Jesus is not only a victim of social forces. Through the punishments which they inflict, he feels himself exposed to and handed over to Death's power. The one who had lived in perfect communion with God his Father, who had known his life and love as no human before him, now finds himself abandoned. Slowly death chokes and strangles the life which had surrounded him. Slowly he sinks into the abyss of futility, despair and God-forsakenness which threatens and ultimately rules all humans. "My God! My God!" he screams, "Why hast thou forsaken me!" (Mark 15:34). Jesus experiences the weight of being full cursed, fully condemned, and irreversibly cast off. In this way Christ bears not only the opposition of social powers, not only the sins of all humans who participate in them, but also the pitiless and irrevocable curse of sin and death. And since God's judgment consists in handing over sinners to this ultimate fate, on the cross Jesus also bears the judgment and wrath of God.

We have argued, however (Section II), that although Jesus really does bear the horror of God's wrath, this wrath is exercised indirectly. Jesus, that is, experiences the abandonment by God, the exclusion from God's presence, that constitute the fitting penalty for all who have turned from God to the powers. Nevertheless, this does not mean that Jesus experiences direct anger and hatred from his Father. We have just shown how complete a unity of wills and of

[16] See esp. Hengel, *Crucifixion*, pp. 22–63.

love between Father and son permeated Jesus' life.[17] As Jesus suffers under the finality of death, then, his Father's attitude continues to be one of love. And when a loving parent watches a beloved child die, the parent's attitude cannot but be one of wrenching, heartfelt grief. For Paul, this giving up of his Son constituted an overwhelming manifestation of the Father's love. "If God is for us," Paul exclaimed, "who can be against us? He who did not spare his own Son, but gave him up for us all, will he not also give us all things with him?" That God's love should go to such length convinced Paul "that neither death, nor life, nor angels, nor principalities, nor things present, nor things to come, nor powers, nor height, nor depth, nor anything else in all creation, will be able to separate us from the love of God in Christ Jesus our Lord" (Rom. 8:32, 38–39).

When we consider not only Jesus' life, where a human being came into communion with God, but also Jesus' death, we begin to realize how profoundly God also came into union with humanity. For on the cross, as the Son suffers abandonment and death, and as the Father suffers grief and loss, God enters into human weakness and suffering and death. As the Son sinks down under the weight of all that Death and Hell can heap upon him, and as the Father above him grieves, all the pain, suffering, fear and hopelessness which afflict humanity pass, as it were, between them.[18] The violence of all these fears and powers threaten to tear the unity of Father and Son apart. As Satan, through the Roman soldiers and the Israelite leaders, taunts Jesus on the cross, he is once again tempted to come down from it, and finally become the conquering Messiah. And yet, as Jürgen Moltmann has said, precisely when "Father and

---

[17] Although we have focused on Jesus' obedience as human obedience in this chapter, we do not mean to say that Jesus was a mere human being who was gradually filled with and joined to God, as classical liberal Christologies assert (Chap. 14). In addition to being fully human, Jesus was also the fully divine Son throughout the course of his obedience. We can clarify this complex relationship, however, only in Vol. II, Chap. 17.

[18] In this context the notion of payment of a "price" *at least equivalent* to the penalty for all sin has a meaning. When we understand Christ's bearing of God's judgment not merely as his bearing of social opposition but also as his bearing of the powers' enmity, we recognize that his crucifixion is their climactic assault upon God. Now that they have God's son in their clutches, Death and Hell exert their utmost violence to annihilate him. In other words, all the force which has been exerted against sinners throughout history is now focused and concentrated at one point. (Something similar is expressed by the notion that Christ's death is a "recapitulation" of all the righteous blood ever shed [Matt. 23:35; cf. note 11 above].) The power of Death which Christ feels coming against him is thus at least "equivalent to" the horror and the pain which afflicts all the condemned. The notion "equivalence" underlines the tremendous strength which these powers have, and gives assurance that there is nothing with which they can afflict us that Christ has not already borne.

Son are most deeply separated in forsakenness," they "at the same time are most inwardly one in their surrender."[19] The unity between Son and Father holds. And, as Hebrews 9:14 tells us, the Spirit also participates, enabling the Son to keep offering up himself. Consequently,

> All human history, however much it may be determined by guilt and death, is taken up into this "history of God".... There is no suffering which in this history of God is not God's suffering; no death which has not been God's death in the history upon Golgotha. There is no life, no fortune and no joy which have not been integrated by his history into the eternal joy of God.[20]

C. Summary

The concrete reality of Jesus' saving work can be helpfully illuminated, as moral influence theorists propose, by tracing the historical and sociological dynamics involved in his earthly history. Nevertheless, its full significance cannot be grasped unless one stresses that, by means of these forces, a struggle between God and deadly supra-human powers was being waged. It is also necessary to stress, as substitutionary theorists do, that Jesus saved us *from* an objective situation which can be described, at least in part, by legal terms. Beyond this, however, theology must also perceive that Jesus saved us *for* communion with God, and that this can best be expressed in relationald terms. Jesus bridges the alienation between God and humanity not only by breaking the dominion of those powers which separate them but by bringing humanity back to God, and by bringing God into human experience, by means of his own person.

Nonetheless, this communion was not fully attained through his death. In dying, Jesus was, in fact, abandoned by and cut off from God. And neither was his triumph over the powers complete. For although they brought themselves under judgment by putting him to death, this was by no means apparent. In fact, in killing Jesus, they seemed to show that his messianic claims were false, and that their opposition to him had been justified. Consequently, the barrier constituted by the powers' dominion could be done away and communion between God and humanity definitively established only through Jesus' resurrection.

---

[19] *The Crucified God*, p. 244.

[20] Ibid., p. 246. We do not interpret this assertion in a universalistic sense, as Moltmann may perhaps intend. For us, to say that God takes upon, and into, himself the sin and pain of all humanity, need not imply that all will participate in this salvation. Although God's action is sufficient to provide salvation for everyone, in our view people must still turn to him and from the history of sin and pain in order to participate in it [cf. Chap. 8].

V. Jesus' Death as a Sacrifice

Before we move on to Jesus' resurrection, we note that one general model often used to explain Christ's work has so far been largely ignored: that of sacrifice. Biblical data concerning sacrifice has so often been used to support the substitutionary (and to a lesser extent the moral influence) theory, that our own view cannot be complete unless we take it into account. Moreover, consideration of this data can help test the adequacy of our own view. We must ask whether the aspects of sacrifice stressed by the substitutionary and moral influence models are consistent with it. In addition, the adequacy of our perspective will be enhanced if we can show that certain dimensions of sacrifice, perhaps hitherto largely unnoticed, correspond to or enhance our explanation of Christ's work.

Most explanations of sacrifice begin either with very ancient, extra-biblical roots of the practice or else with the Old testament's explicit sacrificial literature. Many studies of the former kind have given rise to "gift," "communion," or "life" theories of sacrifice. The latter kind have often supported substitutionary theories.

In line with our view of revelation as history, we begin our inquiry from the actual function of sacrifice in Israel's salvation history. In many different ways, sacrifice had what we might call an "expressive" function. Many sacrifices were expressions of gratitude.[21] Others emphasized or sealed inner attitudes or desires; they underlined the seriousness of sincere cries for help[22] or of vows.[23] In particular, they could seal an agreement or a covenant.[24]

Sacrifice played an important role during Abraham and Sarah's walk in pursuit of the promise. Years of waiting for Yahweh's fulfillment raised gnawing doubts about its reliability. In response to Abraham's desire to "know" that the promise would be fulfilled (Gen. 15:8), Yahweh performed a sacrificial ritual. After Abraham cut some animals in two, Yahweh, enveloped by an eerie darkness, passed a torch between the pieces, repeated the promise, and prophesied its future (Gen. 15:9–21).

This sacrifice, first, was an "ordeal": Yahweh's character and purpose, as well as Abraham's faith, were being put to the test. The sacrifice was a means of vindicating them. Second, the sacrifice illumined past and future history. God's promises, judgments, and future purposes were clarified. Third, although

---

[21] 1 Sam. 6:14-16; 2 Sam. 6:17-18; 1 Kings 3:15; Ps. 27:6, 51:19, 66:13-15, 107:22; John 1:16.

[22] Gen. 46:1-2; Numb. 23:1-5; Judg. 6:19-24, 13:15-20, 20:26, 21:4; 1 Sam. 7: 9-10, 13:8-12; 2 Sam. 24:21-25; 2 Kings 3:27. They are offered to attain forgiveness in Job 1:5 and 42:8.

[23] Numb. 15:3; Judg. 11:30-31; 1 Sam. 2:24-28; Ps. 66:13-15, 116:17-18; Isa. 19:21; John 1:16.

[24] Gen. 31:51-54, Deut. 27:1-8, Josh. 22:34, 1 Kings 8:5, Ezek. 10:19, Ps. 50:5.

Yahweh initiated the sacrifice, human obedience was essential to its completion. Finally, God was not only its initiator but also its primary actor. As Yahweh passed the torch between the halves of the animals, he was declaring, "Let me be torn in pieces if I do not perform this covenant!"[25] Every covenant included sanctions, or penalties, for non-fulfillment. Here Yahweh was taking these sanctions upon himself.

These elements were fundamental to other important Old testament sacrifices, such as Abraham's sacrifice of Isaac (Genesis 22), the Passover (Exodus 12), and the Day of Atonement (Leviticus 16). Most significantly, they may be found in the institution of the covenant (Exodus 19–24) with Israel. This situation was also one of testing: Yahweh came to prove and test the people, that they might truly believe (Exod. 19:9, 20:20). Their response of obedience was essential (Exod. 19:8; 24:3,7). Nevertheless, God initiated the entire process (Exod. 19:9, 11, 17–20: 20:1, 20; 24:9–11). The covenant was sealed when sacrificial blood was thrown both on the Altar, representing Yahweh, and on the people. It was called "the blood of the covenant which Yahweh made" (Exod. 24:8). As in his sacrifice for Abraham, Yahweh committed himself to maintain the relationship and to be torn in pieces rather than to let it fail.

This divine initiation also lay behind the institution of particular features of the covenant. For example, it might at first appear that the priests and the altar were sanctified by the mysterious, indwelling potency of sacrificial blood (Exod. 29:21, 37). Ultimately, however, they were sanctified only by the glorious presence of Yahweh (Exod. 29:43–45; cf. Lev. 9:6, 23–24). In general, Israel's sacrificial system was able to provide atonement not because of any power inherent in her rites or in the things sacrificed. Instead, the entire sacrificial system was a gift given by Yahweh. Sacrifice was efficacious only because Yahweh appointed it as the means whereby people could come to him—and ultimately because God's own commitment, God's own willingness to be torn in pieces for the sake of the covenant, lay behind it.

These biblical dimensions of sacrifice, all too briefly sketched, illuminate in four ways the meaning of Christ's death.[26] First, we note that such sacrifices involve a substitutionary element. Down through their history, Yahweh's people

[25] A covenant "as a commitment has to be confirmed by an oath…Gen. 21:22ff.; 26:26ff; Deut. 29:10ff.; Josh. 9:15-20; 2 Kings 11:4; Ezek. 16:8, 17:33ff.; which included most probably a conditional imprecation: 'May thus and thus happen to me if I violate the obligation.' The oath gives the obligation its binding validity, and therefore we find…the pair of expression: …covenant and oath' (Gen. 26:28; Deut. 29:12, 14, 21; Ezek. 16:59, 17:18)." (TDOT II, p. 256; cf. p. 259 on the standard expression, "to cut a covenant.") In Genesis 15, the sacrifice functions as such an oath. Sacrifice as passing between the halves of animals is found explicitly in Jer. 34:18–20 (cf. 1 Sam. 11:7).

[26] Markus Barth, Was Christ's Death a Sacrifice (Edinburgh: Oliver & Boyd, 1961), pp. 16-27. The understanding of sacrifice outlined here is suggested in large part by Barth.

repeatedly broke the covenant, bringing its sanctions upon themselves. To speak of Christ's death as a sacrifice, then, is to say that in Christ, God stepped in and took those covenant sanctions upon himself, letting himself be torn in pieces rather than forsaking the covenant. Sacrificial language provides another way of saying, as does the notion of ransom, that the estrangement caused when God's people break their relationship with him cannot be overcome unless God steps in and takes the pain and the penalties of that estrangement upon himself.

Second, considered as such a sacrifice, Christ's death helped answer the burning question which many were asking in his day. Many Israelites were wondering whether Yahweh had forsaken them. They wondered whether God would ever vindicate "the poor" who suffered and would ever fulfill his ancient promise. They questioned whether Yahweh was loving, powerful, and just enough to do so (Chap. 14). But if in Christ's sacrifice God had borne the covenant sanctions, this question was answered in two ways. On one hand, the fact that Jesus had to bear these sanctions revealed the depth of their own sin. Whereas Yahweh seemed to have forsaken them, Christ's death showed that they had forsaken God. In addition, it showed that despite this sin, God had remained faithful to them. Yahweh had not forgotten his promise nor forsaken his people. God had remained so faithful that he was willing to take all the sin, evil, and death caused by his people upon himself.

We have argued that the earliest Christians came to this awareness partly by recognizing the parallels between Jesus' fate and that of Isaiah's servant (Section III). Isaiah 52:13—53:12 indicates the close linkage between judicial and sacrificial language. Jesus, like the servant, had been a victim of injustice (Isa. 53:8–9) in which they had participated, and by which they were condemned. Nevertheless, the servant's unjust death had also been an expiatory sacrifice by which his killers were forgiven (Isa. 53:10, 12). Notice that in this passage, which lay at the roots of the growing awareness from which much of the New Testament's understanding of Christ's work developed, neither judicial nor sacrificial models are primary. Instead, they provide means of explaining the servant's historic task of calling Israel to Yahweh and bringing light and justice to the Gentiles.

Third, Christ's death, so understood, had the character of an "ordeal." It was an act by which God and his people were tested, and in light of which Yahweh's historical dealings were illuminated. It was a public expression and manifestation of God's righteous character. This helps explain why one central text which presents Christ's death as an expiation also describes it a public revelation of this kind. Why did God "put forward" Christ "as an expiation"? "This was to show God's righteousness...it was to prove at the present time that he himself is righteous, and the one who justifies through the faithfulness of Jesus Christ" (Rom. 3:25–26).

Fourth, understood as a bearing of the covenant sanctions, Christ's death was not only a revelation of God's righteousness but also of God's love. This explains why Paul could use the sacrificial phrase that Jesus dies "for us (me)" as an exclamation of wonder. For if Christ died "for us" even while we were God's enemies, then how great must be the love of God (Rom. 5:6–10)! It is so great that nothing can ever separate us from it (Rom. 8:31–32; cf. Gal. 2:20)! This also explains how John could describe Christ's expiatory sacrifice, which was the laying down of his life for us, as the greatest revelation of God's love (1 John 3:16, 4:9–10).

These last considerations show that God's judgment and God's love are not so opposed as substitutionary and moral influence advocates have sometimes insisted. God's love is actualized and realized in Christ's death precisely because it involves suffering under the horrible dominion of the powers and the severity of the covenant sanctions to which people are consigned by God's judgment. God's love is overwhelingly great precisely because it is willing to bear these things. Or, to state it alternatively, the seriousness of God's judgment can be apprehended only when one sees that nothing but his supreme act of love could overcome it.

VI. Atonement and Rationality

Despite the many differences between the substitutionary and moral influence models, most versions of each have this in common: they seek to explain Christ's work as the actualization of certain universal principles knowable through reason apart from biblical revelation. As such, they raise a question similar to that discussed under general revelation (Chap. 13): Are the basic features of God's saving work so unusually accessible that God's historical and propositional revelation is not necessary for people to understand them, and perhaps even for them to be saved by means of them? If so, was Jesus' history simply a helpful illustration of how these principles operate but not necessary to the actualization of salvation itself?

Horace Bushnell sought to deduce the main features of Christ's work from a moral law—the law of vicarious love. In this respect, his work was much like that of another moral influence advocate, Albrecht Ritschl. For Ritschl, Kant's ethical concept of the kingdom of ends was funcitonally equivalent to the theological notion of the kingdom of God, and governed his Christology. The notion that God's kingdom is a social reality known of and longed for in many philosophies and religions (such as Leonardo Boff's "fundamental utopia of the human heart") is found in many liberal and liberation Christologies (Chap. 14). It is so central to their understanding of Christ's work that we must consider it first.

Is the kingdom which Christ brought no more than an historical actualization of an universal moral ideal? Ever since the Enlightenment, it has often been argued that the fundamental equality of all humans—whether Jew or Gentile, rich or poor, male or female—is a truth knowable to reason alone. Perhaps Jesus' "Great reversal," which challenged unfair distinctions among people on the basis of race, wealth, or class, involved no more than putting this moral ideal into practice.

Our discussion of the kingdom's coming, however, showed that it involved much more than this (Chap. 15). God's dawning reign involved the transformation of nature. Yet most rational social theories, such as Kant's (whom Ritschl followed in this respect), also argue that nature is governed by unbreakable natural laws. Even more significantly, the kingdom entered into conflict with the depravity of the human heart, which was under the dominion of demonic forces. But the notion such demonic influence conflicts sharply with most moral theories, for which the human will must be free from all such restraints.

We cannot possibly compare our theological notion of God's kingdom with the utopias found in every religion and philosophy. But we have said enough to illustrate our basic point. Many social and moral ideals, like other basic concepts found in general revelation, correspond in certain respects to the kingdom of God. Yet when the logic of these ideals is worked out in detail, they conflict with it in certain important ways. Chapter 13 showed how this is true of certain rational concepts of God. However similar they may be to the biblical God in some respects, by themselves they point to a deity quite different from him. Taken by itself, for instance, the moral argument for God's existence might well lead to the notion of an inflexible legalist who governs the universe without compassion or mercy.

The same is true of the rational explanations of atonement presented in Chapter 16. For instance, Anselm's notions of God's honor and purpose and of sin seem to lead to a God who becomes incarnate and bears our transgressions. Yet by themselves, they lead to a deity who does so only to maintain his laws and execute his purpose, and whose love need not enter the picture. All this suggests that concepts or models derived from philosophy or other religions might correspond to God's revealed truth at certain points. Theology can use some of them to illumine certain features and relationships of this truth in various apologetic contexts. But when the inherent logic of such concepts is pushed beyond the paramaters of biblical revelation, they can come into contradiction with it.

This chapter's discussion of the notion of the devil's deception has yielded similar results. If one begins from the inherent logic of this model, and seeks to extend it too far, it comes into conflict with other features of biblical revelation. But if one restricts it within a certain range, it can usefully show the appropriateness, or the fittingness, of certain of Christ's atoning actions. Much the same can be said for the model of ransom. It can express and make vivid the biblical insistence that sin produces consequences which can only be overcome at dreadful "cost." Yet it functions best in atonement theory not as a premise from which the fundamental character of Christ's work can be deduced but as a way of illuminating the relationship between Jesus and the network of evil whose power he came to break.

The fundamental notions and the inner logic of Christ's saving work, then, cannot be adequately know through reason alone. The various aspects of this work which reason might apprehend do not, by themselves, lead to truly saving, or "integrating" revelation. Christ's work has a unique, unfathomable quality that models, derived from reason and even from Scripture itself, can only partially and one-sidedly apprehend. That is why theology must stop when it has developed the explanatory features of each model as far as the biblical data allows. That is why it often must let different models stand side by side, clarifying their interrelations only up to a certain point.

To be sure, the human mind would prefer to deduce all significant features of Christ's work from a single model. This is probably why the substitutionary and moral influence models have won so many adherents in theology's history. Once one accepts their fundamental premises, they possess a certain self-evident clarity. This can seem preferable to the paradoxes of the Christus Victor motif. Nevertheless, their premises are so different that the deductions made from them are often antithetical, and have placed their proponents at loggerheads. In contrast, the Christus Victor model can better handle the broad, rich diversity of the biblical data on these themes. Though its paradoxes may frustrate the mind's efforts to pull everything together, it is better able to allow the different emphases of Scripture to make their own witness, and to point beyond all models to the unfathomable mystery of Christ's atonement itself.

CHAPTER EIGHTEEN

The Resurrection of Jesus Christ

Theological reflection concerning Jesus Christ is always guided, consciously or unconsciously, by certain urgent questions. Christologies have usually been guided either by the query: "What must I do to be saved?"; or by the concern: "How can I, and how can we all, become fully human?" The resulting Christologies have tended to be either kerygmatic ("from above"), stressing Christ's divine, saving power; or contextual ("from below"), emphasizing his humanity. We, however, have investigated Christ's work primarily in light of a third urgent question: "Is Jesus the fulfillment of God's promise?" For this was the primary question for Jesus' contemporaries, and it is still alive for people today (Chap. 14).

During the last two chapters, however, the overall importance of this question has perhaps become less evident. Out of respect for theological tradition, we have examined numerous concepts emphasized in discussions of atonement. But such careful analysis may have dissected the overall historical flow of Jesus' work. This chapter, then, must restore this continuity. Previous chapters have shown that the meaning of Jesus' life cannot be separated from the meaning of his death, and that neither has full saving significance apart from his resurrection. Our first task, then, will be to exhibit the meaning of this resurrection, regarded primarily as the answer to the question of whether and how Jesus fulfilled God's ancient promise, and as the culmination of Christ's saving work.

The meaning of Jesus' resurrection however cannot be adequately articulated in our modern world without some understanding of its nature. What kind of event was it? Was it a vision, a hallucination, a physical event? To be sure, during the eighteenth and early nineteenth centuries, authors and pastors often focused too exclusively on exactly what "event" had occurred, and they overlooked the importance of its meaning or "interpretation." But today the tide has reversed. Most theologians discuss the resurrection's meaning at great length, but they are extremely hazy as to its historical character. If one's theological "interpretation" is inseparable from the nature of such an "event," we shall have to examine both carefully. To place the resurrection in the proper broad perspective, we will first examine its meaning. Next we shall consider its nature or historical character.

I. The Meaning of Jesus' Resurrection

A. The Cry for Righteousness

Let us recall the primary question in the minds of Jesus' contemporaries. Almost two thousand years before, Yahweh had promised Sarai and Abram that their posterity would become a great nation, by which "all nations of the earth shall be blessed" (Gen. 12:3). Yet throughout the succeeding centuries fulfillment of this promise often seemed far off. Of course, Israel could remember Yahweh's mighty deliverance of the slaves from Egypt, or the victories of David, or the empire of Solomon. Yet long periods were marked by struggle for survival, intermingled with times of subjugation and captivity. And especially since the amazing return from Babylon, a series of stronger empires had subjected Israel under their sway. Within Israel, moreover, the truly righteous seemed to dwindle to an increasingly small "remnant."

These experiences, we have seen, fueled the burning cry for Yahweh's "righteousness." God's righteousness, was not simply an abstract legal standard. Primarily, it was God's saving act, whereby he punished the wicked, vindicated and rescued his people, and established them in peace. By such an act, Yahweh's faithfulness to his promise and his concern for the oppressed would also be vindicated.[1]

Chapters 8 and 9 showed that questions about God's righteousness are very much alive today. They are, in fact, the great eschatological questions. In all nations, most people have heard rumors of the God of Israel and Jesus, and of the kingdom of justice and peace which he once promised. Over the centuries, in fact, this vision has energized countless reformist and humanitarian impulses, even when their proponents were unaware of their ultimate source. Yet today other forces seem to really control history. The yearning for power, security, and status has spawned a world where a few nations have accumulated overwhelming economic wealth and military might. In other countries, most

---

[1] Chap. 8; for a full discussion, see Vol. II, Chap. 7.

people struggle for mere daily survival. Meanwhile, the massive political and economic forces which shape life in the dominant countries have reduced individuals to insignificance and spawned numerous social problems. And the vast arsenals of nuclear power threaten to annihilate all humanity tomorrow.

Who really controls history? What kind of power really determines its destiny? Are those faint visions of justice, of love, and of international reconciliation just empty wishes? Or are they based on something more solid, despite their extremely tenuous fragility? These are the broad and burning eschatological questions of today. In a more specific, Israelite form, they were also the burning questions of Jesus' day.

In Jesus' day God was "on trial." Long ago, Yahweh had called all nations to a trial (Isa. 43:9–13, 44:6–8, 45:20–21, etc.). Over against the various claims and doubts as to who controlled history, Yahweh had boldly proclaimed:

> Turn to me and be saved, all the ends of the earth! For I am God, and there is no other. By myself I have sworn, from my mouth has gone forth in righteousness a word that shall not return: "To me every knee shall bow, every tongue shall swear!" (Isa. 45:22–23).

Christ's work as a whole may be seen within the framework of such a trial. Jesus comes proclaiming that "the time is fulfilled, and the kingdom of God is at hand!" (Mark 1:15). Yahweh is finally fulfilling his age-old promise! Jesus' powerful healing, teaching, and exorcisms seem to confirm this claim (Matt. 11:2–6 and par). Boundless hope arises in the hearts of his disciples and especially among sinners, Gentiles, the poor, and women. Jesus answers the doubts about Yahweh's righteousness, but in a surprisingly "reversed" way: by claiming that God is already establishing a kingdom in which sinners and the oppressed are blessed, but where the "righteous" and the oppressors are judged. But before long, Jesus' opponents quickly put him on trial. His religious enemies accuse him of blasphemy. His political enemies accuse him of insurrection. With surprising ease, Jesus is captured and killed.

In Jesus' death, to all appearances, a verdict had been passed. His enemies' accusations seemed confirmed: the man was a false Messiah, a dangerous insurrectionary. Or, should one's convictions about Jesus' authenticity persist, the verdict was even more crushing. For then Yahweh himself had been defeated. All hopes for God's kingdom, all expectation for fulfillment of the promise, had been ground underfoot by the relentless march of actual history. Seen from the most profound theological perspective, death and the Devil had attacked God and won. Jesus' death confirmed and vindicated their status as the real Lords of the cosmos.

To apprehend the significance of Jesus' resurrection, theology must pause in wonder and horror before the paradox of the cross. Here the one claiming kingship suffered the torture reserved for the lowest criminals and slaves. The herald of hope died in despair. The one living in closest communion with God expired in most bitter abandonment. Until one has grasped the horrible finality of this "verdict," there can be no understanding of the triumph of the resurrection.[2]

To all appearances, Christ's opponents put him "on trial"; their victory was sealed by his death. In reality, God, in his secret and hidden wisdom, was putting Christ's opponents on trial; their condemnation was sealed by his death. Biblically speaking, however, God's righteousness triumphs neither in the mere passing of a sentence nor in the condemnation of the wicked alone. God's righteousness is fully actualized only when it is revealed: only when it vindicates and rescues his people; only when it begins establishing them in life and peace; only when Yahweh's true character becomes known.

Jesus' resurrection was the reversal of that verdict which the powers thought they had passed on Yahweh and his servant. As such, it was the victory and the revelation of God's righteousness. We may consider its significance from three angles: as the triumph of life, as a legal "sentence," and as a manifestation of God's victory. (We shall consider a fourth aspect, Christ's ascension to Lordship, at the close of this chapter.)

B. The Triumph of Life

The significance of Jesus' resurrection is best conceived in dynamic, organic categories. It was the bursting forth of joy and the establishment of God's people in life and peace which nothing could ever again destroy.

Peter's first sermon affirms that death could not hold Jesus, and presents his resurrection as the glad triumph over "corruption" (Acts 2:24–27, 31; cf. 13:35–37). In Peter's second sermon, Jesus is "the leader (*archegos*) of life" (Acts 3:15, cf. 5:31; Heb. 2:10, 12:2). For Paul, Jesus' resurrection reversed the reign of death which had held sway since Adam; Jesus, the last Adam, "became a life-giving spirit" (1 Cor. 15:21–22, 45)." "Christ was raised from the dead by the glory of the Father, [so that] we too might walk in newness of Life."[3] "If, because of one man's trespass, death reigned through that one man, much more will those who receive the abundance of grace and the free gift of righteousness reign in life through the one man Jesus Christ!" (Rom. 5:17).

1. *The Divine Dimension.* But even though the risen Christ is a source of life, the kerygma uniformly affirms that he *was* raised.[4] In other words, Jesus did not

---

[2] "Here we are faced by the night of the real, ultimate and inexplicable absence of God....Here is the triumph of death, the enemy, the non-church, the lawless state, the blasphemer, the soldiers. Here Satan triumphs over God. Our faith begins at this point where atheists suppose that it must be at an end. Our faith begins with the bleakness and power which is the night of the cross, abandonment, temptation and doubt about everything that exists! Our faith must be born where it is abandoned by all tangible reality; it must be born of nothingness, it must taste this nothingness...in a way no philosophy of nihilism can imagine. (Hans Joachim Iwand, quoted in Moltmann, *The Crucified God*, p. 36.)

[3] Rom. 6:4, cf. 1 Cor. 4:10-11; Col. 3:1-4; 1 Pet. 1:4, 21; John 5:21-29.

[4] Acts 2:32, 3:15, 10:40, 13:33; 1 Thess. 1:10; 1 Cor. 15:4; Rom. 8:34, 10:9.

raise himself. His death was not simply an appearance, a fainting swoon, or a fake. The Son really was abandoned to all the finality and horror of death. Consequently, theology cannot, properly speaking, include his resurrection under "the work of Jesus Christ." The New Testament attributes his resurrection to God the Father[5]; or, more properly, to the Father through the Holy Spirit.[6] Jesus' resurrection is intrinsically related to the outpouring of life because of this agency of the Spirit who bestows life.

As we have examined Jesus' life and death, it has slowly become apparent that the saving work which occurred through him cannot be attributed to him alone. From the beginning of his ministry, he was energized and guided by the Spirit (Mark 1:8, 10, 12). Indeed Matthew and Luke locate the Spirit's work even further back at his very human origin (Matt. 1:20, Luke 1:35). We have also noticed how Jesus' mission, empowered by the Spirit, was carried out in continual obedience to, and in continual dependence on, the one whom he called Father. And the mystery of his death involved a unique relationship of love, pain, grief, and abandonment, between Jesus and his Father, to whom he offered himself through the Spirit (Heb. 9:14).

2. *The Human Dimension.* Considered as a divine act, Christ's resurrection was a work of Father and Spirit; the Son was passive. Considered from its human side, however, it was an exaltation of human nature, in the Son, into the very presence of God. We can best explain this as the completion of that process of "recapitulation" which occurred throughout Jesus' life and death.

As early proponents of the Christus Victor model said, through Jesus' continuous obedience to his Father, in harmony with the Holy Spirit, a human nature passed through all its developmental phases in perfect communion with God. This vital, organic union was never infected by sin. It grew amid, and by means of resistance to, all temptations and sufferings which afflict the human race. By maintaining this obedience up to and through death, this human being passed entirely out of the sphere ruled by demonic forces and the penalties they inflict. By being resurrected, then, this human rose into full communion with God.[7]

But how shall we understand the affirmation that human nature now participates in full communion with God? Early patristic theology sometimes conceived of human nature as a universal metaphysical substance, in which Jesus and all other persons participate, and which is now increasingly permeated by an immortal, divine substance (Chap. 14). Yet so far we have found no basis for

[5] One of the earliest New Testament titles for God is "the one who raised Jesus from the dead" Gal. 1:1; Rom. 4:24, 8:11.

[6] Rom. 1:4, 8:11; 1 Tim. 3:16; 1 Pet. 3:18-19.

[7] "He who has died is freed from sin....Christ being raised from the dead will never die again; death no longer has dominion over him. The death he died he died to sin, once for all, but the life he lives he lives to God" (Rom. 6:7-10; cf. 7:1-4, Gal. 2:19-20).

asserting that all humans are being assimilated into a divine substance. It is better to say, at least provisionally, that we are being transformed by divine energies.

For the New Testament tells us that after Jesus' resurrection his living presence is communicated to us through the Holy Spirit. According to the early kerygma, Christ first poured out the Spirit on the day of Pentecost.[8] According to John, the Spirit makes the teachings and the presence of Christ internally real to us.[9] It is through the Spirit that we know that we abide in Christ, and he in us (1 John 3:24, 4:13; cf. Rom. 5:5-6).

In Volume II we will elaborate on the work of the Holy Spirit. There we will substantiate our claim that the basic mode of our participation in Christ is not by means of sharing in the same substance. Instead, it is a more personal, *sympathetic* sharing of experiences, sufferings, and joys. This sym-pathetic union reached a climactic point when Father, Son, and Spirit opened themselves to the depths of human experience on the cross. Now, through the Son's resurrection, all who are joined to him are welcomed into the divine experience of joy and love. This sharing is mediated by the personal, volitional agency of the Holy Spirit. Therefore it demands our personal, volitional response. We do not participate in Christ, and our human nature is not renewed by him, in a passive manner.

3. *Christ's Present Work.* However theology conceives of this participation, the basic resurrection message is that Jesus has entered into a sphere pervaded by divine life, wholly free from the dominion of the powers and their penalties. From that time on, then, Christ's work has had a present, continuing dimension for his people. Many facets of it are conveyed by the phrase, "in Christ."[10] Especially when we speak of the Church (Vol. II, Chaps. 9–14), we will elaborate it further.

Essentially, we may say that those who are in Christ already participate with him in that sphere of life, free from the powers' dominion. To be sure, since all the powers' *activities* have "not yet" been subjected to Christ's reign, they can still afflict his people. Most fundamentally, however, those who are in Christ are no longer under the powers' dominion. They have been irreversibly incorporated into the reign of indestructible life. This is why evil's worst assaults cannot fully extinguish their hope. For no matter how fiercely all the powers of hell may rage, nothing can separate us from God's love in Christ (Rom. 8:35–39).

The certainty of our victory is indicated by speaking of Jesus, and of his resurrection, as the "firstfruits" of our own resurrection (1 Cor. 15:20, 23; cf.

[8] Acts 2:33, cf. Gal. 4:6. Jesus also "baptized" through the Spirit (Acts 1:5, 11:16 with Mark 1:18 and par).

[9] John 14:25-26, 15:26, 16:13-16; cf. Acts 1:2, 1 Cor. 2:12-13.

[10] See *TWNT*, Vol. 2, pp. 541-43 and Alfred Wikenhauser, *Pauline Mysticism* (Edinburgh: Nelson, 1960), esp. pp. 21-33, 50-65.

James 1:18, Rev. 14:4). As apprehended amid early Christianity's eschatological atmosphere, Jesus' raising was no isolated miracle but the beginning of the end-time resurrection of the righteous (Chap. 7).

In the mean time Christ's people are protected and preserved through his "intercession": through his continual bringing of our concerns and situations into God's presence (Heb. 7:25). When human or demonic enemies seek to accuse or frustrate us, it is Christ, "who died—better—who was raised from the dead, who is at the right hand of God, who indeed intercedes for us!' (Rom. 8:34 When we sin, or are worried by consciousness of our sin, Jesus is our advocate or comforter in the Father's presence (1 John 2:1–2; cf. Isa. 53:12).

This present work of the Son cannot be separated from that of the Spirit. The word which John applies to Jesus, *parakletos*, primarily means one who defends in a legal situation; but also one who, by this means, comforts and encourages another amid struggle. *Parakletos* is also the main term with which Jesus describes the Spirit in John (14:16, 26; 15:26; 16:7). Paul speaks of the Spirit's intercession as helping articulate our deepest thoughts and feelings, and thereby enabling us to petition and praise God (Rom. 8:26–27, Gal. 4:6). Like Christ, the Spirit not only is called the Advocate/Comforter, and not only intercedes for us, but is also the "firstfruits" of the coming Glory (Rom. 8:23).

C. The "Legal" Dimension

Since Jesus' resurrection reversed the "verdict" pronounced by his death, certain facets of its meaning can be well expressed by legal terminology. We remember how the early kerygma presented Christ's death primarily as a murder and thus the resurrection primarily as his vindication and his enemies' condemnation. John, moreover, speaks of the world being convicted of sin and of "the ruler of this world" being judged, because Jesus went "to his Father" (John 16:8–11).[11]

In Chapter 17, we argued that legal terminology can express the objectivity, the unvarying consistency, of certain states of affairs. Legal terms do not mean that reality is structured by superior rational laws which even God must obey. But they do indicate, in connection with sin, that God had allowed certain processes, whereby evil repeatedly brings its own murderous consequences upon itself, to operate unhindered until God himself had suffered at their hands.

In connection with Christ's resurrection, legal terms can express that this

---

[11] Moreover, Christ's resurrection is sometimes called the fundamental moment in an important legal process: justification. According to an early formulation, Jesus "was manifested in the flesh, justified in the Spirit." According to Paul, Jesus "was put to death for our trespasses, and raised for our justification" (1 Tim. 3:16, Rom. 4:25). See Markus Barth and Verne Fletcher, *Acquittal by Resurrection* (New York: Holt, Reinhart and Winston, 1964). We will deal with justification fully in Vol. II, Chap. 7.

objective situation has changed. Since the powers have been judged, they no longer have the right to imprison sinners under conditions where God's renewing life does not reach them. Legal terminology can emphasize that this objective situation had to be altered before God's saving life could become subjectively effective.

Nevertheless, certain legal principles (such as "payment of an equivalent ransom remits punishment") do not form the ultimate foundations upon which all relationships between God and Satan, life and death, are based. Satan's dominion over humans begins in a dynamic struggle of wills, of emotions, of minds, of entire persons. Death is the inevitable termination of personal lives lived out in subjection to this dominion. A legal principle (e.g., "sin deserves death") can only broadly describe one result which inevitably issues from such a situation. Theology, then, cannot best articulate death's deepest reality by regarding the committing of a legal infraction, and the assigning of a legal penalty, as its ultimate foundation. Nor is the entire dynamic struggle of wills and persons its secondary expression or result.

In the same way, the life which the risen Christ bestows is not best conceived as based on the legal transfer to us of certain merits which Jesus earned. We have seen that this life is a dynamic reality; we participate in it personally and organically. To be sure, Jesus "acquired" it by obeying the Father throughout his life. Yet this consisted primarily in the growth of an organic union (through "recapitulation"). And when that life is bestowed upon us, it is, as even Anselm recognized, better understood as a gift rather than as an obligatory legal grant.

In short, theology can best articulate God's "work" by means of models which are historical, organic, and personal. By themselves, legal concepts abstract from the living reality of processes and relationships. They can grasp only those features which are clear-cut and precisely definable. Yet once any relationship is understood primarily in terms of laws, its deeper dimensions may be overlooked. When Christ's death, for instance, is regarded primarily as the payment of a penalty, the titanic struggle between divine love and Satanic violence can can easily be obscured. Similarly, by regarding Christian living primarily as a matter of keeping rules, one can become blind to the deepest, volitional roots of sin and obedience.

Proponents of the substitutionary model often argue that rival theories fail to take sin seriously enough. On the contrary, however, any model which explains Christ's work primarily in legal terms risks minimizing the awesome but often subtle volitional power of sin, which enslaves the world and the human heart at a far deeper level than can be described by any set of laws.

On the other hand, Christ's work has a certain decisiveness which historical, organic, and personal concepts (precisely because of their fluidity and dynamism) cannot best represent. Legal concepts can better express the objectivity and definiteness of, and the contrast between, those relationships existing before and after the irreversible triumph of eschatological salvation. Legal conceptuality, then, is essential to satisfactory articulation of Christ's work. Yet it functions somewhat as do propositions in communicating revelation. Revelation is a personal and historical process; yet one which flows, as it were, within certain contours and in a certain direction which only propositions can shape (Chap. 12). Similarly, God's saving work is primarily a personal and historical drama; yet those saving acts centering on Christ have a decisiveness which legal concepts can best articulate.

D. The Manifestation of God's Victory

A biblical trial is not completed with the mere passing of a sentence. It includes the actual punishment of the wicked and the establishment of the righteous in life and peace. And beyond this, it includes the open, public manifestation of the righteousness of the judge. When God's righteousness is manifested in this way, God's act of salvation also becomes an act of revelation.

In Jesus' life and death, Yahweh himself was on trial. Long ago Yahweh had called all nations to a trial (Isa. 45:19–23). Yet passing centuries seemed to show that he could not fulfill his promise, could not rescue his righteous people who called upon him. The stark reality of history seemed to have proven that Yahweh was at best weak and less than the true God; at worst, that Yahweh was unrighteous and unfaithful. Jesus' life, death and resurrection not only vindicated the Son as Yahweh's Messiah but also Yahweh himself. How did this occur?

Jesus' opponents claimed that they were ultimately in control of history. They consisted of intertwined demonic, religious, and political forces (Chap. 15). For all three, deceit (appearing other than they truly were) was essential to their success. Demonic forces operate in hidden ways (cf. Vol. II, Chap. 6). They work through other individuals and structures. Moreover, "Satan disguises himself as an angel of light...[and] his servants also disguise themselves as servants of righteousness" (2 Cor. 11:14–15).

Jesus' religious opponents appeared to be the guardians of Yahweh's revealed religion. Their piety was highly visible and exemplary (Matt. 6:1–6, 23:5–7, Luke 14:7, etc.). Like religious leaders in most times and places, they claimed to be the necessary mediators of divine favor. Yet as they surrounded Jesus to add his blood to that of the prophets, Jesus likened them to "whitewashed tombs, which outwardly appear beautiful, but within they are full of dead men's bones and uncleanness. So you also outwardly appear righteous, but within you are full of hypocrisy and iniquity!" (Matt. 23:27–28).

Jesus' political opponents liked to appear as "benefactors" (Luke 22:25) They built monuments and public works, and they held festivals to display their munificence.[12] Like political leaders in all times and places, they publicized themselves as the promoters and necessary guardians of social good. Yet Jesus contrasted their ways sharply with those of his kingdom. There "whoever

---

[12] See Bruce Malina, *The New Testament World: Insights from Cultural Anthropology* (Atlanta: Knox, 1981), Chap. 2.

would be great among you must be your servant, and whoever would be first among you must be slave of all" (Mark 10:43-44 and par).

Finally, those who complained that Yahweh would or could not deliver them appeared to themselves more righteous than they really were. Like most people in all times and places who find God inactive and far off, they were unaware of factors within themselves that helped keep God at a distance.

To reveal himself as he truly was, God came among us. And what did Israel's religious leaders do? Rather than welcome Yahweh's Messiah and place themselves in his service, they found him an intolerable threat to their institutions and practices. From early on, they found this danger so great that they joined forces with their Roman enemies to eliminate him (Mark 2:6,). And what did the alleged guardians of social order, the apparent creators of world peace do? They found an intolerable threat in Christ's concern for those oppressed by their social system—the poor, the sick, and women. Although Jesus broke no laws and mounted no military threat, these guardians of legality condemned him in violation of those very laws they claimed to enforce.[13]

And what did the multitudes do? At first, when Jesus came with marvelous healings and teachings, the multitudes welcomed him. But when opposition to him grew, when his sayings became harder to understand and even harder to bear, they began to turn against him too. Some simply turned aside. Others fled. Some simply became indifferent. Others cheered for his execution.

Simply by coming among us, God revealed the truth about human and demonic forces. Religious and social institutions that appeared to serve Yahweh and the common good proved irrevocably opposed to God and his kingdom. All those who in one way or another thought that they longed for God's righteousness collaborated with those forces who killed him.

All this, of course, was not revealed until the resurrection. Only then did it become clear that those who had sought to preserve religion, society or their own skins had in fact participated in the murder of God.[14] Only then could the earliest Christians acknowledge as their own the amazed, repentant confession: "Surely he has borne *our* griefs, and carried *our* sorrows; yet we esteemed him stricken, smitten by God, and afflicted" (Isa. 53:4). And only in light of Jesus' resurrection could it be said that God "disarmed the principalities and

---

[13] "What does Pilate do? He does what politicians have more or less always done...he attempts to rescue and maintain order in Jerusalem and thereby at the same time to preserve his own position of power, by surrendering the clear law, for the protection of which he was actually installed!" (Karl Barth, *Dogmatics in Outline,* p. 111).

[14] Chap. 17 showed how those who actually did this are linked to all other humans through a solidarity in sin and evil which can be partially expressed in sociological terms, but which is ultimately a participation in the dominion of the powers. Thus neither the Romans, nor Israel's leaders, nor the Jewish nation as a whole are ultimately more responsible than anyone else for Jesus' death.

powers and made a public example of them, triumphing over them in him" (Col. 2:15). As Hendrikus Berkhof has said, the powers

> are unmasked as false gods by their encounter with Very God....Yet this is only visible to men when they know that God himself had appeared on earth in Christ. Therefore we must think of the resurrection as well as of the cross. The resurrection manifests what was already accomplished at the cross....
>
> Christ has 'disarmed' the Powers. The weapon from which they had heretofore derived their strength is struck out of their hands. The weapon was the power of illusion, their ability to convince men they were the divine regents of the world, ultimate certainty and ultimate direction, ultimate happiness and the ultimate deity for small, dependent humanity. Since Christ we know that this is an illusion. We are called to a higher destiny; we have higher orders to follow and we stand under a greater protector.[15]

In Jesus' resurrection, then, not only were his people established in life, and not only were his enemies judged, but God's character was revealed through all of this. The resurrection revealed that God had indeed fulfilled his age-old promise. Yahweh had indeed sent his Messiah and established his kingdom. What's more, as the early church would come to apprehend with increasing profundity, God's particular way of coming among them (as a humble, suffering servant, especially on the cross) revealed unsuspected depths in the love of God.

II. The Nature of Jesus' Resurrection

So far, we have focused on the meaning of Jesus' resurrection. Yet our vivid language about it as establishing life, judging God's enemies, and revealing God's righteousness can ring strangely hollow in modern ears. Those who think seriously about such exalted claims will wonder: Is all this just mere rhetoric? After Jesus' death did something really occur? If so, exactly what was it? A vision? An hallucination? Or if something more physical in nature was supposed to have occurred, how can we possibly believe in it? In order to clarify the meaning of Jesus' resurrection in today's context, theology must also inquire as to its nature.

A. The Resurrection in Modern Theology

Until the eighteenth Century, almost everyone assumed that Jesus' resurrection was a physical event, though an unusual one. When liberal theologians challenged this assumption, they did so largely in the name of science; therefore they sought to provide alternative historical explanations for what had occurred. Some picked up the suggestion found in Matthew that Jesus' disciples stole his body from the tomb and fabricated the resurrection story (Matt.

---

[15] *Christ and the Powers* (Scottdale, Pa: Herald, 1977), p. 31.

27:64).[16] Others, including Schleiermacher, argued that Jesus did not really die: he fainted, or "swooned," and later made his way out of the tomb.[17]

Even some liberals found such explanations unconvincing. For the disciples had fled in terror and despair from the cross. It is extremely unlikely that they would steal Jesus' body and then, while knowingly proclaiming a lie, exhibit the courage and conviction that founded the church.[18] The "swoon theory" is also highly problematic. How could the Romans, such experts in crucifixion, have failed to be sure that Jesus was dead? How could someone 90 percent dead push away the enormous boulder which sealed his tomb?

Given the weaknesses of such theories, most who rejected the bodily resurrection ceased explaining what happened to Jesus' corpse. They assumed that it had remained in the tomb. They came to regard his resurrection as a series of visions. Those who had been deeply impressed by Jesus' love and power began experiencing his presence as something continuing, which death could not overcome. Given their "mythological" ways of perceiving reality, they spontaneously, and without intentional deception, embellished their experiences with elements from pagan myths and legends.[19]

Today, however, few theologians seek to explain the *nature* of Jesus' resurrection at all; neither in objective, historical terms nor in subjective, experiential ones. Sometimes they argue that the earliest Christians made no effort to affirm that it was a generally observable, spatio-temporal event. Peter, for instance, admits that Jesus appeared "not to all the people but to us who were chosen by God as witnesses, who ate and drank with him after he rose from the dead" (Acts 10:41). Paul, moreover, placed his own vision of the risen Lord in the same list as the earliest appearances (1 Cor. 15:5-8). Of course, the resurrection stories in the Gospels do stress its physical character. Yet they were

[16] E.g., as propounded by H. S. Reimarus (1694-1768). See Charles Talbert, ed., *Reimarus: Fragments* (Philadelphia: Fortress, 1971; [originally published 1774-78]), pp. 153-210.

[17] Friedrich Schleiermacher, *The Life of Jesus* (Philadelphia: Fortress, 1975 [originally published in 1832]), pp. 415-65. For a more recent presentation of such an approach, see Hugh Schonfield, *The Passover Plot* (New York: Random, 1965).

[18] See, e.g., Albert Ross (under the pseudonym Frank Morrison), *Who Moved the Stone?* (New York: Barnes & Noble, 1930), pp. 103-16, 145-65.

[19] This type of explanation was first popularized by D. F. Strauss, who criticized Schleiermacher's "swoon theory" in *The Christ of Faith and the Jesus of History* (Philadelphia: Fortress, 1977 [originally published in 1865]), pp. 121-57. For the fullest development of Strauss' view, see *The Life of Jesus Critically Examined* (Philadelphia: Fortress, 1972; originally published in 1840), pp. 691-744.

composed much later and are colored by legendary elements.[20] One can conclude, then, that the resurrection's nature was a belated, secondary concern for
New Testament writers. Following their lead, then, theology should be concerned about its *meaning*.

This orientation is strengthened by modern ways of studying the resurrection
accounts. Form criticism regards them as shaped largely through concerns and
experiences of early communities. Redaction criticism studies their shaping by
individual biblical writers. Since both methods focus on subjective responses
to the resurrection, questions as to whether anything actually happened to
Jesus can be lost from view. Although this need not be the case, both methods
can lead to or be dominated by the assumption that the resurrection accounts
are largely the creative productions of their authors.[21]

When one supplements this biblical data and these methods of study with
the fact that claims about a bodily resurrection appear problematic to the modern, "scientific" mind, it is small wonder that contemporary theology focuses
almost entirely on the resurrection's meaning. However, if one can say little
about the resurrection as an event (its nature) one will really be able to say little about the meaning of the resurrection. Instead, the meaning of Jesus' resurrection will become equivalent to a subjective illumination of the deeper
significance of his life and/or his death. For Rudolf Bultmann, for instance,
*"faith in the resurrection is really the same thing as faith in the saving efficacy of the
cross."*[22] Jesus' resurrection, that is, was not a distinct historical occurrence,
happening sometime after his death. Instead "Cross and resurrection form a
single, indivisible cosmic event."[23] "Resurrection" is a mythological way of expressing the meaning of Christ's death.

We have argued, however, that Jesus' resurrection contrasted radically with
his death—and with many features of his life. Indeed, the gap between his humiliation and his exaltation is perhaps as profound as any paradox in Christology (Chap. 14). To be sure, Jesus' resurrection did reveal certain truths about
his life (say, that he really was the Messiah) and his death (such as, that the
powers were judged at the cross). Nevertheless, we have seen that the deepest
truths in Scripture are often those which become true, which prove themselves
true in the process of struggle (Chap. 12). In the fullest sense, then, Jesus be-

[20] See Reginald Fuller, *The Formation of the Resurrection Narratives* (Philadelphia:
Fortress, 1980). For more conservative interpretations of the evidence, see John
Alsup, *The Post-Resurrection Appearance Stories of the Gospel Tradition* (Ph. D. disser-
tation, Munich, 1973) and Grant Osborne, *The Resurrection Narratives: A Redactional
Study* (Grand Rapids: Baker, 1984.)

[21] For a critique of form criticism's usual approach, see Moltmann, *Theology of Hope*,
pp. 182-190. For a brief overview of redaction criticism's approach, see Grant Osborne, pp. 32-40. Osborne's work is an effort to utilize redaction criticism without
making such an assumption.

[22] *Kerygma and Myth* (New York: Harper, 1961), p. 41.

[23] Ibid., p. 39.

came the Messiah and the powers were judged, at his resurrection. Had Jesus not been raised, he would have been neither Messiah nor Lord over the powers (cf. Acts 2:36). On the contrary, the powers would have triumphed over him. The significance of Jesus' life and death was not merely illuminated but actualized "in power" (cf. Rom. 1:4) by his resurrection. Moreover, we have insisted that something really new occurred when the Father raised the Son through the Spirit. Life triumphed and was poured out in a qualitatively new manner. Humanity was decisively released from the dominion (even if not from every influence) of the powers.

The significance of Christ's resurrection, then, is more than the subjective illumination of the significance of his life and death. Consequently, we cannot articulate its specific meaning unless we can say something about his resurrection itself, about its nature as an event.

B. The Objectivity of the Resurrection

Response to Christ's resurrection certainly involves more than intellectually affirming that an event having certain characteristics once took place. Jesus' resurrection radically transforms the subjectivity of anyone encountered by it. Still we insist, as we did in discussing eschatology and revelation, that human subjects are most profoundly changed not merely when new depths of their internal experience are opened up but when they are encountered by another person or by significantly altered, objective circumstances. Human subjects open up, blossom, and are transformed in response to realities beyond themselves.

Close examination of the biblical records shows that the earliest Christians understood Jesus' resurrection as the raising of his body. While Peter acknowledged that Jesus did not appear publicly to everyone, he emphasized that those who did see him "ate and drank with him" (Acts 10:41). While Paul added his own vision of Christ to the list of resurrection appearances (1 Cor. 15:5-9), one can hardly assume that he thought of it as like them in every important respect. Indeed, his very inclusion of his own experience highlighted important differences (15:8-9). Paul insists that our coming resurrection, of which Christ is the "firstfruits" (15:23), will be physical, even though the exact relationship between our present mortal body and our future spiritual body remains a mystery (15:35–44).

Of course, early reports of Jesus' resurrection do not stress its physical character as much as do the gospel stories. However, there was no real need for them to do so. The notion of a person or a "soul" living apart from one's body was foreign to the Semitic mindset of the earliest Christians. Indeed, had Jesus reappeared while his body was in the grave, *that* would have called for explanation. (We find no traces of this.) Not until the kerygma had penetrated deeply into the Greek world did the physical characteristics of the resurrection become problematic. This is probably why they were not emphasized before the gospel accounts were written.[24]

Even if the New Testament writers assumed that Jesus' body arose, might this simply have been due to their Semitic mindset? Might they have naively assumed this, whereas it was in fact untrue? Such a supposition can hardly be squared with the early kerygmatic account of Jesus' resurrection, reported by Paul in 1 Corinthians 15:3-7.[25] Its early date shows that the formula must have arisen and converts must have appeared very shortly after Christ's death. Now if Jesus' body were in fact in the grave, his many zealous opponents could have stopped all this by producing it. Even had his corpse been deposited in a little-known location (which hardly fits Matt. 27:62-66 and par), it is unthinkable that they would not have done all they could to recover it. Yet no evidence exists that the kerygma was ever challenged on the basis that Jesus' body had been found.

On biblical grounds it is difficult to show that the New Testament church ever thought of Jesus' resurrection as other than bodily. On general historical grounds theories as to what else could have happened to his body (that the disciples stole it, that Jesus "swooned," etc.) are not plausible. Historically, the origin of the kerygma "is hardly understandable except under the assumption that Jesus' tomb was empty."[26] Our overall conclusion is strengthened in considering the broadest theological horizons within which the resurrection was understood. During the intertestamental period God's promise expanded to include the entire cosmos within its scope (Chap.14). Evil nations seemed to have triumphed for so long, and the righteous seemed to have succumbed to disease and death so often, that fulfillment of the promise seemed inseparable from the overall renewal of the created order. This was one reason why the eschatological resurrection was expected to be bodily. We have also seen that Jesus' miracles heralded the inbreaking of God's kingdom as the fulfillment of this cosmic promise (Chap. 15).

Within this eschatological horizon we can apprehend the full significance of Jesus' resurrection. It was not simply an extraordinary, isolated event *within* history and the cosmos. It was the inauguration of a new direction and of new possibilities *for* history and the cosmos.[27] It was the decisive inbreaking of the new age itself. In raising Jesus from the depths of death and nothingness, the Spirit

---

[24] Osborne, p. 279. Moreover, the legendary or mythological elements that color the gospel stories were separated from their original pagan contexts. They were utilized to help communicate claims about historical, physical reality for those from non-Hebraic cultures (p. 277; cf. our remarks on the relationship of elements of truth from other contexts to the fullness of "integrating revelation [Chap. 13]). Osborne shows this in detail for each gospel's resurrection story.

[25] For what follows, see Pannenberg, *Jesus: God and Man*, pp. 88-106.

[26] Ibid., p. 101.

[27] Moltmann, *Theology of Hope*, p. 179.

and the Father created life anew, *ex nihilo* (1 Cor. 1:28, Rom. 4:17; cf. Vol. II, Chap. 16).

Over against these considerations, the only weighty objection to considering Jesus' resurrection as physical comes from the "modern, scientific" worldview. Yet, as Chapters 6 and 8 showed, even modern science, properly understood, exhibits a limited openness to such an event. And when we realize that Jesus' resurrection confronts all understandings of reality, including science itself, with ultimate claims about the cosmos, we can see clearly why the resurrection can never be interpreted within an framework of any scientific perspective that is regarded as unalterable.

Having affirmed that Jesus' body arose, theology can add few physical details. No information exists as to what actual processes occurred between his burial and his appearances. Jesus' risen body appeared different from his mortal body, so that he sometimes was not recognized. Nevertheless, however different the risen body was, theology can affirm that it was a transformation of his mortal body. However radical that transformation may have been, there was continuity between the beginning and the end points of the process.[28]

Theologically this means that the risen "Christ of faith" is not a spirit or a symbol but the "Jesus of history" himself. Whatever ecclesiology may wish to affirm about the Body of Christ, the body of the risen Christ is a specific person (cf. Vol. II, Chaps. 10 and 13). Jesus' bodily resurrection also means that our concrete, physical humanity, not just our inner experiences and aspirations, has been raised into the very life of God.

III. Conclusions

A. Jesus' Ascension to Lordship

In elaborating three dimensions of meaning in Christ's resurrection (triumph of life, legal sentence, divine victory), we postponed one meaning until we had established that, given its bodily nature, it signified the inauguration of a new direction and of new possibilities for the entire cosmos. But now, having seen that Christ's resurrection broke through all demonic, social, and physical barriers to the creative life of God, we can more fully grasp its significance as his ascension to cosmic Lordship.

To be precise, the kerygma sometimes speaks of Jesus being raised directly to God's right hand (Acts 2:32-33, 5:31). Thus some scholars regard Christ's resurrection and ascension as one event, which was broken down only when legendary accounts of the appearance stories began to picture the whole thing in concrete, "mythological" ways.[29] Other expressions of the early kerygma, how-

[28] Cf. Pannenberg, pp. 74-77. The same may be affirmed of whatever further transformations took place during Christ's ascension.

[29] E.g., Fuller, p. 123.

ever, emphasize Jesus' appearances on earth (1 Cor. 15:5–7; Acts 10:40–41, 13:31). And even those former accounts, which are briefer, also stress that these things were witnessed (Acts 2:32, 5:32), which seems to imply earthly appearances. Further, since the appearances involved some sort of physical contact with Jesus, they required a period before his ascension when he remained on earth. Finally, if Jesus did not appear on earth, then all those personal dimensions of his resurrection—as a joyful time of reunion and instruction with those who had been overwhelmed by his death—vanish beneath his awesome installation as cosmic Lord. Consequently, an historical distinction between Jesus' resurrection and ascension must be made.

Theologically, however, Christ's ascension is a dimension of the meaning of his resurrection. In returning to the ascension, we return to the point from which our theologizing in this volume began. We remember that proclamation of Christ as reigning Lord is the heart of the kerygma. Like the early Christians, we found that this proclamation filled us with hope. Its insistence that Christ "already" is Lord turned our gaze towards the future, from whence he will surely come to consummate his reign. In light of this certainty, all evil, suffering, and death seemed doomed to pass away. We affirmed that those who are grasped by this hope strive to better situations of oppression and pain, knowing that these never need have the last word.

We return to this starting point, however, with a far deeper grasp of its nature and significance. Having cast our sights towards the coming "revelation of Jesus Christ," we turned our gaze towards revelation's present activity and back over its lengthy previous history. We began to understand that long history of the promise—of walking and waiting, of yearning and crying out for God's righteousness—in which we still to some degree participate. We learned that Christ's resurrection could not be understood without apprehending his sufferings, and that the struggle between pain and joy, despair and hope, death and life continues in the Church today.

Perhaps as we return to rejoice in Christ's resurrected, cosmic Lordship, yet with our awareness sobered by our understanding of the cross, our longing may find expression in these words of Paul:

> that I may know him and the power of his resurrection, and may share in his sufferings, becoming like him in his death, that if possible I may attain the resurrection from the dead. Not that I have already obtained this or am already perfect; but I press on to make it my own because Christ Jesus has made me his own. Brethren, I do not consider that I have made it my own. But one thing I do: forgetting what lies behind and straining forward to what lies ahead, I press on toward the goal for the prize of the upward call of God in Christ Jesus (Phil. 3:10–14).

B. Is God Righteous?

In examining Christ's work within the context of the cry for righteousness, we have claimed that it helps answer burning questions about justice which are still alive today. In light of what we have discovered, what response can today's

Church give to the many who wonder: Is God just? Does he care about those who suffer? Will God ever put an end to oppression and murder? Does he have the power to do so? The Church must caution that all such questions will not be resolved with satisfaction until "the Lord comes, who will bring to light the things now hidden darkness and will disclose the purposes of the heart." (1 Cor. 4:5). As long as the eschaton is "not yet" consummated, some such problems will remain shrouded in mystery. Nevertheless, the work of Jesus Christ offers some answers to those who search for hope and meaning in a world permeated by oppression and pain.

First, Jesus' ministry shows that God wills to establish a society where people from every nation, sex, and social class live harmoniously together. God opposes any system where some groups oppress others. God wills that his kingdom come and his will be done "on earth as it is in heaven" (Matt. 6:10).

Second, no one who is sincerely repentant will be excluded from this kingdom due to their imperfections or past sins. Nonetheless, those who do so repent must be willing to surrender everything which places them in positions of power, prestige, or security at the expense of others. Accordingly, this kingdom message is more often "good news" for those who have little to lose in this world than for those who have much to lose. In this sense, God favors those on the underside of things.

Third, Christ's work shows that God is faithful. None had greater cause to doubt God's reliability than the righteous in Israel. Yet Christ's work shows that God's apparent absence is not due to God alone. Jesus' work illuminates the magnitude of those resistant forces which seek to bind all humans, and in which we all participate. It shows that God is distant, at least in part, because individuals and the systems in which they live seek to push God away (cf. Isa. 59:1–15, Rom. 3:9–19). But despite this, God did not forget his covenant nor cease loving his human creatures. God entered that lethal network of resistance and took all the pain of our suffering and sin upon himself.

Unfortunately this lethal network still operates. This suggests, fourth, that experiences of God's apparent absence, and encounters with evil that seems endlessly to triumph, may be fairly normal in the Christian life. People might still come to know God primarily in that walk of hope and doubt, of joy and disappointment, that stretches between promise and fulfillment. The work of Christ shows that God is not really absent from, but is most profoundly present and revealed in, situations which at first seem permeated by suffering and despair.

Fifth, Christ's cross shows that whatever suffering humans may experience, no matter how intense and hopeless the alienation and pain and despair, God has already experienced and borne it. On the cross, Son, Father, and Spirit opened themselves to experience all the grief and hell that humans have ever known. No suffering is so deep that it is not undergirded even more deeply by the suffering, sym-pathizing love of God.

Finally, Christ's resurrection shows that even this deepest suffering was swallowed up by joy and life. Not only does God, through the cross, now participate in our death; but we also can participate in God's presence and life. God has not only saved us *from* the powers but also *for* the joyous fellowship of his kingdom.

Such answers to the questions about God's righteousness, however, will not satisfy everybody. For they do not promise immediate release from suffering, nor immediate experience of undiluted joy. They do not promise to end all concrete injustice, nor even to answer all questions about why injustice persists. For they proclaim not that all of evil's *activity* is abolished but only that evil's *dominion* is. Those who turn to the risen Christ will not experience a salvation entirely free from suffering and death. But they will know salvation in the deepest sense: participation in God's love that nothing, not even the most intense pain, not even the most despairing death, can ever destroy. And when suffering, death, and all the powers' threats and temptations are overwhelmed by such a love—precisely then is their dominion destroyed.

Suggestions for Further Reading

Barth, Markus and Fletcher, Verne. *Acquittal by Resurrection.* New York: Holt, Reinhart and Winston, 1964.

Davies, J.G. *He Ascended into Heaven.* New York: Associated, 1958.

Fuller, Daniel. *Easter Faith and History.* Grand Rapids: Eerdmans, 1965.

Fuller, Reginald. *The Formation of the Resurrection Narratives.* New York: Macmillan, 1963.

Jansen, John. *The Resurrection of Jesus Christ in New Testament Theology.* Philadelphia: Westminster, 1980.

Künneth, Walter. *The Theology of the Resurrection.* St. Louis: Concordia, 1965.

Leon-Dufour, Xavier. *Resurrection and the Message of Easter.* New York: Holt, Reinhart and Winston, 1974.

Ladd, George. *I Believe in the Resurrection of Jesus.* Grand Rapids: Eerdmans, 1975.

Lampe, G.W.H. and MacKinnon, D.M. *The Resurrection: A Dialogue.* Philadelphia: Westminster, 1966.

Marxsen, Willi. *The Resurrection of Jesus of Nazareth.* Philadelphia: Fortress, 1970.

Moule, C.F.D., ed. *The Significance of the Message of the Resurrection for Faith in Jesus Christ.* Naperville, Ill.: Allenson, 1968.

Niebuhr, Richard. *Resurrection and Historical Reason.* New York: Scribner's, 1957.

Osborne, Grant. *The Resurrection Narratives.* Grand Rapids: Baker, 1984.

Ramsey, Michael. *The Resurrection of Christ.* Philadelphia: Westminster, 1956.

Ross, Albert (under pseudonym Morrison, Frank). *Who Moved the Stone? The Evidence for the Resurrection.* New York: Barnes & Noble, 1930.

Selby, Peter. *Look for the Living: The Corporate Nature of the Resurrection Faith.* Philadelphia: Fortress, 1976.

Torrance, Thomas. *Space, Time and Resurrection.* Grand Rapids: Eerdmans, 1976.

Wilckens, Ulrich. *Resurrection.* Atlanta: Knox, 1978.